DOWN THE WARPATH TO THE CEDARS

DOWN THE WARPATH
TO THE CEDARS

Indians' First Battles
in the Revolution

MARK R. ANDERSON

UNIVERSITY OF OKLAHOMA PRESS : NORMAN

Library of Congress Cataloging-in-Publication Data

Names: Anderson, Mark R., 1966– author.
Title: Down the warpath to the Cedars : Indians' first battles in the Revolution / Mark R. Anderson.
Other titles: Indians' first battles in the Revolution
Description: Norman : University of Oklahoma Press, 2021. | Includes bibliographical references and index. | Summary: "A history of the attack on the Continental forces at the Cedars in 1776, when Native American neutrality frayed to the point that hundreds of northern warriors entered the fight between crown and colonies during the American Revolution"—Provided by publisher.
Identifiers: LCCN 2020044856 | ISBN 978-0-8061-6859-3 (hardcover) ISBN 978-0-8061-9081-5 (paperback)
Subjects: LCSH: Cedars, Battle of the, Québec, 1776. | Canadian Invasion, 1775–1776. | Indians of North America—Wars—1763–1814. | United States—History—Revolution, 1775–1783—Participation, Canadian.
Classification: LCC E241.C34 A53 2021 | DDC 973.3/3—dc23
LC record available at https://lccn.loc.gov/2020044856

The paper in this book meets the guidelines for permanence and durability of the Committee on Production Guidelines for Book Longevity of the Council on Library Resources, Inc. ∞

Copyright © 2021 by the University of Oklahoma Press, Norman, Publishing Division of the University. Paperback published 2022. Manufactured in the U.S.A.

All rights reserved. No part of this publication may be reproduced, stored in a retrieval system, or transmitted, in any form or by any means, electronic, mechanical, photo-copying, recording, or otherwise—except as permitted under Section 107 or 108 of the United States Copyright Act—without the prior written permission of the University of Oklahoma Press. To request permission to reproduce selections from this book, write to Permissions, University of Oklahoma Press, 2800 Venture Drive, Norman, OK 73069, or email rights.oupress@ou.edu.

CONTENTS

Preface: New Perspectives and the Significance of the Cedars / vii

Acknowledgments / ix

1. American General, Kahnawake Chief / 1
2. Council Fires / 10
3. Invasion / 20
4. Kahnawake Power / 28
5. "Of One Heart & a Mind" / 37
6. On the Blooming Moon / 45
7. Stopping the Road of Peace and the Door of Trade / 52
8. "Each Nation Sang Its Death Song" / 61
9. "Ordered to Their Alarm Post" / 69
10. "Menaced with Destruction" / 75
11. "Putting a Whole Nation to Shame" / 84
12. Ambushed / 91
13. "A Scene of Savage Barbarity" / 100
14. "To Stop the Enemies Progress" / 108
15. "The Dictates of Humanity" / 117
16. "Put All to the Sword" / 125
17. Reverberations / 132
18. Paths and Detours / 141
19. The Question of Massacre and Historical Currents at the Cedars / 151

Appendix A. Continental Soldiers at Fort Cedars and Quinchien / 159

Appendix B. Continental Captives / 173

Appendix C. The May 27, 1776, Cartel / 175

Appendix D. The July 10, 1776, Continental Congress Resolutions / 180

Notes / 185

Bibliography / 255

Index / 285

PREFACE
New Perspectives and the Significance of the Cedars

The 1776 "Massacre" or Affair at the Cedars does not command much name recognition. Most Revolutionary War historians have evaluated this series of relatively small engagements west of Montreal through the lens of British–American conflict, treating it as an afterthought or sidenote. For example, when the Canadian government considered whether the Battle of the Cedars warranted historic-site recognition with a plaque in the 1920s, historian Victor Morin frankly doubted the event's significance, arguing that it was of only secondary national-historical importance.[1] When mentioned at all in military histories, the encounter primarily serves as a particularly messy example of the rebel American army's collapse in Canada—notable for a cowardly surrender at Fort Cedars and the alleged Indian "massacre" that followed. The few detailed historical examinations of the Cedars to date have been article- or chapter-length efforts, largely focused on proving or disproving atrocities and British complicity in them, or assessing specific American officers' responsibility for their shameful defeat.[2] This work explores these relatively well covered paths in unprecedented detail but also ranges further afield to explore meaningful new historical ground.

The Cedars historiography has largely ignored the event's most important participants—the Indian nations that shaped the strategic situation and sent hundreds of men to both sides of the battle. When the story is expanded to incorporate the Haudenosaunee Iroquois Six Nations, Seven Nations of Canada, and Mississaugas, with their varied interests and objectives, it provides a significantly different, far more complex picture of northern affairs at the beginning of the Revolutionary War. Historian Gavin Watt finally cracked open the door to glimpse at this aspect of the Cedars affair in his 2014 book, *Poisoned by Lies and Hypocrisy*; however, with his work's more extensive scope covering the entire American invasion of Canada, Watt cast only a splinter of light into this vast, unexplored historical space.[3]

The Battle of the Cedars and the fall 1775 skirmishes in Canada that preceded it were the first Indian battles of the Revolutionary War; but military and Native American historians have collectively ignored, glossed over, or dismissed this detail as well. The July 1776 Cherokee battles, or the Saratoga campaign and Battle of Oriskany in 1777, provide common milestones for Indian military entry into the war. Representative of the traditional historiography, Ethan Schmidt omitted the Cedars altogether in his "Timeline of the Major Events of the American Revolution, Including Those Relating to Native Americans," while George F. G. Stanley argued that Indians did not conduct offensive operations until 1777, contending that the Cedars was "essentially defensive in character," without discussing the motivations that drove Six Nations and Mississauga warriors hundreds of miles from Iroquoia and Anishnaabewaki to fight outside their own primary domains.[4]

When considering the campaign afresh and breaking free from historiographical currents, the Cedars serves as an illuminating and informative case study, including the road to battle, events in the field, and the aftermath. Given that the Revolutionary War is commonly recognized as a "catastrophe" for eastern Native nations, an event that "devastated, divided, and transformed" them, a new understanding of the "first Indian battles" is more than a trivial chronological revision.[5] The Cedars shifts the initial focus north, incorporates the Seven Nations of Canada, emphasizes different interests among the key groups that gravitated toward the British or Continentals, and even sheds new light on the Declaration of Independence's charge regarding the king's efforts to employ "merciless Indian savages."

As a fundamental goal, I have aimed to incorporate Native agency as much as possible in this work. Reading Euro-colonial documents "against the grain," it is clear that the affair's strategic environment is well characterized by Michael Witgen's concept of an "Infinity of Nations"—"not actually a world of indigenous nations, but rather a world of bands, clans, villages, and peoples"; and these factions and individuals were most influential in the campaign's origins, execution, and outcomes.[6] The Cedars provides another example to support Pekka Hämäläinen and Samuel Truett's observation that "empires and nations never controlled American space in the ways they intended," and "borderlands are places where stories take unpredictable turns and rarely end as expected."[7]

ACKNOWLEDGMENTS

Important research for this book was directly supported by a generous fellowship from the Massachusetts Society of the Cincinnati.

I particularly appreciate the insightful comments and suggestions from Colin Calloway, Jon Parmenter, and David Preston that improved this book through the review reading process as well as their generous assistance with earlier research questions.

I would also like to thank everyone who contributed in their particular realms, including those who enriched this project with generous answers and conversations in their areas of expertise: Carl Benn, Darren Bonaparte, Travis Bowman, Frank Cecala and John Anson of John Lamb's Artillery Company (living history), Thomas Chambers, Marcio da Cunha of the Light Company of the King's 8th Regiment of Foot (living history); Tom Deer, Don Hagist, James Kirby Martin, Holly Mayer, Michael McDonnell, Thomas Peace, André Robichaud, Albert Smith, Matthieu Sossoyan, Alan Stone, Karim Tiro, Len Travers, and Peter Whiteley; those who helped with research materials or images, especially Julie Bellefeuille and Stephanie Favreau (Centre d'archives de Vaudreuil-Soulanges), Ellen Clark and Rachel Jirka (Society of the Cincinnati), Muir Haman (Vergennes Library), Kathie Ludwig (David Library of the American Revolution), Morgan Swan (Rauner Special Collections Library, Dartmouth University), and Meryl Saxton; my dedicated beta reading team: Kira Anderson, Pam Anderson, and Dave Eblen; the always helpful University of Oklahoma Press team, especially Alessandra Tamulevich, Stephanie Evans, and Adam Kane; and Bob Fullilove for his keen eye in copyediting.

CHAPTER 1

AMERICAN GENERAL, KAHNAWAKE CHIEF

On a fair summer day, August 1, 1775, an exotic stranger walked through the Continental Army camp in Cambridge, Massachusetts. The occasional thunder of artillery fire served as a reminder that the motley assembly of New Englanders around town was at war, having penned the British into Boston for three months. Escorts guided the unusual traveler to Gen. George Washington's Vassall House headquarters, and the staff welcomed Louis Cook, or Atiatoharongwen, into the Georgian manor's parlor.[1]

The guest stood in stark contrast to his genteelly dressed colonial hosts in the formal reception room. Louis Atiatoharongwen was a "tall Indian figure," dark and muscular, dressed and ornamented in "savage" fashion.[2] General Washington received him as "a Chief of the Cagnewaga Tribe"—a powerful Mohawk nation near Montreal.[3] Louis's home village had the "greatest influence" in the Seven Nations Confederacy of Canada, to such a degree that in colonial practice, his village-nation's name of Kahnawake (pron. gah-nah-wah-geh) was often synonymous with the entire confederacy. This was largely due to the village's role as the central council fire, but Kahnawake also held a "central situation" at the head of the St. Lawrence River's Sault St. Louis rapids and proximate to the Lake Champlain corridor connecting Canada to New York and New England.[4]

Louis Atiatoharongwen had undertaken this three-hundred-mile journey to meet the new Continental confederation's principal "war chief" and share goodwill for the American colonies in their escalating military contest with Great Britain.[5] The chief had good cause to be interested in American intentions, especially since colonial soldiers had already intruded into his own nation's lands. On May 10, 1775, Ethan Allen's Green Mountain Boys seized Fort Ticonderoga and Crown Point, key posts that controlled the Kahnawakes' Lake Champlain waterway path to Indian neighbors and the British colonies. The forts also abutted

Probably Louis Atiatoharongwen, at Newport, Rhode Island, in August 1780. Detail from *Indiens du Canada* (ca. 1750–1829), by French officer Jean-Baptiste Verger. The bow design and some clothing elements are more likely figurative than descriptive.

Library of Congress, Prints and Photographs Division (LC-DIG-ds-10898).

hunting grounds shared by both major northern Indian confederacies: the Seven Nations of Canada and the renowned Haudenosaunee Iroquois Six Nations.

Just two weeks after the initial shocks at Ticonderoga and Crown Point, the apparently restless American rebels had brought war even closer to Kahnawake. Colonels Ethan Allen and Benedict Arnold led separate, consecutive raids on Fort St. Johns, over the Quebec border and just thirty miles from Louis's home village. With the sparks of another colonial war landing on their doorstep, the Kahnawakes sought opportunities to direct any flames in favor of their sovereign interests in the newly fluid strategic situation.

From the American perspective, General Washington and the Continentals had their own reasons to cultivate friendly Kahnawake Indian relations. Even before the war's first shots, colonists were already sharing frightening news that "the whole influence of government is exerted to stir up the Canadians and savages to cut our throats," resurrecting the specter of Indian irruptions on the northern frontier.[6] In the century since Catholic Indian mission villages emerged in the St. Lawrence River valley, they had launched innumerable war parties to raid English colonial backcountry settlements, and Kahnawake Mohawks and the Abenakis of St. Francis (Odanak) were the most notorious of these historical boreal Indian opponents. As war opened in 1775, New England fully anticipated that these old enemies would return with similar violence.[7] The British may have conquered Canada from the French in 1760, but in the intervening years, the British king had become the Indians' primary imperial Atlantic partner.

Washington brought his own personal experience with Kahnawakes and other northern Indians to the Cambridge meeting too. After his first military defeat at Fort Necessity in 1754, Colonel Washington watched helplessly as enemy Indians from Canada plundered his fellow Virginians, blatantly disregarding British–French terms of surrender.[8] A year later on the Monongahela, Washington survived the catastrophic British rout by an Indian-French force that included parties from four of the Canadian mission nations. The Virginian vividly witnessed his enemies' effective tactics and "cruel Butcheries" on the field. Coincidentally, Louis Atiatoharongwen fought opposite Washington in that battle, beginning his own ascent to war chief status.[9]

Twenty years later, Louis Atiatoharongwen and General Washington had a far more amicable, comfortable encounter at Vassall House. The Continental commander in chief frankly expressed concern about how to "keep the seven Nations from tak[ing] up Armes Against the Americans." Communicating "tolerably well" in English, Louis reassured Washington with stories of Kahnawake's repeated refusal to fight alongside the king's forces. The general took particular note of the chief's comment that "if any [American] Expedition" were "meditated against Canada," the Indians there would give the Continentals "all their Assistance." This was an important detail. Just one month earlier, the Americans' Continental Congress directed Maj. Gen. Philip Schuyler's Ticonderoga-based army to seize key points in Canada "if practicable," but that enterprise would be doomed from the start if opposed by the Seven Nations Indians.[10]

After this short meeting with Chief Louis, Washington believed their conversation would "have a good Effect." American newspapers hinted at the general's discussions when they reported that "very late intelligence" had been received at headquarters, that "the Canadians and Indians cannot be persuaded by Governor [Guy] Carleton to join his forces, but are determined to remain neuter."[11] Neutrality was all the Americans sought from the northern Indian confederacies at the start of the war.

Before returning home to the banks of the St. Lawrence River, Louis Atiatoharongwen took time to attend another meeting in Massachusetts. Two days later, the chief traveled a couple of miles up the road to Watertown to confer with a Massachusetts House of Representatives committee. In their interview, Louis related intriguing details of a late May incident in Canada. After the Americans raided Fort St. Johns, the governor of Quebec, Guy Carleton, dispatched two well-respected, veteran French Canadian Indian officers to visit Kahnawake. They invited "the several Tribes of Indians to take up Arms against" the upstart New England rebels. The Kahnawakes resisted the overture, despite offers of "half a pound of powder and a drink of brandy" for each man, "and an ox among them for a feast." Indian village leaders contended that "no body had taken Arms against them, and they would not take Arms against any body to trouble them." They "chose to rest in peace," unless attacked.[12] With Louis's credible firsthand account, the Massachusetts committee had little reason to believe that the colonies' "inveterate enemies" of past wars were ready to launch another series of "depredations" on New England's frontiers.[13]

During those meetings in Cambridge and Watertown, Louis Atiatoharongwen dramatically simplified a very complex situation among his own mission village's one thousand inhabitants. He completely glossed over the Seven Nations Confederacy's myriad partisan and national interests—reaching far beyond the 250-mile span from Akwesasne (pron. ak-we-sas-neh) village in the southwest to Wendake (Lorette) on the outskirts of Quebec City, into adjacent hunting grounds and out to Native and colonial neighbors in every direction. The seven

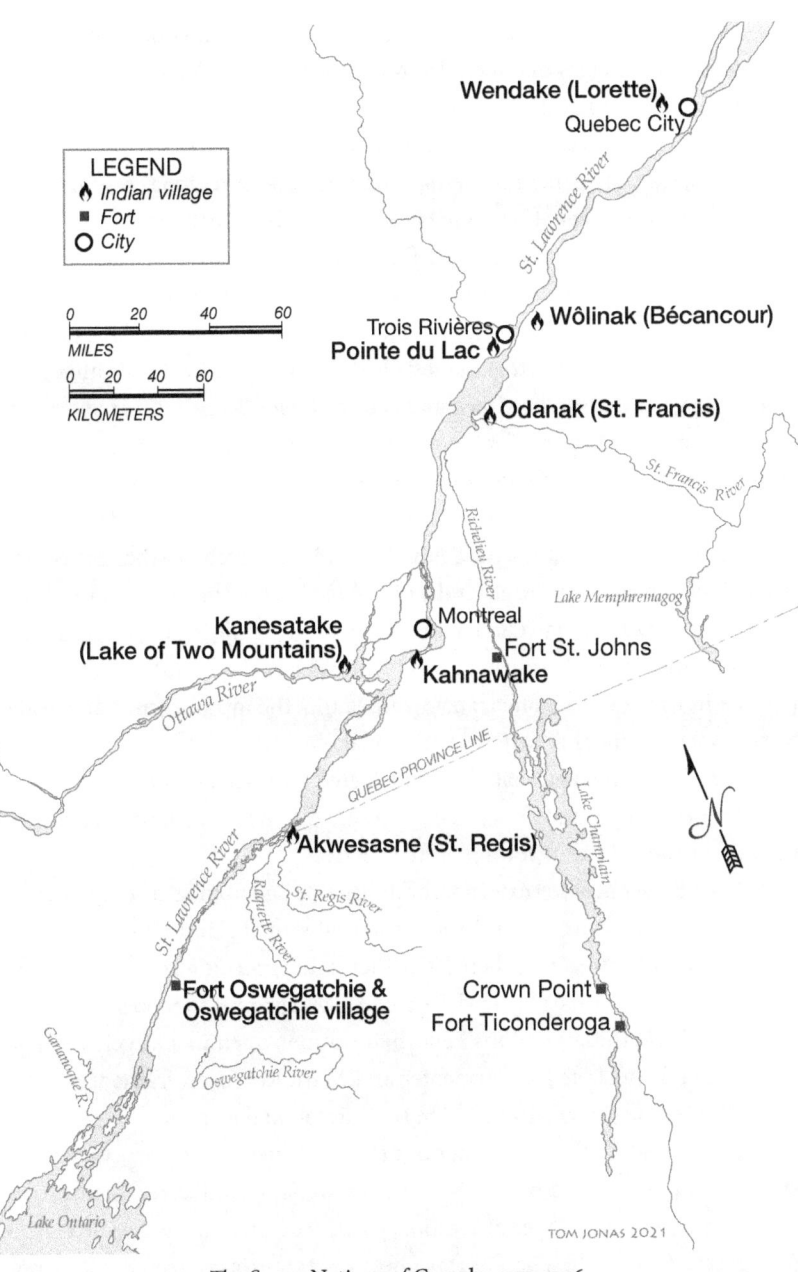

The Seven Nations of Canada, 1775–1776.
Map by Tom Jonas.

different confederacy council fires represented a diverse mix of Jesuit and Sulpician mission villages that included Mohawk-Iroquois, Abenaki, Huron, and Algonquian ethnic groups. Kahnawake and these other nations shared common bonds that encouraged their coordination—proximity to Canadian colonial neighbors, Catholicism, and overlapping interests in regional resources and hunting territories—but they were far from a single unified polity.[14]

At a fundamental level and as a defining characteristic, the Indians' political structure lacked centralized authority. Sachems and chiefs conducted village and confederation governance in council, a forum designed to seek consensus while reconciling diverse, competing interests.[15] The ideal was to be "of one mind," but, by European standards, headmen and councils were "wanting coercive power" to impose unity.[16] As part of this construct, in the absence of a clear consensus, councils were equally free *not* to make decisions, so controversial issues like going to war often remained unresolved at village-nation and confederacy levels.

By the eighteenth century, the Laurentian Indians, much like their Six Nations Iroquois counterparts, were generally disinclined to take up arms, and exploited imperial rivalries through triangular diplomacy by retaining neutral ground as long as possible. They also did not consider themselves subordinate to any colonial power—in 1741, a French official complained that the intransigent Kahnawakes were "a sort of Republic," while Revolutionary War British Indian agent Daniel Claus similarly lamented that they "considered themselves independent & free agents."[17] The community's core political interest was its own sovereignty, not fighting Europeans' wars for imperial objectives.

While villages avoided external commitments and managed competing factions to avoid any sort of dangerous "internal schism," individual chiefs had relative autonomy to act on their own. They could recruit war parties to join a belligerent power or liaise with different external groups to represent partisan interests. These Indian nations kept their options open in a largely informal process that historians Jon Parmenter and Mark Robinson framed as "active neutrality" or "active engagement" in the late colonial wars.[18]

Louis Atiatoharongwen's Cambridge trip characterized this aspect of northern Indian politics, and he served as the diplomatic trailblazer for the Seven Nations' emerging pro-American faction, particularly in Kahnawake and Odanak (St. Francis).[19] In the first half of 1775, these interest groups steered village politics toward closer relations with the Continental colonies. The prorebel faction had complex motivations, derived from community history, demographics, and external contacts. Even during past colonial wars, Kahnawake generally kept good relations with Albany New Yorkers, observing a tacit neutrality that facilitated mutually beneficial, illicit trade across imperial borders in the north. Many Kahnawakes also developed a strong dislike for the British, and Louis Atiatoharongwen was one of them. They had fought the redcoats through most of the last war; and after the peace, individual Indians suffered indignities and mistreatment at the hands of occupying soldiers, and inconsistent British policy occasionally disregarded or infringed on Kahnawake interests.[20]

Louis was also one of several pro-American Kahnawakes with a personal connection to New York or New England. Northern tribes traditionally "replaced" dead community members by ritually killing or adopting captives taken in battles and raids, and a substantial number of Seven Nations Indians were such adoptees, or their descendants. Kin ties held great cultural significance, and beyond immediate personal connection, Indians commonly relied on adopted or intermarried members as ambassadors to their native kin group.[21]

Four prominent American patriot-oriented Kahnawake leaders were known adoptees. Louis Atiatoharongwen was a small child when captured in a 1745 frontier raid on Saratoga. He was soon adopted, and even though his father was African American and his mother Abenaki—some Euro-colonials referred to him as "Black Lewa" or "Louis le Nègre"—this did not affect his path to leadership. As historians Evan Haefeli and Kevin Sweeney described adoptees' status: "Whether Native, European, or African in origin, once they were adopted into a Kahnawake family they were Mohawk. . . . The Mohawks themselves decided who was a Mohawk. Race did not matter. Culture and community membership did." Louis proved himself as a reliable warrior in several Seven Years' War campaigns, becoming a war chief.[22]

Jean-Baptiste Ogagragighte was the eldest adoptee that favored the rebel colonists. He had been captured in a much earlier raid, seventy-one years before the Revolution, and inherited the position of clan sachem upon the death of his adoptive Kahnawake father. Even with his prominent position in the Native community, he maintained loose connections with his colonial roots. In 1739–40, he revisited his past in a trip to Massachusetts, and in 1772 confided to a missionary that he "expressed great affection to his relations in New England."[23] Another adoptee, former Dutch New Yorker Philip Sanórese, was taken from his home as a teenager in the 1740s. Embracing his new Mohawk community, he explicitly declined an opportunity to return to his old colonial life, and became an Indian department interpreter before earning recognition as a chief or "headman."[24] In June 1775, Louis Atiatoharongwen also identified another adoptee as

Kahnawake's "head chief"—John Stacey Ayonwahtha. Nineteen years earlier, Stacey had been captured as a Massachusetts provincial soldier in a Lake George ambush. After the British conquest of Canada, Stacey defied repatriation orders to stay in his new home, married a Kahnawake woman, served as an interpreter, ran a store, and inherited the name Ayonwahtha, specifically conferred with clan sachem status.[25]

In the years before the Revolution, the Kahnawake nation developed another relevant relationship to the American colonies, through Dartmouth College. Over a century of coexistence with French Canadian neighbors, Seven Nations communities developed a "thirst for Learning . . . got by observing the great advantage which the Learned have." Traditionally, mission priests educated willing villagers, but particularly in Jesuit villages like Kahnawake, Odanak (St. Francis), and Wendake (Lorette), this avenue of instruction was at risk—the British did not allow new Jesuit priests to enter Quebec, so these communities wisely foresaw the eventual loss of teacher-priests to death or retirement. In 1772, New England missionaries serendipitously arrived in Kahnawake, desperately seeking Indian students to fulfill the chartered purpose of Eleazar Wheelock's Dartmouth College.[26] Both John Stacey Ayonwahtha and Philip Sanórese welcomed the missionaries and visited the college themselves. By 1775, they both had sons attending the New Hampshire school alongside at least eight other Seven Nations boys.[27] Eleazar Wheelock liked to think that "continual Intercourse" between his institution and the Seven Nations was "the surest Bullwark" for protecting New England colonial backcountry settlements from Indian attack, while the Kahnawakes sustained the Dartmouth tie throughout the war for their own community-strengthening and diplomatic purposes.[28]

As prewar tensions flared, New Englanders and Kahnawakes revived other connections too. Connecticut militia colonel Israel Putnam opened a friendly correspondence with Kahnawake in early 1775, and in March, interpreter Winthrop Hoit visited the village as part of a liaison-spy party sent to Montreal. In the French and Indian War, Putnam had been a short-term Kahnawake captive, and Hoit was actually a captive adoptee, who learned Mohawk for four years before his repatriation. Hoit returned from his 1775 visit to relay Kahnawake reassurances "that if they are obliged for their own safety to take up arms on either side that they shall take part on the Side of their Brethern the English in N[ew] England."[29]

After the Americans seized Fort Ticonderoga in May, Kahnawakes frequently visited the Americans there. Garrison officers and Indians shared information and nurtured friendly relationships. Some Kahnawakes even established a courier network, delivering messages between the fort, their own village, and active patriot Canadians around Montreal.[30] While the Americans grew more comfortable with friendly Seven Nations Indians, the British grew wary.

By June, those British suspicions unintentionally pushed the Kahnawakes even closer to the rebels. Three Massachusetts Stockbridge Indian diplomats entered Canada on a mission to the Seven Nations when they were arrested by the king's soldiers at Fort St. Johns. The redcoats discovered wampum and alarming, "treasonous" letters in the emissaries' packs, so they treated the Indians as spies, roughed them up, bound them in cords, and took them to Montreal.[31] Even if the British had good reason to suspect Stockbridge intentions, by Native protocol, diplomats should have been granted safe passage.

Kahnawake chiefs rushed to Montreal to intervene on the Stockbridges' behalf. In the ensuing encounter, "high threatening words passed between the General and the Indian Sachems." British officers haughtily and indiscreetly declared that they "did not care the Snap of their Finger for all the Indians," and a Kahnawake sachem bitterly responded, "I have not known yet who was my Enemy, . . . but now I shall know who is my Enemy." The king's officers reconsidered the strategic implications of their actions and deescalated the confrontation by permitting the Kahnawakes to escort their Stockbridge friends out of the city. The Indian ambassadors safely returned home, where they told rebel leaders that the insulted Kahnawakes had confided to them that if they "did fight at all, they would fight against the [British] Regulars, for they did not like them."[32]

In early 1775, historical, kin, and educational connections between Kahnawakes and "patriot" Americans helped create an impression that the American Continentals might have little to fear from the Seven Nations. There was far more in motion in Canada, and in the Six Nations Iroquois confederacy though. Active political forces and powerful personalities quickly muddied the picture.

CHAPTER 2

COUNCIL FIRES

While Kahnawake chief Louis Atiatoharongwen was still on his way to Cambridge, more than one hundred Six Nations Iroquois men landed in the bustling fur-trade city of Montreal, completing a St. Lawrence descent from Lake Ontario. Their sudden appearance on July 17 dramatically shifted the scales of Indian alignment in the Revolutionary War's first summer. While the Six Nations were a separate confederation from the Seven Nations of Canada, the two distinct polities had broad historical bonds, kinship ties, and overlapping interests that blurred distinctions between them.[1]

There was a key structural difference that reflected the two confederacies' scale of power and influence; in contrast to the mission-based Seven Nations, each of the Haudenosaunee Iroquois confederacy Six Nations consisted of multiple communities. From east to west, these ethnolinguistic nations were the Mohawks, Tuscaroras, Oneidas, Onondagas, Cayugas, and Senecas. The latter was the most powerful and expansive, with dozens of villages spread over a broad region bounded on three sides by Lake Erie, Lake Ontario, and Seneca Lake, reaching into the Ohio and Susquehanna Valleys.

British Northern Indian Department superintendent Guy Johnson accompanied the Six Nations visitors to Montreal with great effect. He was only thirty-five and had just inherited his office in the past year, following the death of his uncle, Sir William Johnson. The talented, Irish-born Guy held considerable influence in the northern Native world in his own right. Having spent more than half of his life in the Indian Department, the pale, sharp-featured Guy had honed a cross-cultural fluency, and was a skilled operator in two worlds as represented in his Benjamin West portrait. Like his uncle, he ran affairs from the Mohawk Valley—centered around his limestone Georgian manor known as Guy Park—and his interests were intricately intertwined with his close political allies and kin-tied Mohawk neighbors.[2]

Shortly after the Revolutionary War broke out, Guy Johnson felt threatened by patriot neighbors and judged that he could better support the king elsewhere, so

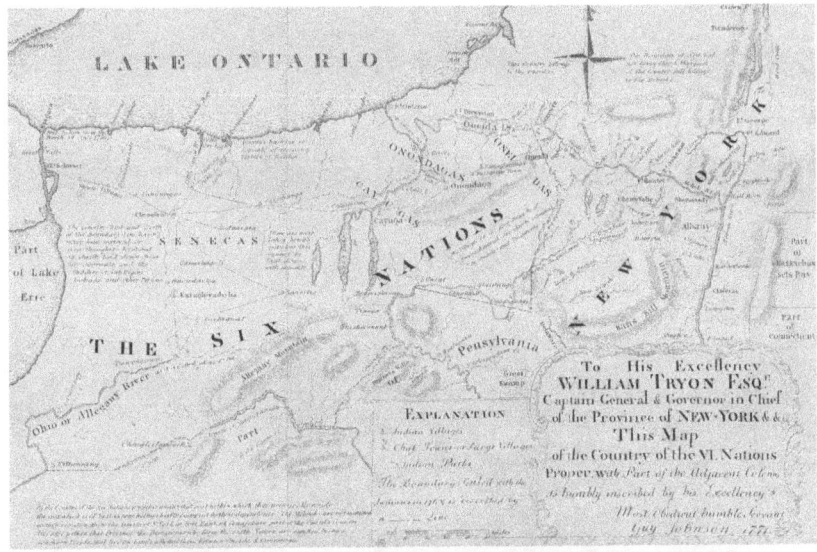

Iroquoia. "To His Excellency William Tryon Esqr., Captain General & Governor in Chief of the Province of New-York & &: This map of the Country of the VI. Nations Proper, with Part of the Adjacent Colonies . . ." Map by cartographer Guy Johnson, 1771.

Lionel Pincus and Princess Firyal Map Division, New York Public Library (b20645561).

he led about two hundred loyal colonists and Mohawks on a circuitous 450-mile route to Canada. He first headed west, through Iroquoia, stopping at the shores of Lake Ontario on June 17. Drawing Indian trade goods from the British stronghold at Fort Niagara, he called a council at the end of the month, attended by more than one thousand Six Nations Indians. Inside the deteriorating earth and timber works of Fort Ontario (Oswego), Johnson diligently followed diplomatic protocol and distributed generous presents to refresh relations and demonstrate the king's generosity and power. He also leveraged Iroquois strategic interests in his speeches, emphasizing his intent to ensure the Six Nations' continued access to British trade goods—well aware that confederacy members expected regular supplies of European cloth, metal wares, firearms, and gunpowder. The British could satisfy these demands via the St. Lawrence–Lake Ontario waterway; the rebel Americans were completely unprepared to meet those needs.[3]

In the Fort Ontario council, Six Nations Indians broadly agreed "to cooperate with his Majesty[']s troops in the defence of the Communication and water Emptying into the River St. Lawrence." Johnson then asked for ten warriors

Benjamin West, *Colonel Guy Johnson and Karonghyontye (Captain David Hill)*, 1776.
Andrew W. Mellon Collection, National Gallery of Art, Washington, DC (1940.1.10).

from each nation to accompany him to Kahnawake, where "he was to kindle up a Council-fire" for the Seven Nations. Scores of Iroquois men were ready to join his trip down the St. Lawrence to Montreal. The attendees played along with the charade that they would be going "to hear what passed between him [Johnson] & the seven Nations" in Canada; but rebel spies reported that Senecas and Onondagas had secretly accepted war belts from Johnson—symbolizing commitments to join their British ally "on the war path." The Indian men accompanying Johnson were self-selected, motivated for distinction through political or military action, and would be moving further away from the peaceful restraints of village sachems and clan matrons. Limited by available watercraft, 220 loyalists and Indians left Fort Ontario with Johnson on July 11, speedily cruising down the lake and the upper St. Lawrence on a sloop and a handful of boats to Fort Oswegatchie, where they transferred to canoes and arrived in Montreal just six days later.[4]

Word immediately spread from the Fort Ontario council, and hundreds of Iroquois confederacy and Lake Ontario Mississauga Indians followed the path to Montreal in a matter of days. With visible support growing each day, Johnson's deputy for Canada, Daniel Claus, also met with local Seven Nations chiefs, encouraging them to reassess their own strategic situation relative to the British government and the rebels. Many of their warriors soon joined the multinational Indian host gathering on the Island of Montreal. On July 26, Governor Guy Carleton and Superintendent Johnson convened an Indian congress in Montreal—1,664 warriors, women, and children crowded into the small city, pleasing merchants and frightening other citizens.[5]

Over five days' ceremonies, British officials liberally distributed traditional diplomatic "presents" to their guests. Guy Johnson kept his Six Nations compatriots inspired and, after appropriate formalities, also "delivered to each of the Canadian Tribes, a War Belt and the Hatchet, who accepted it; after which they were invited to *Feast on a Bostonian and drink his Blood* [italics in original]. An ox being roasted for the purpose and a pipe of wine given to drink, the war song was sung"—the ox was a proxy for the American enemy, hearkening back to old ritual cannibalism traditions when embarking on the warpath. With Johnson's influence and Six Nations representatives' show of power, the "Chiefs and Warriors of the Canada Confederacy . . . unanimously resolved to support their Engagements with His Majesty, and remove all Intruders on the several Communications." The emphasis on "communications"—access to trade goods and freedom of movement—neatly aligned with Johnson's previous Six Nations appeal at Fort Ontario.[6]

The Seven Nations' resolution to support the king was not a complete about-face. Even before Louis Atiatoharongwen embarked on his journey to Cambridge, his village had made token commitments to help British forces defend Quebec. Back in mid-June 1775, some of Governor Carleton's Indian agents visited Kahnawake on the very day that Seven Nations confederacy chiefs were gathering in council to "jointly determine to act in the approach[in]g War only on the defensive." Influenced by pro-British factions and their colonial government guests, the Indians shifted their position and made surprising "Professions of Zeal for the King's service." As a result, the Continental colonies soon heard alarming reports that the Kahnawake "Indians had taken up the Hatchet"; in fact, this specific news was the final straw that prompted the Continental Congress's June 27 decision to invade Canada.[7]

The Seven Nations' June commitment to the British was in fact less straightforward than it might have seemed. Contradictory sources soon reported that the "seven Nations had agreed not to fight the Yankees." A trusted informant even claimed that the Kahnawakes, "to save themselves from being destroyed[,] have ingaged to assist in defending him [Governor Carleton] at Montreal, but to go no further.... This concession was only for self preservation." It was a summer of confusing news, and in part, Louis Atiatoharongwen had gone to Cambridge to help clarify the situation and reassure Continental leaders with his own faction's perspective. The reality in Kahnawake was that, even after the June "commitment" to the governor, Indian agent Claude de Lorimier reported just three Kahnawake warriors in the field with the British.[8]

At least one village in the Seven Nations took the commitment more seriously. By June 18, warriors started joining the loyal colonial defenders of Fort St. Johns, and many of them were from Kanesatake (pron. gah-neh-sa-ta-keh). Twenty river miles west of Kahnawake, Kanesatake village sat at the head of a calm river basin where the Ottawa River enters the St. Lawrence River valley, known as the Lake of Two Mountains. The namesake peaks provided a five-hundred-foot-tall backdrop for the community "situated on a delightful point of land.... Near the extremity of the point their church is built, which divides the village in two parts, forming a regular angle along the waters side." Kanesatake Mohawks lived on one side, and two Anishinaabeg (Algonquian) peoples lived opposite—Nipissings and Arundaks—about six hundred villagers all combined.[9]

Based on strategic geography, Kanesatake's national interests were primarily up the Ottawa waterway, controlling traffic and managing affairs west to the upper Great Lakes. Historically in the colonial wars, Kanesatake Indians,

Henry J. Warre, *Indian Village (Kannasatakee), Lake of Two Mountains, Lower Canada (Quebec)*.
Courtesy Library and Archives Canada (1965-76-79).

especially the Nipissings, had proven to be particularly dedicated allies to the French cause, and this commitment to the neighboring colonial government appears to have transferred to the British. Unlike Jesuit communities in Kahnawake and Odanak (St. Francis), Kanesatake was a Sulpician mission. The Sulpician order was still vibrant and politically active—in fact, its Canadian superior, Etienne Montgolfier, was an extremely outspoken loyalist. Unique among the Seven Nations of Canada, the Kanesatake Indians were tenants, since the missionary order claimed seigneurial property rights to the village and its rich, black-soil lands.[10] Based on these interests and motivators, the Lake of Two Mountains nations generally served as a counterbalance to Kahnawake's recklessly independent and broadly American-oriented tendencies in the factionalized Revolution-era Seven Nations confederacy.

Yet whether the British had a few dozen Indian allies in June, or hundreds in August, Governor Carleton consistently aimed to restrict their operations. He insisted that warriors only be employed defensively, north of the Quebec

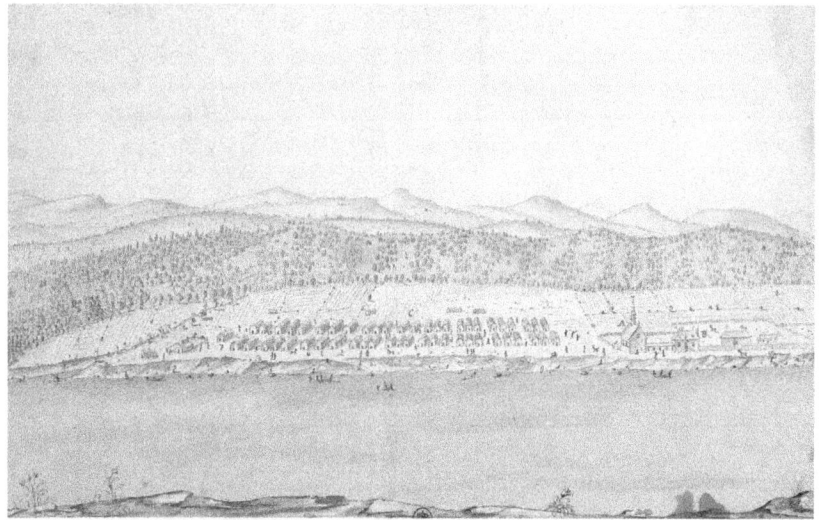

Vue de la Mission du Sault St Louis (Kahnawake), after 1720. The dwelling design and layout were idealized by the artist.
Courtesy Bibliothèque nationale de France (FRBNF40492463).

Province line, "lest cruelties might have been committed and for fear the innocent might have suffered with the guilty." To better manage Indian allies after the massively successful July–August conference, Guy Johnson encouraged them to keep camps on the Island of Montreal near the city, with its trade-goods stores and attentive government officials, and rotate parties of forty or fifty warriors to Fort St. Johns. There, under close Indian Department officer supervision, Indians acted as scouts to "watch the Motions of the Rebels" while remaining north of the provincial border.[11]

Louis Atiatoharongwen certainly would have noticed the increased Indian activity around Fort St. Johns when returning from Cambridge to Kahnawake, "the most respectable of all the Indian villages." Passing through substantial fields of maize, squash, and beans, Louis entered a vibrant town of about ninety houses, laid out in a "regular form" around a large, livestock-busy central commons. Some Kahnawake abodes were Canadian-style stone structures; others were more traditional wooden dwellings or "huts." The large, spired, stone Catholic church anchored the Jesuit mission community and marked the western, upriver limit of habitations.[12]

Almost immediately after Louis returned—hours or a couple of days later—he was called to a Seven Nations grand council. Superintendent Guy Johnson, his deputy Daniel Claus, and interpreter John Butler were in attendance, and they focused their attention on the recently returned chief. As Louis remembered, they asked "for me to take up the Tommy Hawk . . . Against the Americans," and quizzed him on what news he brought from his trip. At this point, he ended the British agents' game by bluntly telling them he was "for the Americans."[13] Basking in confidence, Johnson was seemingly unconcerned by this single recalcitrant war chief's defiance, having rallied all the strategically relevant northern Indian nations to the Crown in recent weeks. Even if less enthusiastic Native parties were leaving Canada for home, about five hundred warriors remained on the Island of Montreal to augment the province's "slender force" of just two British regular regiments.[14]

Back in Iroquoia, however, the situation had taken a dramatic political turn after Guy Johnson's departure for Montreal. Paralleling the Kahnawakes' position in the Seven Nations, an influential Oneida faction encouraged stronger Six Nations relations with the Americans. Oneidas made their own June 1775 declaration of neutrality and actively encouraged the rest of the Iroquois confederacy to follow their example in the budding fratricidal war between Britain and the colonists. Cooperating with New England missionaries Samuel Kirkland and James Dean, this faction opened communications with American officials, while the Continental Congress concurrently directed its own Northern Indian Department commissioners to ask the Six Nations simply to "remain at home, and not join on either side, but keep the hatchet buried deep."[15] The Oneidas' and Americans' goals were conveniently well aligned in this regard.

That summer, Maj. Gen. Philip Schuyler, commander of the Continental Northern Army, had also been appointed as one of the Congress's Northern Indian Department commissioners. His family had long-respected roots in New York–Iroquois affairs, so when Oneidas encouraged their colonial friends to "rekindle" the Albany council fire that summer, Schuyler was a natural choice to be its symbolic "keeper." With a meeting place established, in late July and August the Oneidas assisted the Americans with their call for a Six Nations conference.[16]

On August 21, a Continental soldier in Albany recorded: "there was about 500 Indians, some of all the 6 nations came into the city in order to agree with the United Colonies not to fight against them." The delegations were not truly representative though; historian Ethan Schmidt noted that "only the Oneida and Tuscarora sent leaders of sufficient stature to be able to speak on their respective group's behalf." Still, after a week of preliminary meetings and councils in the old Dutch city, variously conducted at Cartwright's tavern, the Dutch church, and the Presbyterian meetinghouse, the American commissioners and Indian chiefs "smoked the pipe of peace together, and . . . parted good Friends." The Six Nations representatives pledging neutrality in Albany had bypassed formal confederacy processes—such decisions were traditionally made at the central Onondaga council, but the declaration satisfied many.[17]

In Iroquoia, there was temporary comfort that the Six Nations could "live on neutral ground, surrounded by the din of war, without being engaged in it." While some factions favored war, the Albany neutrality conformed with the core confederacy policy followed since the Grand Settlement of 1700–1701, to remain independent and neutral, barring clear and substantial advantage from doing otherwise.[18] As Continental leaders prepared to invade Canada at the end of August 1775, they were reassured that the Six Nations were not an immediate threat too.

General Schuyler had also been fostering friendly bonds with the Kahnawakes that summer. He and his officers met visiting chiefs, including Louis Atiatoharongwen, and repeatedly cautioned American scouts and spies heading for Canada to treat the Indians with respect. In return, Continental officials received reassuring accounts from the Seven Nations, including a report that "the Americans had nothing to fear from them and that they would be supported by the Caughnawagas in their [coming] victorious campaign."[19] On August 22, however, mere days before the invasion of Canada, a rash officer put all this progress at risk. On the marshy shores of Lake Champlain's Missisquoi Bay, just north of the province line, a British-aligned Seven Nations patrol encountered a rebel scout detachment led by Green Mountain Boys militia captain Remember Baker. Despite "express orders not to molest the Canadians or Indians," the captain and five companions rashly opened fire on the warriors, wounding two or three. The Indians returned fire, killing Baker and driving off the rebels.[20]

Schuyler was absolutely aghast when he heard of the Baker affair—especially with news that two Kahnawakes had been killed. Rebel Canadian James Livingston even reported that "owing in a great Measure" to these casualties, more Kahnawakes rallied alongside the British at Fort St. Johns.[21] The general feared the fruits of American–Seven Nations diplomacy might have been catastrophically spoiled by Baker's recklessness, and at the worst possible time.

Schuyler's deputy, Brig. Gen. Richard Montgomery, was already sailing down Lake Champlain with the Continental Northern Army, headed into Canada. As the major general rushed to join his soldiers, he encouraged fellow Indian Department officials in Albany to send Six Nations chiefs after him, emphasizing that "a peaceable message to those of Canada" might help resolve the Baker incident's fallout.[22] The Indian commissioners complied, but it would take a couple of weeks for the Indian delegates—all Oneidas—to make their way north.

General Schuyler did not wait, taking his own measures in the meantime. On the American army's first day in Canada, he issued a public manifesto from the Île aux Noix designed for both Canadian and Indian audiences. Leveraging the wide-ranging connections between the two northern Indian confederacies, Schuyler publicized that "a treaty of friendship has just been concluded with the Six Nations at Albany." He specifically addressed the Baker incident by declaring, "I am furnished with an ample present for their Caghnawaga [Kahnawake] brethren and the other Canada tribes. If any of them have lost their lives, I sincerely lament the loss; it was done contrary to orders, and by scoundrels ill-affected to our glorious cause; and I shall take great pleasure in burying the dead, and wiping away the tears of their surviving relations."[23] Schuyler's manifesto demonstrated functional fluency in Native diplomacy, where protocol held that "accidental" deaths could, and should, be "covered" by gifts to victims' kin. His competent diplomatic and consolatory approaches would prove valuable in coming weeks.

CHAPTER 3

INVASION

French Canadian Claude-Nicolas-Guillaume de Lorimier spent many hot, humid summer days in 1775 roaming the mosquito-thick northern Lake Champlain shores, deep woods, and swamps, searching for intruding American rebels.[1] At any distance, Lorimier would have appeared to be one of his Indian companions—dressed in leather leggings, loincloth, and cotton or linen shirt, his hair pulled back to generally resemble warriors' tight crown tufts on otherwise shaved heads. His gallic, aquiline nose and prominent thick-lidded eyes did not overtly betray his European roots.

Early on, interpreter Lorimier was joined by only two or three close Kahnawake friends on these missions. By late August, he was accompanying parties of a half-dozen Seven Nations, Haudenosaunee Iroquois, or Mississauga warriors. Lorimier's climactic scouting expedition came the day after his thirty-first birthday. He was investigating Missisquoi Bay with some Lake of Two Mountains Arundaks when Captain Remember Baker engaged them in the firefight that left at least two Indians wounded and prompted both parties to withdraw. The next day, Lorimier accompanied another Indian party that returned to recover Baker's abandoned corpse, cut off the rebel's head, and bring it to Fort St. Johns as a trophy.[2]

Claude de Lorimier may only have entered British government service a few months before this incident, but he had prepared for such duty his entire life. Claude, his brothers, and his father all served honorably as colonial military officers for New France, often working with Indian allies. The elder Lorimier even earned the prestigious title "Chevalier of St. Louis" from the king. After the French cession of Canada, the Lorimiers served their new, adopted government with "Zeal and Loyalty." Catholics were ineligible for British military commissions, so in 1766 Claude's father asked Sir William Johnson to employ his twenty-two-year-old son as an Iroquois interpreter. Claude was familiar with many northern Indian cultures and conversant in Native languages from military experience, the fur trade, and Kahnawake village's proximity to the family home in Lachine.[3] In spite of young Claude's credentials, it took nine more

Claude-Nicolas-Guillaume de Lorimier, ca. 1810. Sketch enhanced by Meryl Saxton.
Courtesy Wikimedia.

years and a war until circumstances were right for him to secure a government interpreter position.

In May 1775, days after the rebels raided Fort St. Johns in Quebec Province, Claude de Lorimier attended a Montreal dinner with Governor Guy Carleton. Lorimier, who had recently inherited his father's chevalier title, recounted: "His Excellency said to me that he knew on great authority that my late father and all of my family had always had a great influence over the savage tribes and that he was sure I could be of great service in this new war that was looming on the horizon, if I were willing to serve the [British] king." Lorimier eagerly accepted an Indian interpreter commission, with lieutenant's pay.[4]

Coincidentally, Lorimier had developed a very direct personal connection to Kahnawake. A woman named Sagoouike, whom he called Louise Skeler (Schuyler), was pregnant with their son. The Kahnawakes recognized Lorimier's kin status and gave him the Mohawk name Tiohateken. Lorimier may have been integrated into the village, but he was still quite politically naive. After his appointment, he was confident "that the Indians from Caughnawaga would take the warpath with me and follow me anywhere"; but he confessed afterward that "in this case I ended up looking foolish; no one wanted to follow me."[5] The Seven Nations warriors who later warred alongside the British did so because of their own interests, not because of Lorimier's personal influence.

By September, almost six hundred British soldiers and elite Canadian volunteers had concentrated at Fort St. Johns behind sod-covered earthworks, near the provincial border. British military leaders planned to block rebel entry to Canada there and ordered the fort's commandant to "defend St John's to the last Extremity." Lorimier was one of a few Indian Department officers assigned to escort warriors serving "as scouts and covering parties to the troops at St. John's who were then much exposed."[6]

On September 5, hundreds of Continentals crossed into Canada by ship and bateaux, led by Maj. Gen. Philip Schuyler and Brig. Gen. Richard Montgomery. They established an expeditionary base on Île aux Noix, a swampy Richelieu River island twelve miles south of Fort St. Johns. The following day, General Schuyler sent about five hundred American soldiers to the western river shore, to test the fort. The British commander sent all available Indians to meet them, accompanied by Lorimier, one of his brothers, and a few other Indian officers. The composite war party, sixty to ninety men, included some of Superintendent Guy Johnson's Six Nations Mohawk allies and warriors from different Seven Nations villages. Sotsichoouane, a chief nicknamed "the Grenadier," led some British-allied Kahnawakes. The Indians were unsupported, as the British commander husbanded redcoats and Canadian volunteers behind the ramparts of Fort St. Johns.[7]

The war party had maneuvered through deep, swampy woods to about one and a half miles south of Fort St. Johns when the flash and smoke from a musket salvo came out of the thick brush less than thirty yards away. The British-allied Indians had triggered an ambush. Two warriors fell dead on the spot, but Chief Sotsichoouane reacted almost immediately to seize the initiative, leaping into battle with a spear and a hunting knife to kill three Americans before musket fire dropped him too. Inspired Indians followed his example and drove the Americans back to their entrenchments. When the rebels rallied for a counterattack, the war party "gave them so warm a reception that . . . they retired with precipitation."[8] The next morning, the amateurish Continentals retreated back to Île aux Noix.

The Indians had suffered serious losses in their victory though. Eight warriors died and a similar number were wounded, including Six Nations Mohawks,

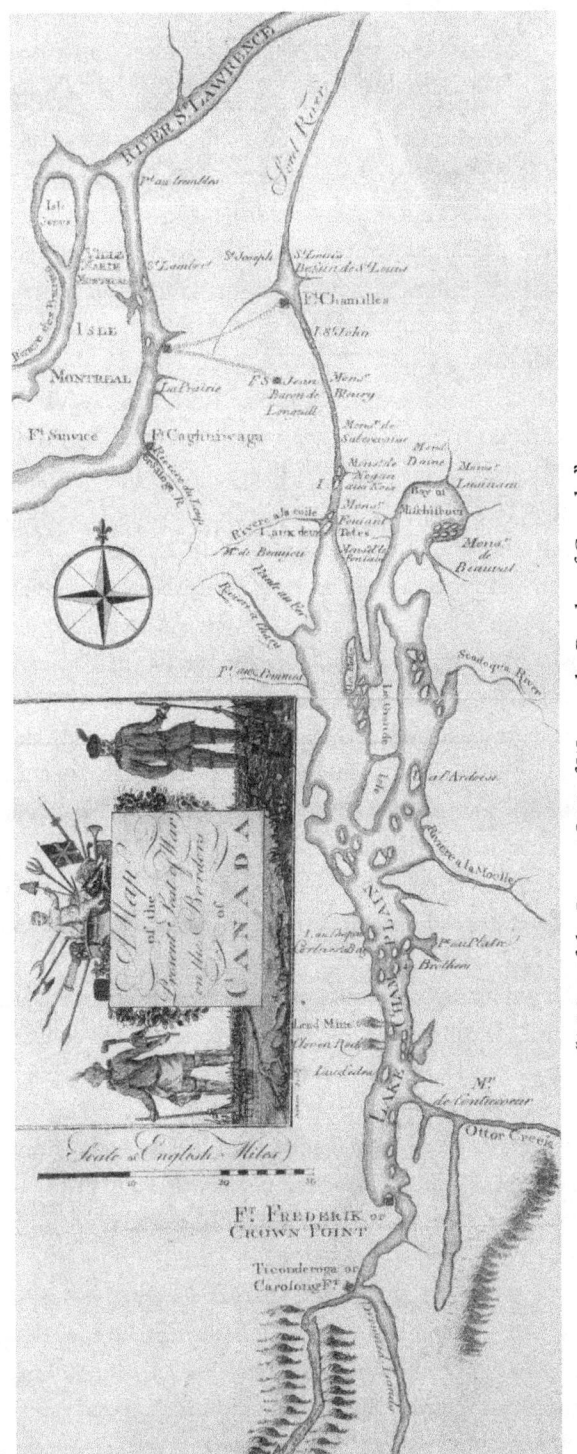

"A Map of the Present Seat of War on the Border of Canada," 1775. © *Fort Ticonderoga Museum Collection. Photograph by Gavin Ashworth.*

Kahnawakes, a Wendake (Lorette) Huron, and a Lake of Two Mountains chief. Mohawk warrior Tekawiroñte—a son of Sir William Johnson—later boasted, "I have Killed so many Yankies at Fort St. John's with this Sword of my Father, they are no Soldiers at all. I kill'd and scalp'd, and kick-d their arses"; but bragging rights meant very little to chiefs who lost credibility when they suffered casualties among their followers, and for Native communities that lost loved ones.[9] The September 6 encounter bode ill for British hopes to keep Indians on the warpath beside them.

The Indians were further astonished by the British army's passivity. The French rarely sat behind fortifications to let Indians fight for them. The warriors were further frustrated that the ungenerous British supplied them with only fifteen shots each for the battle. To make matters worse, Governor Carleton waited a week to praise the Indians publicly and condole their losses. Six Nations Mohawk chief Joseph Brant Thayendanegea certainly remembered this affair when he visited London the next year, reminding Secretary of State George Germain that when Canada was first invaded, only Native warriors had defeated the New Englanders in open battle.[10]

Almost immediately, the bulk of British-allied warriors showed their disgust with their feet. Four days later, Indians who remained took part in another skirmish, repelling a second rebel landing attempt. Interpreter Louis Perthuis and another warrior died in that fight. Lorimier claimed, "When Perthuis was killed, all our Indians abandoned the fort and the English cause within the hour." In reality, perhaps a score of warriors remained for yet another week, and just a dedicated handful stayed longer.[11]

The political situation in Kahnawake and other Seven Nations villages became extremely dynamic. The proximity of warring armies amplified the impact of competing powers' successes and defeats, and Laurentian Indians' strategic calculus faced frequent, rapid changes in variables. Each village responded differently, based on its interests and spheres of influence. Factions buffered the immediate blowback from fighting in a losing battle and provided ongoing diplomatic flexibility—internal parties could "cultivate relations with different powers and prevent domination by any one."[12]

Lake of Two Mountains (Kanesatake) villagers remained the most steadfast supporters of the British colonial government. As soon as the Kanesatakes heard of the rebel invasion, eighty-six warriors rushed to join Guy Johnson on the Island of Montreal. In addition to historic interests, the Lake of Two Mountains Indians' strategic interests were particularly dependent on their connection with the imperial power in Montreal, profiting as a link between the upper Great Lakes and the Atlantic world, via the city. A rebel American victory in Canada would sever access to British goods and markets, seriously diminishing Kanesatake regional power. Encouraged by Sulpician missionaries Jean-Claude Mathevet and François-Auguste Magon de Terlaye, Lake of Two Mountains warriors expected to engage the American invaders immediately. Instead, Johnson asked them to remain in reserve on the Island of Montreal. As the siege of Fort St. Johns wore on, Kanesatake warriors came and went, their numbers rising and falling with British successes and failures.[13]

Superintendent Johnson appreciated the Kanesatakes' dedication but hoped to bring the rest of the Seven Nations back into the British fold as well. Around September 10, he sent some pro-British warriors to Kahnawake village to advocate for the British in a confederacy council that was already in progress. Pro-American Kahnawakes Louis Atiatoharongwen, Thomas Wildman Kaghnectago, and Wendake Huron Jean Vincent had been dominating council conversations to that point. This trio conferred before the council with American volunteer officer Ethan Allen, a liaison to rebel Canadians on the Richelieu River. At Allen's urging, the Indians carried Brigadier General Montgomery's diplomatic request that belligerent Indians "go back to their villages and stay neutral." The men made the mistake of overselling their case though. Allen had only a small Continental guard detachment, but Louis and Vincent claimed they had seen Americans in Canada "as numerous as the leaves of the forest"; in reality, the rebel army was stuck on Île aux Noix, having twice failed to establish a mainland foothold.[14]

Interpreter Lorimier was in this council and recognized the pro-American Indians' exaggerations. He left that night, September 11, and ventured to Fort St. Johns on his own. Lorimier returned to the Kahnawake council the following morning to report confidently that he had not seen a single American soldier on the mainland. With this news, the council-fire smoke figuratively shifted in the opposite direction. About one hundred warriors assembled that same morning and left to fight alongside the British at Fort St. Johns.[15]

The war party did not get far. Just a half-dozen miles out from Kahnawake village, warriors spotted a group approaching from the opposite direction under a white flag. Four Oneidas came forward to introduce themselves, extemporaneously sharing word of the recently concluded Albany conference, emphasizing the Six Nations' commitment to neutrality there. The Oneidas had attended that council and traveled north after its conclusion to deliver messages for the

Seven Nations from the Continental commissioners and Six Nations leaders at the conference.[16]

The Iroquois and Laurentian confederations had deep historic and strategic ties. If the Six Nations had actually agreed not to take any part in the quarrel between the king and his American children, the Canada nations had to weigh carefully the implications. Chiefs called for new deliberations in council, prompting a "great dispute" in the would-be war party. A belligerent element pressed on toward St. Johns, but most warriors returned to Kahnawake with the Oneidas. After incredibly short welcoming formalities and preliminary discussions, Seven Nations sachems sent fleet-footed messengers to ask earnestly the warriors bound for battle to return. The war party accepted and came back to the confederation council.[17]

The Kahnawakes warmly welcomed the Oneida emissaries. In more tranquil times, Indian diplomats would be given a night's rest before addressing a council, but in this urgent case Seven Nations chiefs were so very eager to hear "what had been transacted at Albany by the Six Nations and the Commissioners of the Twelve United Colonies," that their guests consented to just four hours' rest. Later that day, the four Oneidas entered the council house and presented wampum and letters confirming that the Six Nations confederation was committed "not to take any part" in the war, but to "sit still" and see the British government and colonists "fight it out." They also shared the Americans' messages, including apologies for the Baker affair and an invitation for Kahnawake headmen to meet them in council at Albany.[18]

The council chiefs sincerely thanked their guests and announced that the Seven Nations would "be quiet," and that they "were now convinced that Guy Johnson had told them nothing but lies." The Oneidas added a request from General Schuyler for a separate Kahnawake delegation to confer with him as soon as practical at Île aux Noix, as "he desired that they would stand on one side, that no Indian blood might be spilt." Chiefs agreed to send seven headmen with the homeward-bound Oneidas "to hear what he had to say to them," and in regard to Indian diplomacy, they promised that when "St. John's was taken, . . . they should come to [the Six Nations' council fire at] Onondaga, to speak with them."[19] The Oneidas had completely reversed the course of Seven Nations politics at a particularly critical moment.

Indian superintendent Guy Johnson was frustrated by this turn of events, which occurred on the heels of a devastating professional development. On September 10, as the recent Kahnawake council began, Major John Campbell reported to Governor Carleton in Montreal with a commission as the new superintendent of Indian affairs in the province of Quebec. On paper, this effectively terminated Johnson's authority in Canada.[20]

Johnson still continued the fight for the Seven Nations' support. His deputy Daniel Claus formally invited the Oneidas to confer with British officials in Montreal, but Kahnawakes strongly discouraged it, "lest they should be served like the Stockbridge Indians, and be made prisoners." Heeding their warning, the Oneidas declined. When the zealously pro-British Mohawk Joseph Brant Thayendanegea heard of the council discussions and the Kahnawakes' intention to meet with General Schuyler, the war chief exclaimed, "It is over with Johnson; all the Indians will quit him."[21]

On September 17, three days after the confederacy council adjourned, the Oneida quartet returned through Île aux Noix, accompanied by seven Kahnawakes. General Schuyler had unexpectedly departed the island camp for Fort Ticonderoga, suffering from debilitating illnesses. His deputy, General Montgomery, had also just left, moving to the mainland in the Northern Army's third, successful attempt to establish a foothold south of Fort St. Johns. The Kahnawakes and Oneidas crossed the Richelieu River to the rebels' new base and found Montgomery. In a meeting noted for its "great solemnity," the general "prayed the Caughnawagas that they would keep their people on one side, as he would be very sorry to shed any of the blood of his brethren." In return, the chiefs delivered a wampum belt and "assured him that he might depend that not one of the seven nations of Canada Indians should in the least molest them."[22]

When the Indians prepared to leave, Montgomery offered the Seven Nations confederacy "a Present in the name of the Congress." Such presents traditionally went hand in hand with the "words" of Indian treaty agreements. With some embarrassment, the general confessed that his treasurer had not yet arrived with the gift money, but he promised it would be delivered to Kahnawake soon. The general found enough money to diplomatically "ease" the individual Kahnawake ambassadors' return journey though.[23]

The Oneidas' timely intervention secured confederation-level Seven Nations neutrality in mid-September 1775—a diplomatic windfall for the Americans that brought a critical prerequisite for victory in their Richelieu Valley campaign. Some Laurentian warriors would still fight the Americans, and the political situation was never static, but Continental leaders were significantly less concerned by the Seven Nations Indians after September 17. The tide of battle soon followed in the rebels' favor.

CHAPTER 4

KAHNAWAKE POWER

While Brig. Gen. Richard Montgomery conducted his September 17 council with Kahnawake headmen and Oneida diplomats on the western bank of the Richelieu River, his army prepared to advance on Fort St. Johns. Earlier that day, Montgomery had asked Kahnawake grand chief Joseph Kontítie, Louis Atiatoharongwen, and Huron Jean Vincent to help scout enemy positions. Kontítie found his way into Fort St. Johns, meeting four Six Nations Mohawks, a pro-British Kahnawake warrior, self-styled Akwesasne chief Ohquandageghte, and interpreter Claude de Lorimier behind the grass-covered earthworks. Kontítie quietly advised them all to escape the fort before the rebels attacked. The warriors politely dismissed his warning, and he slipped back to American lines.[1]

By dusk, fourteen hundred Americans had crossed from Île aux Noix to establish a new camp in the marshy autumn-tinted woods south of Fort St. Johns. Opposite the enemy post, Maj. John Brown led a separate "corps of observation"—Continental soldiers, rebel-patriot Canadians, and Kahnawake scouts—that stealthily occupied the main crossroads in the north connecting Fort St. Johns with the king's forces in Montreal and the lower Richelieu. That night, Brown's men waited silently amidst the rhythmic sylvan chitter, until they heard a series of strange owl hoots to the west. The Kahnawakes warned that these were calls coming from British-allied Indian "outrunners" for enemies approaching on the Laprairie road. Brown's men set an ambush, surprising an inbound supply convoy. After a short, sharp fight, they seized several wagonloads of goods. The Fort St. Johns garrison responded with a counterattack. With "Englishmen fighting against Englishmen, French against French and Indians of the same Tribe against each other," there was "much bloody adventure on both sides."[2]

In this counterattack, the Kahnawakes were fortunate not to lose a grand chief. During a short pause in the fight, interpreter Lorimier and some Indian associates were surprised when Chief Kontítie appeared from the wooded shadows, saying: "The British are going to be chopped to bits, so come along with

Detail of Louis Atiatoharongwen, from John Trumbull, *The Death of General Montgomery in the Attack on Quebec, December 31, 1775*, 1786. Louis was not present at the battle but was added for allegorical purposes, like many of the personalities represented.
Courtesy Yale University Art Gallery, Trumbull Collection (1832.2).

us." Instead of fleeing with the Kahnawake messenger, steadfast British-allied Indians knocked him unconscious, bound him, and debated whether to kill him. Lorimier intervened and facilitated Kontítie's escape, as the interpreter and his companions returned to battle.[3]

Leading the main American army in the south, General Montgomery heard the musket fire from Brown's initial ambush, and then a second round of fire indicating that the British had counterattacked. Montgomery responded by ordering his reserve to maneuver west around the fort, to support Brown. The general turned to a camp newcomer to lead this mission, "a man of large natural endowments and great force of character," named Col. Timothy Bedel. Contemporary sources spelled his name in numerous ways—Beatle, Beedle, Bedle, Beadle—clearly indicating its pronunciation.[4]

Colonel Bedel rousted his New Hampshire Rangers, who were lying on their arms nearby, fatigued from an eight-day trek that had brought them into Canada just that morning. These rangers were well suited for this sort of fight, hardy backcountry volunteers enlisted to roam New Hampshire's western borderlands to protect settlements from Indian raids. They had only been retasked to join the Northern Army's Canadian invasion when it was evident that the Seven Nations posed no immediate threat to their home colony.[5]

Timothy Bedel was a veteran officer, "tall, spare and of light complexion." For decades, he had served whenever his home colony called; from the forests around Crown Point, to the cold Atlantic siege of Louisbourg, and eventually into the heart of New France for the last campaigns of the French and Indian War. At the start of the Revolutionary War, he was commissioned as an active-duty New Hampshire ranger captain, and was soon given a field colonelcy over all three of that colony's ranger companies, as well as a volunteer detachment.[6]

While Bedel assembled his men to march around Fort St. Johns that night, pro-American Huron Jean Vincent advised General Montgomery to send the force on a path that could cut off the enemy's retreat. A French Canadian guide piped in with a less risky plan, and Montgomery took that recommendation instead. Bedel and his rangers entered the deep woods and lowland muck west of the fort, emerging from the dark to attack the enemy flank near the contested road junction. This prompted the redcoats, loyalist Canadians, and allied Indians to retreat back into Fort St. Johns. Bedel had accomplished his principal objective, relieving Major Brown at the crossroads, but in hindsight, after daylight observation of the terrain, there was widespread agreement that if Montgomery had followed Vincent's advice, Bedel's rangers would have forced the enemy sortie party's surrender or destruction, potentially with decisive impact. Instead, while the Americans successfully encircled Fort St. Johns that night, the resultant siege would endure for weeks.[7]

After the battle, General Montgomery gave Bedel command of all forces north of the fort. With a hodgepodge of Continental detachments, Canadian partisans, and friendly Indians, the New Hampshire colonel was tasked to prevent enemy relief, while extending American influence in the narrow triangle between the Richelieu River and the St. Lawrence.[8] Bedel's advance units soon established posts at Laprairie and Longueuil, the principal towns across the river from Montreal.

General Montgomery also directed Colonel Bedel to take "Charge of the Indians." The colonel had ample Indian experience from both his military and civilian past. As a founding grantee of three townships along relatively remote stretches of the Connecticut River, he almost certainly conducted borderlands diplomacy with regional Abenakis and Seven Nations Indians, and presumably partook in the obscure "privileged" trade between Kahnawakes and his home townships in a region known as Coos Country. In July 1775, New Hampshire recognized Bedel's influence when leaders called on him to use his "utmost Endeavours to get & keep the Friendship of the Indians." Authorities also identified Bedel as a well-qualified candidate to escort Louis Atiatoharongwen on his Cambridge trip, but the colonel was already engaged with his ranger command that summer.[9]

After the September 17–18 crossroads victory, Bedel met Indians on a daily basis, especially Louis Atiatoharongwen and Jean Vincent, the two of whom regularly couriered messages and wampum between Kahnawake and the colonel's field headquarters. A Connecticut officer reported that Indians freely mingling about his camp had "all learned English enough to say Liberty and Bostonian, and all call themselves Yankees." Bedel later boasted that he had cared for the Seven Nations "without the least Complaint on either Side."[10]

On September 20, General Montgomery directed Bedel to inform the Kahnawakes that their diplomatic present, promised in conference three days earlier, had arrived—"£400, York money"—and to ask when they would "come to receive it." In a rush to disprove British Indian superintendent Guy Johnson's public characterization of Americans as "beggarly miscreants, who have nothing to give away to the Indians," Montgomery ignored proper diplomatic form. Timothy Bedel prudently slowed the process. With his "knowledge of Indian ways and respect for Indian know-how," he conducted preliminary discussions and arranged a proper council exchange, resulting in a visit to Kahnawake village a few days later, on September 24.[11]

In his council speech, Bedel reminded the chiefs that he had "always" told them that he desired "peace with my Brethren the Indians," and he respectfully advised them not to be alarmed when Americans approached their village frontiers—that those soldiers were just preparing to fight the British. He concluded with an appeal for Seven Nations villages to follow the example of their Six Nations "Brethren," who were "all united in peace & friendship with each other, & also with their Brethren of the 13 united Colonies."[12] Delivering the United Colonies' diplomatic cash gift with this speech, he "reinforced" the Kahnawakes' fresh neutrality agreements.

In mid-September, after the Oneidas' visit and the American encirclement of Fort St. Johns, Kahnawake chiefs and warriors were emboldened in their safe neutrality. Even as war raged in their neighborhood, the Indians made it clear in several episodes that they were not beholden to either warring power. They flexed their independence, tested allies, and exploited the situation to their advantage. Claude de Lorimier had the misfortune to be embroiled in three of these incidents.

After the crossroads battle, with no Indian war parties in the field, British leaders employed Lorimier on special missions, where he could apply his extensive local knowledge, woodsman's skills, and Indian connections. On the night of September 24–25, the Fort St. Johns commandant asked Lorimier to escort a prisoner past the Americans, to Montreal. After successfully sneaking through enemy lines, the chevalier was surprised to encounter eight Kahnawakes on horseback, led by Thomas Wildman Kaghnectago, a "dyed-in-the-wool rebel" Indian.[13]

The Kahnawakes abruptly stripped Lorimier of his outer garments, dressed him in Indian clothes, and forcibly painted his face with charcoal and vermillion. The chevalier anxiously anticipated that he was going to "be repaid with interest" for Chief Kontítie's rough treatment at the hands of the interpreter's British-allied Indian friends just a week earlier, in the crossroads battle. Lorimier steeled himself to "endure their cruelties," ready to "sing his death song." With a laugh, Wildman and companions revealed that they had only reaccoutered him to get him past any American patrols—they would never "debase" themselves by mistreating a kinsman. With a few more misadventures, Lorimier found his way through Kahnawake village and back to Montreal.[14]

In following weeks, Kahnawakes interrupted Lorimier on two other missions. A scouting effort near the Continental camp at Laprairie ended abruptly when the chevalier's trusted, but drunk Kahnawake companion shouted the Canadian's name within earshot of American sentries. Days later, the interpreter was sent back to Fort St. Johns to consult with the British commandant about a possible breakout, but word reached the wrong ears in Kahnawake village and General Montgomery was forewarned. When Lorimier approached the fort, there were so many Continental patrols about that he had to abort the mission and retreat again to Montreal.[15]

The Americans faced their own frustrations and challenges with the Kahnawakes. On September 25, volunteer officer Ethan Allen made a bold, but ill-conceived bid to seize Montreal. Allen's small force of Continentals and rebel Canadians was surprised to encounter British soldiers, loyal Canadians, Indian Department officers, and a few Indians outside the city. The two sides engaged in an intense fight at Longue Pointe, which ended in the rebel leader's defeat, surrender, and capture.

After this debacle, Lt. Col. Seth Warner was leading Continental operations along the southeast banks of the St. Lawrence, when some Kahnawakes visited his camp. The suspicious Warner considered the Indians to be spies. Having heard that "there were a number of the Caughnawaga Indians in the battle against Allen," the colonel bluntly asked his guests why their nation fought against the Americans "in every battle." The Kahnawakes replied "that Carleton made them drunk, and drove them to it; but they said they would do so no more." Drunkenness was a convenient, sometimes figurative, excuse for factional activity or young warriors' opportunistic fighting; it served as a cross-cultural convention that masked the complexities of Indian "active neutrality."[16]

In mid-October, seemingly out of the blue, friendly Kahnawakes asked General Montgomery to send Continental soldiers to their village, on the pretext that the British were ready to attack. Even though the general did not believe this supposed threat, he sent Maj. Henry Livingston with two companies of New York Continental soldiers to "protect that nation from any Insults Carleton might offer them." American troops established themselves in the neighboring parish of Laprairie, and Major Livingston invited twenty-six Kahnawakes to an elegant dinner including "18 bottles of Claret." During the meal, Livingston's headmen guests shared that their situation had changed; "they feared no invasion from Mr. Carleton," and could defend themselves in any case. This entire escapade could have been a test of American commitment—if true, the rebels must have passed. The Kahnawakes told Livingston that his attitude and actions contrasted with those of the British: "Mr. Carleton had often sent them belts and made speeches to them—But had never din'd with them."[17] This was a telling anecdote, since food and drink were essential components of Native diplomacy.

On the opposite side of the St. Lawrence, Superintendent Guy Johnson had become intolerably frustrated by mid-October. He itched to lead his hard-gained Indian allies into combat, yet Governor Carleton was consistently unwilling to engage the rebels. This became a pivotal moment as Johnson shifted his energies from direct, personal Indian diplomacy to political intrigue and the self-interested subversion of superiors that would characterize his actions for the next few years. He sailed from Montreal for London, to make the case for an aggressive Indian policy and restoration of his authority in Canada. His senior Indian Department officers and zealously anti-American Six Nations Mohawk war chief Joseph Brant Thayendanegea accompanied him, in effect removing these influential agents and allies from events in North America until mid-1776.[18]

Only Connecticut-born Indian Department interpreter John Butler remained behind to represent Johnson's superintendency. Butler was no novice; with a demonstrated aptitude for Indian languages and diplomacy, he had steadily progressed under Sir William Johnson's tutelage in the French and Indian War—progressing through duties as an interpreter, Six Nations war-party liaison officer, and eventually deputy commander of Indian operations. Despite his seemingly insignificant activity into late 1775, historian Paul L. Stevens assessed that "neither the superintendent nor the governor could have chosen an agent better-suited than John Butler to deal with the Six Nations."[19]

One of Butler's first tests came shortly after Johnson's departure for England. Forty-eight Iroquois warriors visited the interpreter-agent, ready to leave Canada after recent British defeats. A Seneca chief asked for "provision[, and] Ammunition sufficient to take us home," as well as "some Cloaths and Little Rum" since it was "growing Cold." Before satisfying their requests, Butler negotiated a further promise from them. He revealed that soon, he too would leave Montreal for Fort Niagara; but he asked "that four or five of the Senecas & Cahugas would stay in Canada untill they should see how affairs were settled between the Kings Troops and their Enemies." When the Iroquois reported their findings to him at Niagara, they would be amply rewarded. The Six Nations warriors acceded to his request. Within days, Butler also met with Anishinaabeg Mississauga warriors who were leaving to rejoin their migratory home bands around Lake Ontario. Butler repeated a similar message regarding future councils and the wealth of stores at Niagara.[20] While Butler's appeals had an air of the forlorn for the moment, he set conditions that promised better returns in the long run. The interpreter-agent saw that he could entice Iroquois and Great Lakes Indian visitors to Fort Niagara, where the rich vaults of trade goods and diplomatic isolation from restraining and opposing voices—Indian and American—would undoubtedly play to the Crown's advantage.

Meanwhile, General Carleton was finally prompted to action in Montreal, coincidentally just a short while after Guy Johnson had quit the scene. In late October, it was clear the military situation was not going to improve, and the increasingly colder and shorter days indicated that little time remained to act. Carleton mobilized forces to attack the rebel Americans and relieve Fort St. Johns, calling in regional militia companies and Seven Nations warriors. Carleton had already abandoned hope for the headstrong, independent Kahnawakes and explicitly excluded them from this appeal. About sixty Indians answered from other nations, and once again, many were "esteemed brave warriors" from Lake of Two Mountains village.[21]

On October 30, General Carleton assembled six hundred Canadian militiamen, 130 British soldiers, and about eighty Indians who embarked in forty boats to attack the rebels across the St. Lawrence. Carleton commanded the operation; Lorimier led the Canadian "brigade," and his older brother François-Thomas de Verneuil de Lorimier guided the Indians. The crossing rapidly devolved into a fiasco. Carleton's hesitant execution and confused signals complicated the demanding amphibious assault attempt, as the rebels offered a dexterous defense from Longueuil. Every time canoes or boats approached the shore, a hail of musket balls tore into watercraft and flesh. Only a few "gallant, but unsupported" warriors and *Canadiens* reached the far bank before Carleton suddenly called off the assault.[22]

When the victorious rebel soldiers combed the riverbanks after the battle, they found seven enemies left behind. The Americans captured two Canadian militiamen and two Lake of Two Mountains Kanesatake warriors. The Continentals also discovered the bodies of three Indian warriors: Akwesasne-dwelling "medal chief" Ohquandageghte and two others, probably Kanesatakes. The Americans took their Indian prisoners back to the main camp and chained them aboard a tiny sloop in the Richelieu River for a month, before sending them to Fort Ticonderoga. Lake of Two Mountains villagers were aggrieved by these losses. As a result, the Americans' Longueuil victory brought unintended repercussions in the spring, when it came time for Indians to consider taking up the hatchet again.[23]

General Montgomery sent one of the Canadian prisoners into Fort St. Johns to prove that Carleton's relief operation had failed. The fort's loyal garrison had put up a noble fight for almost two months, but supplies were running low, and with winter nigh, their limited shelter was shredded from weeks of rebel artillery fire. On November 2, the British commandant agreed to surrender. When news reached Montreal, General Carleton's last few Indian allies left for home.[24] With the rebel army preparing to advance on the city, Carleton ordered officials, soldiers, and military stores onto all available ships for a retreat downriver to Quebec City, the Crown's last remaining stronghold.

Four days after the rebels secured Fort St. Johns, Governor Carleton invited interpreter Claude de Lorimier to join the coming government exodus from Montreal. Initially, the chevalier accepted, but he reconsidered in the few days before departure. Meeting with Carleton again, Lorimier offered an alternative plan—to remain in Montreal and sneak past American patrols to "visit the [Indians'] hunting grounds" over the winter. The interpreter would "gather a war party and return to harry the Americans around Montréal." The governor skeptically consented to Lorimier's audacious proposal.[25]

Before leaving Montreal, the governor also jotted off a last set of orders to Lieutenant Colonel John Caldwell at Fort Niagara, commander of the Eighth Regiment, garrisoning the king's distant up-country posts from Oswegatchie on the upper St. Lawrence to remote Michilimackinac. Even if the rebels controlled the forts' Laurentian line of communications, the garrisons had adequate stores to hold out through the winter and conduct small-scale operations. Unfortunately, Carleton's orders are lost—there is no documentation to show whether the governor asked Caldwell to cooperate with Lorimier, or execute any other specific military missions before the rebels were expelled from Canada and communications were restored.[26]

CHAPTER 5

"OF ONE HEART & A MIND"

The Continental Army marched into Montreal on November 13 after citizens peacefully turned their city over. Following a short rest and refit, Brig. Gen. Richard Montgomery led a few hundred reenlistees downriver toward Quebec City at the end of November. His little corps of 1775 campaign veterans rendezvoused with Col. Benedict Arnold and six hundred survivors of the epic Maine wilderness march. Once united, Montgomery and Arnold blockaded Quebec City in hopes of forcing that well-defended city's surrender.

Most American soldiers in and around Montreal headed home after its conquest, their enlistments expiring by the end of the year. Col. Timothy Bedel of the New Hampshire Rangers stayed with these troops, but his field command had effectively ended. About one-third of his men had reenlisted under General Montgomery as an independent company, and the rest not only faced December demobilization but were "very much distressed for the want of clothing" in the "severe season." They hastened home before the full force of winter struck Canada and New England.[1]

Colonel Bedel himself delayed a few more weeks in Canada before returning to New Hampshire. Indian associates heard he was headed south and asked to join him. They had their own business to attend to in the colonies. A diplomatic contingent, mostly Kahnawakes, was going to meet with Continental Indian commissioners in council at Albany—delivering on promises made in the September 17 conference with General Montgomery. Bedel and twenty-one Indians joined sixty British and Canadian prisoners in tight quarters on a schooner and sloop for a frosty cruise up Lake Champlain, until dangerous ice packs prompted their disembarkation at Crown Point on December 16. Bedel said farewells to his Indian friends, promising to see them again in Cambridge, following their Albany visit. He paid an agent to transport ambassadors and families to Albany, while he took an eastbound path to the warm comforts of his home hearth in the Connecticut River's Coos Country.[2]

Back in Montreal, the rear-area commander, Brig. Gen. David Wooster, had a diplomatic extravaganza of his own shortly after Bedel's Canadian departure. On December 19, a New York colonel reported: "The whole Tribe of Coghnewaga [Kahnawake] Indians, with their Wives and Children, amounting to between 300 & 400, waited on General Wooster & presented him with a Belt of Wampum, promised to maintain a strict Friendship towards us." An "antient" chief also added "that they were ready at any Time to send their young Men to our assistance." Wooster thanked the Kahnawakes and promised to "maintain them in their ancient Rights & protect them against all their Enemies, &c.," renewing bonds between the Indians and the most recent conquerors of Canada.[3]

The southbound Seven Nations emissaries reached Albany several days after parting ways with Colonel Bedel. The delegation included women, children, warriors, and chiefs—five identified headmen among them: Louis Atiatoharongwen, Nicolas Anádanonneh, Paul Oghradouskon, Eneas Sadaresoghsqua, and the septuagenarian, adopted-captive sachem Jean-Baptiste Ogagragighte.[4] While officials prepared for a formal Albany council, citizens welcomed the Indians for several short days and long nights in their snow-covered city of old Dutch gabled brick homes on the Hudson.

Maj. Gen. Philip Schuyler and fellow commissioner Volckert Douw finally convened a treaty council on January 3. Indicative of mutual amenability, both parties agreed to a treaty of "perpetual peace and friendship" after just three days. The Americans promised to protect "the said Caghnawaga nations [sic] . . . in the peaceable enjoyment of all their property, rights & privileges" as long as they refrained from taking up arms against the Americans. The use of "Caghnawaga 'nations'" implies inclusion of the larger Seven Nations confederacy, more than just Kahnawake village itself. In accordance with the united colonies' consistent appeals, the sachems and warriors committed to "observe an Exact neutrality."[5]

The treaty received remarkably scant notice at the time. The Continental Congress did not even make a specific record of it. Without a published copy, it has also been forgotten in historical discussion of early Indian treaties—drawing even less attention because it was signed before American independence and involved a nation in territory outside of what became the United States. This is unfortunate, because the treaty clearly shows Kahnawake's political-military importance to the united colonies at the time—especially in light of its generous terms. In contrast with the July 1776 Treaty of Watertown and September 1778 Treaty of Fort Pitt, the Albany Kahnawake treaty asked nothing more than that its Indian subscribers "should hold a perfect neutrality"—even specifying that "they shall not be called upon to take up Arms to assist the Colonists in their virtuous struggle for Liberties."[6]

After the two parties signed their January 6 treaty, thirteen Indians left Albany's now familiar streets for a long winter trip to the Continental Army camp at Cambridge, Massachusetts, seeking "war chief" Gen. George Washington's assent to this new treaty. Traveling in American-procured wagons, the Kahnawake party followed a roundabout two-hundred-mile southerly route to visit rebel capitals in Connecticut and Rhode Island on their way. During an otherwise pleasant stop in Providence, the chiefs and their hosts first heard "disagreeable intelligence from Canada"—General Montgomery had been killed in a failed New Year's Eve assault on Quebec City. In a seemingly extemporaneous response, concerned Kahnawake ambassadors immediately offered to gather "1500 men for the service of the United Colonies," a stark deviation from the strict neutrality negotiated just two weeks earlier.[7]

When the Kahnawakes came to the Continental Army camp on a cold Sunday, January 21, Washington had already taken measures to ensure his guests would "be so entertained during their stay, that they may return Impress'd with sentiments of Friendship." American officers escorted Indian guests around the fieldworks, and senior leaders feted them at a series of elaborate dinners. John Adams attended one, observing that "Louis, their Principal," spoke "English and French as well as Indian," and that "It was a Savage feast, carnivorous Animals devouring their Pray [sic]. Yet they were wondrous polite." Responding positively to the warmhearted and generous Cambridge reception, Kahnawakes shared hopes that the Americans would "look upon them as assured friends."[8]

By January 27, however, Washington's effusive Indian guests put him in a quandary. During unofficial "out-door's talk," typical of Indian chiefs' precouncil consensus building, headmen revealed "a desire of takeing up Arms in behalf of the United Colonies," with an offer to raise four or five hundred warriors. Initially taken aback, the commander in chief kindly suggested he would delegate any decision to General Schuyler, who had a much better feel for northern affairs. To Continental leaders, Washington confided that he was "a little embarrassed," more concerned about the potential expenses of keeping Indians in arms than the "Impropriety of Incouraging these people to depart from their Neutrality."[9]

The Kahnawakes waited several more days in Cambridge for their friend Timothy Bedel to arrive "before they opened themselves fully" in council, but when Washington shared news that the colonel was unavoidably detained in New Hampshire, they agreed to proceed without him. On January 31, Washington and his northern Indian guests finally met in formal council. Kahnawake chiefs recommitted to the Albany treaty, and Washington signed to show his approval. Then the eldest sachem, Jean-Baptiste Ogagragighte, gave a speech, including the declaration, "I am now in my own Country where I was born (being a New Englander & taken prisoner in his Infancy) and want liberty to raise men to fight for Its defence." As precoordinated in their earlier conversations, the septuagenarian sachem asked Washington to advise General Schuyler "that If he wants men, to call upon us & we will join him." Their Cambridge mission complete, the Indians left within a few days.[10]

To facilitate the Indian ambassadors' return, Washington sent Colonel Bedel a letter tasking him to "Conduct them in the Safest, & most Agreeable manner to themselves, into Canada." Since the commander in chief had also heard that Bedel was commanding a new unit for the Northern Army, he further directed the colonel to "use all the deligence [sic] & dispatch possible, to raise the Said Regiment & march it into Canada." Concurrent with the Kahnawakes' Cambridge visit, and immediately after receiving news of General Montgomery's Quebec City defeat, New Hampshire commissioned Bedel as colonel of a new "Regiment of Rangers" on January 22. A dedicated patriot, Timothy Bedel answered this call even though he had been back with his wife and children less than a month.[11] General Washington's instructions, with competing military and Indian diplomatic responsibilities, offer an early precedent for the incompatibly broad range of duties Bedel would face in coming months.

Colonel Bedel reunited with the Kahnawake delegation in Exeter, where he was discussing regimental business with the New Hampshire Committee of Safety. It was evident the colonel still had Indian affairs "much at heart," as he secured additional travel funds for the diplomats and advised the colony to allocate extra money to the chiefs for "entertainment of their own & the other tribes who would meet to hear the report of their Represent[ative]s" when they returned home.[12] Bedel clearly understood that the Kahnawakes' pro-American message would carry more weight with the Seven Nations in Canada if coupled with appropriate presents.

From Exeter, one group of Kahnawakes left with Bedel for Orford, his regimental muster point; the rest headed for Dartmouth College. Unfortunate circumstances quickly brought the groups back together though, as two Indians unexpectedly died from illness en route to the college. At Dartmouth, schoolmaster Eleazar Wheelock kindly led a funeral service for the fallen ambassadors, with Louis Atiatoharongwen interpreting. Beyond this solemn affair, the

Kahnawakes and Wheelock used the visit to refresh their mutually beneficial relationship linking the Seven Nations directly to Dartmouth, and indirectly to New Hampshire and the American cause.[13]

On his way back to Canada, Louis Atiatoharongwen stopped in Albany, visiting General Schuyler again. He repeated the Kahnawakes' offer of warrior allies, but the general remained noncommittal. As Schuyler revealed when declining a similar Massachusetts Stockbridge proposal, militarily he was in no rush to pay Indian auxiliaries, and diplomatically he was cautious about inflating Indians' sense of importance to the American cause.[14]

As the Kahnawakes concluded their New England tour, Col. Timothy Bedel stayed behind, struggling to surmount enormous obstacles besetting his new regiment. To begin with, Bedel's manpower requirements more than tripled from the last campaign: he needed to recruit eight companies of eighty-six men each, compared with just three companies of sixty-two in 1775. Furthermore, the recruiting pool had markedly shrunk; one-third of Bedel's veterans were serving independently in Canada, and competing New England regiments had already poached many good frontiersmen by enlisting them earlier or on more advantageous terms. Of two hundred rangers accompanying Bedel to the Cedars that spring, only seven had served with him in the St. Johns campaign. Half of Bedel's captains had never served as officers in the field before, and they in turn found themselves forced to fill the ranks with many novice soldiers. To compensate, they did recruit a fair number of recently discharged Bunker Hill veterans, comprising about one-fifth of the 1776 Ranger Regiment. Overall, whether greenhorns or Cambridge camp veterans, many lacked the deep-woods skills and Indian-fighting savvy that New Englanders traditionally associated with the title "ranger."[15]

While Bedel wrestled with recruitment, pay, and logistics, politicians in Exeter badgered him with impatient demands, including a comment that they were "very sorry the inlisting and marching of the men are so much slower than we were made to expect." Infuriated, Bedel impoliticly reminded them in a testy March 19 letter that he had already received marching orders from General Washington and the Continental Congress; the colonial government's job was to supply the regiment, and it was their shortages of cash, equipment, and weapons that still impeded unit mobilization.[16]

In the same letter, however, Bedel also reported that most companies were already on their way to Canada. Based on Washington's guidance for "each company to march as fast as they are raised," Bedel's regiment did not deploy as a complete unit. The first piecemeal detachments snowshoed north to Montreal, where Continental officials pointed them toward Quebec City, to join Brig. Gen. Benedict Arnold's siege. Bedel remained in New Hampshire until the regiment's last elements mustered. Even with extended delays, the last company was significantly understrength, and scores of men marched north unarmed, hoping to find muskets on their way. Spring settled upon New England before the rear guard marched, so instead of heading overland direct to Canada, Bedel led the last echelon west to Crown Point, to embark for Fort St. Johns as soon as the Lake Champlain ice broke up. Bedel's trail detachment reached Canada sometime between April 7 and 20, almost three months after the regiment's establishment.[17] Colonel Bedel had returned to the Kahnawake heartland just four months after his recent military and Indian diplomatic successes there.

Contemporaneous with the Kahnawakes' Albany-Cambridge-Dartmouth tour, other momentous events were taking place out west in Iroquoia. The Kahnawakes' Oneida friends had been equally busy shoring up the foundations of Six Nations neutrality. Their most spectacular and controversial achievement came at Albany in mid-December. Patriot Indian agent and missionary James Dean reported that "a large party of the Six Nations," mostly Oneidas, "came down to deliver up the War hatchet which the patriotic Mr. Johnson had sent to them, for the humane purpose of massacreing the Women & Children upon our defenceless frontiers." Even if this gesture met the spirit of the confederacy's nominal neutrality, it was unpopular in many Iroquois communities since the Oneidas circumvented the Six Nations' council protocols and turned over wampum not given to them.[18]

Politically, by early 1776, the Oneidas already deemed pro-American Seven Nations factions to be "of one heart & a mind" with them, so they invited Laurentian Indian representatives to a crucial Six Nations confederacy meeting at the central council fire at Onondaga village, coming in March. This also accommodated the Seven Nations' mid-September promises to confer with the Iroquois after St. Johns finally fell. A party of Canada Indians—unnamed Kahnawakes and representatives from "adjacent villages"—reached Oneida village on March 11 for preliminary coordination. Then the Oneidas led the group to Onondaga, accompanied by their trusted friend James Dean.[19]

Even before the Six Nations council convened, American missionary Samuel Kirkland reported, "Many of the Indians have observed to me, that they never knew debates so warm, and contention so fierce, to have happened." Starting March 28, Onondaga council discussions were stoked even hotter during five days' deliberations, as sachems tried to negotiate a consensus to address opposing pressures from the ends of their figurative longhouse. In the west, Senecas and displaced Mohawks coordinated efforts with agents of the Crown at a rekindled Fort Niagara council fire, while to the east, the most influential Oneida faction cooperated with American Indian commissioners in Albany.[20]

Even though he did not attend this council in person, John Butler was the key British voice echoed at Onondaga, having been "appointed to the care and charge of the Indian Department in Colonel [Guy] Johnson's absence." The Seneca-speaking Butler and Fort Niagara commandant Lieutenant Colonel John Caldwell exploited every means in their power "to Point out . . . the insidious Designs of the Rebels, and the pernicious Consequences of their joining the King's Enemies," thereby successfully contesting American influence among the Six Nations. They backed their messages with substantial presents. Butler particularly emphasized the Indians' own responsibility to "open the door" to British trade goods by securing the St. Lawrence corridor, now blocked by the rebel army in Montreal. The British messages resonated particularly well with those Mohawks closely allied to the Johnson family, as well as a large Seneca bloc—from a particularly influential nation, containing about half of the Six Nations' population, and inclined toward the warpath as the confederacy's "Keepers of the Western Door."[21] In the grand council, like-minded Seneca, Cayuga, and Onondaga chiefs reiterated the British agent's most meaningful themes in efforts to persuade confederacy sachems to lean toward Great Britain.

The Oneidas, on the other hand, appealed for continued neutrality, advocating reliance on generations-old strategy in the face of unsettling revolutionary conditions in the colonies. The Oneidas, backed by Tuscarora and Kahnawake allies, "manifested an unshaken friendship for the Colonies, and a firm attachment to the Council-fire at Albany." By the time the Onondaga council ended on April 2, the Oneidas' message carried the day with the conservative sachems in council, but a long struggle lay ahead. As historian Paul L. Stevens summarized, the confederacy was "publicly united around its traditional policy but privately divided over perceptions of the League's true interests and loyalties."[22]

The March 1776 Onondaga council clarified the emerging northern Indian camps in this war. An American political commissioner concluded, "The Oneidas, Tuscaroras, the Deputies from Canada, and some other small Tribes appear to be our firm Friends, but the Senecas, Mohawks and the others seem to me to be unfriendly." From Fort Niagara, Butler similarly believed "all the back nations . . . are at the Kings command & will take his side." He further disputed Kahnawake claims to have united the Seven Nations in neutrality, maintaining that "the Kaghnawages are by themselves—& they are Bostonians [Americans]."[23] In the early weeks of spring, both Crown and Continental officials believed they had made considerable progress toward their respective Indian affairs objectives. Events in Canada would soon put the northern Indian world's growing rifts on display, even if they were generally curbed by still-intact peacekeeping protocols between and within the Iroquois Six Nations and the Seven Nations of Canada.

CHAPTER 6

ON THE BLOOMING MOON

During the first two months of the American occupation of Montreal, British Indian Department interpreter Claude de Lorimier followed the example of most loyalists and "dared not speak." By late January 1776, however, economic interests finally prompted Montrealers to raise their voices in the public sphere. The fur trade was the city's lifeblood, and under rebel rule, almost everyone in the city feared they might be prohibited from sending annual shipments up the St. Lawrence and Ottawa Rivers in early May.[1]

Citizens met to discuss their concerns in a couple of public assemblies. On February 2, one of these meetings broke down as pro-American and loyalist Montrealers competed for preeminence. In the midst of a chaotic adjournment, Lorimier emerged from the crowd to make a bold, loud declaration against the occupiers. Patriot Canadians took note of his reemergence and conveyed their concerns to American officials.[2]

A few days later, American commander Brig. Gen. David Wooster announced that he "did not incline to grant passports without the direction of Congress," justifiably concerned that trade goods might be used by the British Great Lakes garrisons and their Indian allies to attack from the west. While the Montreal business community could still petition the Continental Congress for redress, no coarse goods were to be "carried out of the Country[,] unless for the use of the Continental Army."[3] The Americans temporarily barred the trade door between Montreal and the up-country—exactly as British Indian agent John Butler had repeatedly warned Indians in Fort Niagara winter councils.

Before the end of February, General Wooster called Lorimier to headquarters and demanded an accounting for his very public loyalist stand at the citizens' assembly. The chevalier unabashedly "admitted every bit of it." Exasperated and short of patience, Wooster ordered Lorimier to "get ready to leave for New York within six days" as a political prisoner.[4] The French Canadian was slated to join several recently arrested loyalists who were destined for imprisonment in the thirteen colonies.

Lorimier quickly plotted an escape before his arrest, collaborating with lawyer Richard Walker and fur trader James Stanley Goddard. They would head up-country to recruit Indian allies and return to attack the Continental occupiers, just as Lorimier proposed to Governor Guy Carleton back in November. Goddard was an invaluable contributor who had spent fifteen years intimately immersed in the Great Lakes Indian trade. As deputy Indian superintendent Daniel Claus previously assessed, Goddard had more "influence w[i]th the Indians about Lake Michigan" than any other trader, agent, or officer.[5]

The loyalist trio slipped out of Montreal on March 2. Lorimier escaped by disguising himself as an Indian, "out cold" from too much drink, sprawled in the back of a carriage driven by his beloved Kahnawake partner Louise Sagoouike. Deceived, Continental sentries let them pass the city gates. The loyalists reunited at the Lorimier family home in nearby Lachine village, eight miles from the city, where the chevalier gathered essential gear for an onerous 120-mile overland trip to the nearest British-held fort, Oswegatchie on the upper St. Lawrence.[6]

Under bright winter moonlight, the loyalists set out by horse-drawn sleigh, bells removed for silent passage. They crossed the frozen St. Lawrence to the sparsely settled south bank and abandoned their sleigh in Ville Chauve (Beauharnois) that same night. From there, the trio trekked on snowshoes for three miserable days, reaching the Seven Nations village of Akwesasne, also known as St. Regis, on March 6. A friendly Akwesasne Mohawk took them on to Oswegatchie aboard his wicker sleigh in just two and a half more days.[7]

Lorimier, Goddard, Walker, and their Akwesasne sleigh driver cleared the woods and approached the small, snow-blanketed village on the St. Lawrence River's south bank. Smoke from a few score Indian and merchant houses veiled Fort Oswegatchie in the background. Lorimier was probably familiar with both village and fort; his father commanded the post in the French and Indian War, and it was common for Canadian officers' young sons to accompany them on duty.[8]

Like Seven Nations communities downriver, the Oswegatchie Indian village originated as a Catholic mission. It thrived from its 1749 foundation until the French and Indian War brought a disastrous turn. In 1760, Abbé François Picquet, the town's famous warrior-missionary, fled as the British advanced down the St. Lawrence. Most villagers soon followed suit, seeking shelter downriver in Akwesasne, or returning back to native Six Nations lands. In the interwar years, remaining Oswegatchies benefited from proximity to the British-held post, but as the new war dawned in 1775, they opted for neutrality from their ambiguously subordinate position between the Six and Seven Nations. A solitary

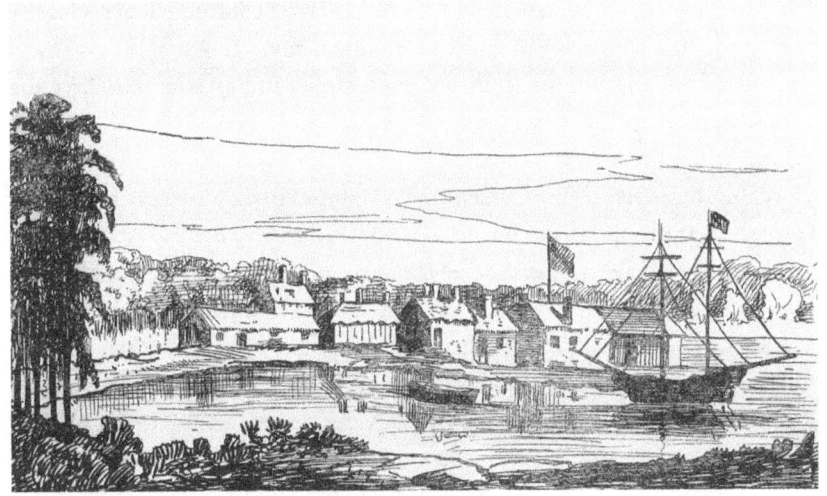

View of Oswegatchee on the River St. Lawrence, July 1765.
Courtesy Library and Archives Canada (C-097658).

contemporary report observed that the villagers would "decline taking up the Hatchet against the Bostonians [Americans]."[9]

Lorimier, Goddard, and Walker recovered a few days in Oswegatchie before conferring with the British fort commandant—Captain George Forster of the King's Regiment of Foot (the Eighth), a veteran of two decades' service, including European campaigning in the Seven Years' War. His North American adventure began in June 1768 when the Eighth shipped to Canada on a regular unit rotation, beginning six years of "Tranquility and boredom" in garrison duty around Montreal and Quebec City. In 1770, Forster received a captaincy and command of the regiment's "elite" light infantry company. More demanding duty came four years later, when the entire regiment was ordered up-country to replace another posted at Forts Niagara, Detroit, Michilimackinac, and Oswegatchie.[10]

Forster's company occupied Fort Oswegatchie, which consisted simply of "four blockhouses joined together by rows of piquetts" about fifteen feet high. The outpost was far more important than its size or stature reflected. In 1768, General Thomas Gage cogently argued: "The Post of Oswegatchi is very Necessary, to protect the Provision which is sent in Boats from Montreal to Oswegatchi, and carried in Sloops from thence over the Lakes, to supply the Forts in the Indian Country." The post was also one of the Crown's "backcountry contact points" for regular interaction with the region's indigenous inhabitants and migrant visitors.

In a year and a half at the remote fort, Captain Forster confronted myriad tasks: mitigating the fortifications' natural deterioration; managing supply storage and shipment for the rest of the regiment; maintaining Indian relations; directing quotidian garrison life for soldiers and families; and whenever time permitted, drilling troops in tactical mechanics.[11]

When the adventurous loyalists met Captain Forster, they pitched a bold "project to raise Indians to burn the [American] shipping" at Ticonderoga. The king's officer abruptly dismissed the idea, and forbade the Canadians from undertaking any enterprise of the sort. The two Anglo Canadians subsequently avoided Captain Forster, and Walker soon disappeared from the scene, but Lorimier worked hard to give the commandant "a better opinion" of his zeal and loyalty. Lorimier and Goddard had already decided to take matters into their own hands and seek support elsewhere, focusing efforts toward an attack on the rebels around Montreal. Goddard left for Fort Niagara, hoping that a direct appeal to the Eighth Regiment's commander, Lieutenant Colonel John Caldwell, might be more productive. Lorimier remained at Fort Oswegatchie until he persuaded Captain Forster to permit him to hunt his own food in mid-March.[12]

In white-blanketed, wooded Native hunting grounds north of Lake Ontario, Lorimier encountered Kanesatake men who had traveled west from Lake of Two Mountains "to follow the chase, according to the custom of their forefathers." Lorimier shared his plans for a springtime attack on the Americans, and these men expressed eagerness to join when the time came. Kanesatake warriors had consistently responded every time Governor Carleton called for support, and they were further motivated by reports that the Americans had mistreated two of their warrior brethren, captured at Longueuil in October.[13] The French Canadian interpreter and Kanesatake hunters parted to continue their late winter hunts.

Elsewhere among barren hardwoods and snow-covered spruce, Lorimier met hunting bands from the Algonquian Ojibwa-speaking Mississaugas of the northern Lake Ontario basin. The Canadian interpreter presumably had some understanding of the Mississauga language and customs, since his father had also been a liaison officer with them during the last war. To most British and French colonists, these people were a mystery; the seasonally migratory Mississaugas lived in small "Parts & Tribes" of family-centric bands, much less observable and comprehensible than village-based Six and Seven Nations peoples.[14]

Politically, imperial powers also struggled to discern consistency in the Mississaugas' allegiances, since these Indians conducted politics at the band level. Their commitments appeared ephemeral since, in the right season, any influential

Anishinaabe could gather a war party when he wished, and individual warriors took up the hatchet whenever there was a promising opportunity to "prove one's worth" in battle.[15]

Like the Lake of Two Mountains Kanesatakes, the Mississaugas needed little encouragement to take the warpath with the British in the Revolutionary War, but for different reasons. In season, Mississauga warriors could take the warpath whenever there seemed promising opportunities for glory, and their lands were distant from any American threat. In the previous summer, twenty-two Mississauga warriors had already patrolled provincial borderlands around Fort St. Johns as allies of the Crown. Two more years into the war, a British officer observed that Mississaugas "never varied nor required holding any Councils to deliberate." As ethnohistorian Joy Bilharz noted, "Unlike the Iroquois, the Mississaugas did not require bribes, threats, cajoling, and constant attention."[16]

Yet when Mississauga hunting parties met Lorimier in late March 1776, they were not yet ready to take the warpath. The men and their wigwam-dwelling families were transitioning from hibernal subsistence hunting to early spring maple sap–gathering sites, and they suspended warfare in the winter, resuming once ice cleared and they could travel by canoe. Presumably in a series of encounters in the deep woods, and on icy bogs and frozen rock-rimmed lakes, Lorimier claimed to meet about one hundred Mississaugas, who told him they would bring 250 "good men" to rally at Gananoque on the May 3 "Blooming Moon" to join his campaign. They promised to send a messenger fifty miles down the St. Lawrence to Fort Oswegatchie, to inform Lorimier when they had assembled.[17] The French Canadian's hunting-ground proselytization had been quite fruitful.

While Lorimier ranged the woods west of Oswegatchie, his compatriot James Stanley Goddard journeyed over 270 miles of snow, ice, melt, mud, and waterways to reach Fort Niagara. Near the end of April, Goddard finally arrived at the remote British fort on the south Lake Ontario shore, ready to persuade the king's officers to support his scheme to attack the rebels around Montreal.

In the imposing three-story stone "castle" headquarters, built a half century earlier by the French, Colonel Caldwell listened to Goddard's proposals. The reticent British commander declined direct commitment. His garrison was typically short of provisions at winter's end, and there was an ever-present chance the rebels might launch a surprise attack on his expansive but undermanned and eroded post. After this rebuff, the persistent Goddard sought an audience with Indian Department officer John Butler.[18]

The senior department agent had laid the groundwork for just such an enterprise, having "spared no pains, nor attention to fix" the Six Nations to the king's interests. In frequent meetings with western Haudenosaunee Iroquois and various Great Lakes chiefs, Butler regularly emphasized the St. Lawrence corridor's importance, pointing out "the Boston people have got possession of Cannada, the only Dore you and your Western Breatherin had a Right to Expect Supplys through." Some Senecas had already indicated their intention to act, "should the Road of peace & the Dore through which our Trade comes be stopped up."[19] General Wooster's February fur trade ban in Montreal had done just that.

After meeting Goddard, Butler held new conferences with the many Iroquois in and around Fort Niagara. He repeated his usual themes, adding warnings that his king was "a Terror to all the World," who could crush the rebels as easily as the Indians could "a Muskitoe." Butler further suggested that the Seven Nations of Canada had recently changed their outlook after discerning "the Wicked & Treacherous design of the Bostonians," and claiming that two hundred Canada warriors were "determined to Clear their Country of them."[20]

John Butler proposed "that a number of your warriors should go in quest of Col [Guy] Johnson"—everyone expected the Indian superintendent to return to Quebec from London as soon as the St. Lawrence cleared in early May. Following Johnson's model from the previous summer, Butler provided a convenient, superficially peaceful pretext for the king's Indian friends to travel to Canada. Once the young men were far from sachems and clan matrons and other restraining forces at home, circumstances could easily lead them onto the warpath. Once substantial Indian support was evident, Colonel Caldwell released a British government Lake Ontario sailing ship to transport the gathering force. Butler suggested to the Indians, "Let them imbark—who desire a speedy interview w[i]th Col Johnson." Some skeptical chiefs at Fort Niagara saw through and denounced Butler's ploy, while others vainly reminded eager young men of their confederacy's neutral stance.[21]

Once again, a substantial number of Six Nations men played along, as more than fifty joined the new expedition, eager to prove themselves in battle and help reopen their access to trade goods. They were principally Senecas, with smaller Cayuga, Onondaga, and Mohawk contingents, and even a few Oneidas. At least one of Sir William Johnson's Indian sons joined them, veteran warrior William Tekawiroñte.[22]

While Butler was busy securing these Six Nations volunteers' commitment, James Stanley Goddard visited a neighboring group of Indians. The loyalist trader used his considerable experience with Anishinaabeg people to solicit

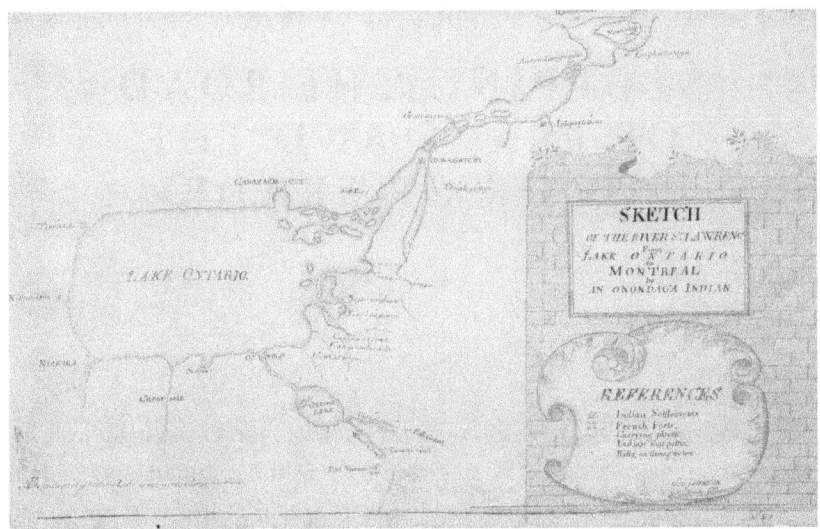

"Sketch of the River St. Lawrence from Lake Ontario to Montreal by an Onondaga Indian." Map by cartographer Guy Johnson, 1759. This map is particularly interesting for its Indian perspective. "Baron Longueills" is the Cedars; "Rarondacks" is Kanesatake.

Map reproduction courtesy of the Royal United Services Institute for Defence and Security Studies and Norman B. Leventhal Map and Education Center, Boston Public Library.

support from Mississaugas across the Niagara River, perhaps as far afield as modern Toronto. These were different bands from those Lorimier had met a few weeks earlier. Forty or fifty responded to Goddard's appeal, agreeing to join the expedition.[23] As they headed for Fort Niagara to join the Iroquois contingents, Goddard pressed on to the upper Great Lakes to gather even more allies for summer campaigns in Canada.

The Indians boarded a large sailing ship, perhaps the *Haldimand*, accompanied by some of John Butler's junior Indian Department men to make sure the warriors were "properly officered" in the field. Circumstantially, Caldwell might have transmitted orders to Fort Oswegatchie with this vessel, authorizing Captain Forster to prudently employ his light infantry company, and historian Paul Stevens further suggested that the colonel probably dispatched "a squad or two of redcoats to watch over Forster's fort while the captain led his garrison out to fight." With fair winds, on May 10 the ship set off on a short, speedy cruise down Lake Ontario and the St. Lawrence.[24]

CHAPTER 7

STOPPING THE ROAD OF PEACE AND THE DOOR OF TRADE

Near the end of March, Claude de Lorimier returned to Fort Oswegatchie from his winter hunting-ground tour. He shared with the British commandant, Captain George Forster, that 250 Mississauga allies were expected in just a few weeks, and that he was "uneasy on the question of provisions." Lorimier shared a plan to use contacts at the nearest settled parish, the Cedars (Les Cèdres), thirty miles upriver from Montreal, to obtain additional supplies through covert loyalist networks. While Forster remained gruffly ill-disposed toward amateur military ventures out of his fort, allied Indian activity may have sparked his interest—he permitted the interpreter to venture downriver.[1]

Dressing himself in Indian garb again, Lorimier ventured three days down the still-frozen St. Lawrence to the Cedars. Upon arriving, he visited the parish priest's home, meeting young Curé Pierre Denaut, a friend with "ardent zeal" for the Crown. The adventurous interpreter shared his schemes and asked for assistance gathering "a fortnight's provisions sufficient for nearly 300 men as soon as the river was navigable." Denaut called wealthy merchant Thomas Denis to come straightaway. The Anglo loyalist proved equally "eager to serve the government," assuring Lorimier that the requested goods "would arrive on time since he [already] had enough on hand to load three bateaux." The French Canadian interpreter returned to Oswegatchie, arriving in early April as the last river ice floated off.[2]

As Lorimier repeatedly demonstrated his energy and dedication to the king's cause, Captain Forster's icy view of Lorimier seems to have thawed in tune with the seasons. When the interpreter reported his successful encounter at the Cedars, the commandant ordered his junior officer, Lieutenant Henry Bird, to lead a few soldiers downriver in three bateaux to recover and protect the promised goods. The redcoat lieutenant already had a dozen years' peacetime service, but the

Rapids on the Approach to the Village of the Cedars, Lower Canada, ca. 1838.
Courtesy Library and Archives Canada (1970-188-PIC-02217).

coming campaign would launch him into a series of "zealous services with the Indians thro' the whole of the war."[3]

Guided by Lorimier, Lieutenant Bird's little detachment skillfully piloted and portaged their bateaux through ice-cold, rushing waters and roaring Laurentian torrents to reach Pointe-au-Foin, above the Coteau-du-Lac rapids and fourteen river miles from the Cedars. As the lieutenant and his men set up camp on a frozen inlet, Lorimier advised them to stay in place with the bateaux, while he ventured solo to scout out their destination. In his now usual Indian disguise, he approached Curé Denaut's presbytery on the morning of April 11.[4]

Lorimier used costume and play-acting to slip past a detachment of rebel American soldiers coincidentally lingering around the priest's house, where he coaxed the priest into his chambers. In a hushed private conversation, Denaut explained that the requested goods were already conveniently hidden at the Coteau-du-Lac portage, between the Cedars and Lieutenant Bird's detachment. Lorimier rejoined the lieutenant and led him to the cache site, where the soldiers helped unearth 125 quarter barrels of provisions—roughly enough to feed two hundred men for two weeks. Soldiers carefully packed the goods into the three bateaux and made an arduous eighty-five-mile return trip to Oswegatchie, fighting the current in their heavily laden vessels.[5]

Despite Lorimier's secrecy, rebel leaders were largely aware of his adventures. Just days after he escaped Montreal, American authorities heard about his passage through Akwesasne, and Brig. Gen. David Wooster informed his superiors that loyalists were opening communication with the king's troops at Oswegatchie and Niagara. Wooster presciently warned of "a plan concerted for those troops, in conjunction with what Canadians can be collected about those places, a number of Indian traders and their workmen, and a number of Savages, to make a descent upon this town." Such intelligence often came from pro-American Kahnawakes, who freely traveled with open ears in the Seven Nations' sphere, where there were few Euro-colonial secrets kept between Indians. Wooster asked a friendly young Lorette Huron, Louis Vincent Sawatanen, to go "among several of their tribes, to see whether he can find out the truth" behind the rumored up-country loyalist agitation.[6]

With spring offering hope for action and success at Quebec City, General Wooster left Montreal on March 27 to lead the main American corps himself. Col. Moses Hazen, commander of the Second Canadian Continental Regiment, was left in temporary command of the rear district until Brig. Gen. Benedict Arnold came upriver to take charge on April 20. The general was still limping from the serious leg wound he received in Montgomery's failed New Year's Eve assault but was ready to apply his energies and bold spirit to this new duty.

On the same day Arnold arrived in Montreal, Colonel Hazen informed him of a fresh report that the "Rascall" Lorimier had been seen at "the Ceadars ... stir[r]ing the Indians to cut our throats here," and of Hazen's own plans to move troops west to counter this brewing threat. General Arnold concurred and quickly issued new orders: Col. Timothy Bedel and the New Hampshire Rangers were to "march Immediately & take post at the Cedars," as well as Carillon, critical portage points upriver from Montreal, on the St. Lawrence and Ottawa, respectively. Bedel was "to prevent any goods being sent to the upper country, and to guard against a surprise from the enemy or their Indians."[7]

Conceptually, Bedel's assignment was simple, but geography significantly complicated matters. The colonel was responsible for two remote points separated by forty river miles, both dozens of miles upstream from supply and reinforcements in Montreal. Furthermore, Bedel was also tasked "to Cultivate a friendship with the Indians and engage them if possible in the service of the united Colonies," resuming his fall role as the army's lead Indian agent.

Bedel also faced serious manpower challenges. The bulk of his New Hampshire regiment was serving far away at Quebec City, so he could cobble together only 260 rangers from his recently arrived trail echelon. Bedel and his officers took advantage of time in the city to procure muskets for their many soldiers who had entered Canada weaponless.[8]

On the same day Bedel received his new orders, he expanded his force through interesting means. He signed on Kahnawake chief Louis Atiatoharongwen as captain of an additional Indian company in his ranger regiment, with a lieutenant and twenty-eight "rank and file." The Indians received an enlistment bonus and were paid at Continental rates.[9] These Kahnawakes would provide valuable scouting service but were not a substitute for conventional Continental troops at the new upriver posts.

To help remediate troop shortages, Arnold augmented Bedel's command with two half-strength companies from Burrall's Connecticut Regiment. Established in January, this regiment's mobilization experiences closely paralleled those of Bedel's Rangers. Col. Charles Burrall had been similarly charged to use "the utmost dispatch to forward the first [companies] that can be got ready," and he too sent small, ill-equipped parties forward in haste. Burrall and most of his troops went to Quebec City, but two of his captains led almost one hundred Connecticut soldiers still in rear areas to join Bedel. Arnold also detached a lieutenant and eleven soldiers from Hazen's Second Canadian Continental Regiment, perhaps to help coordinate with French-speaking locals. A sergeant's detachment of four artillerymen also brought two brass field artillery pieces for the Cedars fort.[10] Altogether, Bedel had about 360 Continentals to guard distant posts at the Cedars and Carillon and secure their lines of communication from the much anticipated Indian and British up-country threat.

Even before the enemy approached, Bedel's corps was already being depleted by another scourge—smallpox. The disease bloomed in the Quebec City siege camp, and it hit Montreal as soldiers headed home at the end of their enlistments. Frightened by the fatal risks of contracting the disease by natural, chance infection, many Continental soldiers "inoculated themselves contrary to orders," to reduce the chance of death. In the process, they rendered themselves ineffective for weeks while fighting the disease, and if not isolated after inoculation, they could spread contagion even further. At Louisbourg in the French and Indian

War, Bedel personally witnessed the devastation smallpox could visit on an army, and he chose to be inoculated in Montreal before heading to the field—this gave him about a dozen days to deploy his forces and establish the two new posts before the disease's most debilitating effects would strike him in a month-long course of symptoms.[11]

When Bedel's and Burrall's men formed in Montreal for their westward journey on April 22, they were largely wearing their own civilian clothes—the ranks appearing as an undifferentiated mass of New England farmers. Officers were primarily distinguished by finer clothing, and some ornamentation like hat lace. Although New Hampshire Committee of Safety authorized the rangers' muster master two hundred yards of cloth for "Indian leggins," shirts, and coats, it appears clothing was issued only to the few men who enlisted without appropriate field wear.[12]

Bedel's column spent its first night in the fur-trade village of Lachine. From there, the soldiers slowly followed the riverside highway west for two days, keeping the gentle St. Lawrence flow on their left as they passed a seemingly uninterrupted string of farms. In Ste. Anne Parish, on the "tip of the Island," the column followed the shoreline north. A couple of miles later, Capt. John Stevens's Connecticut vanguard would have spotted two windmill structures in the distance, one ancient and one functioning, and then a structure appearing like a European stone castle—Fort Ste. Anne (also known as Fort Senneville). Its four corner towers were roughly two and a half stories high, capped with steep roofs. Twelve-foot walls connected the bastions on three sides, and the back wall of the two-story, three-chimneyed manor house formed the fort's southern face.[13]

Estate owner Jean-Baptiste Philippe Jérémie Testard de Montigny was "at first much unwilling" to cooperate with the rebels. Not only was he a dedicated loyalist, but he had just spent the last two years transforming the manor from an abandoned hulk into a beautiful, well-furnished home that he did not wish to see damaged by the occupiers. After brief protests, he resigned himself to his plight and left with his wife and two young sons, temporarily abandoning the place to rebel soldiers.[14]

Later that day, Maj. Isaac Butterfield of the New Hampshire Rangers joined the troops at Fort Ste. Anne. He was acting as Bedel's second-in-command but lacked any military background more substantial than a few months' local duty as a militia major before receiving his Continental commission. Butterfield's most notable qualification might have been his ability to recruit, since he was "well acquainted w[i]th the people & Country" in the neighborhood of his popular Connecticut Valley tavern.[15]

The following morning, April 26, Butterfield ordered Capt. Ebenezer Green and twenty-five ranger volunteers across the Lake of Two Mountains to establish a foothold on the mainland—a vast wedge between the Ottawa and St. Lawrence Rivers known as the Presqu'île (peninsula). Green's band pushed a bateau off into the unknown, unable to distinguish any meaningful details on the low, wooded banks of the distant shore. The soldiers rowed across the placid basin, steering into a slight current from the north. Two miles later, they hauled ashore at the Pointe-de-Quinchien landing, near seigneur Michel-Eustache-Gaspard-Alain Chartier de Lotbinière's water mill and below his manor house. The owner was absent, detained by the Americans as a loyalist prisoner of war at the surrender of Fort St. Johns. With the far shore secure, Major Butterfield and the main body joined Green's advance guard the next day.[16]

From the Pointe-de-Quinchien landing, Major Butterfield led his men on a leisurely paced eleven-mile march south to the Cedars, along the road that roughly followed the shoreline. There were still plenty of farms in "very pleasant country," but on this side of the Lake of Two Mountains, the cultivated strand was interrupted more frequently by woods and marshes.[17] About halfway to their destination, soldiers would have heard a low churning roar from the nearby Les Cascades rapids, the last stretch of dangerous Laurentian falls before the river spread into the calm of Lake St. Louis. A right turn led the column west to its destination, through a final stretch of continuously settled ground along the St. Lawrence.

On April 28, Butterfield and his men reached the Cedars. The parish was named for trees that once stood at the tip of a wide, high-banked peninsula, projecting south into the St. Lawrence's turbulent course. The point overlooked a river waterway where only brave pilots with lightly laden vessels might dare to pass the perilous Coteau-des-Cèdres rapids. Most travelers took the portage instead, using the dirt road running just north of the peninsula. Even someone with Butterfield's limited military experience would see the wisdom of building a fort there. For good or bad, the point was also the hub of the Cedars community. A well-weathered wooden parish church and Curé Denaut's presbytery sat near the middle of the peninsula. Adjoining the church grounds, there was at least one large general store and seigneur Paul-Joseph LeMoyne de Longueuil's estate, including a manor home, barns, and a water mill.[18]

Regional Overview.
Map by Tom Jonas.

Major Butterfield had adequate manpower and plenty of matériel to construct the new fort, but he lacked an engineer. Of five captains, only Daniel Wilkins had any relevant military experience, but despite service at Cambridge and Bunker Hill, he appeared to remain "ignorant as to the art and policy of war."[19] Butterfield's men proceeded to build a fine-looking fort with basic ax and shovel skills, but the structure would have its design limitations.

Challenged by fickle spring weather, the New England soldiers worked through rain and snow, then unseasonable heat in early May. Since the site was surrounded by furrowed farmland, the troops did not have to clear trees for fields of fire, but that also meant they had to travel several hundred yards to harvest the substantial quantities of wood needed for the fort. The men felled and hauled trees, trimmed off branches, and erected clean trunks in predug holes to form a picket stockade. Thick outer logs might have been reinforced by a second row of thinner posts to fill gaps and increase durability. Elsewhere on the line, soldiers raised earthworks by digging a perimeter ditch, and piling the dirt behind to form a rampart wall of about six feet in height. Reinforced by brush and branches, the result was a breastwork, "designed for covering the soldiers from the enemies cannon or small shot."[20]

The precise layout of Fort Cedars is lost to history, but it appears to have encompassed most of the peninsula. The main fortifications formed a north face roughly paralleling the road; the "greater part of them" enclosed "with picquets[,] and the rest with lines of earth," with cannon positions near each end. The fort's other three sides were primarily protected by steep riverbanks, rising eighteen to twenty feet above the water. The soldiers took up quarters in the church and other substantial buildings inside the works.[21]

Col. Timothy Bedel finally joined his men at Fort Cedars on May 6. His trip must have been uncomfortable as his case of smallpox brought a potential host of symptoms at this stage—fever, backache, headache, nausea. By the time he arrived, his skin was probably breaking out in a rash, and pox pustules might even have started taking form.[22] Still, Bedel summoned the strength to survey the fortifications built in his absence.

Examining one of the recently completed breastworks, Bedel agreed that it was "very nice and strong," but he confided to a friend that there was a key weakness in the fort's layout: it was too large. Because the fort covered so much of the peninsula, there were about five hundred meters of fortified line to be manned on the north side, and the colonel assessed that it would take two regiments to properly man them—he had the equivalent of only half of a regiment. If any of the Continental officers had consulted the popular *Military Instructions for Officers Detached in the Field*, they would have read: "The extent of the work must be proportioned to the number of men that are to defend it, . . . too large intrenchments . . . can only be defended by considerable bodies. Excesses of this kind are extremely reprehensible."[23] It was far too late for Bedel to adjust the plan. The Continentals would have to defend Fort Cedars as best they could, stretching the manpower at hand.

As American soldiers labored to complete Fort Cedars, Capt. Louis Atiatoharongwen's Indian company scouted upriver. Their patrols presumably gave some comfort to the Continentals, with someone in position to provide early warning of an enemy advance. Unbeknownst to the soldiers, the Kahnawakes probably gleaned most of their information from conversations with Indian travelers on the river, and in Akwesasne (St. Regis) village, rather than by ranging up the St. Lawrence on traditional long-range reconnaissance.[24]

Back on the Island of Montreal, Capt. Samuel Young from Bedel's Rangers had been left at Fort Ste. Anne with thirty of his own men and a lieutenant's detachment from Stevens's Connecticut company to guard Continental lines of communication. Their first notable action came on April 28, when Young received intelligence that loyalists were sending powder and rum to enemy forces in the west, aboard several canoes. The captain dispatched an ensign and twenty-two men in a bateau on the Lake of Two Mountains to find and interdict this illicit shipment. The Continentals encountered only a single canoe, and finding nothing more than flour and "indian Packs" on board, soldiers gave the inconvenienced Kanesatake occupants a dram of rum for their time, and parted ways.[25]

On the cold, dreary morning of May 5, Capt. John Stevens and a few dozen Connecticut soldiers passed through Fort Ste. Anne on their way up the Ottawa River to establish the Carillon post. The Yankees made a pleasant en route stop at Kanesatake village, and then as Pvt. Benjamin Stevens sarcastically recorded, "In the afternoon we sailed up the river eighteen miles to Caralion [sic], the Grand Place we have been sentenced to." The soldiers established a camp to guard the point where the Ottawa was "interrupted by a succession of rapids and cascades for upwards of ten miles"; but after just four days, Captain Stevens received new orders to abandon the post and rejoin the main body at the Cedars. Passing back by Kanesatake, the Continentals exchanged friendly salutes with Indian villagers, without the slightest hint that Lake of Two Mountains warriors were simply biding time to join Lorimier on the warpath.[26] They would meet again soon, under far different circumstances.

CHAPTER 8

"EACH NATION SANG ITS DEATH SONG"

When Claude de Lorimier returned to Fort Oswegatchie from his provision-gathering trip at the Cedars in early May, he sent a messenger to Gananoque to let his Mississauga friends know that he was ready for them. The weather was decisively trending away from winter; even the first dandelions and strawberries were in bloom. About one hundred Mississaugas paddled down the St. Lawrence and descended on the fort well before midmonth.[1]

Then on May 12, a large vessel suddenly appeared up the St. Lawrence and came to anchor in the basin at the mouth of the Oswegatchie River, completing its swift two-day sail from Fort Niagara. Nearly a hundred Six Nations men and western Mississaugas stepped ashore outside Fort Oswegatchie's main gate, accompanied by a few Indian Department officers. When the Six Nations men looked around and realized a military campaign was brewing, they split into two factions.[2]

The more aggressive element was ready to take up arms, rallying around three confident and persuasive chiefs: Seneca Kanughsgawiat; a "certain Indian, Called Aboyderroy"; and Onondaga Kaquatanawajey, who "was entirely averse to anything of a peaceable nature." They "prevailed on the younger warriors" to join British and Mississauga allies on the warpath. As ethnohistorian Roland Viau described such moments, for "the Iroquoian man, war was unquestionably a privileged means to prove his skill, accumulate exploits, and thus aspire to war chieftaincy." Battlefield success raised a young man's stature at home and established his masculinity, and several could not resist the promising opportunity given at Oswegatchie.[3]

These warriors had no intention of joining British- or Canadian-led expeditions as obedient auxiliaries, but instead embarked on "parallel warfare." Historian Peter MacLeod used this conceptual framework to characterize Indian-French cooperation in the Seven Years' War, when "both parties to the alliance waged a separate war against the common enemy." This applied in the Revolutionary War too. The belligerent Indian faction at Fort Oswegatchie was ready to fight for an "open door" to trade goods, to maintain strategic ties with Britain, and to increase personal prestige, but chiefs and warriors were far less interested in extinguishing the American rebellion or demonstrating obedience to King George III.[4]

In the midst of the hubbub of Indian arrivals, fort commandant Captain George Forster suddenly became an advocate for action—an about-face that is best explained if Lieutenant Colonel John Caldwell actually sent him orders, and possibly reinforcements, with the ship from Niagara. The captain promptly offered wavering Indians additional enticements to "induce them to engage in the enterprize," including promises of trade goods and monetary rewards downriver. Allegedly, he also dangled the prospect of some of the warriors' traditional, tangible measures of success: "free plunder" and prisoner-captives.[5]

With the three chiefs' instigation and Captain Forster's encouragement, twenty-two Six Nations men took up the hatchet at Oswegatchie—predominantly Senecas, some Mohawks and Onondagas, and apparently even a few Oneidas and Cayugas. As a result, about eight score warriors prepared for action, ranging from the "very stout" Mississaugas to the "taller and better proportioned" Senecas. They committed themselves by singing their "war song" in a ritual also known as the death song—a public declaration that a warrior "took his life in his hand."[6]

The other half of the Six Nations men from Niagara had honestly believed they had come to Oswegatchie to obtain a "a speedy interview" with Indian superintendent Guy Johnson upon his return to Canada. This peacefully inclined element really did come just to hear "the Kings words" and receive first shares of presents from England. They were "disgusted at the proceedings of their chief warriors" and soon left for their home villages.[7]

Even at this early moment, Captain Forster undoubtedly recognized a duty to influence the king's new Indian allies on the warpath. Parallel warfare posed immediate practical challenges to British honor. Historian Armstrong Starkey encapsulated them as "the interesting moral question of the responsibility of officers who knowingly employed warriors who they knew would violate European standards." The captain may have also felt obliged to "show the flag," encouraging the Crown's friends and Canadian subjects "who undoubtedly would have otherwise wondered why they should fight George III's battles for him if he wouldn't risk his own troops."[8] Yet even with these compelling motivations, it seems a near certainty that Forster had some form of orders authorizing him to leave his strategic post and join the rapidly emerging and ever-expanding Indian attack on the rebels.

While Captain Forster conducted Indian diplomacy, the rest of his light company immediately broke from mundane garrison routine to join the campaign. Redcoat rank and file filled cartridge boxes and ensured their "short" light infantry muskets, hatchets, and bayonets were in good order. Soldiers and garrison wives probably rushed to mend and patch well-worn, faded brick-red uniforms already at the end of their one-year service lives.[9] Teams pulled casks and bundles from the fort's stores, manhandled them to the river shore, and carefully loaded provisions and ammunition onto bateaux.

Excitement must have filled the air at Oswegatchie that day, but Forster's soldiers were a steady lot, "neither . . . youthful or adventurous in spirit." The average Eighth Regiment soldier was over thirty and had spent almost a decade in uniform; a fifth had been in the ranks long enough to have fought in Europe during the Seven Years' War. After eight years' garrison duty in Canada, they were well practiced in essential skills like bateaux handling, but probably maintained just a marginal tactical proficiency. Their remote post's quotidian demands left little time for regular drill or company exercise.[10]

Captain Forster marshaled "two lieutenants, two serjeants, two corporals, one drummer, and thirty-three private soldiers, of his Majesty's eighth regiment" to leave Fort Oswegatchie. Eleven "English and Canadian gentleman volunteers" joined as well, Lorimier among them. The bulk of the combined force, however, consisted of the "one hundred and sixty savages of different nations"—northern and western Mississaugas and Six Nations Iroquois. On May 12, the redcoat vanguard, loyalists, and warriors rowed sturdy bateaux and paddled more agile canoes from the fort's calm harbor basin into the rushing northeast St. Lawrence current. The campaign "to relieve the citizens of Montreal, from the oppressive tyranny of the rebels" was underway.[11]

One hundred miles downstream, in Montreal and rural western parishes, zealous loyalists covertly prepared for the up-country liberators' long-anticipated arrival by gathering provisions and assembling men to support the king. Lake of Two Mountains Kanesatakes played an important coordination role, using their relative freedom of movement as Indians to communicate up and down the St. Lawrence.[12] The most prominent Canadian loyalist recruiter was none other than Jean-Baptiste Testard de Montigny, recently displaced from his Fort Ste. Anne manor.

Like Lorimier, Montigny's father had earned the Croix de St. Louis for distinguished French and Indian War service, and both elders helped launch their sons on military careers in Canada. Their paths diverged after the British conquest of Canada though, when the Montigny family returned to France. Testard de Montigny only came back to North America in 1773, a year before buying his Fort Ste. Anne estate, yet he was a firm adherent to his new king and quickly developed "great influence" with his neighbors. After rebels took over his home, he sought out loyal militiamen in the area who would be willing to "attack the entrenchments which the Bostonians had at the Cedars, when the moment was right." By May 13, an active Montreal loyalist hinted at Montigny's success, saying "there were many persons who intended to join Captain Fo[r]ster."[13]

These efforts did not pass undetected by the rebels. At Fort Ste. Anne, Capt. Samuel Young received intelligence that *Canadiens* in the nearby inland settlement of Ste Marie were preparing to take up arms under Montigny. On May 14, Young sent ten rangers to "take the fire-arms from the French-men of the village," and they returned with thirty-three muskets and ammunition that had been hidden in and around Ste Marie's twenty-five simple farmhouses.[14]

While Montigny was circulating around the western parishes, loyalists in Montreal clandestinely collected supplies for the coming showdown. Merchant-outfitter Pierre Foretier received input from Montigny and focused his small loyalist cell's efforts on gathering gunpowder, musket balls, and deerskin for moccasins. They stored the goods in the warehouse underneath Foretier's "sumptuous" stone home on Rue St. Pierre, a couple of blocks from the city's southwest Recollet gate. Foretier had to overcome one major obstacle though—Col. John Philip De Haas and his First Pennsylvania Regiment staff had taken quarters in his house. To "deceive the vigilance" of his guests, the merchant hosted a grand supper for the rebel colonel that lasted until three in the morning, while four loyalist compatriots spent the night surreptitiously removing the provisions out from vaults right under the rebel officers' feet.[15]

The loyalists secreted the goods out of Montreal and ferried them across the Lake of Two Mountains by canoe. When the carefully packed supplies arrived in Vaudreuil, on the Presqu'île mainland, parish priest Abbé Louis Beaumont received them at his presbytery-chapel near the Pointe-de-Quinchien landing. Bundles were "deposited in a hole he had had dug in advance, in an autumn fallow field," and to cover any traces, Beaumont pastured a flock of sheep over the cache.[16] In the coming days, these loyalists' collective logistical efforts would substantively aid local Canadians and the force coming down from Oswegatchie.

On their first day's travels from Oswegatchie, Forster's Indian allies, soldiers, and volunteers navigated eighteen miles of mostly smooth-flowing waters, passing multitudinous wooded islets, to land and camp on the north bank above the Rapide Plat. That evening, the king's Indian allies received an unexpected visitor. An Akwesasne chief appeared in their midst, hoping to convince the "party to turn back and not venture any farther." He warned that the brave men "would be slaughtered by the Americans who were very numerous and who were coming in force to take and hold the rapids" at the Cedars.[17] He may have obtained his information direct from the Americans at the Cedars, or perhaps he had talked with some of Louis Atiatoharongwen's Kahnawake scouts visiting his own village.

Normally, such significant military news would prompt Indians to enter long deliberations in council. By Lorimier's sensational account, on this occasion he intervened to interrupt the time-consuming process by directly addressing the messenger. He said, "Uncle . . . my warriors and I thank you for your good intentions. . . . but you must surely know that when a warrior sings the war song he forgets the welfare of his body and recommends his soul to God." With the emotional initiative, the chevalier dismissed the accuracy of the cautious Akwesasne headman's reports and turned the tables to invite him to "come along with us and help us gather up the spoils" from enemy corpses. The chief was swayed and sang his war song, ready to seize the moment and risk his life with the others.[18]

The next day, the force continued downriver to camp above the dangerous Longue Sault rapids. On the third day, May 14, hundreds of men deftly maneuvered bateaux and canoes through a dozen miles of torrents and chutes, until the waters finally flattened out and they could safely ride the central current again. Just a few miles later, past the Raquette River, they steered toward a point of land on the right bank. They had come to the Seven Nations village of Akwesasne (St. Regis), a community of fifty-some "good huts" set around a small, wood church and surrounded by farm fields. In later years, Lorimier dramatically recounted their afternoon arrival: "Our flotilla of small canoes was more impressive than one might have thought. When we got near the village we fired off a fusillade accompanied by every imaginable shriek of joy (the effect was horrifying) and each nation sang its death song." Even though the village had a substantial pro-American faction and close ties to Kahnawake, the population of about four hundred people mobilized to welcome this peculiar multitude that had arrived at their community's doorstep.[19]

The St. Regis mission had been established only twenty-one years earlier, beginning as a Kahnawake colony—an outlet for excess population and dissenting factions, and a refuge from the relentless lure of alcohol around Montreal. The original Mohawk settlers welcomed some Six Nations outmigrants, and they were joined by displaced Oswegatchie Iroquois and Odanak (St. Francis) Abenakis at the end of the French and Indian War. The Abenakis came for refuge after Robert Rogers's famous 1759 destruction of St. Francis, originally "desiring . . . Protection for one Night as their Expression was, or untill their Village was reestablished." Yet even after Odanak was rebuilt a few years later, many Abenaki families were reluctant to leave their new home. Akwesasne Iroquois coaxed and cajoled them and even sought British assistance to encourage their return, but in 1776 about seventy or eighty Abenakis still remained in St. Regis.[20]

When Captain George Forster arrived in Akwesasne village, he called a council to recruit host nation warriors to the king's cause. Trying to maintain neutrality and placating a substantial American-oriented faction, the chiefs "refused to accompany the expedition." Their village-level decisions did not bind individual warriors though. While Forster's efforts were proving fruitless, Lorimier "made a feast" to keep up the war party's spirits and encourage Akwesasnes to join. The Canadian and his allied Indian cohorts "sang the war song and all the warriors of the village joined in"—fifty-four Akwesasne men. Sachems reluctantly "permitted their young men to go," so by the end of the second night in the village, Forster and Lorimier could tally more than two hundred warriors by their side, already four times the strength of the British light infantry company.[21]

Curiously, after everyone had been stirred to action in the previous night's war dance, on May 16 the assemblage uncharacteristically delayed departure until the afternoon, perhaps because of heavy rains. The 260-man composite force traveled just a dozen miles that day before stopping at Pointe-des-Nègres.[22] Indians, soldiers, and volunteers set up camps at the top of Lake St. Francis, a broad, placid twenty-five-mile stretch of the St. Lawrence.

At dawn on May 17, while the rest of the camp rose and prepared for the day's voyage, Lorimier and four Indian friends left in canoes ahead of the others to scout the path. Reaching the familiar Pointe-au-Foin landing, eight miles above the Coteau-du-Lac rapids, Lorimier left his warrior companions behind and traveled overland alone to reconnoiter. He soon met a local Canadian who informed him that "3,000 Americans were coming the next day to take up positions around

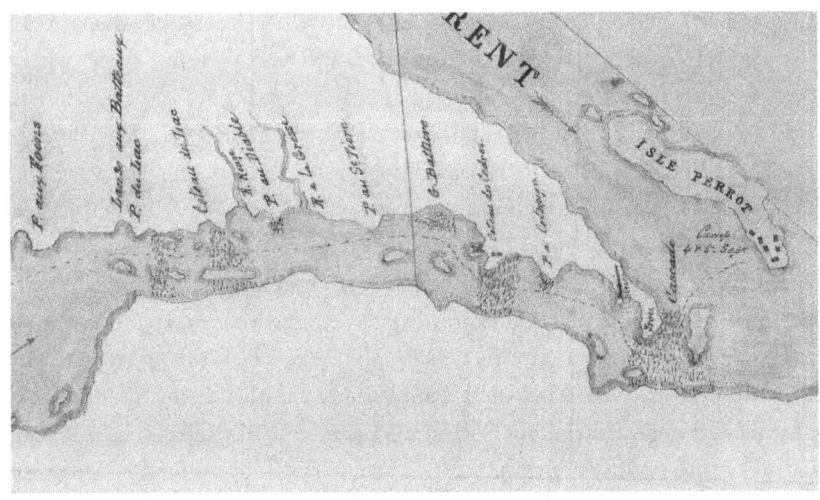

From Pointe au Foin to Les Cascades. Detail from Paul La Brosse, *A Sketch of the River St. Laurence, from La Gallette to the Island of Perrot with the Encampments of the Army, 1760*.
Courtesy Library and Archives Canada (4155643).

the church at The Cedars." When the chevalier rushed back to Pointe-au-Foin with this intelligence, his four Indian companions surprisingly shared that they had already been spotted by rebel-allied Kahnawake scouts on the river. A short time later, Lorimier saw Kahnawakes paddling their canoes back downriver, having had "the fright of their lives" after spotting the main body's fleet of canoes and bateaux headed in their direction.[23]

Lorimier was oblivious to the distinct possibility that his warrior companions had actually consulted amiably with the "enemy" Kahnawakes during their encounter in his absence. During colonial wars, many northern Indian nations observed a "Tacit Neutrality" amongst Native peoples, especially the Six Nations and Canadian mission villages. They avoided fighting each other, focusing their martial energies on European and American foes. Commonly, when out of sight of their non-Native allies, Indians exchanged news and warnings with nominal enemies, rather than blows.[24]

Lorimier led his advance party back upriver, met Forster and the principal chiefs, and shared his newly acquired intelligence. The Indians were "greatly discontented" with this development but reluctantly continued down the lake. By the time they stopped at Pointe-Beaudette, around three o'clock in the afternoon, they had reflected on the situation and expressed their deep reservations about proceeding further.[25] Their tactics and weaponry were ill-suited for attacking a properly manned fort, and chiefs would only lose influence if they sustained losses in a seemingly pointless stationary battle.

The Indians' hesitancy evaporated in a flash when an express messenger arrived from downriver. He brought the first news that General Guy Carleton had "driven the enemy from Quebec," causing "great consternation amongst the rebels." Newly inspired by this strategic turn of events, warriors leapt into their canoes "with great spirit" and furiously paddled down the St. Lawrence "hoping to arrive in time to attack the rebels at the Cedars by break of day." Despite their vigorous pace, dusk began to settle over the river before the Indians could pass the extremely treacherous Coteau-du-Lac rapids. The Indians chose to haul ashore for the night, along with the British soldiers and Canadians, with just ten miles between them and the Cedars.[26] The rebel-allied Kahnawake scouts stole a day's travel and were already spreading word of the enemy approach.

CHAPTER 9

"ORDERED TO THEIR ALARM POST"

On the morning of May 15, Indian scouts entered Fort Cedars, warning the Continental garrison that "there were fifty regulars, and between three and four hundred savages" approaching. Presumably they obtained this information from Akwesasne after the enemy's arrival in that village, since it was delivered a full day before the Lake St. Francis encounter between Claude de Lorimier's Indian allies and the Kahnawake scouts. This fits with a report that attributed the intelligence to some Indians "who had been up the river in a canoe." The last of Capt. Louis Atiatoharongwen's Indian troops appear to have left Fort Cedars immediately after their May 17 encounter with Lorimier's Indians, presumably returning to their village, since they are not mentioned in any records for the next two days.[1]

Maj. Isaac Butterfield received the Indian scouts' report as the fort's acting commander, since Col. Timothy Bedel had gone downriver to attend a council at Kahnawake. When Bedel departed, he was convinced that the picket-and-earthwork fort was "in as perfect tranquility as it had ever been," and he had improved the fort's defensive posture by establishing a twenty-man warning post upriver at the small community of Pointe-au-Diable. Although the long-rumored Indian-British attack from upriver was expected at any time, Bedel had not received any clear indications that the enemy was nearby before he left for Kahnawake. The colonel was probably more concerned at the moment by recent news from the northeast; when shipborne British reinforcements arrived at Quebec City on May 6, the American blockade collapsed like a house of cards—the main army was in a disordered retreat back toward Montreal. One of Bedel's soldiers believed that his colonel was in fact visiting Kahnawake to "make peace with that tribe," to keep them "from raising the Tomehack or scalping knife against us."[2]

In his commander's absence, Butterfield promptly acted on the scouts' warning. Each company at Fort Cedars was "ordered to their Alarm Post to hold them Selv[e]s in Readiness for Battle." Despite Bedel's apparent confidence when he left, the Continental garrison at Fort Cedars faced some serious challenges, especially with logistics. Fort stores held less than two weeks' half-rations, sparking "discontent & dissatisfaction" among the officers, and "very little short of mutiny amongst the soldiers," who were "nearly in a state of starvation." The men were slightly better supplied with ammunition, issued twenty rounds each, which was enough to make cartridge boxes appear more full than empty. Bedel had repeatedly applied to Brig. Gen. Benedict Arnold for additional supplies and important field equipment from Montreal, but the army had precious little to spare.[3]

In the days after receiving the scouts' report, Butterfield sent detachments out to secure additional provisions before the imminent attack. One party guarded stores in a nearby barn, while New Hampshire captain Joseph Estabrook led a mission to a Canadian store about six miles upriver, where his men seized "twenty-five bags of flour." During the night march out, Captain Estabrook employed a questionable tactic, ordering his troops to pass a "bridge with all the noise" to intimidate Indians that the Americans imagined "lay in ambush at the end of the bridge"—an unnecessary measure since the enemy was still many miles upriver. The next morning, the rangers uneventfully returned with the additional food.[4]

Colonel Bedel spent most of May 15 in the Kahnawake council house, still oblivious to the enemy's confirmed approach. He must have been quite uncomfortable, still suffering from his inoculation-induced smallpox—probably with a fever and pox scabbing up all over his body. Yet Bedel persevered in his commitment to Indian diplomatic duties.[5] While no firsthand sources are specifically tied to this conference, the Kahnawakes almost certainly aired their concerns about the American military collapse in Canada. There are two succinct council summaries that could have come from this particular meeting, clearly from sometime in the same early to mid-May timeframe: in one, Dartmouth missionary John Wheelock reported that the Kahnawakes "manifested solid attachment & friendship"; the other was from missionary-agent James Dean, who conveyed that the Kahnawakes "are friendly, but refuse to take up arms in our favour."[6]

Later in the day, council house discussions were interrupted by Indian scouts bringing word for Colonel Bedel that "a body of Savages about 100[,] headed by some English Soldiers number unknown, were come within 9 miles of his Post

[Fort Cedars] with an intention to attack it." The colonel faced a dilemma. His first inclination was to head straight back to his men at Fort Cedars; but Major Butterfield had already received the same warning, and as Bedel remembered, "the Savages in Council Insisted that I should go to Montreal and there Represent the Situation of that part of the Colony"—not just the colonel's western posts, but Kahnawake village too. In a fateful decision, Bedel elected to appease the Indians and go to Montreal first, believing "it could make but two or three hours Difference." The ailing colonel slipped into a Kahnawake canoe, and Indian pilots took him through the Sault St. Louis rapids to the city's riverfront landing.[7]

Late on May 15, Bedel disembarked and struggled up a packed-dirt road to the Continental headquarters in the stately stone Château Ramezay. Bedel's commander, General Arnold, was away. Believing that Bedel was "in very little danger at his post" at the time, the general had rushed down to Sorel, to help rally the main army retreating from Quebec City. In Arnold's absence, Bedel conferred with Col. John Paterson, commander of the Fifteenth Continental (Massachusetts) or Berkshire Regiment, who had been appointed city commandant upon arrival earlier that same day. Paterson had just led his 351 men north to Canada on a three-week march from New York City, but half of them were still waiting on the other side of the St. Lawrence because of widespread bateaux shortages.[8]

After Bedel delivered his alarming intelligence to Paterson, the colonels met with Charles Carroll and Samuel Chase, the remaining commissioners to Canada from the Continental Congress. The duo had traveled north with Benjamin Franklin, to help Canada get on the right political and military path, but they immediately found they could do little to help. Franklin had already given up hope and returned home. Some Americans even believed the commissioners had made the situation worse. As one officer wrote: "Of the Cowardice, mismanagement & confusion at Canada, you will hear enough to sicken you. . . . the small pox & Commissioners of the Congress, ruined the army & our friends. I have not seen a man of any party in the Army or out of it who does not agree that the Commissioners have been the principal means of all the confusion that hath reigned there."[9]

Among the commissioners' misguided or belated interventions, they had addressed one of the western Indians' principal motivators for heading down the warpath to the Cedars. On May 1, the commissioners had reopened the up-country trade, "granting passports to all who shall enter into certain engagements to do nothing in the upper country prejudicial to the Continental interests." Canadian patriot Thomas Walker was a vehement critic, convinced that this measure just gave loyalist traders a ready path to supply British army posts and "their allies the Savages."[10]

When the commissioners heard Colonel Bedel's report of "the approach of some Indians & Soldiers from Detroit [sic] & the upper garrisons with a design to attack our post at the Cedars," it was just one among dozens of crises they were handling. They were also skeptical of this new intelligence, sharing Arnold's assessment that that there really was not "much to fear from that quarter." Despite their doubts, the commissioners supported Colonel Paterson as he hurriedly marshaled reinforcements and supplies for Fort Cedars that night, just in case.[11]

In Montreal, suspicious and frightened Continentals feared a loyalist uprising, so Colonel Paterson chose to remain in the city, rather than leading a Fort Cedars relief force himself. In his stead, one of his regimental field officers, Maj. Henry Sherburne, stepped forward to take command of the party. The talented twenty-seven-year-old major "was honored with the Thanks from the two Commissioners from Congress on the Occasion." Even though he was a Rhode Islander, Sherburne had earned his position in the Massachusetts Fifteenth Continental Regiment with talent and commitment demonstrated at Cambridge in 1775. Brig. Gen. Nathanael Greene praised Sherburne as the only field officer in his previous regiment "that understands the out Lines of his Duty," and senior leaders entrusted him with special, politically sensitive missions. The major also physically fit the part, appearing "bold stout courageous-looking," while soldiers, peers, and leaders commonly used the term "brave" when describing him.[12]

In the morning light of Thursday, May 16, Major Sherburne assembled 140 volunteers from Paterson's regiment outside the "large stone barracks adjoining the North Gate" in Montreal. Over their one short night in the city, the men had drastically improved their weaponry; entering with "fowling-pieces of different sizes and bores and few . . . bayonets," they left with "good, king's arms" drawn from captured stacks in the barracks magazine. Sherburne's ad hoc battalion typified the Continental Army's hodgepodge deployment in Canada, with men drawn from seven of Paterson's companies under three captains. With orders to reinforce the Cedars, the Massachusetts troops marched from the city in hopes of reaching that post before the enemy did.[13]

Sherburne's men brought along three wagons with a "fresh Supply of provisions & Amunition" scrounged overnight from Montreal. Bedel, still frail and afflicted, tried to join the march but fell out eight miles down the road, in Lachine. As he reported, "Sickness absolutely prevented me from proceeding." He would remain out of action for more than a week—a most critical week.[14]

Toward the end of the day, when Maj. Henry Sherburne led his column into Fort Ste. Anne, he could see his next waypoint across the Lake of Two Mountains but was unable to cross the calm two-mile riverine expanse for "want of Batteaus." Continental authorities in Montreal had hesitated to requisition enough bateaux for the mission, apparently out of concern for Canadians' property rights. Tactically, Sherburne wanted enough watercraft to carry his force in one trip—if his men met enemy resistance landing on the Presqu'île, any troops left on the east shore had no way to provide support. With the "many Difficulties in procuring Boats," Sherburne impatiently idled for two critical days at Fort Ste. Anne.[15]

On Saturday, May 18, Major Sherburne finally received more bateaux and led one hundred men across the lake to establish a beachhead at Pointe-de-Quinchien. Waiting with his battalion near the seigneurial manor, Sherburne sent Capt. Theodore Bliss to find local wagons to carry the heavy stores to Fort Cedars, but Bliss was slow to return. After an interminable wait, Sherburne was surprised when a *Canadien* eventually appeared, delivering a letter from the captain that described his "unhappy situation." Bliss reported that he had been captured by locals and Indians within a couple of miles of the landing, and further conveyed his captors' claim that "500 Canadians and Savages" were gathering to attack the landing that night. Sherburne later reported: "This information I thought sufficient to occasion a Retreat, and by Two o' Clock in the Morning got our Men and Provision safe back over the Lake," aborting his otherwise successful first crossing.[16]

The next morning, Sunday, May 19, Major Sherburne ordered his men to reembark at Fort Ste. Anne, but facing a violent south wind, only a single vessel managed to cross the choppy waters before the major abandoned the day's effort. Capt. Ebenezer Sullivan, brother of Brig. Gen. John Sullivan, commanded the one bateau that hauled ashore at Pointe-de-Quinchien. The captain boldly led his twelve-man detachment to the nearest major road junction and found Abbé Louis Beaumont's rectory-chapel home. Sullivan and his men "compelled" the priest to take them to Captain Bliss and found their compatriot to have "received the most humane treatment[,] Contrary to the expectation of all." Sullivan freed Bliss without a fight, and the Americans safely recrossed the lake to the security of Fort Ste. Anne.[17]

During Major Sherburne's march from Montreal and futile crossing efforts, the British and their Indian allies continued to advance on Fort Cedars. On the evening of May 17, the main body stopped above the Coteau-du-Lac rapids, ten miles from Fort Cedars, waiting to cross that extremely dangerous stretch of the

St. Lawrence in daylight. This was prudent; anyone who passed the wrong course "would fall into the great cauldrons, where they must perish without remedy." Sixteen years earlier, British general Jeffery Amherst had lost fifty-five boats and eighty-four men in this passage when advancing on Montreal.[18]

Lorimier and a few eager war chiefs chafed at the main body's measured advance. The chevalier offered to guide a vanguard on a night portage around the rapids and set up an advance position five miles downriver at Pointe-au-Diable. Lorimier was disappointed that there were not many eager Indian volunteers, so he sang his death song once again to motivate or cajole more men—with only slight success. He reported that "the Six Nations Indians didn't show any enthusiasm for my idea." Only fifty warriors joined Lorimier on this night mission. Captain Forster detached Lieutenant Andrew Parke to join them, probably for military oversight. If the intelligence was correct, Lorimier's party might well encounter the enemy.[19]

The advance party completed the portage and a short canoe trip to land at Pointe-au-Diable around ten o'clock that night. The point marked the western extremity of cultivated Canadian land, so Lorimier visited a local farm for the latest word on rebels in the area. The *habitant* shared word that a dozen Americans and some Indians had just been in the tiny community, but after the Kahnawake scouts encountered the advancing British-allied Indians on Lake St. Francis, the enemies had all returned to Fort Cedars.[20]

While each side was clearly aware of the other and was prepared for imminent battle, a decisive moment in the campaign had already passed. Sherburne's "great difficulties" meant that he failed to get reinforcements across the Lake of Two Mountains for three critical days. This dramatically altered the quantitative and morale balance in the upcoming fight at the Cedars. After the campaign, Sherburne recounted a telling anecdote. He described a postbattle meeting with a loyalist Canadian who had been "in Montreal when major Sherburne marched from it, but did not leave till the following day [May 17], when having obtained from the Commissioners a pass to carry a boat load of goods on pretence of trading with the friendly Indians, he carried them to those very Indians who invested the Cedars and was himself in the [coming] engagement against major Sherburne."[21] Despite having a day's head start in his "race" with the Canadian loyalist, the major was waylaid at Fort Ste. Anne for so long that his competitor easily beat him to their common goal. If Sherburne had been properly equipped with bateaux or had assumed more risk in the lake crossing, the course of battle at Fort Cedars might have been quite different.

CHAPTER 10

"MENACED WITH DESTRUCTION"

A dawn glow backlit the clouds around five o'clock on May 18, as Lieutenant Andrew Parke and Indian interpreter Claude de Lorimier arose with their fifty-man Indian vanguard at Pointe-au-Diable and coordinated their morning's efforts. Parke stayed at the camp with some of the older men, while Lorimier and a group of Indian volunteers ventured closer to the enemy. The interpreter noted, "We marched as fast as we could so the enemy wouldn't have time to learn that we were coming"—a pace that undoubtedly helped warm the warriors on an unseasonably cold day. The other Indians, soldiers, and Canadians in the main body were still about five miles upstream, preparing to descend the dangerous Coteau-du-Lac rapids en route to the Cedars.[1]

Lorimier and his Indian companions passed the Pointe-au-Diable settlements, meeting a couple of Canadians, but they did not glean any useful information. With rushing Laurentian waters on their right, the scouts followed the muddy riverside road past several farms and a section of woods. Speeding across yet another wide swath of rutted farmland, they arrived at the Cedars Rapids portage point, upstream of the fort. Crews typically unloaded boats and canoes at this landing when going downriver or reloaded there on the way upstream. Lorimier left those less able and less willing at the portage, and cautiously advanced the last mile to surveil enemy entrenchments on the small peninsula at the Cedars. The Canadian interpreter suggested that his two dozen Indian compatriots advance to cut the rebel line of communications east of the fort, but he was surprised and disappointed by their response: "they refused, saying derisively that this was an honour reserved for the King's troops; they had seen how far back Captain Forster kept himself."[2]

Lorimier summoned his best persuasive skills to goad reticent warrior comrades into action. He explained that when they had exuberantly sung their war songs together at Akwesasne, he feared he "would never be able to measure up to their bravery," but now, if even one man would follow, he would "show them the true meaning of the word." Only a single warrior responded positively—William Tekawiroñte, one of Sir William Johnson's Mohawk sons, also known as William of Canajoharie. Tekawiroñte was a man of action. In just the past year, he had joined Guy Johnson's trek from the Mohawk Valley to Oswego and Montreal, fought the Americans outside Fort St. Johns, returned home to threaten rebel neighbors and boast of his victories, conferred with John Butler at Niagara, and shared pro-British perspectives at the March Onondaga council—all before joining the current expedition. William Tekawiroñte most definitely did not need Lorimier's prodding and enthusiastically replied: "You and I are alike, and the two of us together are capable of putting a whole nation to shame." No one followed his example.[3]

Around seven o'clock that morning, near loyalist Thomas Denis's farm, William Tekawiroñte spotted two rebel soldiers taking aim at Lorimier and himself, "at a distance of about sixty yards, with their muskets resting on a fence." At the last second, the Canajoharie Mohawk warned Lorimier and the two threw themselves into a ditch as musket balls "sang" over their heads. Lorimier and Tekawiroñte leapt to their feet and chased the Americans, who fled toward the fort. Stopping at the same fence the rebels had fired from, the pair lowered their own muskets, coordinated aim, and fired. Lorimier's shot wounded one rebel in the shoulder; Tekawiroñte thought his ball hit the other fleeing soldier in the thigh. Despite injuries, the Americans successfully escaped into Fort Cedars.[4]

While Lorimier and William Tekawiroñte engaged in the day's first exchange of fire, Lieutenant Parke patiently waited at Pointe-au-Diable. When Captain Forster and the main body finally approached on the river, the lieutenant and accompanying Indians took their canoes into the river to join the others. Approximately two hundred Mississaugas, Six Nations Haudenosaunee, and Akwesasne warriors, along with Forster's soldiers, cautiously approached the enemy post. They hauled canoes and bateaux ashore at the Cedars portage point and rejoined Lorimier's hesitant warrior companions, who stubbornly waited for British troops to arrive before advancing further.[5]

The warriors, light infantry men, and Canadian loyalists concealed themselves in the last wooded stand west of the fort, while Captain Forster crept forward to assess the tactical situation. As Lorimier discerned a few hours earlier, the obvious first step was to invest the fort by cutting off rebel communications by seizing the riverside road to the east. This single avenue of approach linked Fort Cedars with both the Pointe-de-Quinchien and Cascades landing points—the

Sauvage Iroquois (Iroquois Indian), 1796.
Library of Congress, Prints and Photographs Division (LC-USZC2-1664).

only practical routes for relief or resupply. Accompanied by Lorimier, about half of the combined Indian force—one hundred warriors—stealthily transited the woods on the far edge of the broad, cleared farmland expanse surrounding the fort, remaining a few hundred yards from the rebel lines.[6]

As the Indians took up positions to control the eastern road, they stumbled upon four or five Americans billeted in a Canadian farmhouse. The warriors opened fire on the rebels, killing one and wounding two. Surprised by terrifying black-and-red-painted warriors, the Continental soldiers tried to flee. One or two men may have reached sanctuary in the fort, but at least one was captured. The

Indians killed another and scalped him for "obstinately refusing to surrender to two savages, when it was not possible to escape."[7]

This scalping was exactly the sort of "horrors of war" that Americans expected in Indian fighting, based on history and legend. To Euro-colonial eyes, scalping was "a mode of torture peculiar to the Indians" that served to escalate the terror of an encounter with enemy warriors. For Indians, scalps were a key means to physically demonstrate success on the warpath. During the French and Indian War, officer Pierre Pouchot noted that his Indian allies' "principal object" was "to bring away prisoners, or to take scalps." Home villages or bands celebrated these trophies as "proof of conquest without encumbrance." Realistically, British officers or Canadians, with their European cultural standards, could only hope to focus warriors' scalping efforts on dead and dying enemies, rather than slightly wounded or uninjured captives, especially women and children.[8]

The Americans inside Fort Cedars were well aware of the enemy's approach after the two short fights east and west of their position. Continental soldiers manned their posts and improved their entrenchments while they awaited both the first sight of the enemy and the return of another detached party. Shortly after midnight, about twenty Connecticut soldiers from Burrall's Regiment had departed the fort to receive a supply shipment at the Cascades landing, four miles to the east. After transferring the goods from bateaux to carts, the detachment headed back to Fort Cedars, unaware that the enemy had surrounded the post during the few hours they were away.[9]

The Connecticut soldiers cautiously guided carts back up the road from the Cascades. Shortly after the fort came into view, the Continentals were startled by musket blasts and balls whizzing past them. Several Indians sprang from concealment and closed for battle. The warriors did not execute their ambush very well; only Pvt. Charles Gillett was killed by the opening volley. The surviving Americans scrambled to the closest farmhouse and "defended themselves vigorously." The ambushing Indians freely exchanged shots with the Connecticut men in the house, since a small rise provided them defilade from Fort Cedars musket fire. Still, a soldier's musket shot found its mark from inside the embattled dwelling, seriously wounding an Indian named Bonheur. Attacking warriors were "enraged and shouted to each other to storm the house and revenge his [apparent] death." Bursting into the house, they were surprised to find it vacant but quickly realized their enemies had escaped into the attic. Rather than recklessly risk their lives by fighting up the single ladderway, the Indians set fire to the house.[10]

Their efforts were jarringly interrupted by a thunderous cannon blast. A three-and-a-half-inch ball ripped through one house wall and out the other side. With this violent distraction, the Connecticut men tore out the gable end of the roof and scampered toward the fort, but pursuing warriors caught wounded private Jabez Lewis before he reached friendly lines. Based on the glimpses of violence seen over their shoulders in flight, his comrades presumed he had been killed. The vengeful Indians did brutally beat Lewis in retribution for Bonheur's wounds, but they dragged him alive to Captain Forster's field headquarters as their captive. Private Lewis, who ultimately survived the life-threatening abuse, suffered the rest of his life from a "Lame and ulcerated leg."[11]

While about half of the allied Indians fought to the east, Forster led his forty light infantry soldiers and about another hundred warriors to secure the woods west of the rebel lines. As a loose group, they cautiously ventured "as near as possible to the enemy," and then individual warriors drew closer on their own. At midday, ranger Zephaniah Shepardson recalled, "we beheld Indians come skiping and runing and out of the woods about half an mile from our camp, war[-]like with all there weapons for war. every time they ran across the level field they came nearer[,] running back and forth oblique."[12]

Captain Forster husbanded his redcoat company behind cover. A rebel defender observed that the British remained "secreted behind old log houses and barns," while Lorimier recounted that "Forster would not budge" from his portage command post, a mile west of the fort, even as Indian allies engaged their common enemy. The captain's cautious approach conformed with light infantry "Rules and Orders" promulgated four years earlier: "The success of any Engagement in a Wood or Strong Country depends upon the Coolness and presence of Mind of the Commanding Officers, and the Silence and Obedience of the Men[,] fully as much as upon their Bravery."[13]

From inside the fort's lines, only "a few guns were fired to let the enemy know they were in the fort. No body killed or wounded." From both ends of the northern wall, Americans soon brought their two brass cannon to bear as well. The eastern gun crew achieved at least one brilliant shot during the resupply convoy fight, but the western battery had no comparable success. At his post near the left end of the line, Private Shepardson observed that "the artillery men could not hit an old barn 40 or 50 rods of(f) [220 to 275 yards]. it would thro[w] the ball about 3 rods [50 feet] to the right every time." In part, he attributed the aiming errors to his belief that the piece had been "reduced" to a four-pounder, but he

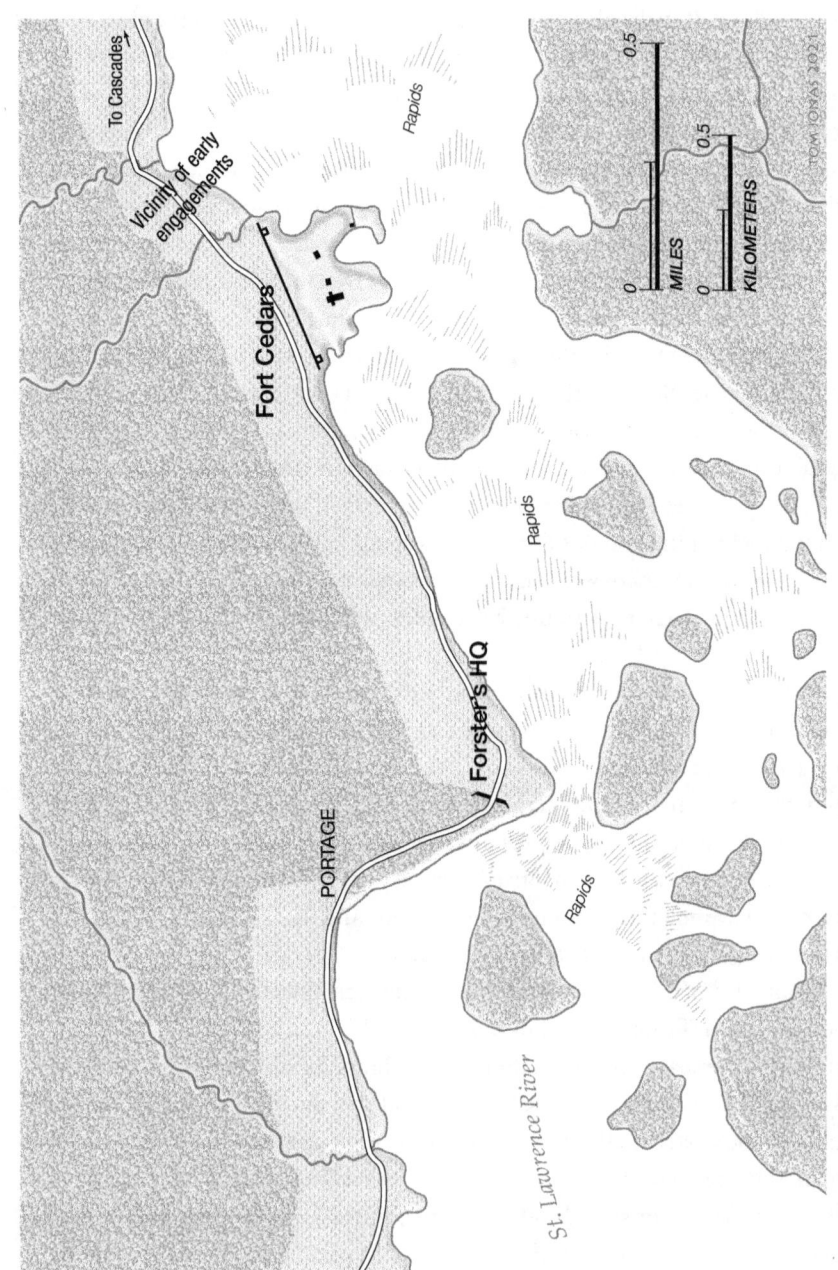

Fort Cedars. Locations and layout of buildings and fortifications are approximated from multiple historical sources. *Map by Tom Jonas.*

also "concluded the young men was no gun[n]ers at that time[,] or fri[gh]ted." He was right on at least one account—the artillerymen had been recruited just a month earlier from recently disbanded New York infantry companies passing through Montreal. Only their leader, Sgt. John McCullough, had meaningful gunnery experience from the siege of Fort St. Johns.[14]

It was the Americans' misfortune that their artillery proved so inaccurate. If the guns inflicted any Indian casualties, they might have made a difference in the fort's ultimate fate. A contemporary source described commonly accepted Indian strengths and weaknesses, noting that they were "excellent men for fighting in the woods," but that the "first cannon makes them scamper like so many dogs." Historian John Mahon similarly concluded that Native warriors "could rarely bring themselves to bear up long under artillery fire."[15] The poorly aimed cannon at the Cedars gave the Indians little cause for concern.

Since the artillerists could not even hit seigneur Paul-Joseph LeMoyne de Longueuil's "superb" barn nearby, the Americans endured intermittent fire from Indians taking cover behind it. Capt. Daniel Wilkins of Bedel's Regiment, a Bunker Hill veteran and "fine gentlemanly Officer," decided to solve the problem himself. He led a party that "rushd out over the breastwork." Lorimier remembered the attacking force as a "body of 180 Americans," certainly an overestimate. Still, only a few score warriors were in the vicinity, so they fled across the long, furrowed fields to rally in the safety of adjacent woods. The Canadian interpreter and his Indian allies soon realized that the Americans "had sortied merely to burn" the barn. When Wilkins's men promptly returned to their lines, warriors crept forward again, and both sides resumed ineffective musket fire.[16]

As Captain Forster assessed the developing tactical situation, he clearly recognized that his force was inadequate for a coup de main assault. Indians were inevitably reluctant to attack fortifications, and he could depend only on his forty disciplined soldiers to attack hundreds of entrenched enemies. So, the captain pursued a less risky approach to take the fort, sending a lieutenant forward under a flag of truce. The Americans met the redcoat officer outside the lines, blindfolded him, and escorted him into the fort. The lieutenant "summoned the enemy to surrender, while it was yet in his power to save their lives," adding Forster's personal warning that "should they not do it immediately, the savages could not be restrained by the small numbers of his troops, from committing acts of cruelty."[17]

Maj. Isaac Butterfield "shewed the greatest marks of terror" at the specter of an Indian massacre. He appeared ready to immediately surrender the fort "but was Prevented by his Men." In a council of war, Capt. Daniel Wilkins and Capt. John Stevens of Burrall's Connecticut Regiment argued that "all the subalterns and all the men were desirious [sic] of fighting." Many of the fort's defenders "cried with vexation" at the suggestion of surrendering without a substantial fight. The captains persuaded Butterfield to delay any decision, and he asked Captain Forster for three more hours to consider his situation and options.[18]

Forster had since received word that an American relief force—Major Sherburne's battalion—was on the way from Montreal, having left the city a few days earlier, so there was some urgency in securing the fort's surrender. The British captain granted the requested three hours, but his lieutenant delivering that reply further unsettled Major Butterfield by informing the American that "the Indians were at present perfectly under his [Forster's] command, and that if the garrison surrendered immediately, he had no doubt but that they would agree to any thing he wished; but if the fort did not surrender, and any of the Indians should be killed, captain Forster could not answer for the consequences." The redcoat lieutenant may also have hinted that Forster's soldiers would soon bring artillery into the fight. Isaac Butterfield reconsidered as his men were "menaced with destruction in case of resistance," and the enemy "boasted of their ability to take it by force." With fleeting assurances that he and his Continentals could be delivered from Indian "savagery," the major replied that he would surrender his post immediately if he and his men were permitted to retire to Montreal "with their arms." Captain Forster refused Butterfield's proposal—by the standards of the day, the rebels' short, passive defense did not warrant the honors of war. Once the flag of truce returned to shelter late that afternoon, "hostilities again commenced."[19]

Soon thereafter, Canadian loyalists brought Forster fresh intelligence from Vaudreuil Parish, just a dozen miles to the northeast. They reported "a reinforcement, with provisions, being landed there from Montreal, under the command of a Major Sherburne." This proved to be the Americans' first crossing from Fort Ste. Anne—the one turned back by loyalist Canadians' deliberate misinformation warning Sherburne he was in danger of attack, and hinting that Fort Cedars had already surrendered. With Sherburne's resultant retreat back to the Island of Montreal, the Canadians bought Forster more time to coerce Butterfield into surrender and avoid pitched battle.[20]

Around sunset, Americans saw the few discernible redcoats withdraw from view, "but the Indians kept up a scatter fire all night." There was no rest in the Continental lines during the dark, moonless night that followed. Some soldiers kept to their arms along the breastworks, while others dug new trenches and further improved fortifications. Despite the Indians' "loose" harassing fire, the Americans "worked like brave boys," many going "without victuals drink or lodgings" through the night.[21]

Captain Forster's British soldiers did not get much rest either. Laboring overnight, the redcoats raised an earthen redoubt anchored on fenceposts, at the point where the riverside road entered the woods before the portage, about five hundred yards from the enemy fort.[22] The Indians and British allies anticipated conquering the fort the next day, one way or another, while the Americans prayed for relief from their dire predicament.

CHAPTER 11

"PUTTING A WHOLE NATION TO SHAME"

With the first signs of daylight on Sunday, May 19, British light infantry soldiers moved back toward Fort Cedars. Under cover of farmhouses and outbuildings, they approached to within 150 yards where they "kept up a fire of musquetry, whenever there appeared any object for its direction." British accounts neglect to mention Indian allies on this morning, but the Americans remembered them well. New Hampshire ranger Zephaniah Shepardson noted how "the Indians disapeard[,] secreted them selves in the grass or small brakes like black snakes on there bellys. So we continued our fire at the Indian ground, grass or brakes." An Abenaki warrior crawled to the west end of the rebel works, along the riverbank, preparing to lay a raking fire down the length of the line. A Continental ensign spotted the Indian though, took aim, and killed him with a well-placed musket shot.[1]

Fort Cedars commander Maj. Isaac Butterfield's most serious exertion during the battle seems to have been in trying to stop his men from being too active in their own defense. Perhaps he remembered Captain George Forster's warning that a single Indian death could have deadly repercussions for the fort's occupants. When Butterfield's "men from time to time sollicited leave to sally on the enemy . . . he not only refused it, but restrained them from firing even from within the lines as much as possible." At one point, Capt. John Stevens actually obtained Butterfield's permission to sortie and drive off some Canadians and Indians firing from a nearby barn until the major, "seeing himself left almost entirely without a guard, became alarmed and sent for Capt Stevents [sic] to return." The captain came back crying with fury.[2]

Zephaniah Shepardson contributed the most morbidly humorous anecdote from Fort Cedars in his campaign reminiscences. He recounted the misfortunes of fellow ranger Nathaniel Bacon, who had "run towards the barracks to take some refreshments"; "on his return running towards his larum post, a musket ball met his head that knockd him down, he sprang up and run crying out im a dead man . . . i must confess i never see a dead man run before now. The ball struck a large button on his cockedup hat and drove the button eye through two thicknesses into his skin towards his skull. So the button savd his Bacon." Ranger Bacon survived, living long enough to submit a pension request forty-three years later that included mention of his Fort Cedars battle wound.[3]

West of the fort, around ten o'clock that morning, Captain Forster unexpectedly received a guest at his command post—Jean-Baptiste Testard de Montigny, the ousted master of Fort Ste. Anne. The volunteer officer brought a "corps of loyal Canadians," thirty men armed and supplied from the stores cached in Abbé Louis Beaumont's Vaudreuil parish grounds. These *Canadiens* did not immediately join the battle though. As Private Shepardson remembered from his perspective inside the fort, "there appeared a very great host of french men in the front, in order to assist the enemy if they stand in need of them."[4]

Despite the Canadians' arrival, the battle was tactically bogged down in a stalemate. Claude de Lorimier fretted, "If we stayed there for long a good number of the Indians would abandon our cause." Slow, inconclusive sieges offered warriors little opportunity to demonstrate bravery, and gave Euro-colonials opportunity to negotiate terms that excluded or minimized opportunities for Indians to gather plunder, captives, and scalps. Lorimier's worries subsided later that morning, when a new war party arrived to bolster Indian spirits.[5]

Hearing that Fort Cedars was under attack, Kanesatake men came to fulfill their winter hunting-ground promises. They had substantial community support, backed by Sulpician missionary priests François-Auguste Magon de Terlaye and Jean-Claude Mathevet, both of whom always supported their flocks' warfare as allies to the king. The village was further encouraged by shifting strategic tides, with recent news arriving direct from Quebec City that British forces had routed the rebels there.[6]

The morning's reinforcements proved helpful around noon, when Captain Forster received word that Maj. Henry Sherburne's rebel relief column was once again attempting to cross the Lake of Two Mountains to relieve Fort Cedars. The British commander turned to Montigny and ordered the Canadian loyalists back to Vaudreuil, to watch the rebels' motions and slow their advance if needed. Forster needed more time to coax Major Butterfield into surrendering Fort Cedars before the rebel reinforcements arrived. Unbeknownst to the British commander, adverse winds would keep Sherburne's main force from crossing that day, but he was adequately prepared for the contingency should they succeed.[7]

New Hampshire ranger Zephaniah Shepardson provided an intriguing story from the second day of battle—a story that does not appear in any leader's account but was somehow conveyed in two 1785 travelers' accounts, describing voyages through the Cedars. During the first evening's truce exchange, Shepardson overheard the British lieutenant warn that soldiers were already preparing cannon to fire on the rebel lines. On the morning of May 19, the New Hampshire private remembered, "we beheld the appearance of three batteries" that "terrifyd our commander Maj[o]r Butterfield very much." Without "a spyglass to view the pretended batterys," the Americans could not tell the guns were actually disguised logs.[8]

If this ploy was true, British and American officers might have avoided mention of this minor detail to save embarrassment from ungenteel deception or at being duped, respectively. In contrast, Shepardson had nothing to gain or lose by recounting the actual story years after the fact. Alternatively, it is equally plausible that the fake-cannon ploy never actually occurred but developed as a local yarn that caught voyagers' attention over the years. An oft-retold legend might even have reached Shepardson decades later to be incorporated as a "false memory" that he fully believed had happened. Available evidence cannot prove or disprove this Fort Cedars vignette.[9]

In any case, American morale was dropping on the second day of battle. A drummer fled down the steep riverbank on the fort's west side, deserting to the British. Meanwhile, three cowardly company commanders also hid on the fort's south side, sheltered from enemy fire under steep riverbanks—Edward Everett, Ebenezer Green, David Downs, and some subaltern officers followed their sad example.[10] Still, most Continental soldiers dutifully kept their posts and put up defiant fire whenever the enemy was visible.

Captain Forster may have sensed that rebel resistance was slackening. Shortly after sending Montigny's *Canadiens* to Vaudreuil, he "assembled the many chiefs" to consult on potential fort surrender terms. Indian allies already had one warrior dead and two wounded, but the British officer claimed that in their conversation he had "overcome the resolution formed by the savages, of allowing no quarters [*sic*]."[11] Once Forster reached an accord with his allies, he, Lieutenant Bird, and a drummer approached the rebel fort under a flag of truce. Rebels received the junior officer and drummer, blindfolded them, and led them into the fort.[12]

Lieutenant Bird invited Major Butterfield to surrender and, along with Captain Forster's proposed terms, shared his commander's warning that "as the disposition of savages is not very certain, I would fain take the advantage of their present favourable turn." Forster promised to secure the soldiers' lives and clothing, but Butterfield was expected to deliver up not only the fort but also "the artillery, ammunition, batteaus, and stores of every kind." The major called another council of war to consider these terms, and he was not only "very sick with the Small Pock" but clearly "much terrified" of the Indians. Low on ammunition and encumbered by sick soldiers, the despondent major argued that it was time to surrender "if their lives could be secured from the savages."[13]

Indomitable Capt. John Stevens, Bunker Hill veteran Capt. Daniel Wilkins, and Capt. Joseph Estabrook disagreed with their commander. They wanted to keep fighting, come what may, even requesting "permission to sally out and fight their way through the enemy," rather than surrender. Butterfield fretted that such a breakout attempt "might induce the enemy to rush on the rest and tomahawk them or to retract from them the benefit of the terms offered." An early secondary account even claimed that the major threatened to fire on Stevens and his followers if they tried to sortie. The captains' belligerent zeal failed to inspire the others. Most officers agreed with their commander—surrender seemed the most prudent course to ensure their men's welfare (and save themselves). Major Butterfield informed Lieutenant Bird that he would accept these terms.[14]

Private Shepardson reported that even after Butterfield agreed to surrender, there was still "a schism or division among the officers." A number of men, "without orders," chose Captain Wilkins to be their "cheif commander . . . to force our way thro . . . Indians and all that should come against us." These patriotic mutineers lost their momentum when Captain Forster and his redcoat company arrived under a flag of truce to accept the fort's surrender. Now it was too late—there was no honorable way to keep fighting. The last-ditch spark of Continental resistance was snuffed out.[15]

On the late afternoon of May 19, Continental soldiers opened the Fort Cedars gates and Captain Forster led six Indians and two score British soldiers inside. The rest of the Indians were kept outside for the rebel prisoners' safety—in hopes of avoiding a pillaging orgy at the moment of surrender. Redcoat drummers entered the fort playing "Yankee Doodle," a tune undoubtedly selected to add insult to the disgraced, submissive rebels. Major Butterfield strictly complied with the terms, turning over the fort's stores, equipment, and two fully operational cannon.[16]

Around five o'clock, the Continentals laid down their arms inside the fort. A British escort party led Major Butterfield's 390 rebels (soldiers and possibly sundry camp followers) outside the fort's lines. Hundreds of Indians impatiently stood by, waiting for their share of the spoils inside. Before the last Americans even cleared the lines, chiefs were already divvying up surrendered weapons in the fort—later reported in New Hampshire as being "the best muskets that belonged to the State." With the surrender complete, Pvt. Benjamin Stevens wrote, "Now we are prisoners. The Lord protect us and keep u[s] from harm."[17]

Hundreds of Continental soldiers began their traumatic prisoner of war experience, unarmed and totally dependent on their conquerors. Forster deliberately kept the rebels outside the lines while Indians scoured the post for material spoils of war, but his plan failed to protect the prisoners completely. At the beginning of the campaign, Forster had reportedly promised "all the plunder to the savages, and that they should strip the prisoners to the skin"; victorious warriors expected to claim personal goods and clothing off the vanquished, even if they spared their lives.[18]

On the other hand, Maj. Isaac Butterfield had apparently believed that in addition to the clothes his men were wearing, his officers were permitted to keep personal baggage. The Indians disagreed. To appease their British allies, victorious warriors might suffer prisoners to keep the clothing on their backs, but personal packs presumably held the choicest plunder—fancy clothing, accessories, and other valuable, portable items like silver dinnerware and watches. These conflicting interpretations of the surrender terms prompted the first "incident" among a series of insults and abuses that would continue over the next week.[19]

Two Indian chiefs decided to seize their just rewards, grabbing what they could off rebel prisoners huddled in a mass outside the walls. The Americans were shocked but did not offer meaningful resistance in their frightened, helpless state. The infamous 1757 Fort William Henry "massacre" was a ready reference point in collective colonial memory, and these first minor depredations at the Cedars were already beginning to parallel that notorious event. The simmering tensions were temporarily relieved when Forster and leading chiefs invited the rest of the warriors inside the fort "to take the plunder which belonged to them."[20]

Before dusk, victorious warriors cleared out of the fort, carrying newfound spoils of war to adjacent camps. Forster ordered the rebels back into Fort Cedars for their own protection, but another wave of dissatisfied Indians took advantage of the corralled prisoners, grabbing whatever they could get without having to resort to bodily violence. British and loyalist accounts dismissively reported that these warriors stripped the captive soldiers "of some watches and money, and perhaps of a laced hat or two," but nothing else, and did not offer "any other insult."[21]

Terrified American soldiers remembered the experience quite differently. Most of their accounts blend several days of serial pillaging in a sentence or two, but Lt. Jean-François Hamtramck remembered that the "Indians immediately took all their clothes, money, and baggage." Major Butterfield also reported: "The savages did plunder the prisoners of almost all their clothes, beginning their pillage and plunder the evening we surrendered."[22]

As twilight faded, British soldiers herded the rebels into their former barracks—for protection from Indian depredations, and for more efficient control if an American relief column were to materialize. Pvt. Zephaniah Shepardson recounted the discomfort with "365 of our men shut up in one room." The rebels stayed in their cramped confines overnight, agonizing over their fates.[23]

Contemporaries and historians have placed almost all blame for the shameful surrender at Fort Cedars on Maj. Isaac Butterfield. Historian Justin H. Smith offered a particularly hostile critique of the major's leadership: "Nearly four hundred plucky fellows—hardly scratched as yet, if scratched at all—were thrown neck and crop to the savages merely to save their commander's skin. . . . It was a clear case of poltroonery." While some historical treatments dismiss or ignore the mitigating circumstances that may have contributed to Butterfield's decision, the basic military facts offer little to dispute their core judgments. The fort's garrison had adequate provisions and ammunition to continue fighting for at least a few more days, the fortified lines were intact, relief was anticipated, and only three or four Americans believed to have been killed, two captured, and three or four wounded.[24]

By conventional standards, the fort had clearly not resisted long enough. The Indians, however, significantly altered the surrender-decision calculus on the scene—they were their own psychological weapon. Historian Colin Calloway observed, "The Iroquois cultivated their reputation as cruel torturers of prisoners as a terror tactic to break the resistance of their foes," and eyewitnesses confirmed their effect at the Cedars, consistently emphasizing Butterfield's fright.[25]

The thickly sown seeds of terror undoubtedly met fertile ground in American colonists' collective memories of French and Indian War "massacres"—particularly Fort Oswego and Fort William Henry. Local interwar oral accounts, and contemporary historical works, repeated the horror-filled aftermath of those sieges. Once the Revolutionary War began, the topic inevitably resurfaced in patriot leaders' discussions and was overtly referenced in at least one early war newspaper report.[26]

Unfortunately, Butterfield never shared the logic underlying his decision to surrender, but smallpox may have been a substantial consideration. Dozens of his men were hors de combat from the disease, and the major's own symptoms could have impaired his judgment in battle. Furthermore, Butterfield and likeminded officers might have remembered that in the last war, sick and wounded soldiers had been the first victims in famous Indian "massacres."[27]

In any case, Major Butterfield appears to have been incapacitated by the responsibility for almost four hundred lives when threatened with unspeakable abuse at the hands of unrestrained Indians. In his panic, the men's immediate welfare apparently outweighed any consideration of military mission. Butterfield failed to meet the basic expectations of a field officer in his situation—as a prevalent contemporary military manual noted, "The obstinate defence of a post is the action where an officer detached singly can acquire the greatest glory; the resistance not proceeding from the number of soldiers destined to defend it, but from the talents of the officer who commands." Isaac Butterfield did not rise to the occasion, and he clearly lacked any hint of intrepidity in critical moments at Fort Cedars.[28]

CHAPTER 12

AMBUSHED

At Fort Ste. Anne, on the windy, rainy morning of May 20, Maj. Henry Sherburne once again directed his provisional battalion into bateaux. Despite the weather, more than one hundred Massachusetts men from Paterson's Fifteenth Continental Regiment and a few New Hampshire ranger guides successfully reached the far shore that morning, on their third consecutive day of crossing attempts.[1] Sherburne had no way to know that Fort Cedars had surrendered to the enemy the day before.

The Continentals unloaded their boats at Pointe-de-Quinchien landing, while detachments requisitioned carts and horses to haul supplies. For the march, Sherburne organized his force in three divisions averaging about thirty-five men each, under Captains Theodore Bliss, Ebenezer Sullivan, and John McKinstry. He also detached ten soldiers to take the boats to a nearby islet, about two hundred yards from the landing, safe from surprise and out of musket range.[2]

Before noon, Sherburne's men stepped out on a nine-mile march to Fort Cedars.[3] Joining the main riverside road, the column of Massachusetts Continentals passed through a mile of closely spaced farmsteads—with houses, barns, and sundry outbuildings. On the landward side, short emerging blades of wheat gave the slightest green tint to the dark, fertile soil. To the west, a forest screen bounded the long, furrowed fields.

These lands sat in a "fief" (or *côte*) known as Quinchien, a name often misinterpreted as being French, *Quinze-Chiens* or *Quinze-Chênes* (fifteen dogs, or oaks). It was actually Algonquian for "rapids," describing the narrow westernmost Ottawa branch that coursed between the Presqu'île mainland and Île Perrot. The appellation broadly applied to the region from the namesake rapids, upstream to the well-used Pointe-de-Quinchien landing, and to a very small river south of the Vaudreuil Parish church.[4] Sherburne's path through the fief appeared clear of enemy threats, but trouble lay ahead.

Marie-Louise de Lotbinière Harwood, *Manoir de Lotbinière en 1765*.
© Centre d'archives de Vaudreuil-Soulanges, Fonds Henry de Lotbinière-Harwood (P006/E20).

A day before, while Fort Cedars was still contested, Captain George Forster told Canadian Jean-Baptiste Testard de Montigny, the displaced master of Fort Ste. Anne, to lead his thirty volunteers back to Vaudreuil Parish from the battle, tasked to find and harass any approaching rebels. Montigny cooperated with local militia captain Jean-Baptiste Lefebvre, who assembled an ad hoc militia company from his home parish and nearby Île Perrot. When Sherburne's hundred-strong rebel force landed at Pointe-de-Quinchien on May 20, the Canadians were clearly outnumbered and avoided contact, but they sent word of the enemy's arrival to Captain Forster.[5]

Back at the Cedars, the British commander had already set further reinforcements in motion. Anticipating Sherburne's imminent arrival, he asked Claude de Lorimier to gather Indians to augment the Canadian volunteers and Vaudreuil militia. Shortly after dawn, three or four dozen eager warriors—including Senecas, Mississaugas, and Abenakis—joined the interpreter. Before the party had left camp, another group of seventeen Canadian volunteers arrived from across the St. Lawrence, ready to join the fight. Jacob Maurer, an "ardent royalist" and former sergeant major in the British commissariat, led the loyalist band, accompanied by one of Lorimier's brothers, probably François-Thomas Verneuil de Lorimier. They promptly joined Claude de Lorimier and the Indian war party. When they left the Cedars before nine o'clock that morning, an American prisoner remembered, the "savages whooped a few times and with the Canadians set out for action."⁶

Along their march route, Lorimier recruited more than a dozen *habitants* in the Cedars and Les Cascades Parishes and armed them with recently captured muskets brought along for that purpose. A short while later, another group of Indians rushed from the Cedars to catch up with the war party, probably after Captain Forster and leading chiefs received news that the rebels had definitely landed at Pointe-de-Quinchien. By the time the party turned left at Les Cascades, it had grown to about thirty Canadians and eighty warriors. Northbound, the force entered a confining forested stretch of the main road, with the Ottawa River's Quinchien branch a few dozen yards to their right. The vanguard probably formed a single well-spaced tactical file with flanking parties covering their left. After a few miles' march, close to noon, they reached the southern edge of Quinchien fief settlement, near Pointe-à-Valois.⁷

Peering over sprout-stippled farmland, the Indian vanguard spied Maj. Henry Sherburne's advancing rebels a little more than half a mile away. The two opposing forces had managed to meet midway between Pointe-de-Quinchien and Fort Cedars. Warriors and *Canadien* volunteers quietly stopped under wooded concealment and assessed the terrain. Lorimier incorrectly believed they had already been spotted by their adversaries—the rebel column appeared to be halting its march at the same time. Unaware of the enemy, the Americans were near a bridge over a small stream, so Major Sherburne was probably following the spirit of common tactical instructions that suggested, "At the passage of defiles, bridges, or fords, the advanced guard should stop at a hundred paces, and form till the whole corps is passed and in order."⁸

From Lorimier's memoirs, a reader would assume that he and his brother were in command, while Lieutenant Parke credited Jacob Maurer as the detachment leader. In reality, though, Indian chiefs were certainly the ones directing warriors into position for a hasty ambush. Ideally, a war party would adopt a half-moon formation, perfect for the "usual flanking and surrounding movements" employed to seize the initiative after springing an ambush. But at this site, the right flank was open to the Quinchien river branch, and the closest cover on the left wing was at the far wooded edge of long farm fields, some two hundred yards from the road, out of effective musket range. Still, Lorimier, Seneca chief Kanughsgawiat, and five other warriors maneuvered around the left flank, aiming for a slight rise to the northwest, while most of the Indians and Canadians positioned

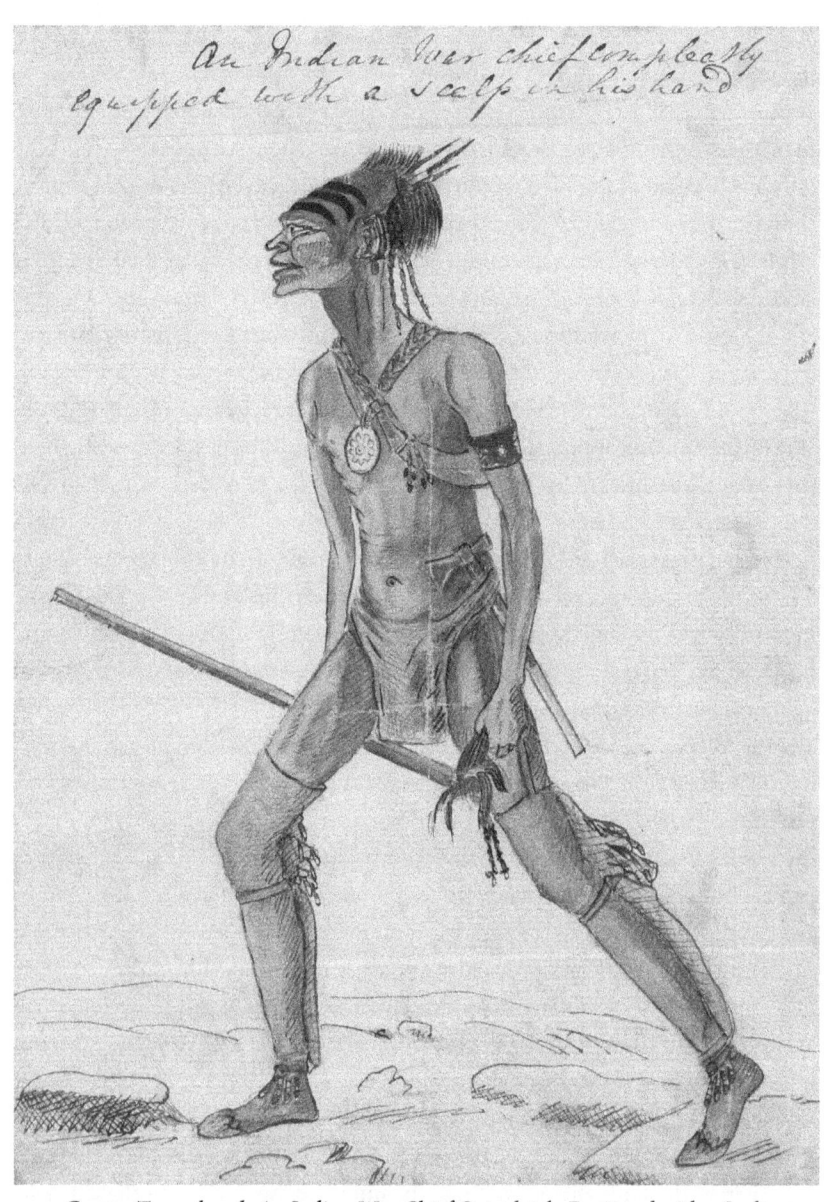

George Townshend, *An Indian War Chief Completely Equipped with a Scalp in His Hand*, ca. 1751–58.
Courtesy National Portrait Gallery, London (NPG4855[73]).

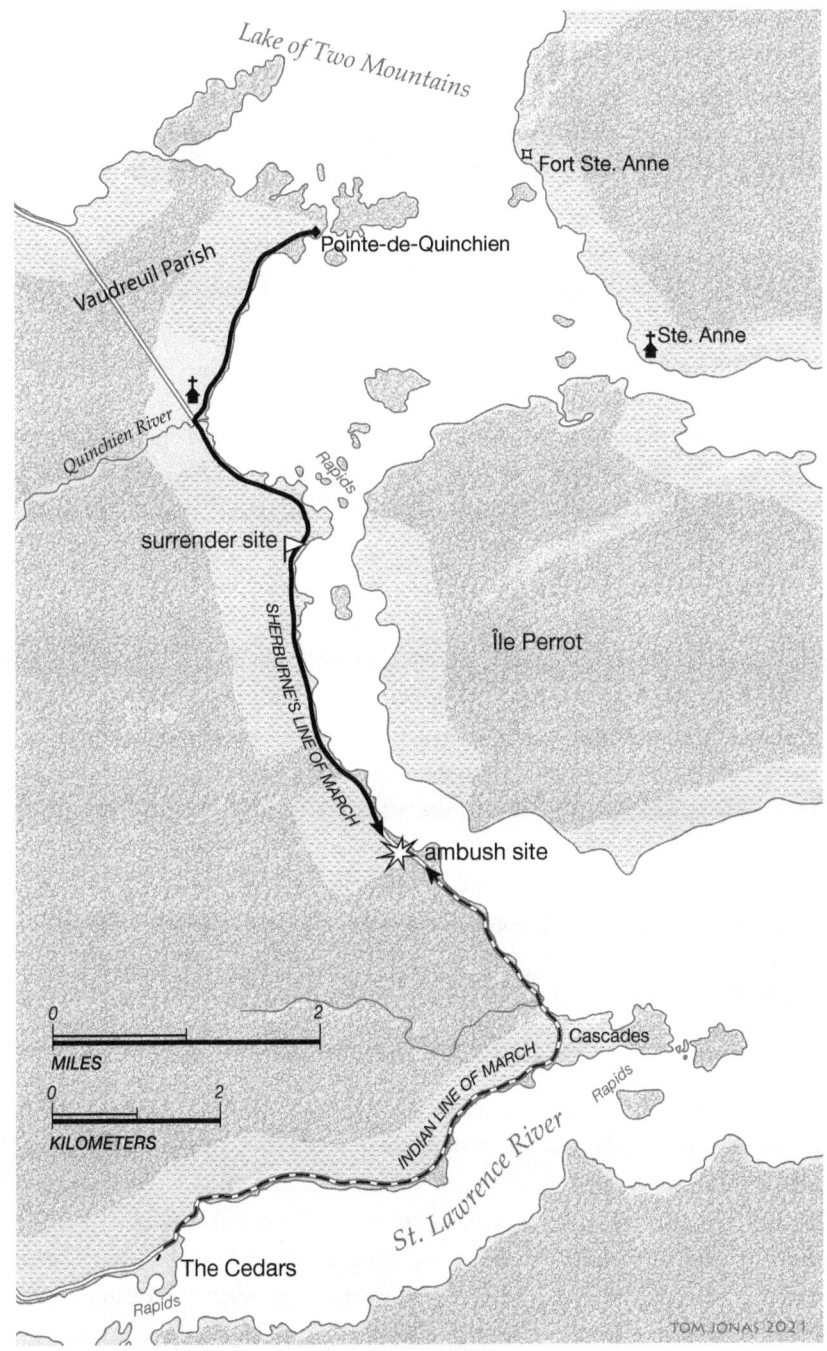

Quinchien Ambush.
Map by Tom Jonas.

themselves astride the main road.[9] Concealed behind the veil of fresh-leafed trees and underbrush, they prepared to unleash their firepower into the face of the approaching enemy column. It was less than ideal, but the loyalist force still held the advantage of surprise.

A Continental soldier described the ambush's opening moment: "As soon as the Americans came opposite to the place the Indians were concealed . . . , the latter rose up and poured upon them a tremendous fire, making at the same time a most hideous noise called the war-whoop, which sounds thus: 'Woo-woo-woo-whoop!'" For those on the receiving end, the surprise musket volley was a jarring assault to every sense—long, flaming muzzle flashes; clouds of smoke; a deafening thunder from exploding powder; the panicked flush of birds; flesh and bone smacked by flying balls; the smell and taste of burnt powder—all before the Indians unleashed their "appalling yells."[10]

French officer Pierre Pouchot described a well-executed Indian ambush in the last war: "At the first moment of the enemy's surprise, they fire upon him, and it is seldom that they fail to bring some of them down"; and with the enemy reeling from the musket volley, the warriors "issue out at once, hatchet in hand, to throw themselves upon them, and do not stop before they are all destroyed." From the Indians' perspective, the Quinchien ambush did not develop so ideally. When the powder smoke thinned, the first rounds appeared to have inflicted minimal damage on the rebel column, and Sherburne's soldiers did not break formation. The Americans undoubtedly flinched at the initial shock, but they kept their wits despite the screams of comrades falling dead and wounded among them. Even after the Indians unleashed their war-whoops, with the potential to "make the stoutest heart that ever existed quake with fear," Sherburne reported, "We stood our Ground, openly exposed to the Enemy, while they were under Cover of Trees."[11]

The Americans' resilience deterred the Indians from closing for immediate hand-to-hand combat. Warriors shifted their tactics in accordance with principles identified by Henry Bouquet after Pontiac's War: "first . . . their general maxim is to surround their enemy. . . . second . . . they fight scattered. . . . The third . . . they never stand their ground when attacked, but immediately give way, to return to the charge." Individual warriors generally understood these tactical basics, but chiefs probably guided the flow of battle, directing smaller parties to advance or retreat.[12]

Sherburne's men "maintained an obstinate engagement" standing in open fields along the road. They caught only the faintest glimpses of Indian forms behind tree trunks and budding underbrush, occasionally unleashing return volleys that shredded branches and leaves without further effect. When Major Sherburne finally spied his adversaries outflanking them, he directed his captains to adjust formation and ordered a retreat. According to the major, this maneuver was all "done with the greatest Order."[13]

The Americans' retreat led them over the same open land along the highway, so they could visually clear their path to avoid a second major ambush, but there were still dozens of farmsteads to pass—sites where houses, barns, and outbuildings could conceal Indian or Canadian skirmishers. Continental captains also had to guide their divisions over several streams, which forced them to slowly funnel men across the small road bridges or risk potentially catastrophic disorder climbing in and out of muddy, cut streambeds. Keeping up a harassing fire, warrior detachments maneuvered around the Americans' flank to cut off the retreat. They mostly remained hidden in the woods to the west, at such a distance from the rebel column on the riverside road that any fire was inaccurate. They were going to achieve more by maneuver than by fire, and as historian Leroy Eid observed, war parties generally "proceeded methodically against adversaries who would not be spooked."[14]

Retreating over a mile, the Continental soldiers reportedly "fought like Lions!" Major Sherburne claimed his men kept disciplined formation "except when occasionally ordered to rush on the enemy in order to dislodge them from barns and other houses in which they placed themselves, which they alwa[y]s effected and did good execution."[15] One of these "rushes" brought about a key moment in the battle.

Claude de Lorimier was making his way north around the enemy flank with six warriors, looking to harass and perhaps cut off the rebel retreat. The seven of them took cover in a barn about a hundred yards from the road. At the same time, ranger Pvt. Joseph Hadley and five other Continentals had been detached to clear the same farmstead. The American squad spotted the Indian party at the barn. Unobserved, Hadley and his compatriots closed inside musket range and took aim. With a single salvo, they dropped a distinctively clad chief and wounded two others.[16]

On the receiving end, Lorimier reported, "One of my Indians was shot seven times through the body and fell dead inside." This was Seneca chief Kanughsgawiat. Another Seneca was hit in the shoulder, and a Mississauga "had part of his nose and his whole upper jaw shot away." The Continentals were apparently using buck and ball, with a musket ball and several buckshot per load. After receiving this devastating, surprise fire, Lorimier recounted, "I would not say that we retreated at this point, but we ran as hard as we could from stump to stump and from hillock to hillock until we reached the river bank."[17]

The Continentals retreated for about forty minutes, covering two miles—a little less than half the distance to Pointe-de-Quinchien landing. Despite their precarious situation, Sherburne proudly reported, "I did not see a dejected Countenance during the whole Conduct." Ultimately, some flanking Indians cut off the division that was leading the retreat. That section was ready to surrender, but the middle division, led by the "active, energetic" Capt. Ebenezer Sullivan, "rushed forwards with their bayonets" forcing their way through the Indians between them.[18] Their success was fleeting.

Jean-Baptiste Testard de Montigny's Canadian volunteers and Jean-Baptiste Lefebvre's militiamen had cautiously approached the battle from Vaudreuil in the north. As Sullivan's counterattack pressed over another bridge, Montigny and Lefebvre led the Canadians to meet the advancing rebels. At the same time, Indians surrounded the Americans' trail division, forcing it to yield. Captain Sullivan "behaved with the utmost bravery & for a long time was the means of securing the party on their retreat," but when his men ran out of ammunition, they were obliged to surrender to the enemy. Sullivan was reportedly the last to surrender.[19]

The Americans might have hoped to surrender to the "civilized" *Canadiens*, rather than submitting to the "savage" Indians, but they threw down their arms so suddenly "that Monsieur de Montigny could not possibly come up before their defeat." Lorimier had also reentered the fight, recounting: "Just as I got up to them with most of my men, they about-faced and came rushing towards us calling out that they wished to surrender." The Indians fell upon the Americans to disarm defeated soldiers and lay claim to them as captives. There was no time to negotiate terms—the Americans were "made prisoners by the savages without any stipulation," and Indian captors deemed them their own private property.[20]

A few weeks later, Major Sherburne would be the first to publicize a narrative of the Quinchien ambush. He emphasized his men's disciplined action, maintaining that they faced about four hundred Indians and one hundred Canadians—five times more than in reality. While the Americans' cohesion and resilience were evident, as eighteenth-century Canadian historian William Kingsford maintained, "The story of Sherburne's holding his ground for an hour against five hundred men . . . is simply a fable."[21]

Sherburne also pointed blame, declaring that the "vile Conduct of Major Butterfield was the unhappy Cause of my Disaster." It is true that Sherburne marched into Quinchien unaware of Butterfield's surrender the previous day, but Sherburne had also failed to cross the Lake of Two Mountains for three consecutive days. Military historian Douglas Cubbison further observed that regardless of the major's vaunted reputation, "he had still permitted his command to be first surprised, and then surrounded."[22]

To Sherburne's credit, casualties at Quinchien were not catastrophic. The major offered several estimates, ranging from twelve to twenty-eight killed and wounded. An escaped captive soldier, perhaps in a better position to gather information from fellow prisoners after the surrender, reported "10 only of Sherburne's party were killed—not one officer."[23]

Sherburne also boasted that "the Enemy lost 22 killed and wounded, among them a Chief of the Seneca Tribe, one of the greatest Warriors they had," but British sources consistently suggested far fewer Indian casualties. Both Lorimier and Captain Forster reported a single man killed and two wounded—all from Lorimier's encounter with Private Hadley's squad. Once again, victory had cost the Indians remarkably little.[24]

In the near term, losses on either side proved less important than the Indians' subsequent treatment of captives. Roughly another hundred rebel soldiers had fallen into warriors' hands as spoils of victory at Quinchien, unprotected by any sort of surrender terms. The Americans' fates were far from secure. As historian Ian Steele observed, "The collision of Aboriginal, colonial, and imperial value systems was seldom displayed as clearly and fatefully as in the taking and treating of captives."[25]

CHAPTER 13

"A SCENE OF SAVAGE BARBARITY"

The encounters at Fort Cedars and Quinchien represented a milestone as the Revolutionary War's first substantial Indian battles. Hundreds of Native warriors from several nations had traveled long distances to fight the Americans. Yet the battles' significance was immediately and enduringly obscured by the controversy surrounding alleged atrocities.

On the afternoon of May 20, Maj. Henry Sherburne's Quinchien defeat underscored essential differences between Euro-American and Native American concepts of war. Continental and British soldiers strove to practice their own conventional prisoner of war standards, while Indian warriors—Six Nations Iroquois, Akwesasnes, Kanesatakes, and Mississaugas—expected physical rewards for taking up the hatchet. It had been only one day since Captain George Forster successfully negotiated Fort Cedars surrender terms that circumvented Indian expectations, but as historian Peter Macleod observed, after several French and Indian War episodes, northern warriors had learned that "their ability to engage freely in parallel war was constrained by the presence of a fort."[1]

Quinchien produced a different sort of battle for its Indian participants, hearkening back to another chapter in the last war—General Edward Braddock's catastrophic defeat at the Monongahela. In both the 1755 and 1776 battles, Native-dominant forces overwhelmed enemies on the field, without a negotiated surrender, leaving far fewer restraints in victory. Historian David L. Preston contended, "There was no other battle during the Seven Years' War in which Natives' cultural expectations of victorious warfare were so abundantly and powerfully realized." The Monongahela became "the standard by which many Native warriors assessed future battlefield success."[2] These memories undoubtedly shaped warriors' expectations for the Cedars campaign, especially at Quinchien.

The past molded American expectations and responses too. Colonial collective memory incorporated several generations' accounts of Indian massacres, scalping, torture, and captivity. When Maj. Henry Sherburne hyperbolically observed, "The Barbarity with which we were treated by the Savages, . . . [was] beyond any thing which can be imagined or described," it played to common assumptions and historical tropes as much as it described his perceived experience. In 1776, American audiences were particularly receptive to accounts from the Cedars that reflected time-honored stereotypes of "savages who threat[e]ned death with every kind of torture."[3]

The true scope of atrocity around the Cedars has remained a subject of heated debate over the centuries. Taken at face value, the few eyewitness accounts are largely partisan, irresoluble, and difficult to assess for accuracy. As historian Thomas Mante perceptively suggested in his early 1770s account of the Fort William Henry "massacre": "Incidents of this kind are almost always exaggerated in the recital; for the impressions of fear are in general too stubborn to yield to the clearest truths." More than two and a half centuries later, historian Ari Kelman similarly observed: "Scenes of violence, especially mass violence, are notorious for breeding unreliable and often unreconcilable testimony."[4] Eyewitness perceptions are distorted in the moment, and fallible memories can be unconsciously warped to conform to expectations and suggestions.[5] While Cedars campaign sources ultimately cannot prove or disprove most atrocity allegations, they can address some specific allegations, identify trends, and bound the nature and scale of violence that followed the battle at Quinchien.

After the rebels' Quinchien battlefield surrender, victorious warriors rushed to claim conquered individuals—captives were their best measure of warpath success; clothing and personal effects were additional spoils of war. Major Sherburne experienced a fraught, firsthand example of this claiming and pillaging. While Canadians Claude de Lorimier, Montigny, and Lefebvre argued over the honor of "capturing" the rebel commander, Lorimier noticed an Indian leading Sherburne away as his own captive. When Lorimier protested, the Indian defiantly declared he had "touched" the major first, cementing his claim by custom.[6] This quickly turned into a potentially deadly situation for the captive.

When the chevalier warned the warrior not to take the prisoner away, he defiantly replied, "You will have a dead body and I will have a scalp," a not unusual resolution for a contested claim. The French Canadian astutely shifted the debate, appealing to the warrior's connection to respected Canadians imprisoned by the rebels. Lorimier protested, "What! You want to kill a prisoner? How would you like to have the Americans kill Colonel [John] Campbell, Captain

[Joseph-Hippolyte] Hertel [de Saint-François], and all our other friends whom I hope to exchange for these men?" The warrior compromised saying, "Keep the bird and I will take his plumes," seizing Sherburne's coat, hat, and vest on the spot.[7]

Wounded Capt. John McKinstry was at the center of an even more dangerous postbattle incident. Lorimier spotted the rebel officer leaning against a fence, suffering from a serious thigh wound. Portneuf, an Abenaki, was stripping McKinstry while the captain tried to offer money in exchange for his life. From past experience, the captain presumably anticipated the worst—he had been in the British colonial force that recovered survivors from the 1757 Fort William Henry "massacre."[8]

When Lorimier asked Portneuf why he was stripping the prisoner, the warrior answered that he "didn't want to get the clothes all bloody when he killed him." Indians frequently killed frail captives unable to keep pace in withdrawal from a battle or raid, like McKinstry with his leg wound. Lorimier confronted the Abenaki: "You want to kill this man without thinking that the Americans may well slaughter perhaps three or four of our friends who are their prisoners as a result." After reflection, Portneuf let Lorimier take the wounded captain, on the condition that he would be exchanged for imprisoned Captain Hertel de Saint-François—a government interpreter at Akwesasne from 1769 to 1770, who had been a valued advocate for that village's Abenaki refugees. Lorimier agreed, sealing the deal and rescuing McKinstry.[9]

During these officers' encounters, other nameless Continentals suffered worse fates. Sherburne reported that after the surrender, "a scene of Savage barbarity ensued; and many of our people were sacrificed to their fury, butchered with tomahawks and other instruments of murder." Another American account noted that the warriors "fell to work ... despatching the wounded by knocking them on the head with their axes and tomahawks, and scalping the dead, that is, tearing the skin and hair from the top of their heads." Given traditional Indian practices that treasured scalps as "proof of valor," there is no reason to doubt these claims in regard to the dead and seriously wounded. A soldier described the Indians' sustained maximization of the terror: "The dead were divested of their clothing and laid by the road-side, where our remaining troops were driven past them like cattle to witness the spectacle, the Indians brandishing their knives and tomahawks over their heads, and howling and screaming like madmen or devils."[10]

After this immediate postsurrender sequence, Canadian and Indian leaders still had to address the last lingering rebel threat to the Presqu'île mainland, the small American detachment left with the bateaux on the islet near Pointe-de-Quinchien landing. Threatening the prospect of near-certain massacre and offering a single alternative, Lorimier coerced Sherburne and fellow captives to cooperate in a ruse that would draw the Continentals from the island to be captured at the landing. Reluctantly, the major called the island detachment to him, and as the boats neared shore, warriors leapt from hiding, jumped into the lake, and grabbed the boats "before the Americans could even think to defend themselves." It was a bloodless victory. Consolidating their gains, warriors herded their captive column south on the highway to rejoin Captain Forster, his soldiers, and their Indian compatriots. As Major Sherburne described it, "After they had stripped us, and killed as many as they thought proper, we were marched off to the Cedars, the Place we were destined to reinforce."[11]

During the daylight hours, while Sherburne's force was being ambushed and abused, Maj. Isaac Butterfield and his fellow prisoners experienced their own tense time at Fort Cedars. More than one hundred "very unruly" Indians appeared ready to kill the captives at the first sign of approaching rebel relief. While Captain Forster and his officers clearly felt responsible for their prisoners' safety in the fort, they had to rely on persuasion and compromise with Indian allies, in lieu of coercive authority or credible restraining force. Forster could only do so much with two score soldiers. In this case, the redcoats herded the rebels back into the wooden church for their own protection.[12]

Tensions at Fort Cedars were ephemerally relieved in the afternoon with the Quinchien war party's victorious return, but the mood soured in an instant with word that they had "lost a principal chief of the Senecas" in battle. Remaining outside the fort, warriors made motions to kill some, maybe all, of the Quinchien captives. There was customary precedent, as Lieutenant Andrew Parke observed: "savages . . . in former wars, sacrificed their prisoners to the *manes* [spirits] of their deceased friends."[13]

Putting himself and his soldiers at risk with "most spirited and decisive conduct," Captain Forster made every effort to prevent massacre. American soldiers believed the "savages were determined to cut off every man of them but were prevented by the officers promising them our plunder." A loyalist account suggested that "to stop their Outrage," Forster gave the Indians a substitute sacrifice of "Eight Yoke of Oxen and some Cows"—a somewhat commonplace practice in late colonial-era parallel warfare. Seneca chiefs presumably played a role in deescalating the situation among the agitated warriors, perhaps with their nation's strategic interests in mind.[14]

Despite Forster's efforts, Continental officers believed the Indians still killed three or four captives that day, but no one could identify alleged victims by name or company. British and Canadian participants denied this claim. There is little in the record to dispute a skeptical nineteenth-century Canadian historian's conclusion regarding these murder allegations, that "the whole evidence is vague in the extreme."[15]

Maj. Henry Sherburne added one more sensational and outrageous detail in later testimony. He maintained that of the three men allegedly murdered, one "was first shot . . . so however as not to kill him[,] and then roasted." The incident was initially reported by a soldier eyewitness who was subsequently unavailable for further questioning, having been taken up-country as a captive. Torture-killing by fire was not unprecedented, but it was generally reserved for occasions when "a nation . . . suffered great losses in war, and it is thought necessary to revenge the death of their warriors slain in battle." These horrific tortures were legendary in the colonies; and such a prospect was certainly running through many soldiers' minds after their battlefield defeat. In this case, though, it is vital to note that after the day of battle, *only* Sherburne—no other Americans, and no loyalists—maintained that such a "roasting" occurred. It seems almost certain that no one was burned to death outside Fort Cedars.[16]

However, another related atrocity legend is the most commonly recirculated and enduring anecdote from the Cedars campaign. The tale claims that Mohawk chief Joseph Brant Thayendanegea rescued Capt. John McKinstry from imminent death by fire at the Indians' hands, when the desperate captive and fellow Freemason "uttered that mystic appeal which the brotherhood of masons never disregard." This story emerged in 1822 after McKinstry's death, was sustained in Joseph Brant biographies, and still circulates in popular Masonic histories.[17]

While the story is enchanting, it is impossible for Joseph Brant to have intervened to save John McKinstry, because the Mohawk chief was visiting England in May 1776. Even though McKinstry family members vouched for the story's accuracy, individuals retelling the incident must have misremembered events over time, confused battles and personalities, and perhaps experienced "imagination inflation." Historians and biographers have suggested alternative origins for the legend, but there is no clear, rational explanation for its distortion between 1776 and 1822.[18]

Sherburne's "roasting" allegation may still have had underlying substance. In addition to the McKinstry incident, Pvt. Jonathan Nocks (Knox) reported, "I was captured by the Indians with my Lieutenant Nathan Lord, & saw him led out to be burnt to death, when he was ransomed, & rescued from death by a British Officer."[19] Other soldiers who similarly observed compatriots "designated for the torture" and led out of sight might have assumed that the act was executed, even if victims were actually rescued. Sherburne was probably just "misinformed as to the actual consummation of such a purpose in the person of any prisoner." Ian Steele unraveled similar cases of incorrectly assumed captive fates in his painstaking analysis of the Fort William Henry "massacre."[20]

Even after their successful interventions to prevent off-battlefield murders, Captain Forster and his officers faced yet another substantial challenge in protecting Quinchien survivors that afternoon. The defeated rebels were still subject to being led up-country by victorious warriors. Captives were the most desirable and substantial proof of battlefield success. In traditional practice, captives could be fully adopted—like the pro-American headmen in Kahnawake—held as slave laborers, or ritually killed in the village.[21]

There was a fourth captive option that Captain Forster used to his advantage. Warriors could also sell captives to Euro-colonials for money or goods, an ascendant practice in the eighteenth century. Lieutenant Parke remembered, "Individuals were bought from them at high prices, and presents to a considerable amount given to the friends of the deceased and wounded Indians." Maj. Isaac Butterfield similarly believed that "Captain Forster and the other officers ... exerted themselves to redeem and rescue the prisoners out of their [the Indians'] hands."[22]

Yet Lieutenant Parke lamented, "All our endeavours proved ineffectual with some of the savages," probably Senecas and Mississaugas, "who would not relinquish their prisoners." Major Sherburne believed the Indians took seven or eight Continentals away that day. Butterfield noted key characteristics of the first captives led off. They included "several young lads"—teenaged soldiers, "one young child" taken from a camp follower, and "all the blacks"—soldiers, servants, and slaves. Among captive soldiers, young men were the most likely candidates for acculturation and adoption in Indian communities. Reflecting eighteenth-century racial attitudes, blacks were particularly valuable captives since they were "saleable plunder" as slaves or servants, with the added benefit that colonial authorities were unlikely to press for their repatriation at the end of a colonial war.[23]

The king's officers undoubtedly acted on humanitarian principles, but Forster also had substantial military considerations to justify his efforts and expense in keeping prisoners together at the Cedars. If warriors had captives under their own control, they would be inclined to promptly return home with living "trophies of their victory," thereby removing themselves from further campaigning. In any case, redcoat soldiers successfully ushered 97 survivors from Sherburne's force into Fort Cedars that day, totaling 487 rebel prisoners temporarily under nominal British control.[24]

The prisoners from Sherburne's battalion had survived traumatic defeat, compatriots' scalpings, murder threats, and captive removals that day. They were undoubtedly happy to join their comrades in the relative safety of the Cedars parish church, even as they were pressed into forty-five pews' floor space in the old wooden structure.[25] Once again, however, any sense of security was fleeting.

Indian warriors may have sold or deferred rights to individual captives, but they still claimed the Americans' possessions as their own. According to Lieutenant Parke, "the savages insisting on their right to pillage the prisoners taken at Quinchien, they could not be prevented from entering the barracks for that purpose, and we do fear they pillaged the prisoners indiscriminately, but they did not otherwise injure them." Warriors who had not fought in the ambush joined in; they too had been denied their just rewards in the Fort Cedars surrender. A New Hampshire ranger remembered, "The indians would climb up in to the windows 10 or 12 feet from the ground, with there tomehacks and scalping knifes," taking things like "money silver buckles buttons silk handkerchiefs and all such light articles as they could carry at a distance." When Major Butterfield protested, Captain Forster "said it was not in his power to prevent it."[26] The British commander accommodated plundering as a relief valve and an acceptable compromise to inhibit further violence against the prisoners.

New Hampshire soldiers later described having "suf[f]ered s[a]vage Barbarity[,] being Strip[p]ed and plundered of Every thing and only Escaped with the Skin of our teeth." As an example, ranger Thomas Gibbs's itemized claim recorded the loss of his gun and powder horn, coat and shoes, new beaver hat, pack and canteen, as well as an ink stand and comb. Prisoners frequently complained that they were left "naked," implying they had been robbed of all garments except britches and undershirts. Even officers reported being "stripped of every part of their clothing that was either comfortable or valuable," and thus were "not in any capacity to appear among gentlemen."[27] By huddling in the church confines, prisoners lost many valuable material goods, but by resisting fight-or-flight instincts, they protected their bodies and lives—from murder, captivity, or exposure in unseasonably cold, inclement weather.

On May 20, most American prisoners at the Cedars survived a figurative gauntlet of terrors, even though British officers, Canadians, and Indian leaders moderated the warriors' bloodiest battlefield practices. There would be more violent incidents in the near future, but on this most charged day, key participants cooperated actively and passively to accommodate cultural differences and avoid a repeat of the widespread violence and "massacres" that occurred at the Monongahela, Fort Oswego, and Fort William Henry. Rather, they managed to bring about an outcome more similar to that at Fort Niagara in 1759, where Sir William Johnson employed his vast cross-cultural skills and connections to act as an "effective broker" to balance and moderate Indian and European conventions. As a result, victorious allies struck a careful compromise, meeting Indian expectations through plunder, scalps, and moderated captive taking so that most prisoners could be returned through Euro-colonial military and diplomatic channels.[28]

CHAPTER 14

"TO STOP THE ENEMIES PROGRESS"

On the clear, frigid morning of May 21, Captain George Forster was forced to weigh his options after the Indians' decisive victory at Quinchien. The path to Montreal appeared clear, but as historian Paul L. Stevens observed, "Forster now found himself overwhelmed by success. He had less than 40 regulars to guard and to safeguard more than 500 rebel prisoners." Even in daylight, Indians brazenly and unrelentingly stripped, pillaged, and threatened the Americans confined in conquered Fort Cedars.[1]

The military opportunities seemed too promising, so Forster decided to press forward, presumably after consultation with allied chiefs. In a few hours, several hundred men—rebel captives, warriors, redcoats, and Canadians—started shuffling up the narrow highway on an eleven-mile march to Vaudreuil Parish. Thirteen prisoners remained in the fort, presumably too ill or seriously wounded to move.[2]

By evening, the ambling procession was only halfway to Vaudreuil. British soldiers guided the rebel prisoners into "old rotten stinking log barnes," sheep stables, and other outbuildings for overnight shelter. The Americans suffered through the frosty night, many now lacking outer clothing, and in the morning, Indians revisited them for further premarch plundering. When the column completed its march to Pointe-de-Quinchien later that day, redcoats ordered enlisted prisoners "to encamp on a certain point of plowd land," near the vacant seigneurial manor. They endured further miseries that night, with "no fires nor wood to fire; nor meat for to cook nor bread to eat," exposed to a "storm of hail and rain" around midnight. They were equally unprotected from "the rage of savage cruelty," with "the thretning promise of death every minute by the indean tomehak." Rebel officers had more comfortable accommodations in Abbé Louis Beaumont's home, the large stone presbytery with its second-floor chapel serving as an interim parish church.[3]

Before continuing the advance onto the Island of Montreal, Captain Forster expected Jean-Baptiste Testard de Montigny to rally a sizable Canadian contingent in Vaudreuil, but he was disappointed when only fifty men showed. Prospects quickly improved though, when fifty Lake of Two Mountains Kanesatakes unexpectedly appeared. With renewed confidence, Forster took another step forward, sending fifty Canadians and twenty Indians across the Lake of Two Mountains that evening under Montigny's command, "to take possession of his own house" at Fort Ste. Anne. The landing was uncontested. The fort's American commander, ranger Capt. Samuel Young, had recently abandoned the post as it became increasingly clear his twenty-man command was alone in the enemy's path.[4]

When dawn light glimmered across the lake on May 23, Captain Forster faced a conundrum at Pointe-de-Quinchien: how could he continue his advance while protecting his prisoners? Slight relief came when Kanesatake's mission priests agreed to care for the captured rebel officers, in Lake of Two Mountains village. Sherburne, Butterfield, and twenty-nine captains, lieutenants, and ensigns stayed there for the next few days, separated from their men's tribulations. Solutions for rank-and-file prisoners remained more troublesome. As Forster moved forward, he left two hundred captives in Vaudreuil, unfed in shabby old barns and sheds, guarded by thirty Canadian militiamen.[5]

Forster's soldiers took the other 250 prisoners with them across the lake and secured them inside Fort Ste. Anne. Redcoats, loyalists, and warriors camped around Montigny's estate, ravaging neighboring properties in quests for food and firewood. That afternoon, Canadian and Indian parties ventured toward Montreal, scouting the next day's advance.[6] There was no sign of rebel opposition yet, but elsewhere on the island, Americans were busy reacting to the Cedars catastrophe.

Four days earlier, when Brig. Gen. Benedict Arnold returned to Montreal from Sorel on the night of May 19, he was greeted with reliable reports that Fort Cedars was under attack—dispelling the illusion of calm in the west. City commandant Col. John Paterson had already dispatched veteran Lt. Col. John Brown to round up scattered elements of Paterson's own regiment across the St. Lawrence at Laprairie, gather warrior allies at Kahnawake village, and "take them with him to join Majr Sherburne." Immediately the next morning, Arnold followed by ordering Capt. David Noble's company from Paterson's regiment to leave the city and reinforce Major Sherburne by bateaux. Later in the day, a Kahnawake "Captain"—perhaps Louis Atiatoharongwen—came to Arnold's headquarters with two or three Indian companions, seeking "a few articles for war" to assist the Americans, presumably prompted by Colonel Brown's visit the day before.[7] The Kahnawakes' apparent commitment to the American cause was a rare positive sign for Arnold at the moment.

Bad news continued to stream into headquarters on May 20, but General Arnold once again demonstrated his "great vivacity, perseverance, resources & intrepidity." Continental leaders were not yet aware of Sherburne's ambush and defeat, but with reports that the small relief column could be facing one hundred British regulars, a thousand "Savages," and Canadians as well, Arnold prepared for the major's likely defeat. The general scraped together one hundred more Continental soldiers and two cannon in Montreal, and personally led them eight miles west to Lachine that evening. The fur-trade village was the key chokepoint before Montreal, the primary portage around the Sault St. Louis rapids, and the site where the principal road headed overland, direct to the city. Joining Colonel Brown and his eighty men already in Lachine, the general emphatically sought "to stop the Enemies progress," and he immediately had the soldiers "cast up a small fort for present defense."[8]

Arnold's keen tactical eye focused on entrepreneur Hugh Heney's property. The general ordered soldiers to anchor defensive lines on Heney's vaulted, stone warehouse, and build adjacent earthworks and batteries astride the Montreal road. He established his own headquarters nearby in Heney's two-thousand-square-foot, two-story stone inn, finding room for a hospital and barracks there as well. The valuable site was also the island terminus for ferry service linking Lachine to Kahnawake.[9]

Giving some of his men a break from earthwork labor, Arnold directed them to investigate Lachine's fur-trade warehouses. They found prodigious supplies, packed in convenient bundles and kegs for up-country shipment. The general confiscated many of these "goods & military stores & provisions" for his men's use, judging that the matériel was "going up to supply our Enemies on the great lakes"—evidently based on little more than arbitrary expediency.[10]

Despite Arnold's defensive efforts, if enemy strength reports were accurate, he still needed additional men to defend Lachine with any confidence. Colonel Paterson could not risk further weakening of the Montreal garrison, but reinforcements still came in from other, unanticipated directions. On May 22, Captain Noble's one hundred Massachusetts soldiers pulled their bateaux back onto Lachine's gravelly shores—returning when it was clear they had failed to reach Sherburne before his defeat. Later that day, Capt. Samuel Young's Fort Ste.

Anne garrison unexpectedly marched into the village from the west. Arnold promptly put Young "under an arrest by reason of his leaving the fort," but maybe a dozen rangers stayed in Lachine to fight. That evening, enterprising Capt. James Wilkinson surprisingly appeared on the Lachine shoreline with yet another one hundred men, mostly from the Second Continental Regiment (New Hampshire). Having just arrived in Canada that day, Wilkinson marched his company where it was most needed. Kahnawakes delivered them by canoe on the final leg across the St. Lawrence. By nightfall, Arnold tallied about four hundred men at Lachine, a theoretically sufficient force to stop the oncoming enemy horde. Now time would tell whether the British and Indians attacked him first, or if he could receive adequate reinforcements to preempt them and pivot to the counteroffensive.[11]

Unbeknownst to Arnold, even larger reinforcements were already on their way from the main army camp downriver. Hearing about increasingly unfavorable developments west of Montreal, the two Continental Congress commissioners circumvented the chaotic military command at Sorel and directly ordered Col. John Philip De Haas and part of his First Pennsylvania Regiment to join Arnold at Lachine, "proceed to Fort Ste Anns & attack Capt. Forster & the Indians under him." The Pennsylvanians were invaluable at this point in the campaign, because so many of them had been inoculated against smallpox or had survived it naturally earlier in their lives. On the afternoon of May 22, De Haas led 300 of his own men out of Sorel, with Capt. John Nelson's 70-man Pennsylvania rifle company attached. Lt. Col. Thomas Williams followed the Pennsylvanians' path later that day with another 160 Massachusetts men, combined from Elisha Porter's Regiment and Paterson's widely scattered Fifteenth Continentals. It would take all of these men a few days to cover the fifty-five miles to Lachine though.[12]

Arnold's relatively quiet night at Lachine was interrupted only by nervous outpost soldiers firing at shadows cast in their direction by the setting crescent moon. The next day, May 23, Arnold used the calm before the storm to visit allies across the river in Kahnawake village. He tried to steady their nerves in the face of the many recent, dangerous Continental setbacks and asked for more warriors to join him in the field. When Arnold returned to Lachine that afternoon, Col. Moses Hazen stayed behind to coordinate with one hundred "Militia Volunteers of the Indian town"—apparently meaning warriors. Pro-American Kahnawakes could finally deliver on their January pledges to General Washington in Cambridge. Two Kahnawake men also headed west to spy for Arnold in the "character of Beaver hunters."[13]

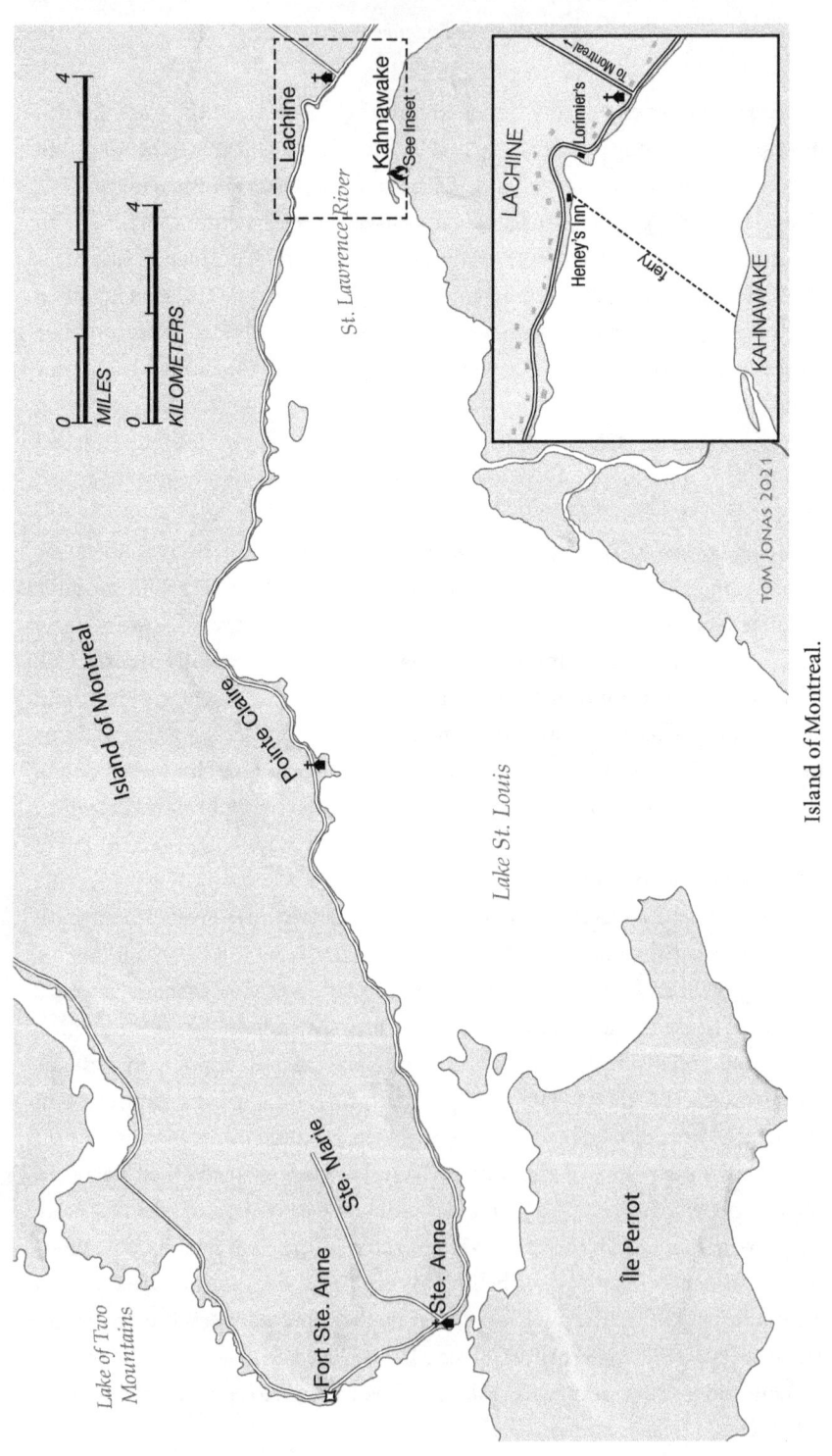

Island of Montreal.
Map by Tom Jonas.

On May 23, an incident outside Lachine foretold the end of mundane fortification building. Late in the afternoon, Lt. Joseph Welch and Pvt. James McElherron wandered along the road "in quest of milk," when an Indian party leapt from an orchard and seized the oblivious duo without a fight. Being led away captive, McElherron slackened his pace, "fell in the rear, wheeled suddenly, and sprang off in retreat." Warriors did not pursue but shot at the escaping private, wounding him in the thigh. He limped into Lachine to warn that the enemy was most definitely nearby. That night, Continentals also believed they heard drums from neighboring Pointe Claire. Battle truly seemed nigh.[14]

Claude de Lorimier interrogated the captive Lieutenant Welch, who "swore there were not more than 250 of them [rebels at Lachine] . . . that they did not expect another blessed soul," and that American officers were itching to retreat. Lorimier passed this seemingly valuable information to Captain Forster, giving the British commander further cause to believe he might drive the rebels from Lachine, continue on to Montreal, and liberate loyal citizens from occupation.[15] The captain and the interpreter would soon find that Lieutenant Welch had misled them, by pure ignorance or design.

At Fort Ste. Anne the next morning, May 24, Captain Forster directed almost five hundred warriors, soldiers, and Canadians down the road to Montreal. Their first destination was Pointe Claire, halfway down the road to Lachine, where Forster again hoped to meet substantial militia reinforcements. Montigny remained behind at the fort with a handful of Canadians, guarding the 250 rebel prisoners locked in the mansion's "chamber and garret."[16]

After completing nine miles' march, Forster reached Pointe Claire later that day only to be disappointed by the militia yet again. Just a few armed Canadians rendezvoused in the parish that was landmarked by its ancient cylindrical stone windmill and a half-moon bay off Lake St. Louis. Arnold's active defensive efforts at Lachine may well have tempered the locals' zeal. Disappointed but persistent, Forster continued on toward the enemy and Montreal.

Later that afternoon, some Montreal loyalists found Forster, still three miles out from Lachine, to deliver new intelligence. One account revealed rebel plans to outflank Forster's corps by marching Colonel De Haas's Pennsylvanians inland, around Mont Real, the high ground northwest of the city. Another warned that Colonel Hazen was leading "three hundred Bostonians" along the St. Lawrence's southeast shore, to outflank Forster far to the west. Lorimier personally vouched for the messengers, believing that they were "incapable of misleading us."[17]

James Duncan, *Pointe Claire from Windmill Point, 12th Aug. 1831*.
© *McCord Museum, Gift of Mr. David Ross McCord (M683)*.

Lieutenant Andrew Parke recorded a quantitative summary of the day's threatening reports: "the rebels had six hundred men, with six pieces of cannon, entrenched at Le Chine [sic]; that two hundred Rifle-men, had marched with two pieces of cannon to reinforce them; that they were calling in all their out-posts, which would by the evening make their numbers fifteen hundred, and the day following would augment them to twenty-five hundred men." With his plans upended by all this news, Forster convened a council of war that unanimously recommended immediate retreat to Point Claire.[18] The highly successful Indian-British western offensive had reached its culminating point.

Once turned back to the west, Indian warriors and Canadian volunteers saw that their opportunity to reap glory and treasure had passed, and most quietly took their own paths home. Reflecting his national and racial biases, Lieutenant Parke believed most Canadians "returned home through fear," while "the fickle disposition of the savages" led them to wander "as their fancy let them." By the time Forster backtracked the short distance to Pointe Claire, 85 percent of his manpower disappeared, leaving him with his forty soldiers and an equal number of stalwart Canadians and Indians. Primary accounts do not differentiate these warriors by nation, but they were probably still a mix of different Six Nations, Seven Nations, and Mississauga warriors. If a stand at Pointe Claire or Fort Ste. Anne might have appeared practical before, Forster now had no choice but to extricate his men from the Island of Montreal.[19]

Interestingly and probably incorrectly, Lake of Two Mountains mission priest François-Auguste Magon de Terlaye later concluded that "loyalist" Montreal merchants had deliberately deceived Captain Forster about rebel strength at Lachine, "because they had packs of merchandise which they would not sacrifice" in a battle there. Yet even if the reports Forster received were slightly inflated, they led him to the correct operational decision. By May 24, the rebels had vast numerical superiority, with more than one thousand men converging on Lachine.[20] The loyalists' timely intelligence actually saved Forster from a very dangerous predicament, especially when opposed by an audacious, experienced commander like Benedict Arnold.

Forster's men retraced their steps overnight to arrive back at Fort Ste. Anne on May 25. The captain was pleased to find that Montigny was already transferring rebel prisoners from the fort to nearby Île aux Tourtes—the uninhabited "Isle of Turtle Doves." This move expedited Forster's retreat by eliminating multiple crossings, and freeing up military manpower—the rebels could be left unguarded on the "desolate island in the middle of the lake."[21]

For the next twenty-four hours, the poor Continental castaways on Île aux Tourtes were "very scantily supplied with provision, barely sufficient to keep them from starving, ... without any covering but the canopy of heaven," and had been stripped to base garments that were far from adequate in still-cold May weather. The harsh deprivation added yet another layer of trauma for prisoners who had already suffered repeated pillaging and near-constant threats of death or captivity.[22] Meanwhile, Captain Forster led his dwindling composite corps back to Pointe-de-Quinchien in twenty-one canoes, ending their two-day misadventure on the Island of Montreal. For the moment, the Lake of Two Mountains served as a valuable obstacle to rebel pursuit.

In large part, Captain Forster gained the time and space to execute his retreat because General Arnold was slow to recognize the fluid situation. For several days, intelligence sources painted a threatening picture that discouraged American offensive action. The scene was finally clarified on May 25 when a New Hampshire ranger captive, Cpl. John Fifield, escaped from Fort Ste. Anne and trekked all the way to General Arnold's headquarters at Heney's Inn. The escapee told Arnold about Forster's advance and subsequent retreat, and scouts soon corroborated the information. Arnold scrambled to take the offensive.[23]

He had already planned a bold combined envelopment operation. Col. Moses Hazen would lead four hundred men in bateaux, "to cut off the Retreat of the Enemy and in such a manners [sic] as to save our Prisoners," via Île Perrot. Arnold and the main body would advance on land to pin Forster's corps at Fort Ste. Anne or perhaps Pointe-de-Quinchien. The general had flexibility in his operational scheme of maneuver because in sharp contrast to Major Sherburne's situation a week earlier, Arnold commanded sufficient bateaux to transport sizable forces on the river and coordinate their efforts with even more men on land. However, De Haas's four hundred Pennsylvanians were waylaid overnight in Montreal by supply shortages, so Arnold simmered another night in Lachine before beginning his advance. On the morning of May 26, scouts came back all the way from Fort Ste. Anne, confirming that Forster had stolen a day's march. Arnold could not move fast enough.[24]

CHAPTER 15

"THE DICTATES OF HUMANITY"

Even in retreat, Captain George Forster and his Indian allies were "much incommoded with his American prisoners." By the time they had recrossed the Lake of Two Mountains, supplies were running low, prompting the captain to put everyone on half-rations. Disgruntled warriors threateningly suggested that they could decrease the number of mouths to feed by killing prisoners. With the situation eroding, senior Indian chiefs took the initiative and asked Forster to arrange a prisoner exchange, relieving them all of this burden.[1]

On May 26, Captain Forster drafted an exchange cartel, and Lieutenant Henry Bird carried it to the rebel officer prisoners in Kanesatake village, seeking their subscription to the proposed agreement. In the cartel preamble, Forster pleaded that the "customs and manners of the savages in war" were "so opposite and contrary to the humane disposition of the British Government," that "the dictates of humanity" compelled him to offer an exchange. Rebel captives would be released for equal numbers and ranks of British soldiers—presumably those surrendered in Canada at Chambly and Fort St. Johns, now imprisoned in the colonies. Majors Henry Sherburne and Isaac Butterfield and the other American officers felt they had no choice in the matter, and they put their signatures on the document.[2]

Forster had a day to craft and coordinate the cartel because Brig. Gen. Benedict Arnold was still at Lachine, waiting to start his pursuit. Before taking the offensive, Arnold embarked on his own far-fetched diplomatic venture, asking Kahnawake allies to visit enemy Indians and deliver his demand for "a surrender of our prisoners." He added a threat to his adversaries—that "in case of refusal, and that any of them [prisoners] were murdered, I would sacrifice every Indian who fell into my hands, and would follow them to their towns, and destroy them by fire and sword."[3] With his military strength growing by the hour, Arnold could afford to test the power of words before resorting to force of arms.

At six o'clock in the morning of May 26, Pennsylvanian Col. John Philip De Haas finally led a Continental advance guard west out of Lachine, trailed by a corps of 600 to 900 soldiers, two field pieces, and perhaps as many as 200 Kahnawake allies. A small bateaux squadron worked its way upriver along the Island of Montreal shoreline, in conjunction with the land advance. That afternoon, De Haas's vanguard completed a vigorously paced eighteen-mile march and approached Fort Ste. Anne, finding it abandoned once again. The Continentals could barely identify redcoats on the opposite side of the lake, two miles away. A few hours later, Americans began spotting British soldiers taking captives off Île aux Tourtes to the Presqu'île mainland, about the same time that Arnold arrived with the main body. They all raged in temporary impotence—the essential bateaux still lagged behind the march, fighting the current.[4]

Captain Forster's soldiers and allied Indians had already spent several hours transferring prisoners from Île aux Tourtes. One of the captives remembered, warriors "took some of our sick into a canoe and drove the rest of us down the island as far as they could get us, through swamps and water as high as our waists." An extremely fatigued American prisoner drowned when forced to cross a creek. Warriors deliberately killed one rebel who was too sick to move, and another who "attempted to hide himself." These prisoner-reported incidents are credible, fitting typical Indian warpath behavior, even if the British later dismissed the claims because surviving Americans could not identify the dead by name.[5]

At least three prisoners effected an escape from Île aux Tourtes during the evacuation. One of the New Hampshire Rangers, Pvt. David Lynds, decided "that he had rather risk his life in the water then with the indians on land," and swam downstream to another island. When American bateaux finally entered the Lake of Two Mountains in the early evening, boatmen also spotted "a naked man up to his middle in the water" and rescued him, probably Pvt. Wentworth Lord. Despite the escapee's miserable condition, he immediately rejoined the ranks to seek vengeance on the Indians.[6]

While General Arnold chomped at the bit in Fort Ste. Anne waiting for bateaux, his Kahnawake emissaries returned from the far shore. British-allied war chiefs defied Arnold's threatening demand to surrender their prisoners and countered that if attacked at Quinchien, "they would immediately kill every prisoner, and give no quarter to any who should fall into their hands hereafter." Eager for vengeance but fearing for captive compatriots, Arnold was "torn by the conflicting passions of revenge and humanity." Colonel De Haas, a respected veteran of both the French and Indian War and Pontiac's War, thought he had successfully advised moderation but was surprised when he returned to the shoreline after a short walk to inspect the fort's surroundings.[7]

General Arnold's passions had since prevailed, and he "ordered every man to prepare for action, and embark in the boats." Five or six hundred soldiers from various units—Nelson's Pennsylvania Rifles, Paterson's Massachusetts Regiment, Burrall's Connecticut Regiment, and others—rushed to remove supplies from fifteen bateaux and clambered in "with zeal and promptitude," even if in somewhat disorganized fashion. A few dozen Kahnawakes joined in three canoes.[8] While their objective was unclear, the infuriated Arnold and his soldiers ached to punish their "savage" enemy.

Arnold slipped into a Kahnawake canoe and "ordered the boats to row immediately" for Île aux Tourtes, less than a mile away. Racing the rapidly setting sun, parties landed on the island, scoured the woods, and recovered "five unhappy wretches, naked and almost starved," hiding in swampy thickets. The recovered soldiers explained that their mates had all been "taken off by the savages just before, except one or two, who, being unwell, were inhumanly butchered." Once the landing parties reembarked, General Arnold "immediately ordered the boats to row for Quinze Chiens [sic]," just another mile away. Any opportunity for an assault landing was dimming with the twilight. Even under a bright, unobscured moon, Arnold's hastily assembled detachment was totally unprepared for night action against disciplined British soldiers and terrifying Indian warriors.[9]

From the Pointe-de-Quinchien shore, Captain Forster had seen Arnold's bateaux flotilla embark. Given the ample warning, the British commander first protected his prisoners. Redcoats urgently ushered an exhausted rebel mass down the road into Vaudreuil's presbytery-chapel, where the rebels found themselves pressed into such tight quarters that they "could neither lye down nor set down nor stand up for the want of strength." Leaving a small guard with the prisoners, Forster then deployed the bulk of his British soldiers at the woods' edge around the primary landing. About a mile downstream to their right, Captain Jean-Baptiste Lefebvre led Canadian militia concentrated near the presbytery-turned-prison. In an adjacent, "well fortified" battery, Captain Pierre de Boucherville commanded militia crews on the two brass artillery pieces taken from Fort Cedars. Scattered warriors covered the rest of the shoreline, hiding behind trees and budding underbrush.[10]

In their dusk approach, bateaux-borne Americans observed "the detachment of British troops employed on the beach, and the Indians ranging themselves on the bank." From a Kahnawake-crewed canoe, Arnold guided his boat squadron

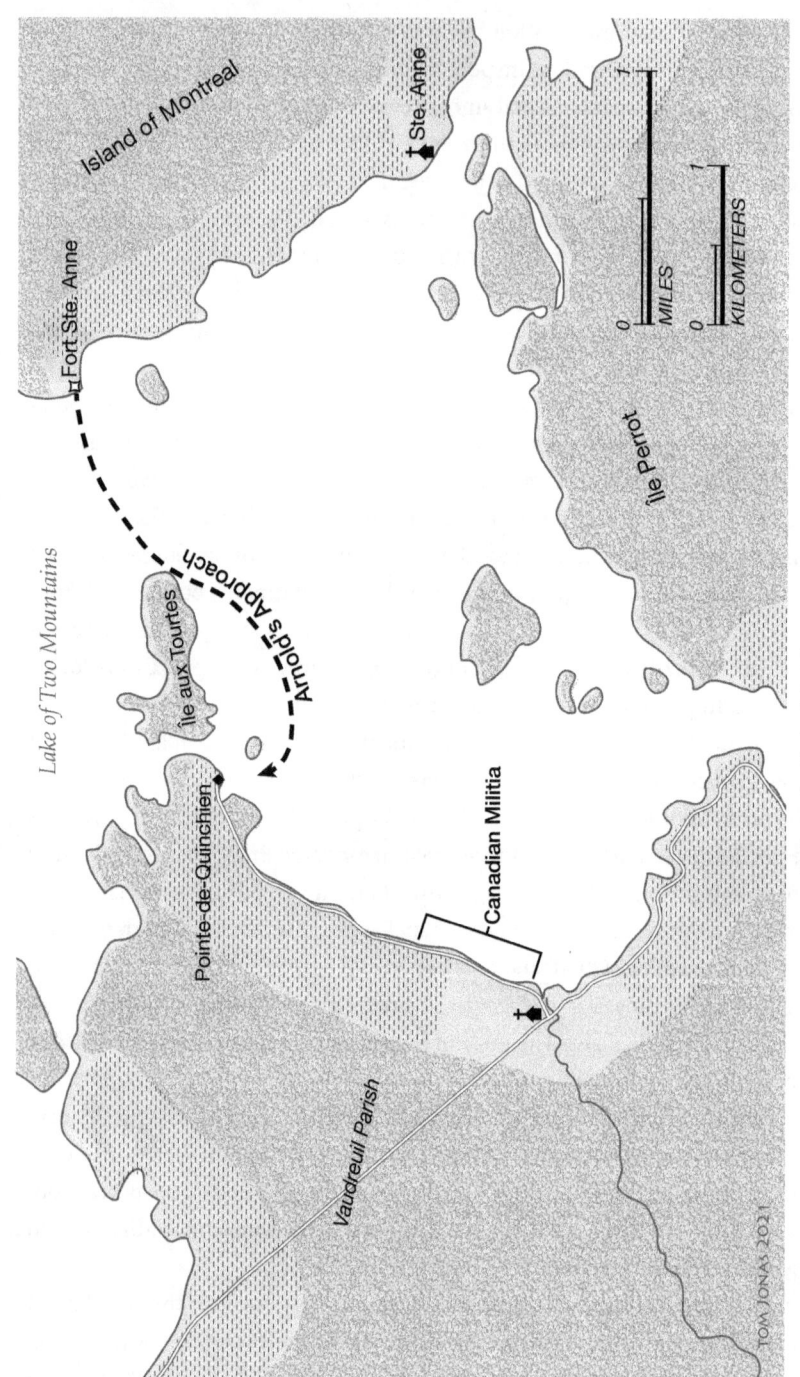

Pointe-de-Quinchien Engagement.
Map by Tom Jonas.

directly toward Pointe-de-Quinchien landing. They "pushed on until within musket-shot of the shore ... and behind every tree were three or four Indians who poured or showered their bullets upon us as thick as hailstones." Pvt. Joseph Badger took note of the enemy's inaccurate fire: "Some shot fell short, some fell near us, and others went over us."[11]

Canadian militiamen soon added artillery fire to the mix. Immediately after the first cannon's roar, "the Indians gave a tremendous yell" and opened "fire from one extremity of the line to the other." Spent musket balls skipped across the water to bounce off pine-sided bateaux. Many troops undoubtedly shared Captain Wilkinson's concerns: "We were eminently exposed to the artillery, every shot plunging beneath or passing over us, and the slightest touch of our fragile craft, would have sent a crew to the bottom, as we were too deeply laden to furnish the smallest relief to each other." The Americans' luck held, however, as all eight long-range artillery shots missed their marks. The cannon proved no more effective in Canadian hands.[12]

For an agonizing moment, Arnold seemed to persevere with an intent to storm the contested shore. Finally, as boats started to close into effective musket range, the general relented and ordered crews to rest on their oars and float downstream because, as Arnold described it, the scene "was so dark we could not distinguish a man on shore, and as we were unacquainted with the ground, and our people much fatigued." Amazingly, the Americans had not suffered a single casualty in their tightly packed boats. Once out of range, crews rowed back upstream to Fort Ste. Anne.[13]

The general's objective that evening was known only to him, if to anyone, but he successfully surveilled the ground and assessed enemy strength at Pointe-de-Quinchien. After Arnold returned to Fort Ste. Anne, he promptly called a council of war, proposing an early morning crossing above or below the point to indirectly attack the enemy—primary sources are unclear on tactical details. There may have been some heated debate, but Arnold's subordinates all agreed to the final plan and left headquarters to prepare their men for action.[14]

The British-allied Indians' apparent tactical ineptitude at Pointe-de-Quinchien is intriguing—they opened fire outside effective range and expended many rounds to no physical effect. A good explanation is rooted in the Indian presence on both sides. As historian Karim Tiro noted, "Natives' qualms about taking the lives of other Natives in this conflict transcended tribal or confederacy identities." Furthermore, by long-standing custom the Iroquois Six Nations and Seven

Nations of Canada "did not fight one another willingly. When the demands of alliances with British or American forces placed other Iroquois in harm's way, they tried to defuse or at least mitigate the threat."[15]

In the Cedars campaign, neither British-allied nor pro-American warriors had compelling reasons to break this convention. A pitched battle would risk Indian casualties, prompt unnecessary prisoner deaths, and do little to advance Native personal or strategic interests. When Kahnawake emissaries visited "enemy" counterparts earlier that day, they had a perfect opportunity to coordinate across battle lines, manipulating the situation to accommodate their own objectives. Circumstantially, in their confederacies' "continuum of cooperative acts," they might well have agreed to demonstrate strength and feign determination by firing out of range and off target, while posing little actual risk to Kahnawakes intermingled among rebel Americans.[16]

In the background of the evening's Pointe-de-Quinchien show of force, American prisoners continued to suffer in the Vaudreuil Parish presbytery. Pvt. Zephaniah Shepardson shared the common fear that if Arnold's force had "even attempted to land, the Indians would perhaps have bu[t]cherd us all in the prison." Redcoat guards struggled to keep their allies outside the crowded sanctuary, as warriors menaced captives by slashing at "the door with their hatchets saying God dam you Bostonies we will do something with your blood."[17] Arnold's aggressive evening approach escalated the urgency for Captain Forster and allied chiefs to resolve their collective captive conundrum by securing a prisoner exchange deal before they faced an actual attack.

With his draft cartel signed by Sherburne and Butterfield, Forster's next step was to persuade General Arnold to accept it as the senior enemy commander in the field. Intending to use Sherburne as a trustworthy exchange advocate, the captain took him "into a council of the Indians then sitting" near Pointe-de-Quinchien. War chiefs emphasized "that it was a mercy never before shewn in their wars, that they had killed so few of their prisoners, but they should certainly kill every man, who should hereafter fall into their hands." Then Lieutenant Andrew Parke took the rebel major and wounded Capt. John McKinstry along to make the case for a timely agreement.[18]

A couple of hours after midnight, Fort Ste. Anne's officer of the day announced a boat in the lake, requesting a parley. After Arnold gave permission to land, Lieutenant Parke and the two American officer prisoners came ashore. Sherburne substantiated Forster's explanation that Indian allies were beyond his control and "determined to kill their prisoners if attacked." To "frustrate their inhuman purpose," Arnold need only sign the document, already subscribed by the captive American officers. At first, the general was "extremely averse from entering into any agreement," but "was at length induced to it, by no other motive than that of saving the prisoners from cruel and inhuman deaths."[19]

Perusing Forster's proposed cartel, two "very insolent terms" drew Arnold's clear indignation. One specified that "those prisoners taken in opposing Government, shall not, on any pretext whatsoever, hereafter take up arms against the Government of Great Britain," while exchanged British prisoners of war would be free to rejoin the war. Another provision made rebel officer prisoners responsible "for all the waste and spoil committed . . . by the detachment under the command of Colonel Bedel," with the implication that Americans had marauded the countryside. Arnold rejected these objectionable terms "with disdain" and sent Parke back to Forster.[20]

After a full day's back-and-forth negotiations, and with Forster's elimination of the disputed provisions, Arnold signed the cartel in the late afternoon of May 27, beginning a four-day cease-fire and opening the path for the prisoner exchange. By agreement, Forster withheld two groups from the immediate prisoner transfer. First, in accordance with the cartel, four captains—John Stevens and Ebenezer Green from Butterfield's detachment, and Ebenezer Sullivan and Theodore Bliss from Sherburne's—volunteered to remain as hostages, guaranteeing American delivery of the promised British prisoners in exchange.[21]

Prisoners from Hazen's Second Canadian Continental Regiment formed another group. Since the Fort Cedars surrender, British soldiers kept Lt. Jean-François Hamtramck's ten enlisted men in irons, away from the other rebels. They were treated "as deserters from the King's troops by their taking up arms against their own military laws . . . traitors to the British government," on the pretense that all Canadian men were embodied in the king's militia under the June 1775 martial law. Hamtramck and his men were not specifically excluded in the written cartel, but Forster verbally forewarned Arnold that they could not be exchanged, insisting "he had positive orders from Government for that purpose." The American general reluctantly conceded, apparently favoring the greater good over principle.[22]

With agreements in place and no immediate opportunity for action at Fort Ste. Anne, General Arnold did not linger. He wrote a letter to the Continental commissioners explaining the cartel, packed his possessions, and headed back to Montreal within the hour. During the cease-fire, he was far more valuable with the main army at Sorel. Colonel De Haas assumed command at the fort, with strict orders to comply with cartel terms.[23]

When Arnold sent the final, signed cartel document to Forster, he took the opportunity to personally excoriate the British captain, observing "that it appeared very extraordinary . . . that he [Forster] could influence the savages to deliver up the prisoners, and could not keep them from being murdered in cool blood, or prevent their being stripped naked, contrary to the agreement made with the garrison at the Cedars." Commissioners Charles Carroll and Samuel Chase carried this theme forward in their correspondence, attacking the "hypocritical, insidious, base, and wicked conduct of a British officer," in which "British troops secure their safety by threats from the savages to murder the prisoners if attacked." In a broader ethical interrogation and key, enduring propaganda point, they added: "If the commanders of British forces cannot control the savages from committing acts of cruelty and barbarity, why do they incite them to arm[s] against us, or act in conjunction with barbarians whose savage customs they condemn? *This same conduct in the French, during the last war, was censured and execrated by the British nation*" [author's emphasis]. They dismissed Indian motivations in all this, peremptorily and ignorantly concluding that "no cause of quarrel subsists between the savages and the Colonies"—surely the British were responsible for leading them to the warpath.[24]

The commissioners did not fault Arnold at all for signing the cartel, but many Continental officers in Canada vehemently believed he should have attacked the enemy instead, regardless of the fatal risk to prisoners. Typical of these outside-the-arena critics, Lt. Col. Joseph Vose mused that "the Cartel was Astonishing to me, & had I have had an own Brother there, I should have been for Pursuing them, & taking them." With a couple of weeks' hindsight, even Colonel De Haas suggested, "Had my Opinion been ask'd I never should have Consented to any thing of the kind as it is possible we might have retaken the whole if we had attempted the attack . . . and because I never would think of giving them up so many prisoners that cost us so much blood and treasure." Internal American sniping over the cartel faded quickly though, as dire circumstances overwhelmed the Continental Army in Canada by early June.[25]

CHAPTER 16

"PUT ALL TO THE SWORD"

More than one hundred miserable American prisoners assembled at Pointe-de-Quinchien landing in the fading sunlight of May 27, ready for repatriation just hours after Brig. Gen. Benedict Arnold signed the exchange cartel. As crews rowed five prisoner-laden bateaux away, the released captives still had one more harrowing experience to endure. On the shoreline, warriors raised muskets and fired at their departing ex-captives—a last assertion of dominance. In this case, they shot mud balls rather than lead, to frighten and intimidate rather than wound.[1]

Disembarking fifteen miles downstream at Chateauguay, near Kahnawake, in accordance with the cartel, the returnees "looked as if they had been dragged by the heels for a hundred miles over the ground." Adverse winds significantly slowed the boats' return, so Captain George Forster delivered the next day's prisoners on a much shorter two-mile trip to Fort Ste. Anne. On the third day, May 29, Forster appealed to Col. John Philip De Haas for American bateaux to complete the last transfer, making a case against further delay by pleading, "It is Intirely out of my Power to put a stop to the Ravages the Savages commit against the prisoners." De Haas sent four boats.[2]

When the last load of prisoners assembled on the shore at Pointe-de-Quinchien, warriors threatened and taunted them, brandishing tomahawks and scalps. Panicked prisoners scrambled for spots in the boats, afraid of being left behind. All those who were exchanged were accommodated, but as the boats entered the lake, the Indians could not let their former captives just float away. Warriors started by shooting at a dog swimming near the bateaux. When they shifted fire, the Americans were convinced that screaming lead balls miraculously missed them, yet once again no one was hit. In a few minutes the former prisoners found comfort among fellow soldiers at Fort Ste. Anne.[3]

Finally free of prisoners and under cartel cease-fire protection, Forster retreated from Pointe-de-Quinchien the next day. His soldiers retained four captain hostages and eleven Canadian Continental prisoners, while the Indians stubbornly held on to at least twenty-three personally claimed captives. At Fort

Cedars, Captain Forster freed Capt. Edward Everett and the thirteen infirm rebel prisoners there, pointing them back to Fort Ste. Anne. Meanwhile, the forty redcoats squeezed hostages, prisoners, remaining provisions, and two captured cannon into three or four bateaux and embarked on a strenuous upstream journey to Fort Oswegatchie. Approaching Coteau-du-Lac portage, Forster's soldiers surprisingly and unceremoniously released the enlisted rebel Canadian prisoners from irons, and "without saying a word," deposited Lieutenant Hamtramck's men on the riverbank to find their own way home.[4]

Reaching Akwesasne, Forster sent Wendake Huron couriers with a final dispatch to the overall British commander, General Guy Carleton. The captain explained that after a highly successful campaign, the Eighth Regiment's light company was finally "under the necessity of retreating to Oswegatchie."[5] Soldiers and warriors returned home, leaving Carleton's army to slowly squeeze the Americans out of Canada from the opposite direction.

At Fort Ste. Anne, a substantial Continental corps remained, waiting to resume the offensive at cease-fire's end. Forty-year-old Col. John Philip De Haas was in command, "an Officer of Experience & well accquainted with military Discipline and the Ettiquettes of an Army . . . a worthy honest man." The ample-framed and keen-eyed colonel was Dutch by birth; his family crossed the Atlantic in his youth, and he grew up in Pennsylvania's western settlements at Lebanon. Coming of age during the French and Indian War, De Haas diligently served his adopted home colony, rising to the rank of captain. A couple of years later, in Pontiac's War, he campaigned as a major with Colonel Henry Bouquet, who observed that De Haas had "been bred in the Service." The Pennsylvanian colonel was also familiar with Indian interaction from his past, as a colonial frontier leader, military diplomat, and officer fighting against and alongside Native warriors.[6]

On May 28, the second day of prisoner repatriation, four Lake of Two Mountains chiefs peacefully approached Fort Ste. Anne en route to Kahnawake. The recently hostile Kanesatakes assured the colonel that "their Tribe had no intention of carrying on a war with us but [were] at peace and that those of their Tribe among the Enemy were leaving them." De Haas diplomatically hosted the emissaries overnight, willing to encourage peace, perhaps with positive memories of campaigning alongside Kanesatake allies during the Bushy Run campaign a dozen years earlier.[7]

The Kanesatake chiefs left in the morning and returned several hours later with news that a major council was planned at Kahnawake in six days, on June 4. As a demonstration of their nation's friendly turn, the Kanesatakes further promised to "bring down all the prisoners they had taken." Some of De Haas's soldiers went to the Lake of Two Mountains village with the chiefs and returned before nightfall with a few freed comrades. The following day, Kanesatake headmen returned to Fort Ste. Anne yet again, this time promising to formally end hostilities by surrendering "the War Hatchet" at the upcoming council.[8]

While De Haas was persuaded that the once-hostile Lake of Two Mountains Indians were now on a path to peace, General Arnold had convinced senior Continental leaders "to take ample vengeance" against their enemies in the west. At cease-fire termination, the general wanted to attack "Capt. Forster & his infernal Crew" and "give not Quarter to the Savages[,] white or Brown," and then punitively devastate Kanesatake and Akwesasne villages for providing enemy warriors.[9] When De Haas sent word that Forster had already retreated from American reach, Arnold narrowed his focus.

On June 1, Arnold directed Colonel De Haas to "immediately take as many of your best men as your Batteaux and Canoes will carry . . . and proceed just before day" to Kanesatake. They were to "surround the town," attack, and "leave not one stone on another or give Quarter to any one." Arnold opined, "This I think no more than a just retaliation for the many murders they have committed on our unhappy countrymen (in cold Blood)." De Haas's staff clearly understood the general's intention to "put *all* to the sword."[10]

Arnold's "no quarter" orders were highly unusual for the Canadian campaign. Just three months earlier, he had suppressed a Canadian loyalist uprising below Quebec City without resorting to "fire and sword." As an episode in colonial–Indian warfare, the most recent historical parallel was Robert Rogers's 1759 punitive destruction of St. Francis (Odanak); but in that case, British general Jeffery Amherst at least winked at customary restraint, specifying, "It is my orders that no women or children are killed or hurt." Even in the Americans' 1779 revenge campaign against the Six Nations, in the aftermath of notoriously bloody frontier raids, Gen. George Washington still emphasized "the *capture* of as many prisoners of every age and sex as possible [author's emphasis]" when destroying targeted Indian villages. As an additional consideration, it is quite clear that Arnold's orders for Kanesatake's destruction did not conform with personal instructions General Washington gave him at the beginning of the 1775 Quebec expedition—that is, to "conciliate the Affections of the . . . Indians to the great Interests of America."[11]

Arnold's violent immoderation may have been rooted in race-based prejudices about Indian "savagery," along with the long colonial tradition of destroying "hostile" villages in war. He also could have considered that these Indians' deliberate disregard of "civilized" Euro-colonial convention provided *jus in bello* justification to annihilate their defiantly "barbarous" villages and villagers. Furthermore, Arnold was undoubtedly exhausted, perhaps inclined to violently lash out at any enemy that actually remained in reach.[12]

Colonel De Haas did not share Arnold's views on inflicting vengeance on Indian villages and was morally distressed when he received the orders for indiscriminate destruction. Even though his troops at Fort Ste. Anne were eager to "revenge the Death" of "slaughtered Brethren," De Haas fabricated an idea that Arnold expected officers to meet in a council of war "to take their opinion" before executing orders. The commanding colonel asked his officers whether the mission was practicable but steered the discussion by emphasizing the key military obstacles: surprise was impossible since geography confined them to landing on the village riverfront; persistent rain meant their firearms might be unreliable; and according to improbable intelligence reports, the enemy could have seven hundred warriors to face just three hundred Continentals transportable via available bateaux.[13]

Off the record, Quartermaster Jacob Shallus revealed further council of war discussions favoring restraint: "The Indians were invited to a Treaty to be held in a few days at Caughnawaga," and that "humanity . . . cry^d aloud against an attempt to kill and destroy Women & Infants." The council recommended not attacking, since "General Arnold was Unacquainted with the intervention of the Circumstances when he issued the orders." When Arnold heard De Haas's decision, he was infuriated, declaring, "None but cowards would hesitate to obey a positive order." He deemed it all "very extraordinary."[14] To De Haas's credit, it was.

Historian Paul L. Stevens concluded that De Haas "wisely circumvented executing this needless order for retribution." When Arnold had initially proposed revenge against the villages, Col. Moses Hazen offered an accurate, dissenting view that "by destroying those Villages we shall be sure of making those Nations our inevitable and durable Enemies, But by saving them we perhaps may regain those Nations to Friendship."[15] In just a matter of days, Native diplomacy would restore functional neutrality in the Seven Nations of Canada; but if De Haas had simply followed orders, both northern Indian confederacies—all thirteen of their member nations, and even associate tribes—may well have cast aside factional differences and united in war against the rebels over Kanesatake's smoldering ruins. De Haas's insubordinate but purposeful subterfuge kept the Revolutionary War from diverting onto Arnold's rash, vindictive, and indiscriminately brutal path at a time when the American cause was already particularly fragile.

De Haas did promptly follow other parts of Arnold's orders, first to withdraw back to Lachine. Then, despite very heavy rain on June 1, the rear guard complied with the general's direction to raze Fort Ste. Anne in retreat. This was done expressly to punish belligerent loyalist owner Jean-Baptiste Testard de Montigny "on acco[un]t of his commanding the Canadians against Sherburne." Quartermaster Shallus observed the conflagration to be "in my opinion as neat a Bonfire as any private Gentleman need set his Eyes upon."[16]

The day after De Haas's men reached Lachine, the colonel received Kahnawake visitors there. The Indians brought along an Oneida guest, one of thirteen Six Nations chiefs (actually all Oneidas) who had come to Canada "on a treaty of friendship to the colonies." Their visit serendipitously aligned with the imminent June 4 confederacy council—which they would attend—but their arrival on the St. Lawrence was actually part of a long Oneida political journey.[17]

In the aftermath of the contentious March–April Onondaga confederacy council, worried Oneidas, Kahnawakes, Tuscaroras, and Oquagas secretly "entered into a defensive league to support each other against the other [Iroquois] nations; being resolved that, if the others join the King's party, they would die with the Americans in the contest." The Oneidas then spearheaded a Six Nations delegation to formally deliver the Onondaga council agreements regarding continued neutrality to the Indian commissioners in Albany. This resulted in a five-day conference attended by hundreds of Indians from five confederacy nations—no Senecas participated—concluding May 7. The assembled chiefs delivered another Iroquois peace belt, and peace-minded Mohawk sachem Abraham reassured the Americans, "You have requested us in the present disturbances to sit quiet. We promise you that we will remain so."[18] Given the dreadful American situation in Canada, this was a positive, timely development.

A couple of weeks after that most recent Albany visit, Oneida chiefs followed up by sending some disturbing news to Maj. Gen. Philip Schuyler. A spy reported that British Indian agent John Butler had recently encouraged a group of Haudenosaunee and Great Lakes Indians to leave Niagara for the St. Lawrence valley. The Oneidas planned to visit Kahnawake to share this information firsthand. Unbeknownst to the correspondents, in the intervening weeks since the spy made his observations, that same Niagara party had already joined Captain Forster, forced the Fort Cedars surrender, and ambushed Sherburne at Quinchien.[19]

In late May, thirteen Oneidas left home to deliver their news to Kahnawake village, stopping en route to talk with General Schuyler. On May 28, Schuyler informed them they had just missed a Kahnawake message and wampum belt sent to their nation, "Intreating Assistance" after the first scout reports of Forster's approach on Fort Cedars. Regretfully, the general also shared sad news, fresh from Canada, that sixty Kahnawake warriors had been killed in an encounter with the king's forces shortly after the Fort Cedars surrender. In a matter of hours, the worried Oneidas rushed north to go "amongst the Canadian tribes to use their influence in preventing them from joining with the British troops, which they were afraid they would."[20] Reaching the St. Lawrence just a couple of days later, the Oneidas were pleased to find that no Kahnawakes had actually been killed. The strategic situation was alarming, but at least it had not devolved into intertribal violence. It was one of these well-traveled Oneida chiefs who met Colonel De Haas in Lachine on June 2.

After the June 4 Kahnawake council, a Seven Nations–Oneida delegation visited General Arnold in Montreal to relay the meeting's outcomes. He reported that "after the usual speeches and ceremonies," Odanak Abenakis, Kahnawakes, and even Kanesatake Mohawks "gave up the hatchet," confirming their neutrality. In this case, unlike the previous September when the Oneidas provided the pivotal influence in the Seven Nations' decision for a general neutrality, Canada confederacy members appear to have made a consensus decision to reassert their neutrality before the Iroquois visitors arrived. The Oneidas may have helped persuade doubtful chiefs, but the Kahnawakes had presumably played a key role in making the case prior to the council that nonalignment was their best course for immediate safety and long-term sovereignty so long as war raged in the St. Lawrence valley. Just a few weeks later, well-informed Dartmouth missionary Sylvanus Ripley reported, "The Caghnawaga Indians tis said have distinguished themselves in their friendship to our Army both when they have been in prosperity & in adversity."[21]

On June 12, eight days after the Indians' short conference with Arnold, Chief Louis Atiatoharongwen met Brig. Gen. John Sullivan, the newest Continental commander in Canada, to share his own personal account of the council. Louis added another detail: unlike the rest of the Seven Nations confederacy, Kanesatake's Algonquian Arundaks—just one of the village's three ethnic groups—steadfastly refused to make peace. The chief further claimed that Kahnawakes wanted the Americans to "Send up Some force which they will Join with to Exterpate" those fifty recalcitrant Arundak warriors. Seven Nations intraconfederacy violence was distinctly uncharacteristic, so this appeal was almost certainly an attempt at political messaging, signaling commitment to a common cause with the knowledge that it was a military impossibility for the overwhelmed, retreating Americans.[22]

The chief also gave Sullivan a letter from Col. Timothy Bedel, arrested by Arnold before the June 4 Kahnawake council, but still working as a de facto Indian agent. Bedel shared important intelligence from Wendake Huron Jean Vincent: the British were coordinating efforts with the recalcitrant Kanesatake Arundaks while blustering that "all the Bostonian Indians at Caughnawaga and elsewhere in Canada wou'd immediately be hanged." The colonel fretted for his Seven Nations friends, who shared that they were "very uneasy not knowing what to do[,] as nobody gives them encouragem[en]t to take up Arms in our behalf, and they are Solicited every day on the King's part." Bedel pleaded in vain for an expedited court-martial trial so he could personally address the friendly nations' concerns through proper in-council Indian diplomacy.[23]

Despite the reassuring Kahnawake council outcomes, the Northern Army in Canada reeled from incapacitating epidemics, inadequate supplies, poor discipline, and "the Infamous Retreat from Quebeck & the Still more Scandalous Surrender of the Post at the Cedars."[24] On June 13, a despondent Continental Army council of war recommended complete abandonment of Canada, to save the other colonies. General Sullivan ordered a retreat up Lake Champlain—the army would move south to protect New England and New York at Crown Point and Fort Ticonderoga.

General Arnold evacuated Montreal just two days later. Before leaving the island, his troops inflicted a last mark of revenge for the Cedars. Claude de Lorimier returned to his widow mother's vacated Lachine home to discover that the "Americans had slaughtered all the livestock, especially those in the poultry yard, after having reduced the orchard to firewood," plundered the house, and half-heartedly tried to torch it.[25]

The Continentals also set fire to Fort St. Johns in retreat, and on June 18, its glow warmed the evening twilight as General Arnold stepped into the rear guard's last boat. His aide Captain Wilkinson recounted that as they drifted away from the Canadian mainland, they "took an affectionate leave of Colonel [sic] Louis, the faithful chief of the Cachnawaga tribe, and the only Canadian who accompanied the army in its retreat from Canada: he cast a sorrowful look at our boat, and retired precipitately into the adjacent forest."[26] Almost a year earlier, the pro-American Kahnawake faction had invited the rebels into Canada, and now one of their most zealous Indian partisans sadly escorted them out.

CHAPTER 17

REVERBERATIONS

The first wave of reckoning for the affair of the Cedars came from Americans who demanded accountability from their officers. On the very day that Brig. Gen. John Sullivan took command of the army in Canada, June 1, he shared his intent to "immediately appoint a Court of Inquiry upon Colo Beadle [sic] & Major Butterfield." Four days later, Brig. Gen. Benedict Arnold sent those two officers and Capt. Samuel Young, all under arrest in Montreal, to the main army camp at Sorel to face justice. Despite their universal condemnation in the Northern Army, both Bedel and Young were convinced of their innocence and eagerly sought trials. Even though the Continental Articles of War targeted eight days from arrest to court-martial, the army's myriad military challenges kept appropriate court-martial boards from assembling in Canada, providing substantial time for the accused officers to compose defenses, gather evidence, and seek character references.[1]

In the interim, General Sullivan's superiors shared their own views on the pending courts-martial. Commander in chief Gen. George Washington told Maj. Gen. Philip Schuyler that if Bedel's and Butterfield's "Conduct was as bad & Infamous as represented, It will surely meet with an Exemplary Punishment." In turn, Schuyler, the Northern Army commander, specifically delegated court-martial authority to Sullivan with encouragement to "take proper Measures and have Good Courts appointed to bring them & Every Other Officer . . . to Tryal that they may be punished according to their Offences. Our Misfortunes at the Cedars were occasioned as It is said entirely by their base & Cowardly Behaviour & cannot be asscribed [sic] to any other Cause." Schuyler ominously added, "If any Officer or soldier in Canada should be Capitally convicted . . . You will Issue Warrants to the proper Officers for Carrying the Sentence into Execution." By the Continental Articles of War, abandoning one's post was a capital offense. The articles did not explicitly discriminate by rank, but in traditional practice capital punishment was reserved for enlisted men; cowardly gentleman officers' lives were inevitably spared, being instead cashiered from service to mark their disgrace.[2]

In mid-July, with the army finally settling into postretreat camp life at Crown Point and Ticonderoga, Capt. Samuel Young was the first to face trial, charged with deserting Fort Ste. Anne in the face of the enemy. Young contended, "If I did anything worthy of confinement or punishment, it was done ignorantly, and not for want of zeal in the cause, as at that time I looked upon myself to be in a defenceless posture." In his July 13 trial, the court accepted this defense, deeming his choices tactically sound or at least forgivable for a junior officer in his position, and found him not guilty. The new Northern Army commander, Maj. Gen. Horatio Gates, approved the verdict. Captain Young rejoined his unit for the rest of the 1776 campaign and then spent the next three years defending New Hampshire's frontier as a scout and captain.[3]

The Bedel and Butterfield trial waited several more days, until July 19, when a board of five colonels, including John Philip De Haas and John Paterson; four lieutenant colonels; and four majors heard prosecution from judge advocate Capt. John Budd Scott, a close ally of Benedict Arnold. By custom, the accused officers represented themselves. If Butterfield offered any defense, it is unrecorded, while Bedel presumably followed the plan drafted during his seven-week camp arrest.[4]

Bedel's defense was built on a witness-corroborated presumption that his command responsibilities were "not limited to the post of the Cedars only, either by Gen[eral] arnolds verbal or writ[t]en orders." Bedel further emphasized Arnold's particular direction before the Cedars—"to attend to the Cultivation of a friendship with the savages"—which explained his presence at the Kahnawake council instead of being at Fort Cedars when the attack began. He further maintained that it was at the Indians' urgent request that he go to Montreal with news of the attack, rather than immediately returning to the fort. He appealed, "If I have erred in Construing the words or meaning of Genl Arnolds orders I hope it will be considered as an error in Judgement, a Defect in the head and not in the heart." Colonel Bedel concluded with a reminder that he had been a stalwart warrior in twelve different campaigns, eight as a commissioned officer, and "never was brought to a Court martial[,] Confined or even Repremanded [sic] before."[5]

Unfortunately for Bedel, a military and political consensus had already predetermined his guilt; he simply could not be acquitted. On August 1, General Gates finally published the court's findings: Col. Timothy Bedel was guilty of "quitting his Post, at the Cedars," and was sentenced to be cashiered—that is, to lose his current commission and command. The court also found Maj. Isaac Butterfield guilty of "surrendering the Post at the Cedars." His sentence carried an implied, but well-understood, taint of cowardice. In addition to being cashiered, Butterfield was "incapacitated forever hereafter to hold a commission in the Army of the United States."[6]

General Gates forwarded the results to the Continental Congress, expressing his hope that despite the court's conservative, moderate sentencing, "the disgraceful example made of the offenders will deter others from committing so flagrant a crime." Americans would have to be satisfied with traditional shaming, rather than radical officer executions *pour encourager les autres*. Outside the army, there was near-universal acceptance of Bedel's and Butterfield's guilt, but mixed sentiment regarding their punishment. A Baltimore newspaper account mentioned that "the two Genius's [sic] who deserted the Cedars" had been "cashiered, a punishment justly due to their Demerits," while congressional delegate Thomas Jefferson matter-of-factly wrote that the duo had been "broke with infamy." General Schuyler did not hide his opinion when the topic of the Cedars came up in a Six Nations conference just days after the verdict was announced, telling Native counterparts: "Our Commander behaved badly, he was a coward and he ought to be put to Death for his Cowardice."[7]

Bedel and Butterfield followed different paths after being court-martialed, reflecting the character of their different sentences. Isaac Butterfield never reentered military service, but his neighbors soon returned him to minor local political offices. When he died in 1801, neighbors overlooked his inglorious military past and honored him with "a numerous and respectable procession from several of the towns in the vicinity of Westmoreland."[8] In contrast, Bedel's military skills and Indian diplomatic talents were in high demand within a few months of the trial, as New England faced the prospect of a 1777 British invasion and Indian raids. Bedel coordinated scouting missions into Canada, maintained communications with friendly Kahnawakes and Odanak Abenakis, and led ranger and Indian forces to protect New Hampshire's frontiers over the next three years. He later represented Coos Country communities in the Vermont and New Hampshire legislatures. His death in 1787 concluded a life of service to the Connecticut Valley settlements, colony, states, and nation.[9]

Even while Bedel and Butterfield were awaiting court-martial in June, generals were rushing reports of the Cedars affair to the government in Philadelphia. On June 15, Congress established a committee to examine the exchange cartel in detail and received an initial report two days later. The committee findings were incomplete; it was clear that more information was needed from Canada. Congress still entered the report into the record, because "silence . . . may be construed by some into a ratification of the said agreement"—the prisoner exchange cartel.[10]

In early June, General Arnold personally dispatched Maj. Henry Sherburne to Philadelphia, "to lay before them a State of this unhappy Affair." Sherburne arrived on Saturday June 22, and Congress recommitted the cartel report to committee the next business day, so members could incorporate his new evidence. Sherburne filled important narrative gaps, corrected interpretive errors, and clearly focused blame on Major Butterfield, while burnishing his own reputation. The updated report added specific details of Indian prisoner abuse and murders and incorporated the alleged captive "roasting" incident.[11]

Historian Charles Butterfield offered a skeptical view of Arnold's choice of Sherburne for this mission, suggesting that the general deliberately employed Sherburne to fashion Bedel and Butterfield as convenient scapegoats for a military failure that was, at root, based on Arnold's own mission orders and disposition of forces west of Montreal. Sherburne benefited from the opportunity as well, using the forum to distract attention from his own Lake of Two Mountains crossing delays and tactical errors entering the Quinchien ambush. However, Sherburne was the best-informed field-grade officer available for the Philadelphia mission, since Bedel and Butterfield were both under arrest.[12]

It is noteworthy that cartel committee member Thomas Jefferson was concurrently preparing the Declaration of Independence. The first word of the Cedars debacle arrived in Philadelphia a day or two before Jefferson was appointed to the committee of five responsible for drafting that historic document. From his earliest drafts, the declaration included a charge that the king had "endeavoured to bring on the Inhabitants of our Frontiers, the merciless Indian Savages, whose known Rule of Warfare is an undistinguished Destruction of all Ages, Sexes, and Conditions." There had been rumors of Indian uprisings encouraged by agents of the Crown in the first year of the war, but none of those had come to fruition. Even by the time Congress adopted the Declaration of Independence, the engagements in Canada—the 1775 skirmishes at Fort St. Johns and, more significantly, at the Cedars—were the only actual examples of the king's employment of "savage" allies. Historical analysis of the "merciless Indian Savages" charge has generally focused on the rumored threats and "conspiratorial fears," while commonly missing its far more concrete link with the Cedars, especially in light of Jefferson's concurrent cartel committee activities.[13]

On July 10, six days after the Declaration's acceptance, the Cedars cartel committee delivered its updated report, with eighteen narrative findings. The most sensational accusations were that Indians put two prisoners to death on the evening of the Fort Cedars surrender, "four or five others at different times, afterwards; one . . . killed on the 8th day after that surrender; that one was first shot, and, while retaining life and sensation, was roasted . . . ," albeit with the caveat that no eyewitnesses were available to confirm the last accusation. That same day, Congress followed with a series of eight resolutions. Most inflammatory, the United States declared that unless the king issued punishment for "all acts contrary to good faith, the laws of nature, or the customs of civilized nations, done by the officers or soldiers of his Britannic Majesty, or by foreigners or savages taken into his service," he was personally responsible for their crimes. In addition to the alleged murders, the king's soldiers were complicit in "plundering the baggage of the garrison at the Cedars, stripping them of their cloathes, and delivering them into the hands of the savages." Asserting its political authority in the war's first formal exchange agreement, Congress also promulgated the cartel committee's judgment that the Arnold–Forster agreement was "a mere sponsion," meaning the general did not have the authority to enter into such an exchange by himself, and that it was therefore contingent on the assembly's approval.[14]

Superficially, Congress followed with ratification of the cartel but immediately added an overriding condition. Before the United States would return any redcoat prisoners, the Congress expected the British commander in Canada "to deliver into our hands the authors, abettors, and perpetrators of the horrid murder committed on the prisoners, to suffer such punishment as their crime deserves; and . . . to make indemnification for the plunder at the Cedars." Delegates could not have seriously expected British compliance, so despite their claim to have ratified the cartel, they effectively negated it—the United States thus conveniently recovered hundreds of prisoners, while the British were left with nothing in return but their four hostages.[15]

Well before Congress issued the Cedars resolutions, American authorities had already been debating whether British actions warranted annulment of the cartel agreement. The congressional commissioners in Canada were early advocates for negation. With Arnold's first report of the cartel, they complained to Congress about the "hyprocritical, insidious, base & wicked Conduct of a British Officer. . . . If the Commander of British forces cannot controul the Savages from Committing acts of Cruelty & Barbarity, why do they incite them to Arm agt. Us or act in Conjunction with Barbarians whose Savage Customs they condemned? This same Conduct in the French during the last War, was censured and execrated by the British Nation." At least among officials in Canada, commissioner Samuel Chase argued that for this reason the Americans could "with safety break the Capitulation made with General Arnold." Colonel De Haas later contributed an observation that because the Indians with Captain Forster had fired on the last boatloads of departing prisoners at Pointe-de-Quinchien, they had "Commenced hostilities before the [cease-fire] time was expired." Therefore, he suggested "in my Opinion we are not bound to perform our part of the Capitulation."[16]

There was direct historical British-colonial precedent for cartel negation. In 1757, after verifying details of the Fort William Henry "massacre," British general James Abercrombie declared that fort's capitulation "null and void because of the 'murdering, pillaging and captivating [of] many of his Majesty's good subjects.'" In 1778, another congressional committee specifically referenced that particular precedent when discussing potential British claims to "Restitution for the Men taken at the Cedars," noting that "on this Occasion the Case of Fort William Henry last War is so fully in Point" that there was nothing more to be said on the subject.[17]

Congress's July 10 Cedars resolutions subsequently took on a life of their own. Historian William L. Stone observed that they were "the indulgence of much crimination and recrimination on the part both of the American and British commanders. . . . The affair of the Cedars excited the strongest feelings of indignation, not only in Congress and among the people, but in the army."[18] Within weeks, the resolutions sparked fights for personal honor and initiated national-level propaganda battles.

Domestic American newspaper audiences were able to read the entire report that summer, which quickly established a consistent patriot understanding of the Cedars affair. Congress's resolutions, the Declaration of Independence, and new reports of Cherokee warfare on the Carolina frontier combined to inflame prejudicial American stereotypes of "merciless Indian savages." The reinvigorated threat of traditional Native enemies helped unite the newly independent states and indicted the villainous king for his cruelty in deliberately employing such barbarous allies.[19]

The first British response to Congress's Cedars resolutions was surprisingly polite. When General Washington delivered the July 10 report to his British counterpart, General William Howe responded with a hope "that the Facts alledged will prove to have been founded upon a Misrepresentation." Farther north, one more proximately involved in the affair, General Guy Carleton, took considerable offense at rebel leaders' "notorious Breach of Faith," fully convinced that the Americans had the basic facts quite wrong: rather than promoting atrocities, British officers had encouraged restraint and even purchased Continental prisoners from Indian allies "at a great price."[20]

Anglo Canadians spearheaded the first loyalist propaganda responses to Congress's Cedars resolutions. The *Quebec Gazette* printed narratives that contradicted many of the rebel allegations, and its published cartel copy included commentary that blamed Arnold for the Americans' perfidy, with a cry of "O! Shame, Where is Thy Blush!" Before year's end, *Scots Magazine* published some Canadian letters on the metropolitan side of the Atlantic, emphasizing Captain Forster's noble choice to offer a cartel and efforts to minimize Indian prisoner abuse, mocking American demands to turn the captain over for "justice."[21]

In 1777, campaign participant Lieutenant Andrew Parke provided particularly valuable ammunition in the stewing propaganda battle. The lieutenant, still on duty in North America, published a fifty-page pamphlet specifically intended to counter Congress's July 10, 1776, narrative and resolutions; he said American accusations had "no foundation in truth, accusing his Majesty's faithful servants and loyal subjects, with the most inhuman acts of unfeeling cruelty." In collaboration with key loyalists and fellow officers, Parke provided a consolidated, credible eyewitness counternarrative, endorsed by campaign commander Captain George Forster. While clearly biased—critical of the rebels and willfully blind to British-Canadian negligence and most Indian "misdeeds"—the narrative captured key details that were missing or misconstrued in Congress's account. Parke's seemingly definitive pamphlet established important facts, serving as a rare example of a British response that was both timely and effective in the ongoing propaganda war. The governor of Quebec, Frederick Haldimand, later commented that it provided "so strong a testimony of the perfidy of the Enemy we have to deal with." He further suggested that since it conveyed the facts so well, it could be "serviceable in negotiating the Exchange of Prisoners"—perhaps even convincing the rebels of their erroneous interpretations of the Cedars affair.[22]

In Britain, the public was already broadly informed of the brutal implications of "savage" warfare in North America, based on past discussion throughout the Seven Years' War. As the Revolutionary War began, British parties began debating the theoretical propriety of employing Indian allies against rebellious American brethren. By late 1776, accounts from the Cedars gave substance to those conversations. Many government members and supporters argued for expanded reliance on their controversial Native American allies, bringing terror

Vignette showing Native Americans roasting a man on a spit. Detail from John Williams, *The Closet*, 1778.
Library of Congress, Prints and Photographs Division (LC-DIG-ds-11617).

on the colonies to decisively terminate rebellion, while opposing voices criticized the "impolitic and anti-christian" use of Indians, who could not be trusted to discriminate between loyalists and rebels, guilty and innocent.[23]

Yet it was not the Cedars, but General John Burgoyne's failed 1777 campaign, that prompted substantial and meaningful parliamentary debate on Native American allies. As an example, Secretary of State Lord George Germain excused government culpability in alleged Indian atrocities, arguing that Burgoyne had insisted that the "savages ... conform to his laws of subordination," but that "when a measure does not answer the expectation of the planner, after he has taken every possible precaution to ensure success, it must surely be unreasonable to blame men, merely for not being able to command events." A year earlier, this argument could have been applied equally well to exonerate Captain Forster at the Cedars. On the other side of the aisle, opposition leader Edmund Burke most vividly mirrored American patriot sentiments in his bold criticism of the government's allies, whose "rewards of danger and warfare consisted in human scalps, in human flesh, and the gratifications arising from torturing, mangling, roasting alive by slow fires, and frequently even devouring their captives."[24] Even if these exaggerations could have come straight from Congress's account of the Cedars affair, it was the Saratoga campaign that remained the focus of subsequent British public conversation.

The British opposition momentarily revisited the Cedars in a 1778 satirical print titled "The Closet." In the upper-right quarter of a multiframe graphic commentary, King George III is depicted in his secret chamber, "the closet," listening to advisers, including "Lord Bute, to whom the Devil whispers." The foul fruits of government policy are represented in four smaller, offsetting frames showing controversial events, including the Indian murder of Jane McCrea, Burgoyne's defeat and surrender, and one titled "The Cedars." The latter features a crude rendition of a prisoner being roasted alive as Indians feast on human flesh, with butchered limbs lying about. In this case, the opposition resorted to a most radical, anti-Indian interpretation of events to make its point.[25]

American propagandists also occasionally referenced the Cedars. In March 1777, a political commentary rallied patriots with an admonishment to "forget not the affairs at the Cedars, when the tyrant's minions delivered your countrymen to the fury of the barbarous Savages." By that summer though, the Jane McCrea murder definitively shifted American attention to civilian-involved incidents, followed by the Wyoming Valley and Cherry Valley "Massacres" that had more substantial and provocative propaganda value. Propagandists made regular claims of the nature that Great Britain "let loose her Indian allies to massacre the unarmed, the aged, the sick, the infant, the matron, wife and virgin"—far more inflammatory than atrocities committed against soldiers.[26] Episodic Indian frontier raids served to sustain this resonant theme for the rest of the war and beyond; as a result, the Cedars never regained its short-lived propaganda potency.

CHAPTER 18

PATHS AND DETOURS

In the aftermath of the Cedars, hundreds of soldiers—prisoners, hostages, and captives—had to find paths back to their comrades or homes. Some took long detours. Others never returned, instead finding new lives in foreign lands.

The cartel-exchanged Americans were the earliest group to reintegrate. Immediately after repatriation, these "naked" and weary soldiers wandered away from Fort Ste. Anne or Chateauguay without a common understanding of their continuing military responsibilities. Some quickly rejoined their units ready to serve, even if they lacked arms and proper dress. A practical contingent went back home, returning to their units at Ticonderoga and Crown Point as soon as they got new clothes or after they had delivered sick comrades to their families. Other misinformed ex-prisoners believed they were forbidden from taking up arms for two, three, or even seven months after the exchange and headed to New Hampshire, Massachusetts, or Connecticut to wait out the term. Many of them reported back to their companies once state officers corrected their erroneous cartel interpretation, or after their assumed "parole" period had expired.[1]

On the British side, the Arnold–Forster cartel called for an equal number of redcoat prisoners of war to be exchanged that summer—those taken in the fall 1775 Canadian campaign. Congress's de facto cartel negation meant that these men from the Seventh and Twenty-Sixth Regiments remained incarcerated for several months longer in Lancaster, Pennsylvania. As an ironic twist, in early August 1776, passing Pennsylvania troops fired into the prison camp to avenge comrades "so barbarously butchered and ill-treated after their surrender to Captain Forster." Lieutenant John André and some soldier prisoners may have been slightly wounded, but local officials otherwise defused the tense situation.[2]

The prisoners' prospects improved later in the year. The British army had netted a thousand new Continental prisoners from the New York campaign, and General William Howe approached General Washington for new exchanges.

Unsurprisingly, Howe raised the topic of the Cedars cartel in these discussions, asking the Americans to honorably deliver the promised redcoat prisoners, or return the exchanged Continental soldiers back to British custody. He further suggested that Washington's and Benedict Arnold's honor were at risk if cartel concerns remained unredressed. Washington replied with dismay, claiming that Howe was well aware that Congress, not he, "had taken upon themselves the consideration of the matter."[3] Despite Congress's "artifices and pretences to evade" the cartel, British and American agents arranged a general exchange, quietly including the redcoats taken in Canada. By late December, Howe reported "the 7th and 26th regiments . . . mostly exchanged." The British still believed they were owed some four hundred prisoners from the Cedars in the transfer ledgers, and they often brought the subject up in public discourse and exchange talks throughout the war. As an example, in 1779 British negotiating officers had the temerity to mock the rebels' Cedars resolutions, deeming it a minor incident "where a few cartouch boxes were wrested into a pretext for invalidating a solemn convention."[4]

Another group of loyal prisoners waited slightly longer to be exchanged—the French Canadian loyalist volunteer officers captured at Fort St. Johns and around Montreal in 1775. Ironically, these were the very men whose names Claude de Lorimier had invoked after Sherburne's Quinchien defeat, when he argued for Indian restraint by promising "we will give these Americans in exchange for our own friends." After General Howe made repeated inquiries, most of these elite Canadians were finally exchanged on May 21, 1777.[5] Several immediately returned to the field as Indian officers in Burgoyne's northern campaign, offering a twofold contribution toward Indian restraint on the warpath to Saratoga: first, these respected veterans were present to directly influence and coordinate with their allies in the field; and second, their exchange might have convinced some warriors that they were not completely cheated after sparing captives at Quinchien and Fort Cedars, thus nurturing trust between agents and allies.

The four American hostages faced an even longer odyssey after the Cedars, serially vexed with hurdles imposed by foes and friends. Brave Capt. Ebenezer Sullivan, still in his mid-twenties, had nobly volunteered for this unpleasant duty alongside fellow captains Theodore Bliss, Ebenezer Green, and John Stevens. The young quartet presumably stepped forward with some expectation of long-term recognition and reward for their virtuous act. They would be disappointed. Once delivered to the Pointe-de-Quinchien camp from their short, paroled respite at Lake of Two Mountains village, it became crystal clear that their experience would be more than just a temporary inconvenience. On the spot, warriors rudely stripped Sullivan and his compatriots down to their base clothing, plundering everything else. Then the redcoats unceremoniously hauled the quartet along to Fort Oswegatchie, more like unwanted cargo than gentleman officers, plagued with "Hunger cold and sickness" and harassed by Indians on the way.[6]

After a few weeks at Oswegatchie, Captain George Forster heard that the rebel army had been driven out of Canada and promptly delivered the hostages back to military authorities in Montreal. There, the four captains were confined in a room with thirty enlisted prisoners, unbefitting their aspirational gentlemanly status. As a further aggravation, Sullivan recounted that Indians were "frequently at the Door of the Prison[,] Menacing[,] telling us we belonged to them and that they would have us out to burn," only leaving when guards called for reinforcements. The hostages' circumstances took a radical turn in early August though, when British deputy quartermaster general Captain John Money arrived to take charge of them.[7]

Money skillfully tightened a psychological vise on the hostages, starting by chipping away at their loyalty to the American cause. He told them about Congress's shocking and dishonorable refusal to honor the cartel, putting the rebel government in the worst possible light. Money also "revealed" that the four hostages were under constant threat, as allied chiefs and warriors demanded they "be given up for the breach of the treaty." He soon moved the hostage quartet into a separate room, ostensibly for protection from threatening Indians, but conveniently making the young captains more susceptible to British exploitation in the process. Then Captain Money dangled the possibility that in their seemingly hopeless, vulnerable position, Sullivan and the others could write letters to facilitate their redemption.[8]

A day after the initial offer, Money led Sullivan and Captain Bliss to meet suave, gregarious General John Burgoyne, who opened conversation by expressing regrets over the plight the hostages faced because of Congress's decisions. While he wanted to ensure the officers were well treated, he too expressed fears that "the Ungovernable temper of the savages might prove dangerous." To alleviate their condition, the British general suggested that Sullivan write his older brother, Brig. Gen. John Sullivan, "of the hard treatment of Congress." Burgoyne reiterated that the rebel government's proclamations were "even so fantastical as to demand Capt. Forster to be given up[,] pretending that he and the british troops had Committed a Massacre at the Cedars." When the incredulous captains challenged him for written proof, the general pretended to search his pockets, found them empty, and promised to deliver the documents the next day.[9]

On August 14, almost three months into his captivity and hostage experience, Ebenezer Sullivan finally took the bait and asked to talk to Burgoyne again. Sullivan explained that he really wanted to write his distressed wife on personal business. The general suggested that the hostage captain could certainly enclose a letter to his wife if he would just correspond with his brother the general, "setting forth the grievance of . . . being detained." Captain Sullivan agreed to write. If Burgoyne really executed the scheme as Sullivan detailed, it was an unusually well-planned British propaganda effort that hit its mark.[10]

Ebenezer Sullivan provided everything the British might have desired. He crafted his letter with a fear that General Burgoyne or Governor Guy Carleton would prevent it from leaving Canada if there was even the slightest hint of discontent or disbelief in their accounts of circumstances. Writing to brother General Sullivan, he expressed shock "that the Congress instead of redeeming us according to the cartel, have not only refused to do it, but have demanded Captain Forster to be delivered up to answer his conduct, in what they are pleased to term the massacre of the Ceadars [sic]." He boldly praised Captain Forster's humanity while criticizing Congress's "unprincipled" cartel negation and hostage abandonment. Sullivan vainly protested, "'Tis not my own confinement but the breach of a treaty (which even savages have ever held sacred) that causes me to write," but his naivete, self-serving arguments, and insubordinate tone directly impeached his virtue.[11]

Facing similar pressures, fellow hostages Captains Theodore Bliss and Ebenezer Green wrote comparable letters that same day, equally ungenerous to Congress. Only John Stevens appears to have declined the opportunity. Green's missive, a stream-of-consciousness exposition marked by extraordinarily odd spelling and grammar, was barely usable for propaganda purposes. Bliss's letter, in contrast, would have answered British propaganda aims; but Sullivan's fraternal ties to a rebel general made his composition far more valuable.[12]

Within days, Burgoyne leaked copies of Sullivan's letter in Montreal, and before the end of the year, it was reprinted in two British magazines and a loyalist New York newspaper. Lieutenant Andrew Parke also featured it in his 1777 *Authentic Narrative* pamphlet, with the comment: "Mr. Sullivan's letter breathes the sentiments of an honest man, who had taken arms in defence of what he thought the liberties of his country, but found himself duped and betrayed by the Congress, the faithless misleaders of the credulous multitude."[13] It powerfully undermined the United States' narrative accounts and controversial resolutions on the Cedars.

After the king's generals reaped their propaganda coup from Sullivan's letter, they had little more to gain from the hostages. The four captains were shipped to British-held New York in September. In March 1777, they were released on parole, unable to reenter active Continental service and subject to British recall at any time. Sullivan, Bliss, Green, and Stevens were essentially trapped in an administrative limbo until the end of the war.[14]

Theodore Bliss found a unique solution. He used a personal relationship with Brig. Gen. Henry Knox to obtain a company command and captain's commission in the Continental artillery. He could not join his men in the field, but he still received pay and accumulated service time while running a Boston tavern.[15] Meanwhile, the other three hostages struggled financially, desperately sought honorable opportunities to satisfy their stifled ambitions, and petitioned Congress for redress. Like many energetic, aspiring young men, Ebenezer Sullivan did not know how best to channel his energy, and more often than not he proved to be his own worst enemy as he insulted officials and appeared to be particularly self-interested. Argumentative and relentless, he had little success until he turned to his brother John as an advocate. General Sullivan used his position to open doors that eventually freed the paroled hostages from a few semantic policy traps and contested government responsibilities that blocked them from fair compensation and advancement.[16]

Paroled hostage Ebenezer Sullivan reached a watershed moment at the end of March 1778 when he went before the Congressional Board of War to address his controversial 1776 letter from captivity. The captain hesitated to make a public recantation while on parole—the enemy could recall him to answer for that—but he made the best case for his actions, highlighting the "danger and distress" the hostages faced in Montreal, and detailing the British officers' skillful hostage conditioning that prompted his controversial letter. Sullivan even drafted a new letter rebutting his original propaganda piece, to be held by Congress until he was ultimately free from parole.[17] After this redemptive process, Congress provided the hostages with basic pay for time in captivity and on parole, relieving their most immediate financial concerns; but other issues remained unresolved.

Some months after Sullivan's meeting with Congress, the British actually recalled the four paroled captains to occupied New York in 1779.[18] British motivations remain opaque—perhaps they had been made aware of Sullivan's potential recantation or Bliss's questionable commission. The hostages returned home a few months later, still on parole. Sullivan, Green, and Stevens continued to fight bureaucratic policy battles over pay, depreciation, and position that outlasted the war—poor reward for their honorable, spur-of-the-moment choice to become hostages in May 1776.

A last group of Cedars veterans faced even wider-ranging, life-changing experiences—those Continentals still held captive by Indians at campaign's end. Great Lakes Mississaugas and Senecas—nations far from British colonial control—held at least twenty-three Americans as their spoils of war. When captors and captives sojourned at Fort Oswegatchie before departing up-country, Captain Forster once again attempted to ransom the rebels. He successfully purchased eleven from Mississauga allies before they ever left his fort, at a rate of sixteen dollars per man. Other captives appear to have been ransomed weeks or months later, after Mississaugas had the opportunity to take them home for public victory ceremonies. This brought the warriors twofold benefits, as "prisoners could still bring honor, but now they brought material reward as well."[19]

Even though the captivity narrative was a popular early American literary motif, none of the men taken at the Cedars left detailed accounts of their time with the Indians up-country. Most stepped into a historical void when separated from comrades, but their experiences can be generalized from other Revolutionary War captivity narratives and historical Indian practices. In the withdrawal from the Cedars, Lt. Jean-François Hamtramck reported that captives were "well used and permitted to go at large," apparently avoiding traditional postbattle restraints—pinioned arms, tumpline leads, and rope bonds when sleeping. Still, they were probably forced to carry their captors' bulky plunder packs and adapt to an Indian diet on long voyages west. In addition to corporeal stresses, captives were inevitably burdened with fear for their fate upon reaching an Indian village, steeped in nightmarish tales from colonial legend. They might be "put to death by inches" through prolonged, fiery torture; or even if spared, in the words of a 1780 captive, there was "no other prospect for the future, than a captivity for life; a final separation from all earthly friends, and situated in an enemy's country!"[20]

One unidentified captive was glimpsed at Fort Niagara in early June 1776, when Mississauga or Seneca captors stopped there with "three Scalps & a Prisoner," on their way home from Canada. Unlike Captain Forster, neither British Indian agent John Butler nor Lieutenant Colonel John Caldwell worried about redeeming the captive; instead, they delightedly commented, "The Fiddle was now getting in Tune for the Americans to dance by." There was no imperative for the officials to stop the victorious warriors. It would be four more years before

Frederick Haldimand, governor of Quebec, finally sent word to Indian allies that "all the King's undutiful Children who are taken in it . . . must be delivered up, to be Corrected by their Father as he shall think fit."[21]

Even if the Cedars captives had relatively mundane journeys west, their condition would have dramatically changed when approaching their captor's village or camp. Warriors followed strict customs for recognition and reintegration in their community, so they readopted their most terrifying warpath appearance—painted and ornamented, brandishing scalps, whooping, and firing guns. They probably transformed their captives too—shaving heads, changing clothes, and applying ceremonial paint for the arrival celebration. Captive colonists frequently assumed this process was a prelude to imminent torture and death. Culturally disoriented captives presumably had similar reactions to a fellow American in 1781, who observed that captors "acted in such a hideous and awful manner, as almost to make our hair stand upright upon our heads, and to fill us with fear and trembling. . . . Their actions are inconceivable. It would seem that bedlam had broken loose, and that hell was in an uproar."[22]

When the warrior victoriously reentered his village or camp, Indian community members determined each captive's fate. In the worst case, the human war trophies would be "compelled to undergo the most painful death, by being burnt alive either at the stake or tree, when a war dance is generally performed." Alternatively, they could be adopted "like a member of the family, enjoying perfect freedom," or "doomed to serve as a slave." There is no direct evidence indicating the full adoption or ritual killing of any Cedars campaign participants, but in the absence of postcaptivity documentation, three men from Burrall's Connecticut Regiment and Primus Chandler, a freed black and New Hampshire ranger, are candidates to have experienced either of these fates. Through historical survivor bias, the few scant records are from those ransomed, released, or escaped.[23]

In most cases, captive men would be kept in a servant/slave status, forced "to do the most menial work, such as cutting firewood, cultivating the fields, harvesting, pounding Indian corn or maize to make sagamité, cooking, mending the hunters' shoes, carrying their game"—Indian women's labor. In the Mississauga world of "scattered, semi-horticultural hunters and fishermen," most colonial captives would have proven themselves to be a long-term community liability—another mouth to feed through lean seasons in the challenging boreal environment. This presumably motivated Mississauga warriors to seek ransoms or arrange convenient circumstances for survivable captive escapes. At least eight such incidents were documented from the two years after the Cedars.[24]

In four exceptional cases, individuals left useful documentary traces of their captive experiences and paths to freedom. Taken captive at Quinchien, Pvt. Benjamin Hardison was eventually purchased from his captor by a British officer, "on condition of laboring with said person to the value of the sum given for his redemption." During the ensuing indenture, Hardison "revised his opinions and became a firm loyalist," eventually settling in Fort Erie, Upper Canada, and rising to regional political prominence. After the same ambush, Drummer James Derry, a twenty-five-year-old from Bedel's Rangers, was "carried into the back country by the indians" and ended up in "the remote parts of Lake superior . . . detained a prisoner, until he made his escape from Detroit in the month of May 1788." He was probably a Mississauga captive, given or sold to a western Great Lakes tribe. Both Hardison and Derry eventually filed for and received back pay from the United States to cover their extended captivities.[25]

Pvt. Randal Hewit's dramatic captive experience contrasts with Hardison's and Derry's bare-bones accounts. Just fourteen or fifteen years old, Hewit was among the youngest American soldiers surrendered at Fort Cedars. When Mississauga captors took him to Oswegatchie, merchant John Grant purchased Hewit and "hired him on" for almost a year—curiously without intervention by Captain Forster, who must have been aware of the rebel's ongoing presence near his fort.[26]

In 1777, Hewit met British Indian agent Daniel Claus at the fort, gathering warriors and supplies for General Barry St. Leger's Fort Schuyler (Stanwix) campaign. Hewit successfully entreated Claus to bring him into his service, and quickly "proved himself . . . a most keen & active woods man acquiring the Indians language very fast & was held in much esteem . . . by the Indians in this country." Working as one of Claus's "Rangers with the Mohawk Indians," he accompanied warriors and loyalists on various enterprises into rebel territory, including the October 1780 Ballston Raid.[27]

Hewit's ranging days ended in June 1781 though, when captured by American-allied Oneida scouts under Lt. Col. Louis Atiatoharongwen, between Crown Point and Johnstown, New York. As a measure of the respect Hewit earned in his service, Daniel Claus subsequently complained that Mohawk allies were "very much concernd & displeased" about the capture. New York authorities examined Hewit and eventually released him on a hefty £100 bail. Unsurprisingly, when Randal Hewit successfully petitioned the United States for a veteran's pension in 1823, he avoided mention of his ranger service under Colonel Claus or participation in border raids alongside "savage" Indians.[28]

Pvt. Reuben Middleton was the fourth Cedars captive with a substantially documented captive journey. As New Hampshire records show, he was a "mulattoe" or "negro" private in Captain Osgood's ranger company, who was surrendered at Fort Cedars, "captured by the Savages and carried, in spite of all his Indeavours to escape[,] some hundred Miles into the Desert." For two years, he was "the sport of unfeeling Monsters whose 'tender Mercies are Cruelty,'" until "his bloody Masters sold him to the French in Montreal, where, with Seven years Servitude he purchased his freedom, and permission to return."[29]

British records fill in some significant and shocking details from Reuben Middleton's "Seven years Servitude" that he neglected to mention in his short state petition account. His Montreal indenture to a silversmith ended after just three years, when Middleton was convicted of raping a ten-year-old girl, fined one hundred dollars, and sentenced to nine months in jail in September 1781. Unable to pay his fine, Middleton faced indefinite imprisonment. To avoid this fate, he appealed to Governor Haldimand for "Pardon & release on his Entering into His Majesty's Service forthwith." He never discussed past rebel army service or Indian captivity but instead claimed that he "came into the Province with a view to render all the services in his Power to His Majesty's Government." The governor approved and the pardoned convict enlisted for life in the Second Battalion of the King's Royal Regiment, where officials thought he would be "usefull as an Artificer."[30]

Middleton honorably served three years in the British provincial ranks until his regiment disbanded in 1784. He soon returned to Boscawan, New Hampshire, applied for and received back pay that encompassed both the time he was indentured in Montreal and that spent in British service.[31] Then Middleton disappeared from the record, apparently returning to a quiet New England anonymity.

Pvt. John Lamont's twentieth-century descendants recorded another apparent Cedars captivity narrative. By the family's traditional account, their eccentric ancestor served alongside Capt. John McKinstry, until after their battlefield defeat Lamont "was carried away a prisoner to the Indian country. His captors planned to put him to death by torture, but among the spoils captured by them was a fiddle which John Lamont snatched up and on which he played so well as to charm the savages from their purpose of killing him. But they compelled him to run the Indian gauntlet, which he did successfully." Then he was "adopted into one of the Indian tribes and was assigned an Indian squaw for a wife. But watching his chance he made his escape, and in due time returned to his own people." Alas, the story is an inherited yarn. Cartel exchange rolls and Lamont's own pension application indicate that he spent ten days or fewer in Indian hands, making his story an impossibility—but a century after the fact, events like the Cedars still possessed enough surrounding drama to sustain this exciting family legend.[32] It is an unfortunate historical feature that the most detailed, gripping, and widely disseminated personal stories from Cedars captives are mythical—Lamont's tale, and the closely related McKinstry-Brant Masonic rescue legend.

CHAPTER 19

THE QUESTION OF MASSACRE AND HISTORICAL CURRENTS AT THE CEDARS

Since the summer of 1776, some people have referred to the event at the Cedars as a massacre. Others have challenged that description, Canadian historian Samuel E. Dawson prominent among them. He wrote an 1874 essay, "The Massacre at the Cedars," specifically to tackle the question of alleged atrocities. With clearly evident national bias, he concluded that "the event stigmatised as the 'Massacre of the Cedars'" was "mythical." Dawson further contended that since the Continental Congress was not addressing real atrocities in its July 10, 1776, Cedars resolutions, the report was little more than a propaganda ploy to rally the newly independent states.[1]

Dawson's essay was clearly prompted by historian George Bancroft's description of the Cedars as a "massacre" in his 1860 *History of the United States.* Notably, Bancroft appears to have been the first to apply the term in any American historical work. And looking back to the Revolutionary War, even contemporary use was quite limited.[2] The Continental Congress did not identify the Cedars as a "massacre"; neither did its officers nor the patriot press. In fact, the controversial July 1776 resolutions actually employed a more moderate legal term: "murder."[3]

Tracing the Cedars "massacre" label to its origins, it curiously appears to have come from British and loyalist sources shortly after the campaign. The first documented use occurred in an August 4, 1776, loyalist's letter, published in the *Scots Magazine* before the end of the year. Hostage captains Ebenezer Sullivan and Ebenezer Green soon followed that document with their own August 14 propaganda-fodder letters from captivity in Montreal—both employed the term but spelled it "massacree." Yet their letters, and Sullivan's subsequent 1778 recantation, imply that British officers first introduced the term into Cedars discussion as they explained Congress's "unfounded" atrocity accusations to the hostages. The British might have deliberately done this as a rhetorical ploy, diminishing the small-scale Cedars affair in implicit comparison to commonly accepted massacre events like that at Fort Willian Henry. Even in published wartime sources, subsequent description of a Cedars massacre was confined to copies of Sullivan's letter promulgated through Lieutenant Andrew Parke's *Authentic Narrative* and loyalist newspaper reprints.[4]

Moving beyond past discussions, a historical reassessment of the Cedars as a massacre properly rests to a considerable degree on the term's definition. However, massacre remains an imprecise term, open to interpretation. Modern meanings vary but trend toward a few common characteristics: large casualty numbers, helpless or unresisting victims, and perpetrators' cruelty or atrocity. Late eighteenth- and early nineteenth-century English-language dictionaries used massacre as a synonym for butchery, carnage, murder, or havoc; but a contemporary French definition adds detail that might better represent Revolutionary War–era British and American usage: "Killing, carnage . . . more commonly said of men who are killed without defending themselves."[5] The disarmed Continental prisoners at the Cedars satisfied the "defenseless" condition, and from the American side of the cultural divide the Indians clearly seemed cruel, so the question of massacre hinges more on the scope and character of the violence.

The biggest obstacle to historical qualification of Cedars campaign atrocities is rooted in the imprecise and conflicting nature of available primary accounts. These key sources generally fail to make a clear distinction between battle deaths and those in postcombat events and provide disputable or imprecise victim quantification. Furthermore, several of them describe a week's events without any chronological specificity. Forensic historical analysis is improved, however, by examining the available primary source evidence for postcombat violence at the Cedars as three discrete incidents.

The first alleged atrocity scene came in the immediate aftermath of the Quinchien ambush battle, where American participants claimed that frenzied warriors killed comrades in cold blood after fighting had stopped. Well-established Indian warfare norms make it plausible that a few soldiers were given deadly blows under the claimed conditions—particularly those who were seriously wounded. Yet those numbers must have been quite small, fewer than ten, based on the best Quinchien casualty estimates.

The second incident came outside Fort Cedars, later that same day, when warriors sought ritual revenge killings for the chief who had died in the Quinchien fighting. On the one hand, Lieutenant Parke's partisan British account is vaguely worded but seems to say that Captain George Forster successfully intervened to prevent any murders of Americans. On the other hand, Sherburne firmly believed two to four of his men were killed there. These contradictory accounts cannot be reconciled—excluding the "roasting" incident, there were perhaps as many as three killings, but quite possibly none.

The last alleged incident occurred during prisoner movement on Île aux Tourtes, eight days after the Fort Cedars surrender. The best evidence seems to indicate that Indians killed at least two Continental prisoners on the island. There are multiple, mutually supporting American primary source claims, and the alleged acts conform with common Indian practices. This is the best-substantiated atrocity event in the entire Cedars affair, even if the few victims were never identified by name.[6]

Summarizing these three incidents, it appears that in the week of May 20, 1776, fewer than a dozen Americans were killed outside European-defined confines of battle, over an eleven-mile expanse from Fort Cedars to Île aux Tourtes. This prisoner death toll would scarcely qualify the Cedars as a military massacre. Although the United States were deeply immersed in what historian Holger Hoock described as the "war of wounds [that] fed the war of words," the Continental Congress's choice to characterize Cedars incidents as "murder" seems most accurate—isolated "unlawful" acts by Euro-colonial standards. The scale of violence at the Cedars clearly did not compare to major atrocity events in the French and Indian War or to later Revolutionary War incidents.[7]

There is one more intriguing aspect of noncombat killing at the Cedars that warrants discussion—the participants' roles in preventing massacre. Contemporary sources emphasized British officers' and loyal Canadians' interventions, yet given Native numerical predominance, those Euro-colonials were in no position to demand or impose restraint. At best they could encourage, negotiate, and reward it. Only a single, anonymous loyalist account credited "sachems" with any specific moderating role, in reference to their urgent requests for an immediate prisoner exchange after the fraught May 26 Pointe-de-Quinchien showdown.[8]

Circumstances, however, suggest that Indians had a far more important role in moderating their own customarily violent practices as the two cultures clashed around the Cedars. In the Native camp, restraint ultimately rested upon individual and noncoercive collective control. Within the "parallel warfare" framework, the Indian contingents had satisfied their most significant objectives upon Sherburne's May 20 defeat: warriors had proven their bravery in battle and could return home with plunder, some with captives or ransom, and a few with scalps; their bonds with the Johnson family and the king were refreshed; they had cleared the St. Lawrence to Montreal by removing the rebels from Fort Cedars; and it was evident that General Guy Carleton's army would soon expel the last rebel occupiers from Canada to restore the flow of trade goods. Other than customary pressures for revenge killings, or tense moments when warriors might execute captives before imminent battle, Indian interests do not seem to have warranted massacre-scale violence, with an ensuing risk of drawing serious British displeasure and possible American retribution.

Moving beyond the single issue of massacre, the affair of the Cedars broadens and deepens our historical understanding of the Revolutionary War, particularly in regards to Native politics, motivations, and warfare principles. As the first Indian battles in the war, the Fort St. Johns skirmishes and the Cedars campaign connect the French and Indian War past with subsequent years of conflict—providing continuity in some aspects and acting as a pivot point in others.

One of the key transitions in 1775–76 came in northeastern Indian politics, as new factional patterns, connections, and conflicts emerged across the Haudenosaunee Six Nations and Seven Nations of Canada. These changes marked a significant break from the past, but after the Cedars, they held with considerable consistency for the rest of the Revolutionary War. Within the Six Nations, new details from the Canadian campaign do not offer any dramatic correction to the common historical understanding of that confederation's progressive wartime fragmentation. However, the paths that Six Nations warriors took to Fort St. Johns and the Cedars serve to reinforce the contested, limited, and factional nature of early Haudenosaunee Iroquois participation and further emphasize the value of an "open door" to trade as a key motivator for early Native action. After the Cedars, the pro-British Seneca, Onondaga, Cayuga, and Mohawk contingents that were represented in the fighting in Canada continued to ally with the king's forces. As the war intruded into Iroquoia, they drew others—from all six nations—to the British Indian Department's Fort Niagara base of operations.

The Oneidas and Tuscaroras, the Six Nations' other major wartime bloc, moved beyond their initial role as chief proponents for neutrality. Even before the Cedars they formed their defensive league with the Kahnawakes to protect common interests against the confederations' increasingly zealous pro-British elements. Yet rapidly escalating events in the summer of 1777 led Oneidas onto the warpath as American partners at Oriskany and Saratoga, and they would maintain this alliance for the rest of the war.

In contrast to the reasonably well developed Six Nations Revolutionary War narrative, the Seven Nations of Canada lack significant historical treatment for the era. The Cedars and its 1775 precedents clearly reveal the complexity of Laurentian Indian politics. The Seven Nations never effectively acted as a single political entity, and village and factional politics took precedence in a way that was rarely observed during the long period of French cooperation in their recent past. After the Cedars, the Seven Nations largely followed the same political and military patterns that were manifested during the American invasion.

At the level of individual Seven Nations villages, the Lake of Two Mountains Kanesatakes remained the outliers as consistent and largely unified British allies—often providing the core cadre for Seven Nations contingents on raids or campaigns. In stark contrast, Kahnawake and Odanak sustained independent and factional political courses, even if their freedom of action was inhibited after British colonial authority was restored in Canada in mid-1776. Given Kahnawake's well-recognized "Bostonian" leanings during the rebels' invasion, that nation was compelled to make token reconciliation efforts before resuming full relations with the British government. Yet both Kahnawake and Odanak retained active pro-American factions, even as fellow villagers accompanied British military expeditions and raids.[9]

The Cedars also marked Akwesasne's rise to a larger political and military role. Even though the village retained factions in both belligerent camps, British officers deemed it a safer, more secure raiding base than Kahnawake or Odanak. At the other end of the confederacy, Wendake Hurons also played a more active role as British military allies after Quebec City's May 1776 relief, but they still had their own pro-American element, spearheaded by Jean and Louis Vincent.

While the Canadian campaign reflected significant northeastern Indian political shifts, it demonstrated continuity in three overarching eighteenth-century Native principles. At multiple levels, the Haudenosaunee Iroquois and Seven Nations continued to conduct "active engagement" with both the British and Americans, keeping opportunities open and buffering negative repercussions from either side; however, in the divisive course of the Revolutionary War, the practice became less functional for the Six Nations. The Cedars also showed the ongoing benefits and limitations of "parallel warfare," as war parties combined efforts with Euro-colonial belligerents to the degree that their campaign objectives aligned and conflicting military customs and values permitted. Warriors also continued to practice "tacit neutrality" to steer violence away from fellow Indians, regardless of nation, balancing the benefits of active engagement with the occasional risks of parallel warfare.

Individual participants also served as important agents of continuity. The Cedars was not the first time many of them interacted, and for many it was not the last. Unfortunately, there is a lack of sufficient historical records to follow most individual Native actors after the Cedars.

Louis Atiatoharongwen is the exception, and his path shows remarkable continuity as a committed British enemy and American ally. Most dramatically, local history placed him with the Oneida contingent at Oriskany on August 6, 1777, immersed in battle against Senecas and Mohawks in the war's most significant break from Native tacit neutrality. Louis continued to accompany Oneidas, serving with the Continental Army from the Saratoga campaign through the end of the war. He also made occasional treks to Kahnawake and Akwesasne to coordinate efforts and gather intelligence. In 1779, George Washington and Philip Schuyler ensured that Louis was rewarded with a lieutenant colonel's commission, making him the Continental Army's highest-ranking Native (and nonwhite) officer.[10]

On the British side, John Butler sustained Sir William Johnson's colonial Indian Department legacy, encouraging and supporting the king's Native allies throughout the Revolutionary War. After the Cedars, Butler was promoted to deputy superintendent, and he continued to encourage and equip Indian allies. British policy changes soon reached North America, so beginning with the 1777 Fort Schuyler (Stanwix) campaign, he could overtly encourage offensive operations. Butler accompanied that expedition, leading Indians and loyalists into the bloody battle at Oriskany. Beginning in 1778, Butler effectively commanded the king's irregular frontier war in the north, launching joint loyalist-Indian forays from Fort Niagara to destabilize the rebels. His own loyalist regiment, Butler's Rangers, became synonymous with the terror that this type of warfare spread across "the whole frontier from the Hudson River to Kentucky."[11]

Claude de Lorimier similarly continued to serve the king after the Cedars. He joined Seven Nations war parties during the rebels' endgame retreat from Canada, in Carleton's aborted fall 1776 invasion, and in Burgoyne's campaign the following year. In August 1777, he received a serious leg wound at the Battle of Bennington and was limited to agent's work at Kahnawake for two years as a result. Once healthy enough to return to the field, Lorimier was the British-appointed leader for a combined 1779 Mohawk Valley raid. However, his Kahnawake, Akwesasne, and Kanesatake allies gave him another sharp reminder of the limits of parallel warfare and the overriding influence of Native tacit neutrality. The warriors rerouted the mission to harass Fort Schuyler; and while the warriors gathered some Continental prisoners and scalps, to Lorimier's chagrin the Indians also met "enemy" Oneidas just out of his sight to exchange information. This affair proved to be his last great adventure of the war, as he had become too physically fragile to undertake further missions.[12]

Lieutenant Henry Bird best represents post-Cedars continuity in the British army officer ranks, particularly since Captain Forster was effectively removed from the war in October 1777. Forster had been promoted to major in another regiment as a reward for his performance at the Cedars and became part of Burgoyne's surrender and another controversial cartel—the Saratoga Articles of Convention. Bird effectively assumed his former captain's mantle as the Eighth Regiment's premier Indian officer. The lieutenant led the redcoat-and-Indian advance party for the 1777 Fort Schuyler–Oriskany campaign where he was again confronted by the limits of parallel warfare. He had to cajole Seneca and Mississauga allies to close on the enemy post, and even then, they set their own pace. Following that campaign, he was transferred west to Detroit and promoted to captain. In 1779, he commenced two years of frontier operations against American forts and settlements in Ohio and Kentucky. He led small redcoat and Canadian detachments, but Shawnee, Wyandot, and Ottawa allies provided the primary fighting force, prompting him regularly to negotiate parallel objectives and follow Captain Forster's Cedars example as he tried to temper or ameliorate violent Indian customs in pursuit of his own mission.[13]

On the Continental side of the war, Timothy Bedel sustained particularly close ties with pro-American Abenakis, including Odanaks, who helped range New Hampshire's frontiers; and on at least one occasion, he coordinated Native operations with Louis Atiatoharongwen. In the 1777 Fort Schuyler campaign, Benedict Arnold heeded Oneida allies' counsel and authorized a brilliant deception scheme that prompted British-allied Indians to abandon their siege. Perhaps his unsuccessful intimidation of Native enemies during the end stages of the Cedars affair had shown him the limited value of direct threats and helped open his mind to alternative approaches. Finally, Philip Schuyler provided substantial diplomatic continuity, extending his family's historical role as leading Albany ambassadors to the Six Nations throughout the war. Even after resigning his army commission, Schuyler remained a Northern Indian Department commissioner. He steadfastly pursued nominal Six Nations neutrality until all hope ended with the Continental Army's 1779 expeditions into the heart of Iroquoia. Schuyler also advocated for the proper care of Oneida and Tuscarora allies and was a chief proponent for a formal postwar peace with the confederacy.[14]

Reflecting on the historical consequence of the Cedars, a past historiographical moment reveals some reasons why the event's significance was largely overlooked and even dismissed for more than two hundred years. In 1893, Canadian historian William Kingsford's twelve-volume *History of Canada* provided an inordinately detailed discussion of the affair at the Cedars. Even though Kingsford judged that "the event itself is utterly unimportant; it was without significance and led to no result," he confessed that he "felt it a duty to narrate at length the affair at the Cedars, for the facts, imperfectly known, continue to be constantly misrepresented."[15] The author of this book was prompted by a similar sense of duty to uncover the truth and correct common historical errors, even if the results indirectly challenge Kingsford's primary conclusions about the Cedars campaign's irrelevance. Particularly at the beginning of the Revolutionary War, the Cedars campaign was important and had significance, and its results affected confederacies, villages, factions, and individuals across the northeastern Native world. Yet, Kingsford's negative conclusions were conventional for his time. What has prompted such a drastic historical revision of the affair at the Cedars?

In the century after Kinsgford wrote *The History of Canada*, the rise of New Indian History, Modern Military History, and Borderlands Studies has expanded our conceptual horizons and range of investigation to look beyond settler-colonial frontier narratives, "drums and trumpets," and nation-state perspectives. Historical methods have improved, and the digital age has provided unprecedented access to rich, but widely dispersed veins of essential source material. These developments facilitated a new interpretation of the Cedars that encompasses the Indians' role in shaping the campaign's outcomes; the scope, significance, and meaning of Indian participation; the question of massacre; the continuity and transition of various Native historical patterns; and the affair's subsequent impact on the war. These meaningful points demonstrate the ways in which the relatively small Cedars campaign improves our broader historical understanding of Indian involvement in, and Native peoples' impact on, the Revolutionary War from its very beginning.

APPENDIX A
Continental Soldiers at Fort Cedars and Quinchien

Status Sourcing

exchanged = unless otherwise noted, from A list of Prisoners belonging to the Continental Army, taken at the Cedars, rg360 i29 r36 pp233-45, M247, NARA
pension = information obtained from M804, NARA, pension claim

New Hampshire Rangers Staff—2 exchanged = 2 total

Butterfield, Isaac Maj.—exchanged
Hibbard, Thomas Adjutant—exchanged

Daniel Carlisle's Company, New Hampshire Rangers— 20 exchanged = 20 total

Aldridge, Luke Drummer—exchanged
Amsden, Thomas Pvt.—exchanged
Bacon, Nathaniel Fifer—exchanged
Beman, Joseph Pvt.—exchanged
Butler, Jonathan Pvt.—exchanged
Chapman, Stephen Pvt.—exchanged
Colborn, Nathaniel Pvt.—exchanged
Gibbs, David Pvt.—exchanged
Gibbs, Isaac Pvt.—exchanged
Gibbs, Joshua Pvt.—exchanged
Gibbs, Thomas Sgt.—exchanged
Houghton, Edward Pvt.—exchanged per pension / not on POW List
Jordan, Eleazar Pvt.—exchanged
Pierce, Joshua Pvt.—exchanged
Shepardson, Zephaniah Pvt.—exchanged
Wheelock, James Pvt.—exchanged

Whitcomb, Thomas Pvt.—exchanged
White, Joshua Pvt.—exchanged
Willard, Henry Pvt.—exchanged
Willard, John Pvt.—exchanged

Joseph Estabrook's Company, New Hampshire Rangers— 1 captive + 1 escaped + 27 exchanged = 29 total

Estabrook, Joseph Capt.—exchanged
Adal, John Pvt.—exchanged
Binton, Andrew Pvt.—exchanged
Bower, Elisha Pvt.—exchanged
Calkin, Solomon Pvt.—CAPTIVE per pension (see appendix B)
Church, Joseph Pvt.—exchanged
Coats, Benjamin Pvt.—exchanged
Dunfee, Cornelius Pvt.—exchanged
Fuller, Jonathan Sgt.—exchanged
Griggs, John 2nd Lt.—exchanged (orig. Wait's company)
Hardwick, William Pvt.—exchanged
Harvey, Timothy Pvt.—exchanged
Hill, Alpheus Cpl.—exchanged
Holbrook, Amos Pvt.—exchanged
Holbrook, Benjamin Ens.—exchanged
Larrabee, William Pvt.—exchanged per pension / not on POW List
Little, Robert Pvt.—exchanged
Lynds, David Pvt.—ESCAPED per Shepardson, "Reminiscence," 18 / not on POW List (see chap. 15)
Miller, James Drummer—exchanged
Montgomery, Martin Pvt.—exchanged
Murphy, William Pvt.—exchanged
Pettibone, George Pvt.—exchanged per pension / not on POW List
Richards, Charles Pvt.—exchanged
Serjeants, Lemuel 1st Lt.—exchanged (orig. Wait's company)
Skinner, Jonathan Sgt.—exchanged
White, Asa Pvt.—exchanged
Wilson, Peter Pvt.—exchanged
Wright, John Pvt.—exchanged
Wright, Moses Pvt.—exchanged

Edward Everett's Company, New Hampshire Rangers—
1 escaped + 24 exchanged = 25 total

Everett, Edward Capt.—exchanged
Barnes, James Pvt.—exchanged
Blodget, Ebenezer Pvt.—exchanged
Brown, John Pvt.—exchanged
Burdeen, Nathaniel Pvt.—exchanged
Chamberlin, Daniel Pvt.—exchanged
Chamberlin, Ebenezer Lt.—exchanged
Chamberlin, Ephraim Pvt.—exchanged
Clarke, Michael Pvt.—exchanged
Cooley, John Cpl.—exchanged
Fifield, John Cpl.—ESCAPED per pension (see chap. 14)
Gates, Ezra, Jr. Pvt.—exchanged
Gates, Ezra, Sr. Pvt.—exchanged
Gates, Jacob Pvt.—exchanged
Gates, Stephen Pvt.—exchanged
Judkins, Job Pvt.—exchanged
Leavit, John Pvt.—exchanged
Meeder, Lemuel Pvt.—exchanged
Mordock, Benjamin Sgt.—exchanged
Pitts, Thomas Pvt.—exchanged
Powers, Nahum Pvt.—exchanged
Rollins, Benjamin Cpl.—exchanged
Tyler, John Sgt.—exchanged
Wells, Paul Sgt.—exchanged per pension / not on POW List
Wheat, Joseph Pvt.—exchanged

Ebenezer Green's Company, New Hampshire Rangers—
1 captive + 1 hostage + 19 exchanged = 21 total

Green, Ebenezer Capt.—HOSTAGE (see chap. 18)
Chamberlin, Abner Pvt.—exchanged
Chamberlin, Benjamin Ens.—exchanged
Chamberlin, David Pvt.—exchanged
Chamberlin, Elias Pvt.—exchanged
Dimmer, Joseph Pvt.—exchanged

Eustis, Daniel Pvt.—exchanged
Evans, John Pvt.—exchanged
Gillet, Simon Pvt.—CAPTIVE per pension (see appendix B)
Glines, John Pvt.—exchanged per pension / not on POW List
Hopkins, Josiah Pvt.—exchanged
Morris (or Martin), Jonathan Pvt.—exchanged
Powell, John Pvt.—exchanged
Rogers, Nathaniel, Jr. Pvt.—exchanged
Rogers, Pearley Cpl.—exchanged
Rowe, John Pvt.—exchanged
Shieldhas, Alexander Pvt.—exchanged
Skinner, Ephraim Cpl.—exchanged per pension / not on POW List
Skinner, Joseph Pvt.—exchanged
Smith, Aaron Pvt.—exchanged
Woodworth, Joel Pvt.—exchanged per pension / not on POW List

James Osgood's Company, New Hampshire Rangers— 3 captive + 54 exchanged (+ 1 unknown?) = 57 or 58 total

Abbot, Philip Pvt.—exchanged
Abbott, Elias Pvt.—exchanged
Abbott, Ezra Pvt.—exchanged (listed twice on POW List?)
Abbott, Nathaniel Chandler Pvt.—exchanged
Basford, James Pvt.—exchanged
Basford, Joseph Pvt.—exchanged
Betton, John Pvt.—exchanged
Brown, Colton Pvt.—exchanged
Brown, John Pvt.—exchanged
Brown, Scott Pvt.—exchanged
Burbank, Wells Pvt.—exchanged
Carleton, Edward Cpl.—exchanged
Carney, John Pvt.—exchanged
Carter, Hubbard Sgt.—exchanged
Cass, Joseph Pvt.—exchanged
Cass, Nathan Pvt.—exchanged
Cotton, Caleb Pvt.—exchanged per pension / not on POW List
Cutler, William Pvt.—exchanged
Danford, Edward Pvt.—exchanged

Danford, Joshua Cpl.—exchanged per pension / not on POW List
Eastman, Ezekiel Pvt.—exchanged
Fahey, William Pvt.—exchanged
Fellows, Joseph Pvt.—exchanged
Fifield, Benjamin Pvt.—exchanged
Foss, Timothy Pvt.—exchanged
Fowler, Samuel 1st Lt.—exchanged
Foye, James Pvt.—exchanged per pension / not on POW List
Freeman, Titus Pvt.—*unknown, poss. captive* (not confirmed at Cedars) (see appendix B)
Hagatee, Barnabas Pvt.—exchanged
Hardaway, Jonathan Pvt.—exchanged
Hardaway, Joseph Pvt.—exchanged
Hill, Charles Ens.—exchanged
Hinkley, Christopher Pvt.—exchanged
Hopkins, William Pvt.—exchanged
Kingsbury, Joseph Pvt.—CAPTIVE (see appendix B)
Kingsbury, Samuel Pvt.—exchanged per pension / not on POW List
Kinsman, Nathan Pvt.—exchanged
Middleton, Reuben Pvt.—CAPTIVE (see appendix B/chap. 18)
Murphy, James Pvt.—exchanged
Paine, Noah Pvt.—exchanged
Pangbourn, Richard Pvt.—exchanged
Peck, Matthew Pvt.—exchanged
Robinson, Jonathan Pvt.—exchanged
Scott, Charles Pvt.—exchanged per pension / not on POW List
Simonds, William Pvt.—exchanged
Smart, Richard Pvt.—CAPTIVE per pension / not on POW List (see appendix B)
Smith, Aaron Pvt.—exchanged
Smith, Jeremiah Pvt.—exchanged
Smith, John Pvt.—exchanged
Spalding, Azel Pvt.—exchanged
Spear, Elisha Pvt.—exchanged
Spear, Joshua Pvt.—exchanged
Vandevort, Jacob Pvt.—exchanged
Walker, Nathaniel Pvt.—exchanged
Webster, Benjamin Cpl.—exchanged

Webster, John 2nd Lt.—exchanged
Webster, Stephen Sgt.—exchanged
Young, Daniel Pvt.—exchanged

Jason Wait's Company, New Hampshire Rangers—
13 exchanged = 13 total

Flood, Amos Pvt.—exchanged
Gray, Joseph Pvt.—exchanged
Gustin, Josiah Pvt.—exchanged
Hall, Benjamin Pvt.—exchanged
Johnson, Aaron Pvt.—exchanged
Johnson, David Pvt.—exchanged
Johnson, Isaac, Jr. Pvt.—exchanged
Johnson, Josiah Pvt.—exchanged
Murdock, Oliver Pvt.—exchanged
Puffer, Amos Pvt.—exchanged
Puffer, Simeon Pvt.—exchanged
Rice, Aaron Pvt.—exchanged
Willis, Elisha Cpl.—exchanged

Daniel Wilkins's Company, New Hampshire Rangers—
1 captive + 61 exchanged = 62 total

Wilkins, Daniel Capt.—exchanged
Abbot, Joshua Cpl.—exchanged
Alld, William Pvt.—exchanged
Allen, John Pvt.—exchanged
Beamine, George Pvt.—exchanged
Blodget, Jacob Pvt.—exchanged
Boutwell, Amos Pvt.—exchanged
Boyd, Samuel Pvt.—exchanged
Bradford, William Ens.—exchanged
Brown, Alexander Pvt.—exchanged
Brown, William Pvt.—exchanged
Caldwell, James Sgt.—exchanged
Campbell, Robert Sgt.—exchanged
Chandler, Primus Pvt.—CAPTIVE / not on POW List (see appendix B)
Clarke, Ephraim Pvt.—exchanged

Clarke, James Pvt.—exchanged
Cochran, James Pvt.—exchanged
Cochran, Robert Pvt.—exchanged
Curtice, Isaac Pvt.—exchanged
Curtis, Lemuel Pvt.—exchanged
Curtis, Stephen Pvt.—exchanged
Dickey, Joseph Pvt.—exchanged
Dutton, Roger Pvt.—exchanged
Farnham, John Pvt.—exchanged
Farrer, Joseph Pvt.—exchanged
Fifield, Jonathan Cpl.—exchanged
Gilbert, Lareford Pvt.—exchanged
Glover, Henry Pvt.—exchanged
Hamblet, William Pvt.—exchanged
Hartshorn, James Pvt.—exchanged
Harwood, James Pvt.—exchanged
Holt, Jabez Fifer—exchanged
Holt, Obadiah Pvt.—exchanged
Jewell, James Pvt.—exchanged
Kemp, Reuben Pvt.—exchanged
Kittridge, Solomon Pvt.—exchanged per pension / not on POW List
Lamson, Jeremiah Pvt.—exchanged
Livingston, Robert Pvt.—exchanged
Lovejoy, Joseph Pvt.—exchanged
Mallady, Thomas Pvt.—exchanged
Martin, Timothy Pvt.—exchanged
McAllester, Benjamin Pvt.—exchanged
McClintock, Jonathan Pvt.—exchanged
McKeen, Hugh Pvt.—exchanged
McLeary, Thomas Pvt.—exchanged
McNeal, Jonathan Colwell Sgt.—exchanged
Mills, John 2nd Lt.—exchanged
Nichols, Aaron Pvt.—exchanged
Phelps, John Pvt.—exchanged
Robbins, John Pvt.—exchanged
Robby, William Lt.—exchanged
Roby, Philip Abbot Pvt.—exchanged

Stearnes, Isaac Pvt.—exchanged
Sternes, Samuel Cpl.—exchanged
Stevens, Thomas Pvt.—exchanged
Warren, Josiah Pvt.—exchanged
Weston, Sutherick Cpl.—exchanged
Wiley, John Pvt.—exchanged
Wilkins, Andrew Pvt.—exchanged
Wilkins, Daniel Pvt.—exchanged
Wilkins, Sylvester Pvt.—exchanged
Wood, Samuel Pvt.—exchanged

Samuel Young's Company, New Hampshire Rangers (with Sherburne's battalion)—1 captive + 2 exchanged = 3 total

Cleveland, Solomon Pvt.—exchanged
Derry, James Drummer—CAPTIVE per pension (see appendix B/chap. 18)
Hadley, Joseph Pvt.—exchanged

Staff, Paterson's Fifteenth Continental Regiment (Massachusetts)—1 exchanged = 1 total

Sherburne, Henry Maj.—exchanged *in negotiations*, not on POW List

Moses Ashley's Company, Paterson's Fifteenth Continental Regiment (Massachusetts)—25 exchanged = 25 total

Bruce, Abner Pvt.—exchanged
Chaplain, Joseph Pvt.—exchanged
Clary, Oliver Pvt.—exchanged
Cole, Timothy Pvt.—exchanged
Curtis, Joel Pvt.—exchanged
Curtis, Nathan Pvt.—exchanged
Davis, Hezekiah Pvt.—exchanged
Deverin, John Pvt.—exchanged
Ingram, Benjamin Pvt.—exchanged
Long, William Pvt.—exchanged
Mattoon, Abel Pvt.—exchanged
Mattoon, Sylvanus Pvt.—exchanged
Miller, Jeremiah 2nd Lt.—exchanged
Norton, Elijah Pvt.—exchanged

Perrin, Daniel Pvt.—exchanged
Perrin, Jesse Pvt.—exchanged
Raymont, William Pvt.—exchanged
Read, David Pvt.—exchanged
Read, Ezra Pvt.—exchanged
Taylor, James Pvt.—exchanged
Taylor, Willis Pvt.—exchanged
Walker, Caleb Sgt.—exchanged
Whitehead, Elisha Pvt.—exchanged
William, Ebenezer Pvt.—exchanged
Winston, Isaac Pvt.—exchanged

Theodore Bliss's Company, Paterson's Fifteenth Continental Regiment (Massachusetts)—4 exchanged + 1 hostage = 5 total

Bliss, Theodore Capt.—HOSTAGE (see chap. 18)
Adams, Joseph Pvt.—exchanged
Bryant, Stephen Pvt.—exchanged per pension / not on POW List
Durban, Thomas Pvt.—exchanged
Ferren, Jonathan Pvt.—exchanged per pension / not on POW List

John McKinstry's Company, Paterson's Fifteenth Continental Regiment (Massachusetts)—2 captive + 2 possible captive or unknown +14 exchanged + 7 unknown = 25 total

Company Roll Source: rg93 f91 p3, July 1776, M246, NARA

McKinstry, John Capt.—exchanged *in negotiations*, not on POW List (see chap. 15)
Barkins, William Pvt.—*unknown* (struck through on July 1776 roll)
Bennett, William Pvt.—exchanged
Church, Elisha Fifer—CAPTIVE per July 1776 roll (see appendix B)
Cleveland, Josiah Pvt.—exchanged per pension / not on POW List
Coventry, James Pvt.—*unknown* (struck through on July 1776 roll)
Fann, William Pvt.—exchanged
Gray, Daniel Pvt.—*possible captive* (struck through on July 1776 roll) (see appendix B)
Hatch, Obed Pvt.—exchanged
Higgins, R. Pvt.—*unknown* (struck through on July 1776 roll)
Hogg, John Pvt.—*unknown* (struck through on July 1776 roll)

Hollister, Jesse Sgt.—CAPTIVE-WOUNDED per pension (see appendix B)
Hollister, Joseph Pvt.—exchanged
Kellyon, Jonathan Pvt.—*unknown* (struck through on July 1776 roll)
Lemmon (Lamont), John Pvt.—exchanged + pension (see chap. 18)
Murray, Michael Pvt.—exchanged
Phelps, Joel Pvt.—exchanged
Phelps, Othniel Pvt. or Sgt.—exchanged
Roberts, Nathaniel Pvt.—exchanged
Scott, John Pvt.—*possible captive* (struck through on July 1776 roll) (see appendix B)
Stephens, David Pvt.—*unknown* (struck through on July 1776 roll)
Van Volkinburg, Francis Pvt.—exchanged
Van Volkinburg, George Pvt.—exchanged
Webb, David Pvt.—*unknown* (struck through on July 1776 roll)
Welch, Isaac Pvt.—exchanged

David Noble's Company, Paterson's Fifteenth Continental Regiment (Massachusetts)—2 exchanged = 2 total

Kingsley, Elias Pvt.—exchanged
Storey, Triston Pvt.—exchanged

Samuel Sawyer's Company, Paterson's Fifteenth Continental Regiment (Massachusetts)—5 exchanged = 5 total

Goodwin, Paul Pvt.—exchanged
Johnson, William Pvt.—exchanged
Kimball, Hezediah Pvt.—exchanged
Stewart, Joseph Pvt.—exchanged
Wilkins, Joseph Pvt.—exchanged

Ebenezer Sullivan's Company, Paterson's Fifteenth Continental Regiment (Massachusetts)—5 captive + 1 escaped + 14 exchanged + 1 hostage = 21 total

Sullivan, Ebenezer Capt.—HOSTAGE (see chap. 18)
Ceathe, Jeremiah Pvt.—exchanged
Eggleston, Moses Pvt.—exchanged
Goodwin, Ephraim Pvt.—exchanged
Hardison, Benjamin Pvt.—CAPTIVE per pension (see appendix B/chap. 18)

Hardison, Stephen Pvt.—exchanged
James, John Pvt.—CAPTIVE per pension (see appendix B)
Jenkins, John Pvt.—exchanged
Jones, Samuel Pvt.—exchanged per pension / not on POW List
Lord, Nathan 2nd Lt.—exchanged
Lord, Wentworth Pvt.—ESCAPED per pension (see chap. 15)
Meachum, Ichabod Pvt.—CAPTIVE per pension (see appendix B)
Nocks, Jonathan Pvt.—exchanged
Parkey, Jonathan Pvt.—exchanged
Pasco, Jonathan Pvt.—CAPTIVE per pension (see appendix B)
Pray, Samuel Pvt.—exchanged per pension / not on POW List
Shean, Richard Pvt.—exchanged
Stillianes, Rook Pvt.—exchanged
Tuke, Mark Pvt.—exchanged
Whitehouse, Enoch Cpl.—exchanged
Wooster, John Pvt.—CAPTIVE per pension (see appendix B)

William Wyman's Company, Paterson's Fifteenth Continental Regiment (Massachusetts)—2 exchanged = 2 total

Frisk, Isaac Pvt.—exchanged
Wentworth, James Pvt.—exchanged

David Downs's Company, Burrall's Connecticut Regiment— 40 exchanged + 1 killed = 41 total

Downs, David Capt.—exchanged
Bennett, Elijah Pvt.—exchanged
Bill, Judah Pvt.—exchanged
Calkins, Joseph Pvt.—exchanged
Clary, James Pvt.—exchanged (double-listed on POW List)
Crocker, Oliver Cpl.—exchanged
Doty, Joseph Pvt.—exchanged
Gillett, Charles, Jr. Pvt.—exchanged
Gillett, Charles, Sr. Pvt.—KILLED MAY 18 (see chap. 10)
Goodrich, Abner Pvt.—exchanged
Gray, Samuel Pvt.—exchanged
Hall, John, Jr. Pvt.—exchanged
Hambleton, Josiah (or Joshua) Pvt.—exchanged

Jackson, Elijah Pvt.—exchanged
Jackson, John Pvt.—exchanged per pension
Jewett, Caleb Pvt.—exchanged
Johnson, Samuel Ens.—exchanged
Kingsbury, Jeremiah Pvt.—exchanged
Knapp, Jonas Pvt.—exchanged
Laughlin, James Pvt.—exchanged
Manning, David Pvt.—exchanged
Maxum, Jacob Pvt.—exchanged
McIntire, Benjamin Pvt.—exchanged
McKee, Michael Pvt.—exchanged
Parsons, Isaac Pvt.—exchanged
Randall, David Pvt.—exchanged
Reen, John Pvt.—exchanged
Reno, Simeon Pvt.—exchanged
Rice, Asa Pvt.—exchanged
Roberts, Rozil Pvt.—exchanged
Rusco, David Sgt.—exchanged
Smith, Jehiel Pvt.—exchanged
Strong, David Sgt.—exchanged
Toby, Ephraim Pvt.—exchanged
Warner, Amasa Pvt.—exchanged
Weller, William Goodrich Pvt.—exchanged
Whitcomb, Simon Pvt.—exchanged
Wilcox, Stephen Pvt.—exchanged
Williams, William Pvt.—exchanged
Willis, Reuben Pvt.—exchanged
Youngs, Benjamin Pvt.—exchanged

**John Stevens's Company, Burrall's Connecticut Regiment—
5 captive + 1 poss. dead + 46 exchanged + 1 hostage = 53 total**
Company Roll Source: rg93 r27 f198 pp2–3, November 25, 1776, M246, NARA

Stevens, John Capt.—HOSTAGE (see chap. 18)
Bailey, Uriah Abrahams Pvt.—CAPTIVE per roll (see appendix B)
Baldwin, David Pvt.—exchanged
Barce, Hezekiah Pvt.—exchanged

Bow, Edward Pvt.—exchanged
Bradford, Elisha Pvt.—exchanged
Clary, James Pvt.—exchanged
Cleveland, Jonas Pvt.—exchanged
Cleveland, Josiah Pvt.—exchanged
Cole, John Pvt.—exchanged
Davis, Julius Pvt.—CAPTIVE per roll (see appendix B)
Dean, Reuben Pvt.—exchanged
Dufee (or Dupee), Simeon Pvt.—exchanged
Evens, John Pvt.—exchanged
Fellows, David Sgt.—exchanged
Fellows, Obel Pvt.—exchanged
Fellows, Samuel Pvt.—exchanged
Fisher, Eleazar Pvt.—exchanged
Fitch, Samuel Pvt.—exchanged
Flemming, Thomas Pvt.—exchanged
Foot, Ebenezer Evert Pvt.—exchanged
Green, John Pvt.—exchanged
Green, Samuel Drummer—exchanged
Gridley, Isaiah Pvt.—exchanged
Hawley, Zadock Pvt.—exchanged
Henderson, Joseph Pvt.—exchanged
Herrington, John Pvt.—exchanged
Hewit, Benjamin Sgt.—exchanged
Hewit, Ephraim Pvt.—exchanged
Hewit, John Pvt.—exchanged
Hewit, Randal Pvt.—CAPTIVE per roll + pension (see appendix B/chap. 18)
Jakways, Daniel Pvt.—exchanged
Kellogg, Eldad Pvt.—exchanged
Ledgard, John Pvt.—exchanged
Lewis, Jabez Pvt.—exchanged-*wounded* per pension (see chap. 10)
Lyon, Enos Pvt.—exchanged
McGoon, John Pvt.—exchanged
Merrel, Titus Pvt.—exchanged
Moon, Paul Pvt.—exchanged
Palmeter, Amaziah Pvt.—exchanged
Patterson, Matthew 2nd Lt.—exchanged

Payne, Rufus Sgt.—CAPTIVE per pension (deserted per roll / see appendix B)
Porter, Zachariah Fifer—exchanged
Preston, David Pvt.—exchanged
Raymond, Seth Pvt.—exchanged
Smith, Jedediah Cpl.—exchanged
Spencer, Abner Pvt.—CAPTIVE per pension (see appendix B)
Spencer, Jabez Pvt.—exchanged per pension (see POW List note below)
Squire, John Pvt.—DEAD per roll (no clear indication killed at Cedars)
Stevens, Benjamin Pvt.—exchanged per pension (see POW List note below)
Stevens, Oliver Pvt.—exchanged per pension (see POW List note below)
Stevens, Zebulon Cpl.—exchanged
Webster, Abraham Pvt.—exchanged per pension (see POW List note below)

POW List note: *There are no privates' names starting with S–W from Stevens's company on the POW List, indicating a portion of the list might be lost; based on the company roll, up to twelve other privates could be missing from the POW List.*

Hamtramck's Detachment, Hazen's Second Canadian Regiment (Continental)—1 captive + 11 released = 12 total

Hamtramck, Jean-François Lt.—released (see chap. 16)
Monty, Claud Pvt.—CAPTIVE per pension (see appendix B)
+ ten others released (unnamed)

William Johnston's Artillery Company (New York)— 5 exchanged = 5 total

Buck, Abiah Mattross—exchanged
Edy, James Mattross—exchanged
Fitzgerald, Michael Gunner—exchanged
McCluar, Matthew Mattross—exchanged
McKallough, John Sgt.—exchanged

Fort Cedars Totals:

12 captive + 2 escaped + 311 exchanged + 2 hostage + 2 (max.) killed + 11 released = 340

Quinchien Ambush Totals:

8 captive + 1 escaped + 69 exchanged + 2 hostage + 9 unknown = 89

APPENDIX B
Continental Captives

Name	Company	Age	Notes
Bailey, Uriah A. Pvt.	Stevens's	unk	"prisoner with the enemy" on November 25, 1776 roll
Calkin, Solomon Pvt.	Estabrook's	29	11 days at Kanesatake per pension (see note in chapter 16)
Chandler, Primus Pvt.	Wilkins's	unk	Blaine[1]
Church, Elisha Fifer	McKinstry's	unk	per July 1776 unit roll
Davis, Julius Pvt.	Stevens's	unk	"prisoner with enemy" on November 25, 1776 roll
Derry, James Drummer	Young's	25	(see chap. 18)
Freeman, Titus Pvt.	Osgood's	unk	possible/circumstantial—Knoblock[2]
Gillet, Simon Pvt.	Green's	20	about four weeks per pension
Gray, Daniel Pvt.	McKinstry's	unk	"captured by Iroquois, sold to British" (possibly post-Cedars)[3]
Hardison, Benjamin Pvt.	Sullivan's	19	see chap. 18
Hewit, Randal Pvt.	Stevens's	14–15	see chap. 18
Hollister, Jesse Sgt.	McKinstry's	24	about twelve days per pension
James, John Pvt.	Sullivan's	22	until October 1776, exchanged in Elizabethtown NJ per pension
Kingsbury, Joseph Pvt.	Osgood's	16	at least through June 1778, returned[4]
Meachum, Ichabod Pvt.	Sullivan's	17	nine weeks, escaped to British, exchanged July 1777 per pension

(continued)

Name	Company	Age	Notes
Middleton, Reuben Pvt.	Osgood's	unk	see chap. 18
Monty, Claude Pvt.	Hamtramck's	15	seven or eight months per pension
Pasco, Jonathan Pvt.	Sullivan's	16	nearly one month, escaped, returned to camp by 25 December 1776 per pension
Payne, Rufus Sgt.	Stevens's	26	one year, seven months, exchanged in New York per pension
Scott, John Pvt.	McKinstry's	unk	captured (possibly post-Cedars)[5]
Smart, Richard Pvt.	Osgood's	unk	short period, escaped per pension
Spencer, Abner Pvt.	Stevens's	unk	"prisoner with the enemy" on November 25, 1776, roll
Wooster, John Pvt.	Sullivan's	24	more than one year, until about September 1777, escaped per pension

1. James G. Blaine, *Zachariah Chandler: An Outline Sketch of His Life and Public Services* (Detroit: Post and Tribune, 1880), 31.
2. Glenn A. Knoblock, *"Strong and Brave Fellows": New Hampshire's Black Soldiers and Sailors of the American Revolution, 1775–1784* (Jefferson, NC: McFarland, 2003), 44, 209.
3. Secretary of the Commonwealth, *Massachusetts Soldiers and Sailors of the Revolutionary War* (Boston: Wright and Potter, 1896–1904), 6:765.
4. *DRNH*, 13:201; Mary K. Talcott, ed., *The Genealogy of the Descendants of Henry Kingsbury of Ipswich and Haverhill, Mass.* (Hartford, CT: Hartford Press, 1905), 127.
5. *Massachusetts Soldiers and Sailors of the Revolutionary War*, 13:920.

APPENDIX C
The May 27, 1776, Cartel

Initial Draft

Source: Parke, *Authentic Narrative*, 31–35. This is a published copy of the cartel. There do not appear to be any extant versions of the original cartel in either form. Another copy of this initial version is included in the Papers of the Continental Congress, but it appears to have been copied later than that presented here: Copy of original Prisoner Cartel, Vaudreuil, May 26, 1776, rg360 i29 r36 pp251–52, M247.

After the maturest deliberation on the customs and manners of the savages in war, which I find so opposite and contrary to the humane disposition of the British Government, and to all civilized nations, and to avoid the inevitable consequences of their customs in former wars, (which by their threats and menaces I find is not changed), that of putting their prisoners to death to disencumber themselves, in case of being attacked by an enemy, I have, therefore, in compliance with the above disposition in government, and the dictates of humanity, thought fit to enter into the following articles and agreement with Major Henry Shelburn [*sic*], and the under-subscribing officers, in the name of the power they were employed by, and of the officers and soldiers who shall be released by this agreement, and whose rank and numbers shall be indorsed on this cartel.

I. That there shall be an exchange of prisoners faithfully made, returning an equal number of his Majesty's troops, and of the same rank with those released by this agreement, as soon as possible, within the space of two months, allowing a moderate time for casualties that may render the performance of this article impracticable.

II. That those prisoners taken in opposing Government, shall not, on any pretext whatsoever, hereafter take up arms against the Government of Great Britain.

III. That they shall be conducted in safety, with all possible convenience and dispatch that circumstances will permit, to the south shore of the river St. Laurence, from which they are to repair to St. John's, and return to their own country immediately, without committing any waste or spoil on their march thither; allowing ten or twelve to go to Montreal to transact their private affairs.

IV. That the prisoners so returned, shall not, under any pretext whatsoever, either by words, writing, or signs, give the least information to Government's enemies, now in arms; or by any other kind of means, by which his Majesty's service may be hurt, to their adherents or others.

V. That the batteaux or other conveyances made use of to transport the prisoners to the south shore of said river, and the people necessary to conduct them, shall return unmolested.

VI. That hostages be delivered for the performance of these articles, to the full, according to the sense and spirit of the agreement, without any equivocation whatsoever.

VII. That the security of the subscribers be given to the inhabitants for all the waste and spoil committed on them by the detachment under the command of Colonel Bedel, on fair accounts, attested and signed, being delivered, for which the hostages are not to be answerable.

It being our full intention to fulfil the the [sic] above articles, we mutually sign, and interchange them as assurances of performance, signed at Vaudriel, this 26th day of May, in the year of our Lord one thousand seven hundred and seventy-six.

By order of Captain George Forster, commanding his Majesty's forces at Vaudriel.—And^w. Parke, Lieutenant in the King's or 8th regiment of foot. Chev^r. Lorimier, Fer^d. de Montigny.
Hen^y. Sherburne,
Isaac Butterfield,
Theodore Bliss,
Daniel Wilkins,
John Stevens,
Eben^r. Sullivan.

The cartel has indorsed on the back,

Two majors	2
Nine captains	9
Twenty-one subalterns	21
Four hundred and forty-three privates	443
Total	475

Final Cartel

This copy of the finalized cartel appears to be the earliest, and presumably the most accurate: Copy of the Cartel, Enclosed in by general Arnold, May 27, 1776, rg360 i162 v1 r179 pp78–81, M247. Other copies can be found at Copy of the Cartel between George Forster and Benedict Arnold, May 27, 1776, CO 42/35 (microfilm), fol. 56, LAC; PRO 30/55/2, National Archives (UK); George Washington Papers, MSS 44693, reel 036, 3209a, LOC; and a partial copy covering only the later terms regarding prison exchange mechanics in Cartel at Fort St Anne, May 27, 1776 [contemporary transcript], Orderly book of the 1st Pennsylvania Battalion of Foot, Society of the Cincinnati. Substantive differences from the Parke version are noted by asterisk, with Parke content following in brackets.

After the maturest Deliberation on the Customs and manners of the savages in War, which I find so opposite & contrary to the humane Disposition of the british Government and to all civilized Nations, and to avoid the inevitable Consequences of *savage [*their] Customs in former Wars, (which by their Threats and menaces I find is not changed) that of putting their prisoners to Death to disincumber themselves in case of being attacked by their enemy, I have therefore in Compliance with the above Disposition in Government, and the Dictates of Humanity, thought fit to enter into the following Articles and Agreement with *General Arnold in the Name of the Power he is employed by [*Major Henry Shelburn {sic}, and the under-subscribing officers, in the name of the power they were employed by], and of the Officers & Soldiers who shall be released by this Agreement, whose rank and numbers shall be endorsed on this Chartle [Cartel].

1st. That there shall be an exchange of Prisoners faithfully made, returning an equal number of his Majesties Troops of the same rank with those released by this Agreement, as soon as possible, within the space of two months, allowing a moderate Time for Casualties that may render the performance of this Article impracticable.

[deleted former 2d. That those prisoners taken in opposing Government, shall not, on any pretext whatsoever, hereafter take up arms against the Government of Great Britain.]

2d. [previous III.] That the prisoners shall be conducted in Safety with all possible Convenience and Dispatch that Circumstances will permit, to the South shore of the River Saint Lawrence from which they are to repair to Saint Johns & return to their own Countries immediately without Committing any Wastes or spoil on their march thither allowing ten or twelve to go to Montreal to transact their private Affairs.

3d [previous IV.] That the prisoners so returned shall not under any pretext, whatsoever, either in words, Writing, or Signs, give the least Information to Government Enemies*, their Adherents now in arms, in the least prejudice to His Majestys service. [*now in arms; or by any other kind of means, by which his Majesty's service may be hurt, to their adherents or others.]

[not in Arnold V. That the batteaux or other conveyances made use of to transport the prisoners to the south shore of said river, and the people necessary to conduct them, shall return unmolested.]

4th [previous VI.] That Hostages be delivered for the performance of Articles to the full, according to the sense and spirit of the Agreement without any Equivocation whatsoever.

6th [sic] [previous VII.] That the security of the Subscribers be given to the Inhabitants for all the Waste & spoil committed [on them] by the Detachment under the command of Col. Bedel, on fair Accounts, attested and signed, being delivered & for which the Hostages are not to be answerable.

It being our full Intention to fulfill the above Articles, We mutually sign and interchange them as Assurances of performance,
Given under our Hands this 27th Day of May 1776
Vaudreuil
signed Geo: Forster Captn. Commadng the King's Troops

Article 1st.[?] The prisoners shall be sent to the south shore of the St Laurence within one League of Caghnawaga and from thence to St. Johns & their own Country, except twelve who have Liberty to go to Montreal for which purpose six Days shall be allowed and Hostilities to cease on both Sides.

4th. Four Captains shall be sent to Quebec, as Hostages and remain there until prisoners are exchanged.

6th. The Continental Troops from principle have ever avoided plundering. Upon proof being made of any Waste committed by Colonel Bedels Detachment Reparation shall be made.

Given under my hand this 27th of May 1776
St. Anns

signed Geo: Forster Captn.　　　signed B. Arnold B General of the
Commanding the King's Troops　　　　　　　　　　Continental Troops

Two Majors
nine Captains
twenty Subalterns
Four hundred and forty three Soldiers.

But if the prisoners can be conducted in less Time, this Truce to cease on the Return of the last Boats employed on this Service on notice given

signed Geo: Forster Captn.
Commandg the Kings Troops

May 27th 1776 Answer. If Captn Forster wd chuse to have Hostilities commence in less time than six Days it will be perfectly agreable to Me provided the Time is fixed on and notice given this Evening.

signed B Arnold, B. Genl.

APPENDIX D
July 10, 1776, Continental Congress Resolutions

Journals of the Continental Congress, July 10, 1776[1]

That, having made diligent enquiry into the facts, they find, that a party of 390 continental troops, under the command of Colonel Bedel, was posted at the Cedars, about forty three miles above Montreal; that they had there formed some works of defence, the greater part of them picketed lines, the rest a breast work of earth, with two field pieces mounted:

That, on Wednesday the 15 of May, Colonel Bedel received intelligence, that a party of the enemy, consisting of about 600 regulars, Canadians and Indians, were on their way to attack his post, and were then within nine miles of it:[2] that Colonel Bedel, thereon, set out himself for Montreal, to procure a reinforcement; whereupon, the command of the Cedars devolved on Major Butterfield:

That, on Thursday, a reinforcement, under the command of Major Sherburne, marched from Montreal for the Cedars, while a larger detachment should be getting ready to proceed thither with Brigadier General Arnold:

That, on Friday the 17th,[3] the enemy, under the command of Captain Foster [sic], invested the post at the Cedars, and, for two days, kept up a loose, scattering fire; that Major Butterfield proposed, from the very first, to surrender the post, and refused repeated solicitations from his officers and men to permit them to sally out on the enemy:

That, on Sunday afternoon, a flag being sent in by the enemy, Major Butterfield agreed to surrender the fort and garrison to Captain Foster, capitulating with him, whether verbally or in writing does not appear, that the garrison should not be put into the hands of the savages, and that their baggage should not be plundered:

That, at the time of the surrender, the enemy consisted of about 40 regulars, 100 Canadians, and 500 Indians,[4] and had no cannon; the garrison had sustained no injury from their fire, but the having one man wounded;[5] they had twenty rounds of cartridges a man, 30 rounds for one field piece, five for another, half a barrel of gun powder, 15 lbs. of musket ball, and provisions sufficient to have lasted them twenty or thirty days: Major Butterfield knew that a reinforcement was on its way, and moreover, was so near the main body of the army, that he could not doubt of being supported by that:

That, immediately on the surrender, the garrison was put into the custody of the savages, who plundered them of their baggage, and even stripped them of their clothes;

That Major Sherburne, having landed on Monday the 20th, at Quinze Chenes [sic], about nine miles from the Cedars, and marched on with his party, consisting then of 100 men, to within four miles thereof, was there attacked by about 500 of the enemy:[6] that he maintained his ground about an hour, and then, being constrained to retreat, performed the same in good order, receiving and returning a constant fire for about forty minutes; when the enemy, finding means to post advanced parties in such a manner as to intercept their farther retreat, they also were made prisoners of war:

That they were immediately put into the custody of the savages, carried to where Major Butterfield and his party were, and stripped of their baggage and wearing apparel:

That two of them were put to death that evening, four or five others at different times, afterwards; one of whom was of those who surrendered on capitulation at the Cedars, and was killed on the 8th day after that surrender; that one was first shot, and, while retaining life and sensation, was roasted, as was related by his companion, now in possession of the savages, who himself saw the fact;[7] and that several others, being worn down by famine and cruelty, were left exposed in an island naked, and perishing with cold and hunger:

That, while Major Sherburne was in custody of the enemy, Captain Foster required of him, and the other officers, to sign a cartel, stipulating the exchange of themselves and their men for as many, of equal condition, of the British troops in our possession; farther [sic], that notwithstanding the exchange, neither themselves nor men should ever again bear arms against the British government; and for the performance of this, four hostages were to be delivered, which, they being under the absolute power of the enemy, did sign:

That on Sunday, the 26th, the prisoners were carried to Quinze Chenes, when it was discovered that General Arnold was approaching, and making dispositions to attack them:

That Captain Foster, having desired Major Sherburne to attend a flag, which he was about to send to General Arnold, for confirmation of the cartel, carried him into the council of Indians, then sitting, who told him "that it was a mercy never before shewn in their wars, that they had put to death so few of the prisoners; but that he must expect, and so inform General Arnold, that they should certainly kill every man who should thereafter fall into their hands:"

That Captain Foster joined in desiring that this bloody message should be delivered to General Arnold; and moreover, that he should be notified, that if he rejected the cartel, and attacked him, every man of the prisoners would be put to instant death:[8]

That General Arnold was extremely averse from entering into any agreement, and was at length induced to do it by no other motive than that of saving the prisoners from cruel and inhuman death, threatened in such terms as left no doubt it was to be perpetrated, and that he did in the end conclude it, after several flags received from Captain Foster, and a relinquishment by him of the unequal article restraining our soldiers from again bearing arms:

That the prisoners, so stipulated to be given up to the enemy, were not in the possession of General Arnold, nor under his direction, but were, at that time, distributed in various parts of the continent, under the orders of this house:

That four hostages were accordingly delivered to Captain Foster, who were immediately plundered and stripped by the savages; and on his part, were delivered 1 major, 4 captains, 16 subalterns, and 355 privates, as specified in a certificate of Captain James Osgood and others, of whom no specification by their names or numbers has yet been transmitted; that he retained 12 Canadians, alleging in his justification, express orders so to do; and that, living in a military government, they were to be considered even in a worse light than deserters from his majesty's armies; these he carried away in irons, but afterwards released: that he permitted the Indians to carry into their countries several others, natives of the United States, for purposes unknown:

That, during the time of their captivity, not half food was allowed the prisoners; they were continually insulted, buffeted, and ill treated by the savages; and when the first parties of them were carried off from the shore to be delivered to General Arnold, balls of mud were fired at them, and at the last parties, musket bullets.

Whereupon,
The Congress, came to the following resolutions:
Resolved, That all acts contrary to good faith, the laws of nature, or the customs of civilized nations, done by the officers or soldiers of his Britannic Majesty, or by

foreigners or savages taken into his service, are to be considered as done by his orders, unless indemnification be made, in cases which admit indemnification, and in all other cases, unless immediate and effective measures be taken by him, or by his officers, for bringing to condign punishment the authors, abettors, and perpetrators of the act:

That the plundering the baggage of the garrison at the Cedars, stripping them of their cloathes, and delivering them into the hands of the savages, was a breach of the capitulation on the part of the enemy, for which indemnification ought to be demanded:

That the murder of the prisoners of war was a gross and inhuman violation of the laws of nature and nations: that condign punishment should be inflicted on the authors, abettors, and perpetrators of the same; and that, for this purpose, it be required that they be delivered into our hands:

That the agreement entered into by General Arnold was a mere sponsion on his part, he not being invested with powers for the disposal of prisoners not in his possession, nor under his direction; and that, therefore, it is subject to be ratified or annulled, at the discretion of this house:

That the shameful surrender of the post at the Cedars is chargeable on the commanding officer: that such other of the prisoners as were taken there, shewed a willingness and desire to fight the enemy;[9] and that Major Sherburne, and the prisoners taken with him, though their disparity of numbers was great, fought the enemy bravely for a considerable time, and surrendered at last but on absolute necessity: on which considerations, and on which alone, resolved, that the said sponsion be ratified; and that an equal number of captives from the enemy, of the same rank and condition, be restored to them, as stipulated by the said sponsion:

That, previous to the delivery of the prisoners to be returned on our part, the British commander in Canada be required to deliver into our hands the authors, abettors, and perpetrators of the horrid murder committed on the prisoners, to suffer such punishment as their crime deserves; and also, to make indemnification for the plunder at the Cedars, taken contrary to the faith of the capitulation; and that, until such delivery and indemnification be made, the said prisoners be not delivered:

That, if the enemy shall commit any further violences, by putting to death, torturing, or otherwise ill treating the prisoners retained by them, or any of the hostages put into their hands, recourse be had to retaliation, as the sole means of stopping the progress of human butchery; and that, for that purpose, punishments of the same kinds and degree be inflicted on an equal number of the captives from them in our possession, till they shall be taught to respect the violated rights of nations:

That a copy of the above report and resolutions be transmitted to the commander in chief of the continental forces, to be by him sent to Generals Howe and Burgoyne.

NOTES

Abbreviations

AA4	Peter Force, ed. *American Archives*, 4th Series.
AA5	Peter Force, ed. *American Archives*, 5th Series.
APS	American Philosophical Society.
Avery Journal	David Avery Journal. David Avery Papers. Connecticut Historical Society; published as David Avery, "The Northern Campaign: From the Diary of the Rev. David Avery, Chaplain in Col. John Paterson's Regiment." *American Monthly Magazine* 18 (Jan.–June 1901) and 19 (July–Dec. 1901).
Butterfield Testimony	Major Butterfield's testimony respecting a breach of the Convention at the Cedars, June 1776. In *AA5*, vol. 1, ed. Peter Force.
DCB	*Dictionary of Canadian Biography* (online), http://www.biographi.ca/en/.
DRHNY	Edmund B. O'Callaghan, ed. *The Documentary History of the State of New York*, vol. 1; and *Documents Relative to the Colonial History of the State of New-York*, vols. 6–10.
DRNH	Nathaniel Bouton, ed., *Provincial Papers: Documents and Records Relating to the Province of New-Hampshire from 1764 to 1776*, vol. 7; *State Papers: Documents and Records Relating to the State of New-Hampshire from 1776 to 1783*, vol. 8; *Provincial and State Papers: Miscellaneous Documents and Records Relating to New Hampshire at Different Periods*, vol. 10; and Isaac W. Hammond, ed., *Town Papers: Documents Relating to Towns in New Hampshire*, vols. 11–13.

Estabrook-Wilkins Testimony	Captains Eastabrook's [sic] and Wilkins's Testimony respecting a breach of Convention at the Cedars. *AA5*, vol. 1, ed. Peter Force.
EWC	Eleazar Wheelock Collection. Rauner Special Library. Dartmouth College.
GJP	Guy Johnson Papers. Beinecke Rare Book and Manuscript Library. Yale University.
Hamtramck Testimony	John Hamtramck, July 11, 1776, Notes of Witnesses' Testimony concerning the Canadian Campaign. In *PTJ*, vol. 1.
HMNF	Historical Section of the General Staff. *A History of the Organization, Development and Service of the Military and Naval Forces of Canada From the Peace of Paris in 1763 to the Present Time.*
HP	MG21-Add.MSS., Haldimand Papers. Sir Frederick Haldimand. Unpublished Papers and Correspondence, British Library (microfilm), LAC.
IIADH	Francis Jennings, ed. *Iroquois Indians: A Documentary History.*
JBJ	John Butler Journal. Beinecke Rare Book and Manuscript Library. Yale University.
JCC	Worthington C. Ford, ed. *Journals of the Continental Congress, 1774–1789.*
LAC	Library and Archives Canada.
LDC	Smith, Paul H., ed. *Letters of Delegates to Congress, 1774–1789.* 25 vols. Washington, DC: Library of Congress, 1976–2000.
LOC	Library of Congress.
M246	RG93, Revolutionary War Rolls, M246, NARA.
M247	Papers of the Continental Congress, M247, NARA.
M804	RG15, Revolutionary War Pension and Bounty-Land Warrant Application Files, M804, NARA.
MACC	James Sullivan, ed. *Minutes of the Albany Committee of Correspondence, 1775–1778.*
NHHS	New Hampshire Historical Society.

NH Rolls	Isaac W. Hammond, ed. *The State of New Hampshire: Rolls of the Soldiers in the Revolutionary War, 1775, to May, 1777* . . . ; and *Rolls and Documents Relating to Soldiers in the Revolutionary War.*
NYPL	New York Public Library.
OB1P	Orderly Book of the 1st Pennsylvania Battalion of Foot, Society of the Cincinnati.
PGWRWS	W. W. Abbot, ed. *The Papers of George Washington, Revolutionary War Series.*
PSP	Philip Schuyler Papers. NYPL.
PSWJ	James Sullivan, ed. *The Papers of Sir William Johnson.*
PTJ	Julian P. Boyd, ed. *The Papers of Thomas Jefferson.*
Sherburne Testimony	Major Sherburne's Testimony on the Affair of the Cedars. In *PTJ*, vol. 1.
SKC	Samuel Kirkland Collection. http://elib.hamilton.edu/kirkland. Hamilton College Library.
UMPRDH	Le Programme de recherche en démographie historique, Université de Montréal. https://www.prdh-igd.com/en/Acces.

Notes to Preface

1. Victor Morin to J. B. Harkin, April 12, 1924, Historic Sites—Battle of Cidres [Cedars], 1775 [*sic*], fol. 310, Department of Canadian Heritage fonds, R5747-0-8-E.
2. For traditional treatments, see Edgar Aldrich, "The Affair of the Cedars and the Service of Colonel Timothy Bedel in the War of the Revolution," *Proceedings of the New Hampshire Historical Society* 3 (June 1897–June 1899): 194–231; Samuel E. Dawson, "The Massacre at the Cedars," *Canadian Monthly* 5 (Apr. 1874): 305–23; and Justin H. Smith, *Our Struggle for the Fourteenth Colony: Canada and the American Revolution* (New York: Knickerbocker Press, 1907), 2:357–87.
3. Gavin Watt, *Poisoned by Lies and Hypocrisy: America's First Attempt to Bring Liberty to Canada, 1775–1776* (Toronto: Dundurn, 2014). Paul L. Stevens's expansive dissertation considered Indian involvement at the Cedars in even more detail that showed the situation's complexity; but based on its format, it has effectively been limited to an academic audience; Paul L. Stevens, "His Majesty's "Savage" Allies: British Policy and the Northern Indians during the Revolutionary War, The Carleton Years, 1774–1778" (PhD diss., State University of New York at Buffalo, 1984).

4. Nathan Schmidt, *Native Americans in the American Revolution: How the War Divided, Devastated, and Transformed the Early American Indian World* (Santa Barbara, CA: Praeger, 2014), xxvii; ("essentially defensive...") George F. G. Stanley, "The Six Nations and the American Revolution," *Ontario History* 56 (Dec. 1964): 225.
5. ("catastrophe") James H. O'Donnell, "The World Turned Upside Down: The American Revolution as a Catastrophe for Native Americans," in "The American Indian and the American Revolution," ed. Francis Jennings, papers written for a conference of the Newberry Library Center for the History of the American Indian, 21–22 February 1775 (unpublished), 80; ("devastated...") Schmidt, *Native Americans in the American Revolution*, title.
6. Michael Witgen, *An Infinity of Nations: How the Native New World Shaped Early North America* (Philadelphia: University of Pennsylvania Press, 2012), 20.
7. Pekka Hämäläinen and Samuel Truett, "On Borderlands," *Journal of American History* 98 (Sept. 2011): 338.

Chapter 1

1. Although contemporary practice generally identified Indians by either European or Native names, the author prefers a construction of combined names in this work.
2. (descriptions) Ludwig von Closen, *The Revolutionary Journal of Baron Ludwig von Closen*, trans. and ed. Evelyn M. Acomb (Chapel Hill: University of North Carolina Press, 1958), 37–38; Edward Bucknam and Seth Wales to Colonel Ba[y]lley and Colonel Hurd, June 20, 1775, Nathaniel Bouton, ed., *Provincial Papers. Documents and Records Relating to the Province of New-Hampshire from 1764 to 1776* (Nashua, NH: Orren C. Moore, 1873), 7:525 (hereafter cited as *DRNH*); ("tall Indian figure") Peter S. Du Ponceau, "The Autobiography of Peter Stephen Du Ponceau," in James L. Whitehead, ed., *Pennsylvania Magazine of History and Biography* 63 (Apr. 1939): 222; Franklin B. Hough, *A History of St. Lawrence and Franklin Counties, New York...* (Albany, NY: Little, 1853), 197.
3. ("a Chief...") George Washington to John Hancock, August 4–5, 1775, W. W. Abbot, ed., *The Papers of George Washington, Revolutionary War Series* (Charlottesville: University Press of Virginia, 1985–), 1:229 (hereafter cited as *PGWRWS*). Historically, English-speakers spelled Kahnawake in several phonetic variations of "Caughnawaga."
4. ("greatest influence," "central situation") John Wheelock, "The present state & situation of the Indian Tribes in the Province of Quebec," May 1779, 779301, Eleazar Wheelock Collection, Dartmouth College (hereafter cited as EWC); Jean-Pierre Sawaya, *La Fédération des Sept Feux de la Vallée du Saint-Laurent: XVIIe au XIXe Xiècle* (Sillery, QC: Septentrion, 1998), 51–52.
5. "Petition from Capt Vincent an Indian..., June 24, 1785," i42 v8 r56 p83, Papers of the Continental Congress, M247 (hereafter cited as M247), National Archives and Records Administration (hereafter cited as NARA); Edward Bucknam and Seth Wales

to Jacob Bayley and John Hurd, June 20, 1775, and John Hurd to New-Hampshire Committee of Safety, July 27, 1775, *DRNH*, 7:525, 569.
6. ("the whole influence...") "Boston, December 19," *Norwich Packet* (CT), December 22, 1774. See also "New-Haven, Dec. 14," *Connecticut Courant* (Hartford), December 19, 1774; Eleazar Wheelock to Roger Sherman, March 22, 1775, 775222, EWC.
7. Although Seven Nations villages cooperated throughout most of their history, they only appear to have formalized that confederacy name after the British conquest of Canada. See Denys Delâge and J-P Sawaya, "Les origines de la Fédération des Sept-Feux," *Recherches amérindiennes au Québec* 31, no. 2 (2001): 43; Jean-François Lozier, "History, Historiography, and the Courts: The St Lawrence Mission Villages and the Fall of New France," in *Remembering 1759: The Conquest of Canada in Historical Memory*, ed. Phillip Buckner and John G. Reid, (Toronto: University of Toronto Press, 2012), 117.
8. Account by George Washington and James Mackay of the Capitulation of Fort Necessity, July 19, 1754, and George Washington's Account of the Capitulation of Fort Necessity [1786], W. W. Abbot, ed., *The Papers of George Washington, Colonial Series* (Charlottesville: University Press of Virginia, 1983), 1:160, 172–73; (Kahnawakes and Kanesatakes) Jon W. Parmenter, "At the Wood's Edge: Iroquois Foreign Relations, 1727–1768" (PhD diss., University of Michigan, 1999), 313, 318.
9. ("cruel Butcheries") George Washington to Francis Halkett, April 12, 1758; *Papers of George Washington, Colonial Series*, 5:125; (Monongahela, Louis) David L. Preston, *Braddock's Defeat: The Battle of the Monongahela and the Road to Revolution* (New York: Oxford University Press, 2015), 135, 161; Eleazar Williams, "Life of Colonel Louis Cook," Papers of Franklin B. Hough Papers, New York State Archives; Barbara Graymont, "Atiatoharongwen," *Dictionary of Canadian Biography* online, http://www.biographi.ca/en/ (hereafter cited as *DCB*).
10. ("keep the seven...") "Petition from Capt Vincent an Indian..., June 24, 1785," i42 v8 r56 p83, M247; ("tolerably well") John Hurd to New-Hampshire Committee of Safety, July 27, 1775, *DRNH*, 7:569 [also *AA4*, 2:1041–42]; ("if any...") George Washington to John Hancock, August 4–5, 1775, *PGWRWS*, 1:229; (invasion) June 27, 1775, Worthington C. Ford, ed., *Journals of the Continental Congress, 1774–1789* (Washington, DC, 1905), 2:109 (hereafter cited as *JCC*).
11. ("have a good Effect") George Washington to John Hancock, August 4–5, 1775, *PGWRWS*, 1:229; ("very late intelligence," "the Canadians and Indians...") "Cambridge, August 3," *Essex Journal*, August 4, 1775.
12. Massachusetts House of Representatives, August 4, 1775, Peter Force, ed., *American Archives*, 4th Series (Washington, DC: M. St. Clair Clarke and Peter Force, 1837–1853), 3:306 (hereafter cited as *AA4*); Report of the Committee to confer with Lewis..., Massachusetts House of Representatives, August 3, 1775, *AA4*, 3:301–2. The Canadians were La Corne St. Luc and Pierre Hertel de Beaubassin.
13. ("inveterate enemies," "depredations") Massachusetts Provincial Congress, July 8, 1775, *DRNH*, 7:562. Carleton and his agents made multiple attempts to recruit Seven Nations allies, but Indian agent Claude de Lorimier reported that until mid-June,

only a single "scoundrel" Kahnawake joined them; Claude de Lorimier, *At War with the Americans: The Journal of Claude-Nicolas-Guillaume de Lorimier*, trans. and ed. Peter Aichinger (Victoria, BC: Press Porcepic, 1987), 27–28. See also Diary, September 10–27, 1774, Daniel Claus and Family Fonds, MG19-F1 v21 pt. 2 (microfilm C-1483 image 896), Library and Archives Canada (hereafter cited as LAC); "New-Haven, Dec. 14," *Connecticut Courant* (Hartford), December 19, 1774.

14. (common interests) Thomas G. M. Peace, "Two Conquests: Aboriginal Experiences of the Fall of New France and Acadia" (PhD diss., York University, Toronto, 2011), 264. Exact council fire locations are unclear and apparently changed over time, but historian Jean-Pierre Sawaya identified Kahnawake Iroquois, the Wendake Hurons (Lorette), the Odanak (St. Francis) and Wôlinak Abenakis, the Pointe du Lac Algonquins, the Kanesatake Iroquois, Nipissing and Algonquins, and the Akwesasne Iroquois as Seven Nations members; Jean-Pierre Sawaya, "Les Amérindiens domiciliés et le protestantisme au XVIIIe siècle: Eleazar Wheelock et le Dartmouth College," *Historical Studies in Education/Revue d'histoire de l'éducation* 22, no. 2 (Fall 2010): 25.

15. Sawaya, *La Fédération des Sept Feux*, 69–70; William N. Fenton, *The Great Law and the Longhouse: A Political History of the Iroquois Confederacy* (Norman: University of Oklahoma Press, 1998), 29, 359; Jon W. Parmenter and Mark P. Robinson, "The Perils and Possibilities of Wartime Neutrality on the Edges of Empire: Iroquois and Acadians between the French and British in North America, 1744–1760," *Diplomatic History* 31, no. 2 (Apr. 2007): 204. For an observant outsider's view of Indian conduct in council, see Tench Tilghman, *Memoir of Lieut. Col. Tench Tilghman, Secretary and Aid to Washington . . .* , ed. S. A. Harrison (Albany, NY: J. Munsell, 1876), 86, 94, 99. Historical terminology is inconsistent, but "sachem" often refers to hereditary clan positions, while "chief" can describe any leader formally or temporarily recognized for merit, reputation, or prestige.

16. ("wanting coercive power") Arthur Lee, "Extracts of Some Letters, from Sir William Johnson, Bart. to Arthur Lee, M.D. F.R.S. on the Customs, Manners, and Language of the Northern Indians of America," *Philosophical Transactions of the Royal Society of London* 63, no. 1 (Jan. 1973): 144.

17. "History of Kahnawá:ke," Mohawk Council of Kahnawá:ke, http://www.kahnawake.com/community/history.asp; Karim Tiro, "The Dilemmas of Alliance: The Oneida Indian Nation in the American Revolution," in *War and Society in the American Revolution: Mobilization and Home Fronts*, ed. John Resch and Walter Sargent (DeKalb: Northern Illinois University Press, 2007), 218; Colin G. Calloway, *The American Revolution in Indian Country* (Cambridge: Cambridge University Press, 1995), 35; Gerald R. Alfred, "The Meaning of Self-Government in Kahnawake," Research Program of the Royal Commission on Aboriginal Peoples (July 1994), [n.p.]; Gretchen Lynn Green, "A New People in an Age of War: The Kahnawake Iroquois, 1667–1760" (PhD diss., College of William and Mary, 1991), 300–301; David Blanchard, *Seven Generations: A History of the Kanienkehaka* (Kahnawake, QC: Kahnawake Survival School, 1980), 202; ("a sort of Republic") M. de Beauharnois to Count de Maurepas, September 21, 1741, Edmund B. O'Callaghan, ed., *Documents Relative to the Colonial History of the*

State of New-York (Albany, NY: Weed, Parsons, 1855–58), 9:1071 (hereafter cited as *DRHNY*); ("... independent & free agents") "Memorandum of the Rebel Invasion of Canada in 1775," Daniel Claus, CO 42/36 (microfilm), fols. 37–38a, LAC.

18. ("internal schism") Peace, "Two Conquests," 355, 348–49; Mary Druke Becker, "'We Are an Independent Nation': A History of Iroquois Sovereignty," *Buffalo Law Review* 46, no 3 (Oct. 1998): 983–84; ("active neutrality") Parmenter and Robinson, "Perils and Possibilities of Wartime Neutrality," 175–76. See also Tiro, "Dilemmas of Alliance," 217, 222; William N. Fenton, "Factionalism in American Indian Society," in *Actes du IVe Congrès International des Sciences Anthropologiques et Ethnologiques, Vienne, 1–8 Septembre 1952*, vol. 2 (Vienna: Adolf Holzhausen, 1965), 338; Caitlin A. Fitz, "'Suspected on Both Sides': Little Abraham, Iroquois Neutrality, and the American Revolution," *Journal of the Early Republic* 28, no. 3 (Fall 2008): 301; Thomas Peace, "Maintaining Connections: Lorette during the Eighteenth Century," in Thomas Peace and Kathryn M. Labelle, eds., *From Huronia to Wendakes: Adversity, Migration, and Resilience, 1650–1900* (Norman: University of Oklahoma Press, 2016), 80; Stevens, "His Majesty's 'Savage' Allies," 1457–58.

19. An Odanak Abenaki delegation visited Cambridge and Watertown two weeks after Louis; George Washington to Philip Schuyler, August 14, 1775, *PGWRWS*, 1:305; Report of the Committee appointed to confer with the Chief of the St. François Tribe, Massachusetts House of Representatives, August 17, 1775, *AA4*, 3:339–40.

20. Theodore G. Corbett, *A Clash of Cultures on the Warpath of Nations: The Colonial Wars in the Hudson-Champlain Valley* (Fleischmanns, NY: Purple Mountain Press, 2002), 71, 82; José E. Igartua, "The Merchants and *Négociants* of Montreal, 1750–1775: A Study in Socio-Economic History" (PhD diss., Michigan State University, 1974), 54; Walter S. Dunn, *Opening New Markets: The British Army and the Old Northwest* (Westport, CT: Praeger, 2002), 47; Franklin B. Hough, *A History of St. Lawrence and Franklin Counties*, 184; Du Ponceau, "Autobiography," 222; (mistreatment) D. Peter MacLeod, *The Canadian Iroquois and the Seven Years' War* (Toronto: Dundurn, 1996), 181–82, 186–87; (interests) Jean-Pierre Sawaya, *Alliance et dépendance: Comment la Couronne britannique a obtenu la collaboration des Indiens de la vallée du Saint-Laurent entre 1760 et 1774* (Sillery, QC: Septentrion, 2002), 25, 66–67; Alan Taylor, *The Divided Ground: Indians, Settlers, and the Northern Borderland of the American Revolution* (New York: Alfred A. Knopf, 2006), 36–37; Stevens, "His Majesty's 'Savage' Allies," 95.

21. (kin relations) Stevens, "His Majesty's 'Savage' Allies," 374; Gerald R. Alfred, *Heeding the Voices of Our Ancestors: Kahnawake Mohawk Politics and the Rise of Native Nationalism* (Toronto: Oxford University Press, 1995), 49; E. J. Devine, *Historic Caughnawaga* (Montreal: Messenger Press, 1922), 296–97.

22. Williams, "Life of Colonel Louis Cook"; ("Black Lewa") Edward Bucknam and Seth Wales to Colonel Ba[y]ley and Colonel Hurd, June 20, 1775, *DRNH*, 7:525 [also *AA4*, 2:1041–42]; ("Louis le Nègre") Lorimier, *At War*, 28; ("Whether Native ...") Evan Haefeli and Kevin Sweeney, *Captive Histories: English, French, and Native Narratives of the 1704 Deerfield Raid* (Amherst: University of Massachusetts Press, 2006), 245,

251; Graymont, "Atiatoharongwen"; Hough, *History of St. Lawrence and Franklin Counties*, 182; Preston, *Braddock's Defeat*, 135.

23. Ebenezer Parkman, *The Story of the Rice Boys, Captured by the Indians, August 8, 1704* (Westborough, MA: Westborough Historical Society, 1906), 4–5; (visits) Emma L. Coleman, *New England Captives Carried to Canada between 1677 and 1760 during the French and Indian Wars* (Portland, ME: Southworth Press, 1925), 1:324–26; ("expressed great . . .") Copy for the Press of Mr. Ripley's Tour, 21 September 1772, 772521.2, EWC. Ogagragighte is transcribed several different ways. Originally named Timothy Rice, he was captured in Chauncey (now Westborough), Massachusetts.

24. Zadock Steele, *The Indian Captive: Or a Narrative of the Captivity and Suffering of Zadock Steele*. . . . (Montpelier, VT: E. P. Walton, 1818), 62–63; Neil Goodwin, *We Go as Captives: The Royalton Raid and the Shadow War on the Revolutionary Frontier* (Barre: Vermont Historical Society, 2010), 46, 76; (declined repatriation) "General Return of the English prisoners . . . ," June 25, 1750, *DRHNY*, 10:214; (interpreter for Indian department) Journal of Indian Affairs, May 29, 1764, and Daniel Claus' Account, Expenses for Canada [1773–75], James Sullivan, ed., *The Papers of Sir William Johnson* (Albany: University of the State of New York, 1953), 11:207, 13:718, 720, 721 (hereafter cited as *PSWJ*); ("headman") Richard Montgomery to Philip Schuyler, September 24, 1775, *AA4*, 3:840. Sanórese was also known as Philip Philips, perhaps his original name. Ethnohistorian Nancy Hagedorn sums up Sanórese's biographical vagaries: "Much of this information is very sketchy, and subject to further revision." Nancy L. Hagedorn, "'A Friend to Go between Them': The Interpreter as Cultural Broker during Anglo-Iroquois Councils, 1740–70," *Ethnohistory* 35, no. 1 (1988): 73.

25. ("head chief") "Petition from Capt Vincent an Indian . . . June 24, 1785," i42 v8 r56 p83, M247; Collection Élisée Choquet P60, S2, D265, p9, Bibliothèque et Archives nationales du Québec; "Stacey, John" and "A YON WAH THA," Charles Cooke, Iroquois personal names, 1900–1951, American Philosophical Society (hereafter cited as APS). See Len Travers, *Hodges' Scout: A Lost Patrol of the French and Indian War* (Baltimore: Johns Hopkins University Press, 2015). Historical sources offer various accounts of Stacey's background, but evidence most clearly connects Kahnawake chief Stacey with a previous life as Pvt. John Stacey, reported missing after Hodges's September 1756 ambush. See September 26, 1772, appendix entry in Eleazar Wheelock, *A Continuation of the Narrative of the Indian Charity School, Begun in Lebanon in Connecticut; Now Incorporated with Dartmouth-College, in Hanover, in the Province of New-Hampshire* (Hartford, CT, 1773), 40, and *Vital Records of Ipswich, Massachusetts, to the Year 1850* (Salem, MA: Essex Institute, 1910), 1:349. Special thanks to Len Travers for identifying key resources regarding Stacey's precapture life.

26. ("thirst for Learning . . .") Eleazar Wheelock, Copy for the Press of Mr. Ripley's Tour, September 21, 1772, 772521.2, EWC. See also Colin G. Calloway, *New Worlds for All: Indians, Europeans, and the Remaking of Early America* (Baltimore: Johns Hopkins University Press, 1997), 180; Peace, "Maintaining Connections," 77, 98; Wheelock, *Continuation of the Narrative* (1773), 11; Colin G. Calloway, *The Indian History of an*

American Institution: Native Americans and Dartmouth (Hanover, NH: Dartmouth College Press, 2010), 193. Kanesatake, a Sulpician mission, did not face this same missionary-education crisis.

27. (host to missionaries) Diary and Account Book, Mission to the Caughnawaga Indians, 1772–1774, Ms 772900-3, EWC; (visits) Wheelock, *Continuation of the Narrative* (1773), 8–9; Sawaya, "Les Amérindiens domiciliés," 26, 28–29; Frederick Chase, *A History of Dartmouth College and the Town of Hanover, New Hampshire*, vol. 1 (Cambridge, MA: University Press, 1891), 315. By Sawaya's accounting, there were four or five Caughnwagas, five St. Francis Abenakis, and one Lorette Huron at Wheelock's school in 1775.

28. ("continual Intercourse," "surest Bullwark") Eleazar Wheelock to David MacCluer, March 20, 1775, 775220.1, EWC.

29. ("that if . . .") John Brown to the Committee of Correspondence in Boston, March 29, 1775, James P. Baxter, *Documentary History of the State of Maine* (Portland, ME: Lefavor-Tower Company, 1910), 14:240–41 [also *AA4*, 2:244]. Unfortunately, none of the Putnam-Kahnawake correspondence is extant.

30. (communication) Philip Schuyler to Continental Congress, July 28, 1775, *AA4*, 2:1745; Philip Schuyler to George Washington, August 6, 1775, *AA4*, 3:50; Deposition of Pierre Charlan, August 6, 1775, Historical Section of the General Staff, *A History of the Organization, Development and Service of the Military and Naval Forces of Canada from the Peace of Paris in 1763 to the Present Time* (Quebec: King's Printer, 1919), 2:68 (hereafter cited as *HMNF*).

31. The Stockbridges' original message was intended to reassure the Kahnawakes that the rebels had only taken Fort Ticonderoga in self-defense, requesting them "to take no part in the present dispute"; Stockbridge Indians to the Caghnawagas, May 13, 1775, James Sullivan, ed., *Minutes of the Albany Committee of Correspondence, 1775–1778* (Albany: University of the State of New York, 1923), 1:129 (hereafter cited as *MACC*); ("take no part") Barnabas Deane to Silas Deane, June 1, 1775, "Correspondence of Silas Deane, Delegate to the Congress at Philadelphia, 1774–76," in *Collections of the Connecticut Historical Society*, vol. 2 (Hartford: Connecticut Historical Society, 1870), 248. At Ticonderoga, Arnold and Allen gave the Stockbridges letters to deliver to Kahnawake, probably some of those found in the packs. Allen's message was particularly belligerent, explicitly calling the Seven Nations to join the Americans in arms. Benedict Arnold to Thomas Walker, Ticonderoga, May 20, 1775, and Ethan Allen to "The Councillers at Koianawago . . . ," May 24, 1775, both enclosed in Guy Carleton to Dartmouth, June 7, 1775, CO 42/34 fols. 148–50. Wampum—strings or belts of beads in meaningful patterns—was used to communicate and formalize diplomatic messages between northeast Indian nations.

32. ("high threatening . . . ," "did fight at all . . .") Extract of a Letter from a Gentlemen at Stockbridge to a Gentlemen of the Continental Congress, June 22, 1775, *AA4*, 2:1060–61; ("did not care . . . ," "I have not known . . .") *MACC*, 1:131–32. A report of the Stockbridges' Montreal affair reached the Continental Congress on June 29, 1775, *JCC*, 2:110–11.

Chapter 2

1. Guy Johnson to Lord Dartmouth, October 12, 1775, Kenneth Davies, ed. *Documents of the American Revolution, 1770–1783* (Dublin: Irish University Press, 1976), 11:142.
2. Harley L. Gibb, "Colonel Guy Johnson, Superintendent General of Indian Affairs, 1774–82," *Papers of the Michigan Academy of Science, Arts and Letters* 27 (1941): 596; Jonathan G. Rossie, "Johnson, Guy," *DCB*; Barbara Graymont, *The Iroquois and the American Revolution* (Syracuse, NY: Syracuse University Press, 1988), 64.
3. Extracts from the Records of Indian Transactions under the Super-Intendency of Colo. Guy Johnson during the year 1775, in Francis Jennings, ed., *Iroquois Indians: A Documentary History* (Woodbridge, CT: Research Publications, 1984) (hereafter cited as *IIADH*); Memorandum from Colonel Maclean to Colonel Johnson, July 8, 1775, Guy Johnson Papers, Beinecke Library, Yale University (hereafter cited as GJP).
4. ("to cooperate . . .") Extracts from the Records of Indian Transactions under the Super-Intendency of Colo. Guy Johnson during the year 1775, PRO, CO 5/77, *IIADH*; (ten men, war belts) Benjamin Davis Deposition, August 8, 1775, Philip Schuyler Papers (hereafter cited as PSP), New York Public Library (hereafter cited as NYPL) (microfilm); ("he was to kindle . . .") Speech of the Onondaga Sachem Onwasgwinghte, Conference . . . at German-Flats, August 13, 1776, Peter Force, ed., *American Archives*, 5th Series (Washington, DC: M. St. Clair Clarke and Peter Force, 1837–53), 1:1046 (hereafter cited as *AA5*); Cayuga Chief Fish Carrier speech, "At a Meeting," May 5, 1776, and ("to hear what . . .") Keyangorachta speech, June 29, 1776, John Butler Journal, Beinecke Library, Yale University (hereafter cited as JBJ); (220) Guy Johnson to Lord Dartmouth, October 12, 1775, *DRHNY*, 8:636.
5. "Memorandum of the Rebel Invasion of Canada in 1775," Daniel Claus, CO 42/36 (microfilm), fols. 37–38a, LAC; Graymont, *Iroquois in the American Revolution*, 67; (1,664 Indians) Journal of Colonel Guy Johnson from May to November, 1775, *DRHNY*, 8:659; Marie-Thérèse Benoist to François Baby, August 14, 1775, Hospice-Anthelme Jean-Baptiste Verreau, ed., *Invasion du Canada, Collection de Mémoires Recueillis et Annotes* (Montreal: Eusèbe Senecal, 1873), 308.
6. ("delivered to each . . .") Philip Schuyler to John Hancock, December 14, 1775, i170 v1 r189 pp222–23, M247; (cannibalism) Daniel K. Richter, "War and Culture: The Iroquois Experience," *William and Mary Quarterly*, 3rd ser., 40, no. 4 (Oct. 1983): 534n22; Graymont, *Iroquois in the American Revolution*, 68; ("Chiefs and Warriors . . .") "Quebec, August 10," *Quebec Gazette*, August 10, 1775.
7. This council apparently occurred between June14 and 18. ("jointly determine to act . . .") James Dean to Jonathan Trumbull, "A Short Acco of a Tour undertaken 9th March 1775 . . . to Canada," *AA4*, 2:1595; ("Professions of Zeal . . .") Guy Carleton to Guy Johnson, Montreal, June 19, 1775, GJP; ("Indians had taken . . .") Report of Dirck Swart, June 20, 1775, *MACC*, 1:91.
8. ("seven Nations had . . .") An Account of the voyage of Captain Remember Baker, begun the 13th day of July . . . , *AA4*, 2:1735; Report of Gerrit Roseboom, July 14, 1775,

MACC, 1:155 [also *AA4*, 2:1670]; ("to save themselves...") Eleazar Wheelock to the Congress at Exeter, June 28, 1775, 775378.1, EWC; James Dean to Jonathan Trumbull, "A Short Acco of a Tour undertaken 9th March 1775... to Canada," *AA4*, 2:1595; Lorimier, *At War*, 28.

9. (Fort St. Johns) Guy Carleton to Lord Dartmouth, August 14, 1775, *HMNF*, 2:69; Lorimier, *At War*, 28; ("situated...") Alexander Mackenzie, *Voyages from Montreal through the Continent of North America to the Frozen and Pacific Oceans in 1789 and 1793 with an Account of the Rise and State of the Fur Trade* (New York: A. S. Barnes, 1903), 1:lvii; (three nations) Stevens, "His Majesty's 'Savage' Allies," 89–90; "Memorandum on Six Nations and Other Confederacies," November 18, 1763, *PSWJ*, 4:242; (population estimate) "Present State of the Northern Indians," November 18, 1763, *DRHNY*, 7:582; and John A. Dickinson and Jan Grabowski, "Les Populations Amérindiennes de la Vallée Laurentienne, 1608–1765," *Annales de Démographie Historique* (1993): 57. Kanesatake had many spelling variations, most commonly Canasadaga, and was also referred to as the Lake of Two Mountains village; Brenda Katlatont Gabriel-Doxtater and Arlette Kawanatatie Van den Hende, *At the Woods' Edge: An Anthology of the History of the People of Kanehsatà:ke* (Kanesatake, QC: Kanesatake Education Center, 1995), 25. The Anishinaabeg villagers may have called their home Oka, the modern Canadian town's name; Algonquins of Ontario, *History of the Algonquins*, http://www.tanakiwin.com/wp-system/uploads/2013/10/a-History-of-the-Algonquins.pdf. Arundaks were often simply described as "Algonquins," or "Roundocks."

10. (land claims) George Heriot, *Travels through the Canadas, Containing a Description of the Picturesque Scenery on Some of the Rivers and Lakes...* (Philadelphia: M. Carey, 1813), 248–49; Sawaya, "Les Amérindiens domiciliés," 27–28; Lucien Lemieux, "Montgolfier, Étienne," *DCB*; Evan Haefeli and Kevin Sweeney, *Captors and Captives: The 1704 French and Indian Raid on Deerfield* (Amherst: University of Massachusetts Press, 2003), 67; Olivier Maurault, "Oka: Les vicissitudes d'une mission sauvage," *Revue Trimestrielle Canadienne* 16 (June 1930): 147; Gordon M. Day, "Nipissing," in *Handbook of North American Indians*, vol. 15: *Northeast*, ed. Bruce G. Trigger (Washington, DC: Smithsonian Institution, 1978), 790. Montgolfier was also the Catholic diocese's Montreal region vicar general.

11. (Province line, "watch the Motions...") "Memorandum of the Rebel Invasion of Canada in 1775," Daniel Claus, CO 42/36 (microfilm), fol. 38b, LAC; (camps/scouts) Guy Johnson to Dartmouth, October 12, 1775, and ("lest cruelties...") Guy Carleton to Lord Dartmouth, October 25, 1775, Davies, *Documents of the American Revolution*, 11:142, 166. Claude Lorimier described a long-range Lake Champlain scout with a single Kahnawake companion going far south of the provincial line, but this appears to have been done on his own, before Carleton and Johnson established their policy for Fort Saint Johns. Lorimier, *At War*, 28.

12. ("the most respectable...") John Long, *John Long's Voyages and Travels, in the Years 1768–1788*, ed. Milo Milton Quaife (Chicago: Lakeside Press, 1922), 9; ("regular form")

Louis Antoine Bougainville, *Adventure in the Wilderness: The American Journals of Louis Antoine de Bougainville, 1756–1760*, ed. and trans. Edward P. Hamilton (Norman: University of Oklahoma Press, 1964), 125; Kahnawake Longhouse, "History and Culture," http://www.kahnawakelonghouse.com/index.php?mid=2&p=1; (ninety houses—1785) Joseph Hadfield, *An Englishman in America, 1785: Being the Diary of Joseph Hadfield*, ed. and ann. Douglas S. Robertson (Toronto: Hunter-Rose, 1933), 49; ("hutts") Francis Grant, "Journal from New York to Canada, 1767," *New York History* 30 (1932): 308.

13. "Petition from Capt Vincent an Indian . . . , June 24, 1785," i42 v8 r56 p83, M247. This source includes firsthand narration by Louis.

14. (departures) Journal of Colonel Guy Johnson from May to November, 1775, *DRHNY*, 8:660; (about 500) Guy Johnson to Lord Dartmouth, October 12, 1775, Davies, *Documents of the American Revolution*, 11:142; ("slender force") Extracts from the Records of Indian Transactions under the Super-Intendency of Colo. Guy Johnson during the year 1775, PRO, CO 5/77, *IIADH*.

15. Declaration of neutrality, [June 1775], Samuel Kirkland Collection, Hamilton College Library (hereafter cited as SKC); (Dean and Kirkland) Graymont, *Iroquois in the American Revolution*, 65; Fenton, *Great Law and the Longhouse*, 586–88, 592; David J. Norton, *Rebellious Younger Brother, Oneida Leadership and Diplomacy, 1750–1800* (DeKalb: Northern Illinois University Press, 2009), 63–65; Karim M. Tiro, "Ambivalent Allies: Strategy and the Native Americans," in Donald Stoker, et al, eds. *Strategy in the American War of Independence: A Global Approach* (New York: Routledge, 2010), 128; James K. Martin, "A Contagion of Violence: The Ideal of *Jus in Bello* versus the Realities of Fighting on the New York Frontier during the Revolutionary War," *Journal of Military Ethics* 14, no. 1 (May 2015): 60; ("remain at home . . .") A Speech to the Six Confederate Nations . . . from the Twelve United Colonies, July 13, 1775, *AA4*, 2:1880–81. Samuel Kirkland visited Philadelphia early in the summer to help craft Congress's Six Nations policy and messaging.

16. (council fire) A Speech to the Six Confederate Nations . . . from the Twelve United Colonies, July 13, 1775, *AA4*, 2:1882–83; (council fire keeper) Graymont, *Iroquois in the American Revolution*, 69; Fenton, *Great Law and the Longhouse*, 594; Philip Schuyler to John Hancock, June 29, 1775, i170 v1 r189 p4, M247; Ralph T. Pastore, "The Board of Commissioners for Indian Affairs in the Northern Department and the Iroquois Indians, 1775–1778" (PhD diss., University of Notre Dame, 1972), 32. Sir William Johnson had moved the council fire from Albany to Johnson Hall, but Guy Johnson abandoned it when he left for Canada, creating the opportunity to "rekindle" Albany's fire. Reflecting the dynamic situation in Canada, Oneidas declined the commissioners' request to invite Kahnawakes to join the upcoming Albany council, claiming that Guy Johnson had disrupted affairs in the north; Proceedings of the Commissioners of the Twelve United Colonies with the Six Nations, August 15, 1775, *DRHNY*, 8:606–7.

17. ("there was about 500 ...") Aaron Barlow, "The March to Montreal and Quebec, June–Dec.] 1775," *American Historical Register* 2 (1895): 642; ("only the Oneida ...") Schmidt, *Native Americans in the American Revolution*, 130; Graymont, *Iroquois in the American Revolution*, 70–72; ("smoaked the pipe ...") Notes from a conference, August 1776, PSP; At a treaty continued with the Indians of the Six Nations at Albany, August 31, 1775, *DRHNY*, 8:609–22.
18. ("live on neutral ground ...") James E. Seaver, *Life of Mary Jemison: Deh-he-wa-mis; The White Woman of the Genesee* (New York: Miller, Orton & Mulligan, 1856), 112–13; Fenton, *Great Law and the Longhouse*, 330, 346, 348, 365; Robert W. Venables, "'Faithful Allies of the King': The Crown's Haudenosaunee Allies in the Revolutionary Struggle for New York," in Joseph S. Tiedemann, Eugene R. Fingerhut, and Robert W. Venables, eds., *The Other Loyalists: Ordinary People, Royalism, and the Revolution in the Middle Colonies, 1763–1787* (Albany: State University of New York Press, 2009), 139; (neutrality, avoiding provocation) Ralph T. Pastore, "Congress and the Six Nations, 1775–1778," *Niagara Frontier* 20 (1973): 95; Tiro, "Dilemmas of Alliance," 216–17.
19. (Louis visits Schuyler) Williams, "Life of Colonel Louis Cook"; (orders) Orders to Capt. Remember Baker, July 27, 1775, and Inquiries to be made by Major Brown, [undated, late July 1775], Orderly Book of Philip John Schuyler, 58, 65, Huntington Library; ("the Americans had ...") Lorimier, *At War*, 28; John Brown to Jonathan Trumbull, August 14, 1775, *AA4*, 3:135–36. Eleazar Williams's Louis Cook biography must be treated carefully—Williams frequently exaggerated and fabricated facts, but he also had intimate access to community history, just one generation removed from the Revolutionary War era.
20. (August 22) Journal of Colonel Guy Johnson from May to November, 1775, *DRHNY*, 8:660; ("express orders ...") Philip Schuyler to Commissioners for Indian Affairs, August 31, 1775, *AA4*, 3:493; (location) "Account of a Skirmish happened on Lake Champlain," *Quebec Gazette*, August 31, 1775.
21. (Baker affair reactions) Philip Schuyler to Jonathan Trumbull, and Philip Schuyler to Commissioners for Indian Affairs, August 31, 1775, *AA4*, 3:469, 493; Oliver Wolcott to Philip Schuyler, September 1, 1775, PSP; ("owing in a great measure," casualties) James Livingston to Philip Schuyler, [August 1775], Manuscripts and Archives Division, New York Public Library Digital Collections; Lorimier, *At War*, 28; Journal of Colonel Guy Johnson from May to November, 1775, *DRHNY*, 8:660. These contemporary casualty reports vary in detail: Lorimier, present, recorded two Algonquins wounded (probably Kanesatake Arundaks); Johnson reported three Indians wounded; Livingston told General Schuyler that two Kahnawakes were killed—perhaps reflecting the common conflation of that nation with the rest of the Seven Nations.
22. ("a peaceable message ...") Philip Schuyler to Commissioners for Indian Affairs, August 31, 1775, *AA4*, 3:493.
23. (manifesto) Philip Schuyler to the Inhabitants of Canada, September 5, 1775, *AA4*, 3:671–72.

Chapter 3

1. Later in life, Lorimier documented his exploits in an invaluable memoir, *Mes Services pendant la Guerre Americaine de 1775* (published in the 1870s, and in translation a century later as *At War with the Americans*—the original manuscript is apparently lost). Claude-Nicholas-Guillaume de Lorimier, *Mes Services pendant la Guerre Americaine de 1775: Memoire de M. de Lorimier*, ed. Hospice-Anthelme Jean-Baptiste Verreau (Montreal: Eusebe Senecal, 1871). As an Indian interpreter and cultural broker, Lorimier is the rare primary source who regularly identified Native participants by name or nation. On the other hand, his memoir must be carefully assessed for accuracy. Historian Gavin Watt identified Lorimier's "tendency to gasconade," and even in the chevalier's day, a British officer noted that the Canadian had "an unhappy failing of mistaking facts"; Gavin K. Watt, "Action at Sabbath Day Point, March 20, 1777," *Journal of the American Revolution* (June 5, 2017), https://allthingsliberty.com/2017/06/action-sabbath-day-point-march-20-1777/; Alexander Fraser to Frederick Haldimand, July 12, 1779, MG21-Add.MSS.-21780, fols. 54–55, Haldimand Papers, Sir Frederick Haldimand, Unpublished Papers and Correspondence, British Library (microfilm), LAC (hereafter cited as HP).
2. Lorimier, *At War*, 28; Chevalier Lorimier to Guy Carleton[?], December 1, 1777, 21777, HP. Lorimier identified them as Algonquins, presumably meaning Kanesatake Arundaks.
3. Douglas Leighton, "Lorimier, Claude-Nicolas-Guillaume de," *DCB*; ("Zeal and Loyalty") Petition of Jean-Baptiste Lorimier to James Kempt, November 20, 1829, C Series, v268, fol. 802, LAC; Chevalier Lorimier to William Johnson, July 5, 1766, *PSWJ*, 5:306; Michel Brunet, "The Conquest Hypothesis Applied," in Cameron Nish, ed., *The French Canadians, 1759–1766: Conquered? Half-Conquered? Liberated?* (Vancouver, BC: Copp Clark, 1966), 139.
4. Lorimier, *At War*, 27.
5. Lorimier, *At War*, ("that the Indians . . .") 27, (Tiohateken) 31, (Louise) 45; individual record #564286, Le Programme de recherche en démographie historique, Université de Montréal, https://www.prdh-igd.com/en/Acces (hereafter cited as UMPRDH); (significance of naming) Fenton, *Great Law and the Longhouse*, 308. Sagoouike was descended from adoptees on both sides of her family: her grandfather, captured in the 1704 Deerfield raid, and her mother, taken in the same 1745 Saratoga raid that brought Louis Atiatoharongwen to Kahnawake. Son Martin was born out of Christian wedlock that December; Collection Élisée Choquet P60, S2, D265, p3, Bibliothèque et Archives nationales du Québec. Claude and Louise were married in the Catholic Church in 1783.
6. ("defend St. John's . . .") Richard Prescott to Charles Preston, [September 5, 1775], State of the Troops Under Command of Major Charles Preston . . . on the 17th day of September last . . . , November 1, 1775, and Narrative of the siege (attributed to John André), September 17, 1775, Arthur G. Doughty, ed., "Appendix B—Papers Relating to the Surrender of Fort St. John's and Fort Chambly," *Report of the Work of the Public*

Notes to Chapter 3   199

Archives for the Years 1914 and 1915 (Ottawa: J. de L Taché, 1916), 7, 13, 18; November 21, 1775, Henry Livingston, "Journal of Major Henry Livingston, of the Third New York Continental Line, August to December, 1775," *Pennsylvania Magazine of History and Biography* 22 (1898): 29–30; ("as scouts . . .") Guy Johnson to Dartmouth, October 12, 1775, Davies, *Documents of the American Revolution*, 11:142.

7. (Sotsichoouane) Lorimier, *At War*, 29–30, *Mes Services*, 248; (unsupported) Guy Johnson to Dartmouth, October 12, 1775, Davies, *Documents of the American Revolution*, 11:143 [also *DRHNY*, 8:636]. Sotsichoouane could be the same as Sohterowane (or Sagtaghroana), a Seven Nations chief at the 1770 German Flats conference. *PSWJ*, 12:838. Six Nations Mohawk chief Joseph Brant Thayendanegea specifically mentioned Nipissing participation, but did not clarify whether he meant Kanesatake Nipissings or those from Nipissing homelands east of Lake Huron. The Answer of Thayendanagea . . . to the Right Honble Lord George Germain, May 7, 1776, *DRHNY*, 8:78.

8. "Account of the Battle . . . ," *Quebec Gazette*, September 14, 1775; "Memorandum of the Rebel Invasion of Canada in 1775," Daniel Claus, CO 42/36 (microfilm), fols. 38b–39a, LAC; ("gave them so warm . . .") Guy Johnson to Dartmouth, October 12, 1775, Davies, *Documents of the American Revolution*, 11:143 [also *DRHNY*, 8:636].

9. Guy Johnson to Dartmouth, October 12, 1775, Davies, *Documents of the American Revolution*, 11:143 [also *DRCHSNY* 8:636]; "Petition from Capt Vincent an Indian . . . June 24, 1785," i42 v8 r56 p83, M247; Journal of Colonel Guy Johnson from May to November, 1775, *DRHNY*, 8:660–61; Lorimier, *At War*, 30; ("I have Killed . . .") November 7, 1775, J. Howard Hanson and Samuel Ludlow Frey, eds., *The Minute Book of the Committee of Safety of Tryon County* (New York: Dodd Mead, 1905), 95–96; Isabel T. Kelsay, "Tekawiroñte," *DCB*.

10. (fifteen shots) Marie-Thérèse Benoist to François Baby, September 7, 1775, Verreau, *Invasion du Canada*, 310; (Carleton's recognition) Francis Le Maistre to Guy Johnson, September 13, 1775, GJP; Speech of Thayendenegeh, March 14, 1776, *DRHNY*, 8:671.

11. (disgust/retirement) Guy Johnson to Dartmouth, October 12, 1775, Davies, *Documents of the American Revolution*, 11:143; The Speech of Thayendenegeh, March 14, 1776, *DRHNY*, 8:671; (September 10 fight) Rudolphus Ritzema, "Journal of Col. Rudolphus Ritzema," *Magazine of American History* 1 (1877): 100; ("When Perthuis . . .") Lorimer, *At War*, 28–29; Narrative of the siege (attributed to John André), September 19, 1775, Doughty, "Papers Relating to the Surrender of Fort St. Johns," 19.

12. ("cultivate relations . . .") Calloway, *American Revolution in Indian Country*, 64.

13. (86 Kanesatakes) Journal of Colonel Guy Johnson from May to November, 1775, *DRHNY*, 8:660; (Montreal centrality) Christian A. Crouch, "Surveying the Present, Projecting the Future: Reevaluting Colonial French *Plans* of Kanesatake." *William and Mary Quarterly* 75, no. 2 (Apr. 2018): 337; François-Auguste Magon de Terlaye to Daniel Claus, August 16, 1775, Claus Fonds, fol. 204, LAC.

14. (Wildman and Vincent, "go back to . . . ," "as numerous . . .") Lorimier, *At War*, 29; (request to convey message) "Petition from Capt Vincent an Indian . . . June 24, 1785," r56 v8 p83, M247. Many sources identify Jean Vincent as a Kahnawake, but in

his June 24, 1785, "Petition" he self-identified as a Wendake (Lorette) Huron. Long, *Voyages and Travels*, 211–13; Peace, "Maintaining Connections," 87–88, 90n61, 91.

15. Journal of Colonel Guy Johnson from May to November, 1775, *DRHNY*, 8:661; At a meeting with the four warriors of the Six Nations who were sent . . . to the Caughnawagas, September 30, 1776, *AA4*, 3:1275–76. See also Stevens, "His Majesty's 'Savage' Allies," 434.

16. At a meeting with the four warriors of the Six Nations . . . , September 30, 1776, *AA4*, 3:1275–76. The Oneida delegates were warriors Henry Cornelius, Jacob Aksiaktatye, Peter Saristtago, and Hanyost T'hanaghghanegaeaghu, accompanied by interpreter George Fulmer. Volckert Douw to John Hancock, September 6, 1775, i67 v1 r81 p63, M247; Norton, *Rebellious Younger Brother*, 72, 82; Joseph T. Glatthaar and James Kirby Martin, *Forgotten Allies: The Oneida Indians and the American Revolution* (New York: Hill and Wang, 2006), 96–97; Stevens, "His Majesty's 'Savage' Allies," 434. Saristtago is identified in "Journal of the Proceedings," *AA4*, 3:1275, but in another account is named "Quedon"—actually Queder, an Iroquoian form of Peter. "Report of the Deputys," September 24, 1775, r172 i153 v1 pp176–77, M247 [also *AA4*, 3:798]. In the Albany treaty discussions, Six Nations chiefs had dissuaded the Americans from attacking the confederation's allies, specifically mentioning Kahnawake, and claiming, "Our path of peace reaches quite there." At a treaty continued with the Indians of the Six Nations at Albany, August 31, 1775, Proceedings of the Commissioners of the Twelve United Colonies with the Six Nations, *DRHNY*, 8:623.

17. (messengers) Report of the Deputies of the Six Nations sent to Canada, September 24, 1775, *AA4*, 3:798; ("great dispute") At a meeting with the four warriors of the Six Nations . . . , September 30, 1776, *AA4*, 3:1276. The Oneidas said Guy Johnson was actually with the element that initially continued on toward St. Johns.

18. (rest) Mary Druke Becker, "Linking Arms: The Structure of Iroquois Intertribal Diplomacy," in Daniel K. Richter and James H. Merrill, eds., *Beyond the Covenant Chain: The Iroquois and Their Neighbors in Indian North America, 1600–1800* (University Park: Pennsylvania State University Press, 2003), 36; Daniel K. Richter, *Facing East from Indian Country: A Native History of Early America* (Cambridge, MA: Harvard University Press, 2003), 135; ("what had been transacted . . .") At a meeting with the four warriors of the Six Nations . . . , September 30, 1776, *AA4*, 3:1276; ("not to take . . . ," "sit still," "fight it out") At a treaty continued with the Indians of the Six Nations at Albany, August 31, 1775, Proceedings of the Commissioners of the Twelve United Colonies with the Six Nations, *DRHNY*, 8:622; Speech to the Chiefs and Warriours of the Six Nations . . . , August 31, 1775, *AA4*, 3:496.

19. ("be quiet," "were now convinced . . . ," "he desired . . . ," "to hear . . . ," "St. John's was taken . . .") At a meeting with the four warriors of the Six Nations . . . , September 30, 1776, *AA4*, 3:1276; Volckert Douw to John Hancock, September 6, 1775, i67 v1 r81 p63, M247; Norton, *Rebellious Younger Brother*, 82.

20. (Campbell) Daniel Claus to Frederick Haldimand, March 22, 1779, 21774, HP; Journal of Colonel Guy Johnson from May to November, 1775, *DRHNY*, 8:661; Jonathan G.

Rossie, "The Northern Indian Department and the American Revolution," *Niagara Frontier* 20 (Autumn 1973): 56.

21. ("lest they should...," "It is over...") Report of the Deputies of the Six Nations sent to Canada, September 24, 1775, *AA4*, 3:798.

22. ("great solemnity") Samuel Mott to Jonathan Trumbull, October 6, 1775, *AA4*, 3:972; ("prayed the Caughnawagas...," "assured him...") At a meeting with the four warriors of the Six Nations..., September 30, 1776, *AA4*, 3:1276; Report of the Deputies of the Six Nations sent to Canada, September 24, 1775, *AA4*, 3:798. The Oneidas' narrative timeline in "At a meeting with the four warriors..." is confusing, appearing to date their Île aux Noix return on the 14th; but key external details indicate that it was almost certainly the 17th, including Schuyler's absence, and Montgomery being on the mainland, but with no reference to the September 17–18 night battle.

23. ("a Present...") Philip Schuyler to George Washington, September 20, 1775; *PGWRWS*, 2:20; (traditional gifts, "word") Albany Committee Chamber, September 2, 1775, Proceedings of the Commissioners of the Twelve United Colonies with the Six Nations, *DHRNY*, 8:629; Wilbur R. Jacobs, *Diplomacy and Indian Gifts: Anglo-French Rivalry along the Ohio and Northwest Frontiers, 1748–1763* (Stanford, CA: Stanford University Press, 1950), 5, 41, 48–49, 60; Wilbur R. Jacobs, *Wilderness Politics and Indian Gifts: The Northern Colonial Frontier, 1748–1763* (Lincoln: University of Nebraska Press, 1966), 13, 17; (cash option) Peter Way, "The Cutting Edge of Culture: British Soldiers Encounter Native Americans in the French and Indian War," in Martin Daunton and Rick Halpern, eds., *Empire and Others: British Encounters with Indigenous Peoples, 1600–1850* (Philadelphia: University of Pennsylvania Press, 1999), 136–37; Gail D. MacLeitch, *Imperial Entanglements: Iroquois Change and Persistence on the Frontiers of Empire* (Philadelphia: University of Pennsylvania Press, 2011), 197, 200; (treasurer not arrived) Richard Montgomery to Timothy Bedel, September 20, 1775, W. T. R. Saffell, ed., *Records of the Revolutionary War: Containing the Military and Financial Correspondence of Distinguished Officers* (Philadelphia: G. G. Evans, 1860), 19; At a meeting with the four warriors of the Six Nations..., September 30, 1775, *AA4*, 3:1276.

Chapter 4

1. (Kontítie in the fort) "Petition from Capt Vincent an Indian... June 24, 1785," i42 v8 r56 p85, M247; (conversation in fort) Lorimier, *At War*, 30; (visit on morning of attack) September 18, Antoine Foucher, "Journal Tenu pendant le Siege du Fort Saint-Jean, en 1775, par Feu M. Foucher, Ancien Notaire de Montreal," *Le Bulletin des Recherches Historiques* 40 (Mar. 1934): 139. Kontítie is spelled "Contethye" in "Petition from Capt Vincent...." Verreau's and Aichinger's transcriptions spell Ohquandageghte as "Hotgouentagehle," while another contemporary account has "Otgwendagoghte"; Extract from a journal of meeting at Onondaga..., March 21–April 3, 1776, *AA4*, 5:1101–2. Deputy Superintendent Daniel Claus recorded earlier that Ohquandageghte

was a "medal chief," recognized by the British colonial government but not his own people, and that he had "no certain place of Abode"; Journal of Daniel Claus, July 8, 1773, *PSWJ*, 13:621. The medal chief was a native Onondaga. "Ohquandageghte," *DCB*.
2. ("outrunners," "much bloody adventure...") Josiah Priest, *The Fort Stanwix Captive, or New England Volunteer, Being the Extraordinary Life and Adventures of Isaac Hubbell among the Indians of Canada and the West, in the War of the Revolution*... (Albany, NY: J. Munsell, 1841), 6–7; Isaac Hubbell petition, S. 36601, RG15, M804, NARA (hereafter cited as M804); ("Englishmen fighting...") Narrative of the siege, September 18, 1775, Doughty, "Papers Relating to the Surrender of Fort St. Johns," 19. Connecticut veteran Isaac Hubbell's account is largely unreliable, a confused mix of different events related decades later; but key elements place him, and some of his narrative details, in the September 17–18 fight.
3. ("The British are...") Lorimier, *At War*, 31; Narrative of the siege, September 29, 1775, Doughty, "Papers Relating to the Surrender of Fort St. Johns," 21; September 18, 1775, Foucher, "Journal,"139.
4. ("a man of...," alternate spellings) Ezra S. Stearns, *Genealogical and Family History of the State of New Hampshire: A Record of the Achievements of Her People in the Making of a Commonwealth and the Founding of a Nation* (New York: Lewis Publishing, 1908), 3:1341.
5. (eight-day trek) Timothy Bedel to New-Hampshire Committee of Safety, October 27, 1775, *AA4*, 3:1207; Bayze Wells, "Journal of Bayze Wells of Farmington, May, 1776–February, 1777, at the Northward and in Canada," *Collections of the Connecticut Historical Society* 7 (1899): 252; (reassignment) Committee of Safety to Timothy Bedel, August 7, 1775, *DRNH*, 7:573.
6. ("tall, spare...") Edgar Aldrich, "Memorial to Col. Timothy Bedel," *The Granite Monthly: A New Hampshire Magazine* 47 (Nov.–Dec. 1915): 501; Aldrich, "Affair of the Cedars," 197. Alan Stone assisted with research for Bedel's colonial war service records.
7. (advice) Israel Morey to New-Hampshire Committee of Safety, October 6, 1775, *DRNH*, 7:621 [also *AA4*, 3:980]; "Petition from Capt Vincent an Indian... June 24, 1785," i42 v8 r56 p85, M247; Benjamin Trumbull, "A Concise Journal or Minutes of the Principal Movement Towards St. John's of the Siege & Surrender of the Forts There in 1775," *Collections of the Connecticut Historical Society* 7 (1899): 144.
8. (units) Timothy Bedel to New-Hampshire Committee of Safety, September 23, 1775, *AA4*, 3:779; Richard Montgomery to Timothy Bedel, September 20, 1775, Manuscripts and Archives Division, NYPL.
9. ("Charge of...") Timothy Bedel to John Sullivan, June 12, 1776, Otis G. Hammond, ed., *Letters and Papers of Major-General John Sullivan, Continental Army* (Concord: New Hampshire Historical Society, 1930), 1:233; ("privileged" trade) Sawaya, "Les Amérindiens domicilies," 21–22, 25 (author's translation); Jonathan Elkins, "Reminiscences of Jonathan Elkins," in *Proceedings of the Vermont Historical Society for the Years 1919–1920* (Montpelier: Vermont Historical Society, 1921), 190; Thomas Kendall to Eleazar Wheelock, August 1, 1773, 773451, and Eleazar Wheelock to Jonathan Trumbull, Sr., June 19, 1775, 775369.2, EWC; ("utmost Endeavours...") Letter of

Instructions to Col. Timothy Bedel from Committee of Safety of N.H., July 7, 1775, Timothy Bedel Papers, fol. 33, New Hampshire Historical Society (hereafter cited as NHHS); (escorting Louis) John Hurd to New-Hampshire Congress, July 27, 1775, *AA4*, 2:174. In Bedel's September 1775 Kahnawake council speech, he mentioned he "always" desired peace, implying a more enduring past connection. Col. T Bedel's Speech to the Indians in Canada, 1775, Timothy Bedel Papers, fols. 21–22, NHHS.

10. (Louis, messages) Israel Morey to New-Hampshire Committee of Safety, October 6, 1775, *DRNH*, 7:621 [also *AA4*, 3:980]; ("all learned English...") Samuel Mott to Jonathan Trumbull, October 6, 1775, *AA4*, 3:974; ("without the least...") Timothy Bedel to John Sullivan, June 12, 1776, Hammond, *Papers of Major-General John Sullivan*, 1:233.

11. (£400, "come to receive it") Richard Montgomery to Timothy Bedel, September 20, 1775, Saffell, *Records of the Revolutionary War*, 19; ("beggarly miscreants...") Richard Montgomery to Philip Schuyler, September 19, 1775, *AA4*, 3:797; ("knowledge of Indians ways...") Colin G. Calloway, "Sentinels of the Revolution: Bedel's New Hampshire Rangers and the Abenaki Indians on the Upper Connecticut," *Historical New Hampshire* 45, no. 4 (Winter 1990): 277; (September 24) Richard Montgomery to Philip Schuyler, September 24, 1775, *AA4*, 3:840.

12. Col. T Bedel's Speech to the Indians in Canada, 1775, Timothy Bedel Papers, fols. 21–22, NHHS. The speech document does not identify when and where it was delivered, but the author is confident that contextual details clearly indicate it was given at Kahnawake, almost certainly on September 24, and no earlier than September 18.

13. Richard Prescott to Charles Preston, undated, and Narrative of the siege, September 24, 1775, Doughty, "Papers Relating to the Surrender of Fort St. Johns," 8, 20; Chevalier Lorimier to Guy Carleton[?], December 1, 1777, 21777, HP; ("dyed-in-the-wool...") Lorimier, *At War*, 32–33.

14. Lorimier, *At War*, 34–35.

15. Lorimier, *At War*, 36–38.

16. ("there were a number...," "in every battle," "Carleton made them drunk...") Seth Warner to Richard Montgomery, September 27, 1775, *AA4*, 3:953; (drunk excuse) MacLeitch, *Imperial Entanglements*, 35; W. J. Eccles, *The Canadian Frontier, 1534–1760*, rev. ed. (Albuquerque: University of New Mexico Press, 1983), 78; (factional neutrality) Fitz, "'Suspected on Both Sides,'" 301, 303, 304. Other than Warner's rumors, there is no evidence confirming Kahnawake participation in Allen's defeat—possibly another example of conflating Kahnawakes with other Seven Nations members. Historian James Ingram discusses circumstances in which Indians in conference "frequently referred to rebellious groups as being 'drunk,' meaning only that they had lost their good sense." Ingram, *Indians and British Outposts in Eighteenth-Century America* (Gainesville: University Press of Florida, 2012), 149–50n45.

17. Richard Montgomery to Philip Schuyler, October 20, 1775, *AA4*, 3:1132; ("protect that nation...") October 18, 1775 ("18 bottles...," "they feared no invasion...," "Mr. Carleton...") October 21, 1775, Livingston, "Journal," 18, 23–24; Rachel B. Herrmann, "'No Useless Mouth': Iroquoian Food Diplomacy in the American Revolution," *Diplomatic History* 41, no. 1 (2017): 30.

18. Extracts from the Records of Indian Transactions under the Super-Intendency of Colo. Guy Johnson during the year 1775, PRO, CO 5/77, *IIADH*, reel 32; Daniel Claus to Frederick Haldimand, March 22, 1779, 21774, HP; Gibb, "Colonel Guy Johnson," 600–604.
19. "Narrative of Lt. Col. Butler's Services in America," May 1785, 21875, HP; Ernest Cruikshank, *The Story of Butler's Rangers and the Settlement of Niagara* (Welland, ON: Tribune Printing House, 1893), 12; R. Arthur Bowler and Bruce G. Wilson, "Butler, John (d. 1796)," *DCB*; John Butler, "Declaration of Colonel John Butler Received by Notary Beek, Montreal, 27 October 1787," *Rapport de l'Archiviste de la Province de Quebec pour 1924–1925* (Quebec: Ls-A. Prouls, 1925), 395; ("neither the superintendent . . .") Stevens, "His Majesty's 'Savage' Allies," 520.
20. ("provision . . . some Cloaths . . . growing Cold," "that four or five . . .") Speech by the Six Nations and part of the seven Nations of Canada in Montreal, and (Mississaugas) October 21, 1775, journal entry, JBJ.
21. Guy Carleton to Dartmouth, October 25, 1775, Davies, *Documents of the American Revolution*, 11:166; Extracts from the Records of Indian Transactions under the Super-Intendency of Colo. Guy Johnson during the year 1775, PRO, CO 5/77, *IIADH*, reel 32; ("esteemed brave warriors") Long, *Voyages and Travels*, 35.
22. Lorimier, *At War*, 38–40; ("gallant, but unsupported") James McGill to Isaac Todd, November 4, 1775, Richard A. Roberts, ed., *Calendar of Home Office Papers of the Reign of George III, 1773–1775, Preserved in the Public Record Office* (London: Her Majesty's Stationery Office, 1899), 483.
23. (Ohquandageghte and two others) Lorimier, *At War*, 40; October 30, Livingston, "Journal," 25–26; James McGill to Isaac Todd, November 4, 1775, Roberts, *Calendar of Home Office Papers*, 483; (prisoner mistreatment) François-Auguste Magon de Terlaye to Andrew Parke, October 9, 1776, Andrew Parke, *An Authentic Narrative of Facts Relating to the Exchange of Prisoners Taken at the Cedars* (London, 1777), 47; Richard Montgomery to Philip Schuyler, November 24, 1775, *AA4*, 3:1695.
24. (Indian departure) Guy Carleton to Dartmouth, November 5, 1775, Davies, *Documents of the American Revolution*, 11:173.
25. Lorimier, *At War*, 40–41, *Mes Services*, 262 (author's translation).
26. (orders) Henry Hamilton to George Germain, August 29–September 2, 1776, Davies, *Documents of the American Revolution*, 12:211. The up-country posts were placed under Carleton's command after the start of the war, because British army commander General Thomas Gage no longer had communication with them; Guy Carleton to Guy Johnson, June 19, 1775, GJP.

Chapter 5

1. ("very much distressed . . .") New-Hampshire Committee of Safety to Philip Schuyler, November 18, 1775, *AA4*, 4:23; A Pay Roll of Colonel Timothy Bedel's Company, 1775, r49 f49 pp6–7, RG93, M246, NARA (hereafter cited as M246). Charles Nelson

(a lieutenant in Bedel's company) led fifty-nine 1775 rangers in a new company reenlisted through April 1776, Bedel accounts, r49 f49 p52, M246.
2. Timothy Bedel to James Holmes, December 16, 1775, Military Papers, Letters, PSP; December 15 [sic] entry, United States of America from Brigr Genl Wooster to Col Timothy Bedel, r49 f49 p45, M246; George Washington to Philip Schuyler, January 27, 1776, *PGWRWS*, 3:201–2.
3. December 19, Ritzema, "Journal," 104. On December 22, loyalist Montreal notary Simon Sanguinet recorded a cynical account of the same event, but Ritzema's journal entry appears more consistent with circumstances; Simon Sanguinet, "Témoin Oculaire de l'Invasion du Canada par les Bastonnois: Journal de M. Sanguinet," in Hospice-Anthelme Jean-Baptiste Verreau, ed., *Invasion du Canada: Collection des Mémoires Recueillis et Annotes* (Montreal: Eusèbe Senécal, 1873), 91–92.
4. Philip Schuyler to John Holmes, January 12, 1776, Orderly Book of Philip John Schuyler, p261–62, Huntington Library; (headmen) Comments on a meeting with Caughnawaga sachems, January 1776, PSP. Schuyler spelled Nicolas's name Natanoghne. Oghradouskon and Sadaresoghsqua appear in several contemporary phonetic forms.
5. ("perpetual peace . . . ," "the said Caghnawaga . . . ," "observe an Exact . . .") Rough draft of a treaty between Indian Commissioners and the Caghnawaga Nation, January 3–6, 1776, and Comments on a meeting with Caughnawaga sachems, January 1776 (January 6 treaty signature), Notes from a conference, August 1776, Philip Schuyler, PSP; Philip Schuyler to George Washington, February 14, 1776, *PGWRWS*, 3:313 [also *AA4*, 4:1146]; Philip Schuyler to President of Congress, January 10, 1776, *AA4*, 4:623. The author has been unable to locate an extant transcript of the original treaty, only Schuyler's draft and comments.
6. ("should hold a . . .") Comments on a meeting with Caughnawaga sachems, January 1776 (January 6 treaty signature), Notes from a conference, August 1776, Philip Schuyler, PSP. On March 29, the Continental Congress merely noted receipt of a copy of an Albany treaty, perhaps this one. *JCC*, 4:240. The Watertown Treaty with the "St. John's and Micmack Tribes" called for mutual defense and a commitment of "600 strong men out of the said Tribes," while the Fort Pitt Treaty committed the Delawares to supplying "such a number of their best and most expert warriors as they can spare," and "free passage through their country" to American troops. Baxter, *Documentary History of the State of Maine*, 24:188–93; "Treaty with the Delawares: 1778," https://avalon.law.yale.edu/18th_century/del1778.asp.
7. Philip Schuyler to James Holmes, January 12, 1776, Orderly Book of Philip John Schuyler, p261–62, Huntington Library; Philip Schuyler to George Washington, January 5, 1776, *PGWRWS*, 3:34 [also *AA4*, 4:582]; February 17, 1776, Voted . . . for W. Torrey, and July 1, 1776, Sundry accounts of Wm. Williams, Esq., and Nath. Wales, Esq., Charles J. Hoadly, *The Public Records of the Colony of Connecticut, from May, 1775 to June, 1776, inclusive* . . . (Hartford, CT: Case, Lockwood, and Brainard, 1890), 242, 478; ("disagreeable intelligence . . . ," "1500 men . . .") "Providence, January 20," *Massachusetts Spy*, February 2, 1776. Note the continuity between the Kahnawakes'

Providence offer and their pre-Quebec-disaster offer to Wooster a month earlier in Montreal, discussed above.

8. (arrival, "be so entertained") George Washington to John Hancock, January 24, 1776, *PGWRWS*, 3:180–81 [also *AA4*, 4:841]; Jeduthan Baldwin, *The Revolutionary Journal of Col. Jeduthan Baldwin, 1775–1778*, ed. Thomas William Baldwin (Bangor, ME: The De Burians, 1906), 23, 24; George Washington to Philip Schuyler, January 16, 1776, *PGWRWS*, 3:112–13 [also *AA4*, 4:696]; George Washington to John Hancock, January 19, 1776, *AA4*, 4:773; John Adams to Abigail Adams, January 24, 1776, and ("Louis, their Principal . . .") Diary of John Adams, January 24, 1776, John Adams Papers, Digital Edition, Massachusetts Historical Society; "Philadelphia, Feb. 7," *Constitutional Gazette*, February 14, 1776; "Extract of a letter from Cambridge, January 28," *Pennsylvania Packet*, February 12, 1776; ("look upon them . . .") "Philadelphia, Feb. 7," *Constitutional Gazette*, February 14, 1776.

9. ("out-door's talk," "a desire . . . ," "a little embarrassed . . . ," "Impropriety . . .") George Washington to Philip Schuyler, January 27, 1776, *PGWRWS*, 3:201–2 [also *AA4*, 4:873]; Philip Schuyler to President of Congress, February 23, 1776, *AA4*, 4:1481–82; Colin G. Calloway, *The Indian World of George Washington: The First President, the First Americans, and the Birth of the Nation* (New York: Oxford University Press, 2018), 221. Kahnawake itself probably had fewer than three hundred warriors within the nation.

10. ("before they . . .") George Washington to Philip Schuyler, January 27, 1776, ("I am now . . . ," "that If he . . .") Speeches of the Caughnawaga, St. Johns, and Passamaquoddy Indians [January 31, 1776], and George Washington to Philip Schuyler, February 1, 1776, *PGWRWS*, 3:201–2, 223, 239 [also *AA4*, 4:873, 893, 908]. By Timothy Bedel's account records, the party apparently left on February 1, but a contemporary newspaper account dated February 3 mentions the Indians were "to set off in a day or two." His Excellency George Washington's Indian Acct. with Colonel Bedel, r49 f49 pp48–49, M246; "Extract of a letter from Cambridge, February 3," *New-York Journal*, February 22, 1776.

11. ("Conduct them . . . ," "use all the deligence . . .") George Washington to Timothy Bedel, February 1, 1776, *PGWRWS*, 3:234 [also *AA4*, 4:908]; George Washington to Philip Schuyler, January 27, 1776, *AA4*, 4:873; ("Regiment of Rangers") Timothy Bedel Commission, January 22, 1776, Timothy Bedel Papers, folder 9, NHHS; New-Hampshire House of Representatives, January 20, 1776, *AA4*, 5:14–15; Ebenezer Thompson to Josiah Bartlett, January 29, 1776, Josiah Bartlett, *The Papers of Josiah Bartlett*, ed. Frank C. Mevers (Hanover, NH: University Press of New England, 1979), 40.

12. ("much at heart") Timothy Bedel to Eleazar Wheelock, February 17, 1776, 776167, EWC; ("entertainment of their own") John Philips to Eleazar Wheelock, February 12, 1776, Isaac W. Hammond, ed., "Correspondence between Rev. Eleazar Wheelock and Others, of Dartmouth College, and John Phillips, LL.D., 1765 to 1787," *Collections of the New Hampshire Historical Society* 9 (1889): 96; His Excellency George Washington's Indian Acct. with Colonel Bedel, r49 f49 pp48–49,

M246; New-Hampshire Committee of Safety to Major Bellows, January 31, 1776, *AA4*, 4:901; Proceedings of the New-Hampshire Committee of Safety, February 2, 1776, *AA4*, 4:1485; (funds) Timothy Bedel to New-Hampshire Committee of Safety, March 8, 1776, *AA4*, 5:140.
13. (two groups, deaths, funeral) Wheelock's Diary, February 18–23, 1776, Chase, *History of Dartmouth College*, 353; Eleazar Wheelock to John Philips, February 27, 1776, Hammond, "Correspondence between Rev. Eleazar Wheelock and Others," 98. See also John Philips to Eleazar Wheelock, February 12, 1776, Hammond, ed., "Correspondence between Rev. Eleazar Wheelock and Others," 96; His Excellency George Washington's Indian Acct. with Colonel Bedel, r49 f49 pp48–49, M246.
14. (Louis in Albany) Philip Schuyler to George Washington, March 9, 1776, and February 14, 1776, *PGWRWS*, 3:443, 313 [also *AA4*, 5:148, 4:1146]; (Stockbridges) Philip Schuyler to President of Congress, February 23, 1776, *AA4*, 4:1481–82.
15. Israel Morey to New-Hampshire Committee of Safety, March 7, 1776, *AA4*, 5:117; Timothy Bedel to New-Hampshire Committee of Safety, March 8, 1776, *AA4*, 5:140; Israel Morey to New-Hampshire Committee of Safety, [undated], *AA4*, 5:427. Company establishment was seventy-six privates, ten noncommissioned officers and musicians, and four officers. New-Hampshire House of Representatives, January 20, 1776, *AA4*, 5:14–15; Guy Chet, *Conquering the American Wilderness: The Triumph of European Warfare in the Colonial Northeast* (Boston: University of Massachusetts Press, 2003), 126; Jeremy Belknap, *The History of New Hampshire* (Boston, 1791), 2:297. Recruiting losses, returning veterans, and Bunker Hill experience are estimated by comparisons between "A list of the Prisoners belonging to the Continental Army, taken at the Cedars," *AA5*, 1:167–68 [also rg360 i29 r36 pp233–43, M247] and 1775 Bedel accounts and Pay Rolls of Capt. James Osgood's, Capt. John Parker's, and Col. Timothy Bedel's companies, r49 f49 pp6, 9, 26, 29, 32, 52, M246, and rolls in George C. Gilmore, *State Senators, 1784–1900: New Hampshire Men at Bunker Hill* (Manchester, NH: John B. Clarke, 1899). The limited experience and skills of Bedel's 1776 regiment parallel the grossly expanded Rogers's Rangers in the late French and Indian War, described in S. Brumwell, "The British Army and Warfare with the North American Indians," *War in History* 5 (1998): 161.
16. ("very sorry . . .") New-Hampshire Committee of Safety to Colonel Bedel, March 13, 1776, *AA4*, 5:208–9; New-Hampshire [Committee of Safety] to Henry Gerrish, March 12, 1776, *AA4*, 5:26; Timothy Bedel to New-Hampshire Committee of Safety, March 19, 1776, *AA4*, 5:428; Israel Morey to New-Hampshire Committee of Safety, [n.d.], *AA4*, 5:427.
17. Timothy Bedel to New-Hampshire Committee of Safety, March 19, 1776, *AA4*, 5:428; ("each company . . .") George Washington to Timothy Bedel, February 1, 1776, *AA4*, 4:908–9; John Hancock to New-Hampshire House of Representatives, January 20, 1776, *DRNH*, 8:40–41; David Wooster to Seth Warner, January 6, 1776, *AA4*, 4:588; (weapons shortages) Capt. Samuel Young's Petition, June 12, 1797, *DRNH*, 12:413–14; Petition of Samuel Fowler, December 30, 1783, *DRNH*, 11:203; (Osgood's underway March 25, after April 7) Frye Bailey, "Colonel Frye Bailey's Reminiscences,"

in *Proceedings of the Vermont Historical Society for the Years 1923, 1924 and 1925* (Bellows Falls, VT: P. H. Gobie Press, 1926), 32; James Osgood to Meschech Weare, March 19, 1776, *DRNH*, 8:104; Reminiscence of Shepardson's military service in 1776 . . . , Zephaniah Shepardson Papers, MS B Sh47, Vermont Historical Society (hereafter cited as Shepardson, "Reminiscence"), 1–2; "Narrative of John Peters," Colonel John Peters Papers, New-York Historical Society (hereafter cited as NYHS), 4; (by April 20) Moses Hazen to Edward Antill, April 20, 1776, 21687, HP; Benedict Arnold to Philip Schuyler, April 20, 1776, *AA4*, 5:1099.

18. ("a large party . . .") James Dean to Eleazar Wheelock, December 25, 1775, 775675.2, EWC; Philip Schuyler to John Hancock, December 21, 1775, i170 v1 r189 p225, M247; Don R. Gerlach, *Proud Patriot: Philip Schuyler and the War of Independence, 1775–1783* (Syracuse, NY: Syracuse University Press, 1987), 87; (controversy) "At a Meeting," Niagara, May 7, 1776, JBJ; Stevens, "His Majesty's 'Savage Allies,'" 531.

19. ("of one heart . . .") James Deane to Philip Schuyler, March 18, 1776, SKC [also *AA4*, 5:769]; ("adjacent villages," March 11) Samuel Kirkland to Philip Schuyler, March 11, 1776, SKC [also *AA4*, 5:773, with variations in transcription]; James Dean to Samuel Kirkland, March 22, 1776, Maryly B. Penrose, ed., *Indian Affairs Papers: American Revolution* (Franklin Park, NJ: Liberty Bell Associates, 1981), 39. The "adjacent villages" were probably Akwesasne (St. Regis) and Odanak (St. Francis).

20. ("Many of the Indians . . .") Samuel Kirkland to Philip Schuyler, March 12, 1776, *AA4*, 5:772.

21. (Butler influence) Extract from the Journal of James Deane, Interpreter to the Six Nations, March 30 and April 1, 1776, *AA4*, 5:1102–3; ("appointed to the care . . .") John Butler to Alexander McKee, February 29, 1776, William A. Smy, *The Butler Papers: Documents and Papers Relating to Colonel John Butler and His Corps of Rangers, 1711–1977* (Victoria, BC: W. Smy, 1994), 1: n.p.; (early 1776 entries, "open the door") January 24, 1776, JBJ; ("to Point out . . .") "Narrative of Lt. Col. Butler's Services in America," May 1785, 21875, HP; ("Keepers . . .") Anthony F. C. Wallace, *The Death and Rebirth of the Seneca* (New York: Vintage Books, 1972), 21; Calloway, *American Revolution in Indian Country*, 134; Graymont, *Iroquois in the American Revolution*, 86; Paul L. Stevens, *A King's Colonel at Niagara, 1774–1776* (Youngstown, NY: Old Fort Niagara Association, 1987), 42–43. Seneca population was estimated at four or five thousand total, about one thousand warriors. Report of His Excellency William Tryon Esquire . . . , June 11, 1774, *DRHNY*, 8:452; Enumeration of Indians within the Northern Department, November 18, 1763, *DRHNY*, 7:582; Stevens, "His Majesty's 'Savage' Allies," 76–77.

22. ("manifested an unshaken friendship") Samuel Kirkland to Philip Schuyler, March 12, 1776, *AA4*, 5:772; Stevens, "His Majesty's 'Savage' Allies," 584, ("publicly united . . .") 587; Graymont, *Iroquois in the American Revolution*, 90–91.

23. ("The Oneidas . . .") Samuel Chase to John Adams, April 18, 1776, Robert J. Taylor, ed., *Papers of John Adams* (Cambridge, MA: Belknap Press, 1979), 4:130; ("all the back nations . . . ," "The Kaghnawages . . .") Oneida Chiefs to Philip Schuyler, May 22, 1776, SKC [also *AA5*, 1:867; and *DRHNY*, 8:689].

Chapter 6

1. ("dared not speak") Sanguinet, "Témoin Oculaire," 98.
2. Lorimier, *At War*, 43–44.
3. ("did not incline . . .") David Wooster to Committee of Congress, July 5, 1776, *AA5*, 1:7; Sanguinet, "Témoin Oculaire," 97; ("carried out of the Country . . .") [Additional] Orders to Colo Hazen [from David Wooster], Ms. 1711, Sol Feinstone Collection, David Library of the American Revolution (since February 2020, incorporated into the American Philosophical Society as the David Center for the American Revolution). Even with his Indian commissioner responsibilities, General Schuyler supported Wooster's decision. Philip Schuyler to John Hancock, March 12, 1776 (transcript), rg360 i170 r189 v1 p354, M247.
4. ("admitted every bit of it," "get ready to leave") Lorimier, *At War*, 44.
5. Lorimier, *At War*, 40–41; (Goddard) Lieut Gorrells Journal . . . *PSWJ*, 11:711–13; Robert Rogers' Commission to James Stanley Goddard, September 12, 1766, John Parker, ed., *The Journals of Jonathan Carver and Related Documents, 1766–1770* (St. Paul: Minnesota Historical Society Press, 1976), 196–97; Journal of Indian Affairs [November 4–13, 1767], *PSWJ*, 12:385; W. Steward Wallace, *The Pedlars from Quebec and Other Papers on the Nor'Westers* (Toronto: Ryerson Press, 1954), 3; ("influence . . .") Daniel Claus to William Johnson, August 10, 1768, *PSWJ*, 6:318–19; Parker, *Journals of Jonathan Carver*, 15–16.
6. (March 2) Chevalier Lorimier to Guy Carleton[?], December 1, 1777, 21777, HP; ("out cold") Lorimier, *At War*, 44–45.
7. Lorimier, *At War*, 45–46; (Ville Chauve) Lorimier, *Mes Services*, 267; (March 6) Moses Hazen to Edward Antill, March 10, 1776, 21687, HP. Historically, Akwesasne was spelled in phonetic variations of Aughquisasne.
8. Long, *Voyages and Travels*, 19; (father) Malcolm MacLeod, "Lorimier de la Rivière, Claude-Nicolas de," *DCB*; (young sons' service) Eccles, *Canadian Frontier*, 101.
9. Hough, *History of St. Lawrence and Franklin Counties*, 79; MacLeod, *Canadian Iroquois and the Seven Years' War*, 168–69; (subordinate position) Benedict Arnold to Philip Schuyler, June 10, 1776, *AA4*, 6:977; ("decline taking up the Hatchet") Examination of Mr. Gerrit Roseboom, July 14, 1775, *MACC*, 1:155 [also *AA4*, 2:1670].
10. Richard Cannon, *Historical Record of the Eighth, or, the King's Regiment of Foot* (London, 1837), 61–65; William L. Potter, "Redcoats on the Frontier: The King's Regiment in the Revolutionary War," in *Selected Papers from the 1983 and 1984 George Rogers Clark Trans-Appalachian Frontier History Conferences*, ed. Robert J. Holden (Vincennes, IN: Eastern National Park and Memorial Association, 1985); (arrival) *Quebec Gazette*, June 16 and 23, 1768; ("Tranquility and boredom") Patrick Mileham, *"Difficulties Be Damned," The King's Regiment, 8th, 63rd, 96th: A History of the City Regiment of Manchester and Liverpool* (Knutsford, UK: Fleur de Lys, 2000), 19; (1770 promotion) *A List of the . . . Officers . . . the Army* (London: War Office, 1771), 62.
11. ("four blockhouses . . .") Grant, "Journal," 305; (fifteen feet) Pierre Pouchot, *Memoir from the Late War in North America between the French and English*, trans.

Franklin B. Hough (Roxbury, MA: W. Elliot Woodward, 1866), 2:107–8; ("the Post...") Thomas Gage to Shelburne, April 3, 1767, Clarence Edwin Carter, ed., *The Correspondence of General Thomas Gage... 1763–1775* (New Haven, CT: Yale University Press, 1931), 1:125; ("backcountry contact points") Ingram, *Indians and British Outposts*, 6; Stevens, *King's Colonel at Niagara*, 11; Michael N. McConnell, *Army and Empire: British Soldiers on the American Frontier, 1758–1775* (Lincoln: University of Nebraska Press, 2004), xvi, 88–89, 96, 148.

12. ("project to raise...") Chevalier Lorimier to Guy Carleton[?], December 1, 1777, 21777, HP; ("a better opinion") Lorimier, *At War*, 46–47. Forster's senior lieutenant, Andrew Parke, met with Carleton in Montreal shortly before the fall of Fort St. Johns, but there is no evidence Forster received any specific orders to guide his decisions to support the loyalists or commit his troops. Stevens, "His Majesty's 'Savage' Allies," 505–6, 509; Stevens, *King's Colonel at Niagara*, 43.

13. ("to follow...") Mackenzie, *Voyages*, 1:lviii; François-Auguste Magon de Terlaye to Andrew Parke, October 9, 1776, Parke, *Authentic Narrative*, 46–47.

14. Peter Jones, *History of the Ojebway Indians; with Especial Reference to Their Conversion to Christianity* (London: A. W. Bennett, 1861), 138–39; Michael A. McDonnell, *Masters of Empire: Great Lakes Indians and the Making of America* (New York: Hill and Wang, 2015), 5, 202; "Over 200 Years of History" and "The Mississaugas," https://heritagemississauga.com/indigenous-heritage/; (father) Malcolm MacLeod, "Lorimier de la Rivière, Claude-Nicolas de," *DCB*; Bougainville, *Adventure in the Wilderness*, 151; Peter Schmalz, *The Ojibwa of Southern Ontario* (Toronto: University of Toronto Press, 1991), 15; Marian M. Gibson, *In the Footsteps of the Mississaugas* (Mississauga, ON: Mississauga Heritage Foundation, 2006), 39–40; Brian Osborne and Michael Ripmeester, "Kingston, Bedford, Grape Island, Alnwick: The Odyssey of the Kingston Mississauga," *Historic Kingston* (1995): 86; ("Parts & Tribes") William Johnson to Thomas Gage, March 16, 1764, *PSWJ*, 4:368.

15. James G. E. Smith, "Leadership among the Indians of the Northern Woodlands," in *Currents in Anthropology: Essays in Honor of Sol Tax*, ed. Robert Hinshaw (The Hague: Mouton, 1979), 310, 314; Cary Miller, *Ogimaag: Anishinaabeg Leadership, 1760–1845* (Lincoln: University of Nebraska Press, 2010), 117; Osborne and Ripmeester, "Odyssey of the Kingston Mississauga," 86; ("prove one's worth") Basil Johnston, *Ojibway Heritage* (Lincoln: University of Nebraska Press, 1990), 68–69; Witgen, *Infinity of Nations*, 19.

16. (Fort St. Johns) Guy Carleton to Dartmouth, August 14, 1775, Davies, *Documents of the American Revolution*, 11:74; (twenty-two Mississaugas) July 24, 1775, *MACC*, 1:155 [also *AA4*, 2:1670–71]; ("never varied") Richard Lernoult letter, April 11, 1777, CO 42/36, fols. 132–135, cited in, and ("Unlike...") Joy Bilharz, *Oriskany: A Place of Great Sadness, a Mohawk Valley Battlefield Ethnography* (Boston: Northeast Region Ethnography Program, National Park Service, 2009), 81.

17. (Mississauga lifeways) Jones, *History of the Ojebway Indians*, 135–36; Brian Osborne and Michael Ripmeester, "The Mississaugas between Two Worlds: Strategic

Adjustments to Changing Landscapes of Power," *Canadian Journal of Native Studies* 17, no. 2 (1997): 262; "First Nations Gallery," http://www.mississauga.ca/portal/residents/firstnationsgallery; Johnston, *Ojibway Heritage*, 146–47; Pouchot, *Memoir*, 2:91; James M. Hadden, *Hadden's Journal and Orderly Books: A Journal Kept in Canada and upon Burgoyne's Campaign in 1776 and 1777, by Lieut. James M. Hadden, Roy. Art*, ed. Horatio Rogers (Albany, NY: Joel Munsell's Sons, 1884), 40; Lorimier, *At War*, 46–47; (three weeks, 250 "good men") Chevalier Lorimier to Guy Carleton[?], December 1, 1777, 21777, HP (author's translation). Lorimier's memoirs describe the meeting date as "when the April moon would be full," on April 3, which would be far too early. Based on his narrative chronology, Lorimier must have meant the May moon, known by the Anishinaabeg as the "Blooming Moon." Gananoque ("the meeting place") is at the mouth of the river of the same name, twenty miles east of modern Kingston, Ontario, in the Thousand Islands region.

18. Stevens, "His Majesty's 'Savage' Allies," 575–76, 588. Governor Carleton gave Caldwell a last set of orders from Montreal in November, but their content is unknown, so it is impossible to determine their impact on the colonel's response. Henry Hamilton to George Germain, August 29–September 2, 1776, Davies, *Documents of the American Revolution*, 12:211.

19. ("spared no pains") Copy of a letter from Colonel [John] Butler [to Guy Carleton], July 28, 1777, CO 42/37 (microfilm), fol. 99, LAC; ("the Boston people . . .") January 22, 1776, ("should the Road of peace . . .") January 23, 1776, and February 24, 1776, Niagara, Meeting with the Onondagoes, Cahugas, & Tederichrunas, JBJ; James Dean to Philip Schuyler, March 10, 1776, r172 i153 v2 pp81–82, M247.

20. ("a Terror . . . a Muskitoe,") "At a Meeting," May 7, 1776, and ("the Wicked & Treacherous . . . determined to Clear . . .") "Brothers Warriors & Sachems now Assembled," undated, JBJ. Butler specifically excluded the Kahnawakes and "some few" Odanak (St. Francis) Abenakis from the list of the Seven Nations' staunch "Friends to Gov[ernment]."

21. ("that a number . . . ," "Let them imbark . . .") Oneida Chiefs to Philip Schuyler, May 22, 1776, SKC [also *DRHNY*, 8:689]; "At a Meeting," May 5, 1776, and June 29, 1776, JBJ.

22. (Cayugas and Onondagas) Conference of the Commissioners for Indian Affairs with the Six Nations of Indians, at German-Flats, August 13, 1776, *AA5*, 1:1046–47; (more than fifty men) Oneida Chiefs to Philip Schuyler, May 22, 1776, SKC [also *DRHNY*, 8:689]; (principally Senecas, Oneida element) Major Sherburne's Testimony on the Affair of the Cedars (hereafter cited as Sherburne Testimony), Julian P. Boyd, ed., *The Papers of Thomas Jefferson* (Princeton, NJ: Princeton University Press, 1950), 1:399–400 (hereafter cited as *PTJ*); (William Johnson) Lorimier, *At War*, 51; Stevens, "His Majesty's 'Savage' Allies," 590–91. A rebel spy offered an alternative account, reporting that assembled Indians "had been kept drunk for some time before, and went contrary to the Inclinations of the sachems of all the six Nations." Philip Schuyler to John Hancock, July 17, 1775, i170 v1 r189 p409, M247.

23. (Goddard Mississaugas) Remarks & Observations upon Indn. Politics..., *IIADH*, reel 33; Daniel Claus Papers, MG19-F1, v1, 255, LAC; (one hundred Indians total) Oneida Chiefs to Philip Schuyler, May 22, 1776, SKC [also *DRHNY*, 8:689].
24. ("properly officered") "Narrative of Lt. Col. Butler's Services...," May 1785, 21875, HP; ("a squad or two...") Stevens, *King's Colonel at Niagara*, 53; (May 10) Samuel Kirkland sent a May 22 report saying the British-allied Six Nations party had embarked "twelve days ago," Oneida Chiefs to Philip Schuyler, May 22, 1776, SKC [also *DRHNY*, 8:689]. Of three government Lake Ontario ships, the snow *Haldimand* seems the likely choice to have carried so many people; Robert Malcomson, *Warships of the Great Lakes: 1754–1834* (New York: Knickerbocker Press, 2004), 24–26, 155. The memoir of a contemporary French Canadian notary, not involved in the campaign, noted that "Capt. Foster [sic]... was *ordered to leave Oswegatchie*... to drive out a party of 300 Americans established at the Cedars" [author's emphasis]; Michel-Amable Berthelot, "Extraits d'un Mémoire de M. A. Berthelot sur L'Invasion du Canada en 1775," in Verreau, *Invasion du Canada*, 236 (author's translation).

Chapter 7

1. ("uneasy on the question...") Lorimier, *At War*, 47.
2. ("ardent zeal") Henri Têtu, *Notices biographiques; les évêques de Québec* (Quebec, 1889), 432 (author's translation); Jean-Baptiste A. Allaire, *Dictionnaire biographique du clergé canadien-français*, vol. 1 (Montreal: Imprimerie de l'École catholique des sourds-muets, 1910), 155; ("a fortnight's...," "eager to serve...," "would arrive...") Lorimier, *At War*, 47; No. 91—Mr. Thomas Denis, "Court of Enquiry of Damages," MG23-GV7, LAC. Despite his last name, Denis was reputedly of English origin; individual record # 81377, UMPRDH; Robert Hunter Jr., *Quebec to Carolina in 1785–1786: Being the Travel Diary and Observations of Robert Hunter, Jr., a Young Merchant of London*, ed. Louis B. Wright and Marion Tinling (San Marino, CA: The Huntington Library, 1943), 60.
3. Lorimier, *At War*, 47; ("zealous service...") "Memorial of Lieut. Col. Henry Bird," February 11, 1818, Pioneer and Historical Society of the State of Michigan, *Collections and Researches Made by the Pioneer and Historical Society of the State of Michigan* (Lansing, MI, 1896), 25:656. Bird appears to have served as an ensign less than a year with the Thirty-First Regiment in England before taking a half-pay lieutenant's commission in the Eightieth Regiment from October 1764 to February 1768, when he joined the Eighth. Kenneth G. Yates, "His Majesty's 47th Regiment of Foot in Canada: 1777–1782," *Journal of the Society for Army Historical Research* 74, no. 300 (1996): 216n36; *A List of the... Officers...* (1767) 199, (1768) 198, (1769) 61; Worthington C. Ford, *British Officers Serving in the American Revolution, 1774–1783* (Brooklyn, NY: Historical Printing Club, 1897), 28.
4. Lorimier, *At War*, 47; (April 11) Copy of Intelligence received from Montreal at Quebec the 14th of May..., CO 42/35 (microfilm), fols. 22–23, LAC.

5. Lorimier, *At War*, 47; (125 quarter barrels) Copy of Intelligence received from Montreal at Quebec the 14th of May . . . , CO 42/35 (microfilm), fols. 22–23, LAC. There is no record of an enduring American presence at the Cedars before April 28; it may have been a patrol to interdict fur-trade smuggling. Ration estimates are based on fifty pounds per quarter barrel, and a one-pound ration of both flour and meat per man each day.
6. (Akwesasne) Moses Hazen to Edward Antill, March 10, 1776, 21687, HP; ("a plan concerted . . . ," "among several . . .") David Wooster to Philip Schuyler, March 5, 1776, *AA4*, 5:417. Wooster did not mention Louis Vincent Sawatanen by name, but details clearly describe him. Sawatanen, a nephew of pro-American Jean Vincent, left his studies at Dartmouth on February 15, specifically to help the American cause. Eleazar Wheelock to David Wooster, February 6, 1776, 776156, EWC; Memorial of Revd. Eleazar Wheelock, April 2, 1779, v10 r52 p387, M247; Peace, "Maintaining Connections," 79; Jonathan Lainey and Thomas Peace, "Louis Vincent Sawatanen: A Life Forged by Warfare and Migration," in Kristin Burnett and Geoff Read, eds., *Aboriginal History: A Reader*, 2nd ed. (Toronto: Oxford University Press, 2016), 112.
7. ("Rascall," "the Ceadars . . . ," "march Immediately . . . ," Carillon) Moses Hazen to Edward Antill, April 20, 1776, 21687, HP; ("to prevent any goods . . .") Benedict Arnold to Philip Schuyler, April 20, 1776, *AA4*, 5:1099.
8. ("to Cultivate . . .") Colonel Bedel's Defence, Isaac W. Hammond, ed., *Rolls and Documents Relating to Soldiers in the Revolutionary War* (Manchester, NH: John B. Clarke, 1887–89), 4:57 (hereafter cited as *NH Rolls*); (muskets) Samuel Fowler to the House of Representatives, December 30, 1783, *DRNH*, 11:203; *DRNH*, 4:48; Capt. Samuel Young's Petition, June 12, 1797, *DRNH*, 12:413–14.
9. A Pay Roll of Capt Lewi's Company of Indians . . . from the 20th of April to the 15th June 1776, r49 p43, M246. Louis's pay was actually the equivalent of a slightly higher artillery captain. Circumstantially, Schuyler and/or Arnold probably authorized Bedel's limited Indian enlistments, but there is no extant documentation.
10. ("the utmost dispatch . . .") John Hancock to Jonathan Trumbull, January 20, 1776, Letters relating to the years 1775 & 1776, Peter Force Collection, Library of Congress (hereafter cited as LOC); Philip Schuyler to President of Congress, February 10, 1776, *AA4*, 4:990; (Canadians) John Hamtramck, July 11, 1776, Notes of Witnesses' Testimony concerning the Canadian Campaign, *PTJ* (hereafter cited as Hamtramck Testimony), 1:451. The artillery men belonged to a new company formed in Montreal from reenlisted soldiers. Muster Roll of a Part of a Company of Artillery . . . Commanded by Wm. Johnston, November 29, 1776, r116 f19 p11, M246. Thanks to Frank Cecala and John Anson of John Lamb's Artillery Company (living history) for additional information.
11. ("inoculated themselves . . .") Charles Carroll of Carrollton to Charles Carroll of Annapolis, May 5, 1776, Ronald Hoffman, *Dear Papa, Dear Charley: The Peregrinations of a Revolutionary Aristocrat as Told by Charles Carroll of Carrollton and his Father, Charles Carroll of Annapolis . . .* (Chapel Hill: University of North Carolina Press, 2001), 2:904; (disease details) Elizabeth A. Fenn, *Pox Americana: The Great*

Smallpox Epidemic of 1775–82 (New York: Hill and Wang, 2001), 19–20; (Bedel inoculation) Bailey, "Reminiscences," 32.

12. ("Indian leggins") New-Hampshire Committee of Safety to Colonels Morey and Bellows, 21 January 1776, *AA4*, 4:811; Israel Morey to New-Hampshire Committee of Safety, 7 March 1776 and [undated, after March 13, 1776], *AA4*, 5:117–18, 427; (Burrall's) Charles M. Lefferts, *Uniforms of the American, British, French, and German Armies in the War of the American Revolution, 1775–1783* (Old Greenwich, CT: WE, 1976), 90. Morey's March 7 letter mentioned the need to provide some clothing before New Hampshire companies marched, but none of the loss claims and only one pension application mention any clothing issue. Ephraim Chamberlin W25060 p6, M804.

13. Benjamin Stevens, "Diary of Benjamin Stevens, of Canaan, Conn," *Daughters of the American Revolution Magazine* 45, nos. 2–3 (Aug.–Sept. 1914): 138; Wells, "Journal," 264; (Fort Ste. Anne) Claude Perrault, *Montréal en 1781: Déclaration du fief et seigneurie de L'ile de Montréal . . .* (Montreal, 1969), 145; Agenda Paper, Fort Senneville, Windmill and Sir John Abbott Summer Residence, No. 1962-11, 5–6, Department of Canadian Heritage fonds, R5747-7-0-E, 1539, LAC; *Site Historique et Archéologique du Fort-Senneville*; Report of architect Peter J. Stokes, April 1962, 2, Department of Canadian Heritage fonds, R5747-7-0-E, 1546, LAC; Louis Franquet, *Voyages et mémoires sur le Canada* (Quebec: Imprimerie Générale A. Coté, 1889), 41; Alexander D. Angus, *Old Quebec in the Days before Our Day* (Montreal: Louis Carrier, 1949), 196–97; Désiré Girouard, *Lake St. Louis, Old and New* (Montreal: Poirier, Bessette, 1893), 180.

14. ("at first much unwilling") April 25, Wells, "Journal," 264; Bailey, "Reminiscences," 34; (restoration) *Site Historique et Archéologique du Fort-Senneville*. Given their very similar names, it is often difficult to differentiate Jean-Baptiste-Philippe-Jérémie Testard de Montigny from his younger brother Jean-Baptiste-Pierre Testard Louvigny de Montigny, and father Chevalier Jean-Baptiste-Philippe Testard de Montigny. See "Le Lorimier et Le Montigny des Cèdres," *Le Bulletin des Recherches historiques* 47 no. 4 (Feb. 1941): 40–46; individual record #106944, UMPRDH; David A. Armour, "Testard de Montigny, Jean-Baptiste-Philippe," *DCB*; and François Béland, "Testard Louvigny de Montigny, Jean-Baptiste-Pierre," *DCB*.

15. (Butterfield arrival) Bailey, "Reminiscences," 32; April 25, Wells, "Journal," 264; ("well acquainted . . .") New-Hampshire General Court to George Washington, January 21, 1776, *PGWRWS*, 3:162; (militia major) New-Hampshire Provincial Congress, August 24, 1775, *DRNH*, 7:577; Charles Butterfield, *In the Shadow of Cedars* (Keene, NH: Historical Society of Cheshire County, 2013), 45, 51–52.

16. Bailey, "Reminiscences," 33; Stevens, "Diary," 138; (Pointe-de-Quinchien) Sébastien Daviau, *Manoir seigneurial de Michel Chartier de Lotbinière et la pointe Quinchien* (Vaudreuil-Dorion, Musée régional de Vaudreuil-Soulanges, September 15, 2014); Adhémar Jeannotte, *L'histoire de Vaudreuil* (Vaudreuil, QC: Société de Généalogie Vaudreuil-Cavagnal, 2015), 1; (Lotbinière) Marcel Hamelin, "Chartier de Lotbinière, Michel-Eustache-Gaspard-Alain," *DCB*. The seigneurial manor was near the west end of the modern Taschereau bridge, where traces of the millrace can still be seen. *Partez*

à la découverte de Vaudreuil-Dorion (Vaudreuil-Dorion, QC: Ville de Vaudreuil-Dorion, 2008), 5.
17. ("very pleasant country") Bailey, "Reminiscences," 33.
18. Jean-Luc Brazeau and Isabelle Aubuchon, *Les sépultures du coteau des Cèdres, 1750–1780* (Vaudreuil, QC: Centre d'histoire La Presqu'île, 2014), 19–20; Pouchot, *Memoir*, 2:96–97; s.v. "St. Lawrence, river," in Joseph Bouchette, *A Topographical Dictionary of the Province of Lower Canada* (London: Longman, Rees, Orme, Brown, Green, and Longman, 1832), n.p.; Mario Filion, *Histoire du Haut-Saint-Laurent* (Sainte-Foy, QC: Les Éditions de l'Institut québécois de recherche sur la culture, 2000), 145.
19. ("ignorant . . .") Shepardson, "Reminiscence," 3.
20. (weather) Stevens, "Diary," 138; Charles Carroll of Carrollton to Charles Carroll of Annapolis, April 30, 1776 [May 1 postscript], Hoffman, *Dear Papa, Dear Charley*, 2:902; Roger Stevenson, *Military Instructions for Officers Detached in the Field: Containing a Scheme for Forming a Corp of a Partisan* (Philadelphia, 1775), 13–14; David A. Simmons, "Military Architecture on the American Frontier," in *Selected Papers from the 1983 and 1984 George Rogers Clark Trans-Appalachian Frontier History Conferences*, ed. Robert J. Holden (Vincennes, IN: Eastern National Park and Memorial Association, 1985); ("designed for covering . . .") Francis Holliday, *An Easy Introduction to Fortification and Practical Gunnery* (London: G. Robinson, 1774), 186.
21. ("greater part . . . ," "with picquets . . .") Sherburne Testimony, 396; (banks) s.v. "Soulange," in Bouchette, *Topographical Dictionary*, n.p.; terrain characteristics supported by General James Murray's map of the St. Lawrence (1761), microfiche NMC17350, LAC. Pvt. Zephaniah Shepardson specified that the works extended beyond the buildings, being "fifteen or twenty rods" (72–100 meters) from them to the northern earthworks. Shepardson, "Reminiscence," 4, 8. There is no historical fort map, and the site was largely destroyed in the early twentieth century to build a massive hydroelectric plant. The most useful fort descriptions come from Shepardson and Lorimier.
22. (symptoms) Elizabeth A. Fenn, "Biological Warfare in Eighteenth-Century North America: Beyond Jeffery Amherst," *Journal of American History* 86, no. 4 (2000): 1559; Fenn, *Pox Americana*, 19–20. Jeduthan Baldwin's detailed account of his own smallpox, begun three weeks later, seems to broadly parallel Bedel's sparsely recorded symptoms. May 28, 1776, Baldwin, *Revolutionary Journal*, 49.
23. ("very nice . . . ," too large, two regiments) Bailey, "Reminiscences," 33; ("The extent . . .") Stevenson, *Military Instructions*, 10–11. The five-hundred-meter frontage estimate is based on Pvt. Zephaniah Shepardson's descriptions, overlaid on the detailed but imprecise Murray Map, and a map-overlaid satellite image in Brazeau, *Sépultures du coteau des Cèdres*, 39.
24. (Kahnawakes at Cedars) "Hartford, June 10," *Continental Journal* (Boston), June 13, 1776.
25. (Young) Bailey, "Reminiscences," 33; ("indian Packs") Wells, "Journal," 264; Stevens, "Diary," 138; Copy of Intelligence received from Montreal at Quebec the 14th of

May . . . , CO 42/35 (microfilm), fol. 22, LAC. Historian Paul L. Stevens suggested that this incident was a potential cause for Seven Nations' discontent with American occupation, but there is nothing in either primary account that indicates particular Indian displeasure with the encounter. Stevens, "His Majesty's 'Savage' Allies," 618.

26. ("In the afternoon . . .") Stevens, "Diary," 138; ("interrupted by a succession . . .") Mackenzie, *Voyages*, 1:lviii–lix; (May 9 departure) Wells, "Journal," 265.

Chapter 8

1. (blooms) Stevens, "Diary," 138; (Gananoque) Lorimier, *At War*, 48.
2. Stevens, *King's Colonel at Niagara*, 53.
3. (three war chiefs) Stevens, "His Majesty's 'Savage' Allies," 590; ("certain Indian . . . ," "was entirely . . . ," "prevailed on . . .") Conference of the Commissioners for Indian Affairs with the Six Nations of Indians, at German-Flats, August 13, 1776, *AA5*, 1:1046; ("the Iroquoian man . . .") Roland Viau, *Enfants du néant et mangeurs d'âmes: Guerre, culture et société en Iroquoisie ancienne* (Cap-Saint-Ignace, QC: Boréal, 1997), 202 (author's translation); Daniel K. Richter, *Ordeal of the Longhouse: The Peoples of the Iroquois League in the Era of European Colonization* (Chapel Hill: University of North Carolina Press, 1992), 36; Tiro, "Ambivalent Allies," 125–26.
4. ("both parties . . .") MacLeod, *Canadian Iroquois and the Seven Years' War*, x; Armstrong Starkey, *European and Native American Warfare, 1675–1815* (Norman: University of Oklahoma Press, 1998), 32; Ian K. Steele, *Warpaths: Invasions of North America* (New York: Oxford University Press, 1994), 217; McDonnell, *Masters of Empire*, 272.
5. ("induce them . . . ," "free plunder") Sherburne Testimony, 399; (prisoners) Hamtramck Testimony, 452. According to Sherburne, when American prisoners of war later confronted Forster about his recruitment methods, he did not deny offering these enticements.
6. (twenty-two Six Nations men, war song) Lorimier, *At War*, 48–49; (principally Senecas, Oneidas) Sherburne Testimony, 400; ("very stout," "taller . . .") July 23, 1776, Ebenezer Elmer, "Journal Kept during an Expedition to Canada in 1776," *Proceedings of the New Jersey Historical Society* 2 (1846–47), 158–59/161; ("took his life . . .") Lewis H. Morgan, *League of the Ho-dé-no-sau-nee, or Iroquois* (New York: Dodd, Mead, 1922), 1:332; Pouchot, *Memoir*, 2:242–43; Viau, *Enfants du néant et mangeurs d'âmes*, 89.

    Primary sources do not specifically identify Cayugas participating in the campaign, but a previous version of the official historic site plaque did. Filion, *Histoire du Haut-Saint-Laurent*, 99. Paul L. Stevens identified Cayuga passengers among those sailing from Niagara, without further mention in the campaign. Stevens, *King's Colonel at Niagara*, 53.

7. ("a speedy interview") Oneida Chiefs to Philip Schuyler, May 22, 1776, SKC [also *DRHNY*, 8:689]; ("the Kings words," presents) "At a Meeting," May 5, 1776, JBJ;

("disgusted ...") Conference of the Commissioners for Indian Affairs with the Six Nations of Indians, at German-Flats, August 13, 1776, *AA5*, 1:1046–47.

8. ("the interesting moral question ...") Starkey, *European and Native American Warfare*, 102; Walter H. Mohr, *Federal Indian Relations, 1774–1788* (Philadelphia: University of Pennsylvania Press, 1933), 37; Troy Bickham, *Savages within the Empire: Representations of American Indians in Eighteenth-Century Britain* (New York: Oxford University Press, 2005), 269; ("who undoubtedly ...") Potter, "Redcoats on the Frontier."

9. (uniforms) McConnell, *Army and Empire*, 64–65.

10. ("neither ...") Mileham, *"Difficulties Be Damned,"* 19; (demographics) Sylvia Frey, *The British Soldier in America: A Social History of Military Life in the Revolutionary Period* (Austin: University of Texas Press, 1981), 24 (Table 5) The 8th (King's) Regiment of Foot, 1782, data adjusted for 1776; (garrison life) McConnell, *Army and Empire*, 62, 99, 150; Stevens, *King's Colonel at Niagara*, 10.

11. ("two lieutenants ... ," "to relieve ...") Parke, *Authentic Narrative*, 21–22; Lorimier 46–48. The British force may have included every effective man in the unit; the company was authorized three officers, two sergeants, three corporals, two drummers, and thirty-eight privates, but units were rarely at full strength. This is another indication that Caldwell probably sent some reinforcements aboard the ship, to hold the fort in Forster's absence. Lieutenant Andrew Parke provided the total of 160 Indians, while Lorimier specified that 22 were Six Nations men from Niagara. While Lorimier claimed to have recruited 106 Indians in the hunting grounds, this probably was the actual number of northern Mississaugas that joined him at Oswegatchie. Overall, based on these numbers, the best estimated force composition at campaign's start is 106 northern Mississaugas, 32 western Mississaugas via Niagara, and 22 Six Nations warriors.

12. François-Auguste Magon de Terlaye, October 9, 1776, Parke, *Authentic Narrative*, 46; Pierre Foretier, "Notes and Reminiscences of an Inhabitant of Montreal during the Occupation of that City by the Bostonians from 1775 to 1776," *Annual Report of the Department of Public Archives for the Year 1945* (1946): xxiii; Lorimier, *At War*, 52.

13. (Montigny background) "Le Lorimier et Le Montigny," 43, 47; Jean-Baptiste Philippe Jeremie Testard de Montigny, Famille Testard de Montigny, MG18 H7, LAC; ("great influence," "attack the entrenchments ... ," "there were many persons ...") Sanguinet, "Témoin Oculaire," 128–29 (author's translation).

14. ("take the fire-arms ...") Bailey, "Reminiscences," 34; (Ste. Marie) Perraut, *Montréal en 1781*, 169.

15. (outfitter) Igartua, "Merchants and *Négociants* of Montreal," 84, 87–88; ("deceive the vigilance ...") Foretier, "Notes and Reminiscences," xxiii–xxiv; Edouard-Z. Massicotte, "Le bourgeois Pierre Fortier," *Bulletin des Recherches historiques* 47 (1941): 176–79; (Rue St. Pierre) Perrault, *Montréal en 1781*, 35; Joanne Burgess, "Foretier, Pierre," *DCB*; ("sumptuous") Mary W. Alloway, *Famous Firesides of French Canada* (Montreal: John Lovell & Sons, 1899), 155–56. Foretier's account is undated. The event

must have occurred after De Haas's April 28 Montreal arrival. "Extract of a Letter from Montreal, May 1, 1776," *Constitutional Gazette* (New York), May 18, 1776.

16. (Vaudreuil presbytery-chapel) Michel Bélisle, *Saint-Michel de Vaudreuil: Une Église Seigneuriale* (Vaudreuil, QC: Le Centre d'Histoire La Presqu'île, 1993), 4; Jeannotte, *L'histoire de Vaudreuil*, 9; Archibald Chaussegros de Léry McDonald, *Les Seigneuries de Vaudreuil et Rigaud* (Quebec: Les Publications Généalogiques, 1995), 32; ("deposited in a hole...") Foretier, "Notes and Reminiscences," xxiv.
17. ("party to turn back...," "would be slaughtered...") Lorimier, *At War*, 48.
18. ("Uncle...," "come along...") Lorimier, *At War*, 48–49. British accounts do not mention any events between Oswegatchie and Akwesasne.
19. ("good huts," church) Grant, "Journal," 307; ("Our flotilla...") Lorimier, *At War*, 49; (population) Stevens, "His Majesty's 'Savage' Allies," 93–94. Lorimier describes the entire trip from Oswegatchie to Akwesasne in two days, while Parke describes it taking three—Parke's account provides specific dates and better fits the overall timeline. The pro-American element approached General Wooster in late 1775, requesting a Dartmouth minister and schoolmaster for their community. Davenport Phelps to Eleazar Wheelock, January 1, 1776, Chase, *History of Dartmouth College*, 344–45; Solomon Walcutt to Eleazar Wheelock, December 18, 1775, 775668, EWC; "Memorandum of what I can recollect relative to the Settlement of St. Regis...," Daniel Claus, March 11, 1784, 21774, HP.
20. (foundation of St. Regis) Jack A. Frisch, "The Abenakis among the St. Regis Mohawks," *Indian Historian* 4 (Spring 1971): 27–28; Darren Bonaparte, "The History of the St. Regis Catholic Church and the Early Pastors," http://www.wampumchronicles.com/catholicchurch.html; Darren Bonaparte, "The History of Akwesasne from Pre-Contact to Modern Times," http://www.wampumchronicles.com/history.html; Gerald F. Reid, *Kahnawà:ke: Factionalism, Traditionalism, and Nationalism in a Mohawk Community* (Lincoln: University of Nebraska Press, 2004), 12; Parmenter, "At the Wood's Edge," 339; ("desiring...") A Meeting with Aughquisasnes [contemporary copy], *PSWJ*, 7:110; (Abenaki refuge) Jack A. Frisch, "Tribalism among the St. Regis Mohawks: A Search for Self-Identity," *Anthropologica* 12, no. 2 (1970): 209; (Abenaki numbers) Stevens, "His Majesty's 'Savage' Allies," 93–94.
21. ("refused to accompany...," "permitted...") Cannon, *Historical Record of the Eighth*, 68; ("made a feast," "sang...") Lorimier, *At War*, 48–50; (fifty-four Akwesasnes) Parke, *Authentic Narrative*, 21–23. While Cannon is a secondary source, his 1837 account seems well informed, including other mundane, plausible details missing from Parke's narrative. Lorimier's primary source account appears to combine two days at Akwesasne into one, while Parke's notably fails to mention Captain Forster in Akwesasne at all.

The only clearly identified Akwesasne warrior is Téhérése, rewarded by the British for his "considerable Service to Captn Forster in his affair at the Cedars," but who subsequently turned to be a pro-American spy and agitator. Alexander Fraser to Frederick Haldimand, August 7, 1779, 21780, HP. Burial records and Lorimier's memoirs imply that several Abenaki Akwesasnes took the warpath as well.

Historian Paul L. Stevens postulated that "chief" Ohquandageghte's death at the late-October Battle of Longueuil would have motivated Akwesasnes to vengeance, but primary sources indicate the chief was actually "detested" in the village, and not even considered an accepted member. Stevens, "His Majesty's 'Savage' Allies," 498–99; Journal of Daniel Claus, July 9, 1773, *PSWJ*, 13:621.

22. (Pointe-des-Nègres) Lorimier, *At War*, 49; (afternoon departure) Parke, *Authentic Narrative*, 22; (rain) Charles Cushing to his brother, July 8, 1776, *AA5*, 1:129. The author has been unable to identify Pointe-des-Nègres, presumably somewhere between modern Cameron's Point and South Lancaster, Ontario.

23. ("3,000 Americans . . . ," "fright of their lives") Lorimier, *At War*, 49–51. Lorimier specifically mentions Kahnawake chief Philip Sanórese, but it is unclear if it is a specific reference to his presence on the scene or a general comment on his ardent pro-American partisanship. A private reported two New Hampshire Rangers traveling upstream with Kahnawake scouts that day, so they may have been with the Indians for some or all of this mission. Shepardson, "Reminiscence," 6.

24. ("Tacit Neutrality") Richard Shuckburgh to Thomas Pownall, October 30, 1753, *PSWJ*, 1:390; August 2, 1708, and 23 Febry [1745], Peter Wraxall, *An Abridgment of the Indian Affairs* (Cambridge, MA: Harvard University Press, 1915), 58, 244; Jon W. Parmenter, "After the Mourning Wars: The Iroquois as Allies in Colonial North American Campaigns, 1676–1760," *William and Mary Quarterly* 64, no. 1 (2007): 40, 44, 50; Fenton, *Great Law and the Longhouse*, 266, 316, 446; Parmenter and Robinson, "Perils and Possibilities of Wartime Neutrality," 196; Richard Aquila, *The Iroquois Restoration: Iroquois Diplomacy on the Colonial Frontier, 1701–1754* (Detroit: Wayne State University Press, 1983), 149; Tiro, "Dilemmas of Alliance," 227. See chap. 19 for further discussion of Lorimier's enduring ignorance of this arrangement.

25. (Pointe-Beaudette arrival, "greatly discontented") Parke, *Authentic Narrative*, 22.

26. ("driven the enemy . . . ," "great consternation . . . ," "with great spirit," "hoping to arrive . . .") Parke, *Authentic Narrative*, 22; Lorimier, *At War*, 50. This news might have been delivered by Wendake (Lorette) Huron or Kanesatake messengers, and/ or Joseph-Marie La Mothe; La Requête de Joseph La Mothe . . . , undated, RG1-L3L v118 fol. 57648, LAC.

Chapter 9

1. ("there were fifty regulars . . .") Captains Estabrook's and Wilkins's Testimony respecting a breach of Convention at the Cedars, *AA5*, 1:166 (hereafter cited as Estabrook-Wilkins Testimony); (May 15) Stevens, "Diary," 138; Wells, "Journal," 265–66; Sherburne Testimony, 396; ("who had been . . .") "Hartford, June 10," *Continental Journal* (Boston), June 13, 1776. Many other details of this news story are grossly inaccurate. The Kahnawake scouts' temporary disappearance from the record could be another example of pan-Indian tacit neutrality—other Indians may have suggested that the scouts leave Fort Cedars before the upcoming attack, or they

may have opted to depart on their own to remove the risk they might be involved in Indian-on-Indian violence around the fort.
2. ("in as perfect...") Colonel Bedel's Defence, *NH Rolls*, 4:57; ("make peace... raising the Tomehack...") Shepardson, "Reminiscence," 3. No primary sources precisely date Bedel's Fort Cedars departure. Estimates vary from "two days before the Siege of the Cedars," to "4 or 6 days before the attack." Bailey, "Reminiscences," 38; Hamtramck Testimony, 451. It is clear that Bedel left the fort before the first substantiated reports arrived on May 15.
3. ("ordered to their Alarm Post...") Wells, "Journal," 265–66; Stevens, "Diary," 138; ("discontent... very little short of mutiny...") Colonel Bedel's Defence, *NH Rolls*, 4:57; ("nearly in a state...") Shepardson, "Reminscence," 6. The most reliable supply assessment comes from Estabrook-Wilkins Testimony, 166. Estabrook's name is variously spelled Eastabrook or Easterbrook as well.
4. ("bridge...," "lay in ambush...") Shepardson, "Reminscence," 6; ("twenty-five bags...") Stevens, "Diary," 138.
5. Bedel's smallpox symptoms are estimated from his April 21 inoculation date and a schedule of typical symptoms, biased to the few details known about his case. Bailey, "Reminiscences," 32; Fenn, *Pox Americana*, 19–20. A junior officer remembered that Bedel "was recovered" when he left the fort, but this may have been relative. Hamtramck Testimony, 451. Historian Elizabeth Fenn posed the question "Did Bedel pass the infection on to the Kahnawakes?" Given the circumstances, the Kahnawakes' intimate historical familiarity with the disease and expansive cross-cultural knowledge, and the lack of reported deaths among village headmen, it is doubtful that Bedel's visit had any real impact on the village, particularly in relation to the armywide outbreak throughout Canada. Fenn, *Pox Americana*, 72–73; John J. Heagerty, *Four Centuries of Medical History in Canada, and a Sketch of the Medical History of Newfoundland* (Toronto: Macmillan, 1928), 1:39–40, 80–81; Rénald Lessard, *Au temps de la petite vérole: La médecine au Canada aux XVIIe et XVIIIe siècles* (Quebec: Septentrion, 2012), 36–37.
6. ("manifested solid attachment...") John Wheelock, "The present state & situation of the Indian Tribes in the Province of Quebec," May 1779, 779301, and John Wheelock to Eleazar Wheelock, June 1, 1776, 776351, EWC; ("are friendly...") Philip Schuyler to George Washington, May 26, 1776, *AA4*, 6:578. In his May 1779 "The present state...," Wheelock reported attending a major Kahnawake council "just before our retreat from Canada," which based on his travels would have been sometime after April 22, and well before May 30. Dean left Canada on May 19. Ammi R. Robbins, *Journal of the Rev. Ammi R. Robbins, a Chaplain in the American Army in the Northern Campaign of 1776* (New Haven, CT: Yale College, 1850), 22.
7. ("a body of Savages...") Commissioners to Canada to John Hancock, May 17, 1776, Paul H. Smith, ed., *Letters of Delegates to Congress, 1774–1789* (Washington, DC: Library of Congress, 1976–2000), 4:23–24 (hereafter cited as *LDC*) [also *AA4*, 6:588]; ("the Savages...," "it could make...") Colonel Bedel's Defence, *NH Rolls*, 4:57.

8. ("in very little danger...") Benedict Arnold to Samuel Chase, May 15, 1776, *AA4*, 6:580; Frank A. Gardner, "Colonel John Paterson's Regiment," *Massachusetts Magazine* 8, no. 1 (Jan. 1915): 27; Thomas Egleston, *The Life of John Paterson, Major-General in the Revolutionary Army* (New York: G. P. Putnam's Sons, 1894), 50; (Berkshire Regiment) Abel Mattoon, S42913 p4, M804; (351 men) Return of the Regiments going on Command to Canada..., April 19, 1775, *AA4*, 5:985; (Paterson arrival) May 15, 1776, David Avery Journal, David Avery Papers, Connecticut Historical Society (hereafter cited as Avery Journal) [also Avery, "Northern Campaign," 18:236]; (bateaux shortage) Benjamin Franklin to Philip Schuyler, May 12, 1776, *LDC*, 3:666.
9. ("Of the Cowardice...") James Caldwell to Elias Boudinot, June 11, 1776, Thomas Addis Emmett Collection, Manuscripts and Archives Division, NYPL.
10. ("granting passports...") Commissioners in Canada to John Hancock, May 1, 1776, *AA4*, 5:1166; Copy of Intelligence received from Montreal at Quebec the 14th of May..., CO 42/35 (microfilm), fol. 22, LAC; ("their allies...") Thomas Walker to Samuel Adams, May 30, 1776, Samuel Adams Papers, NYPL.
11. Commissioners to Canada to Philip Schuyler, May 16, 1776, ("the approach...," "much to fear...") May 17, 1776, Smith, *LDC*, 4:5, 25.
12. ("was honored...") "Extract of a Letter from Major Henry Sherburne,... dated New-York, June 18," *Providence Gazette*, June 29, 1776 [also *AA4*, 6:598]; Edward R. Sherburne, *Some Descendants of Henry and John Sherburne, of Portsmouth, N. H.* (Boston: New-England Historic Genealogical Society, 1904), 22; John Greenwood, *The Revolutionary Services of John Greenwood, of Boston and New York, 1775–1783*, ed. Isaac J. Greenwood (New York: Devine Press, 1922), 122n; L. E. Rogers, *The Biographical Cyclopedia of Representative Men of Rhode Island* (Providence, RI: National Biographical Publishing, 1881), 150–51; ("that understands...") Nathanael Greene to Samuel Ward, Sr., October 16, 1775, Nathanael Greene, *The Papers of Nathanael Greene*, ed. Richard K. Showman (Chapel Hill: University of North Carolina Press, 1976), 1:134; (special missions) George Washington to John Hancock, April 15, 1776, *PGWRWS*, 4:70; Israel Putnam to President of Congress, April 4, 1776, *AA4*, 5:787; John Hancock to Israel Putnam, April 10, 1776, *AA4*, 5:843; ("bold...") Bailey, "Reminiscences," 35; (bravery) Greenwood, *Revolutionary Services*, 26; William Augustus Patterson to Council, 1779, Samuel Hazard, ed., *Pennsylvania Archives, Selected and Arranged from Original Documents* (Philadelphia: Joseph Severns, 1853), 7:167; Charles Carroll of Carrollton to Charles Carroll of Annapolis, May 27, 1776, Hoffman, *Dear Papa, Dear Charley*, 2:912.
13. (May 16 departure, 140 men) "Extract of a Letter from Major Henry Sherburne,... dated New-York, June 18," *Providence Gazette*, June 29, 1776 [also *AA4*, 6:598]; ("good, king's arms") May 14 and 17, 1776, Avery Journal; ("large stone barracks...," "fowling-pieces...") Greenwood, *Revolutionary Services*, 25; (volunteers) Love Roberts deposition, John Wooster, W26091 p10, M804; (orders) Commissioners to Canada to John Hancock, May 17, 1776, *LDC*, 4:24.

14. (wagons) Greenwood, *Revolutionary Services*, 26; ("fresh Supply . . .") Commissioners to Canada to John Hancock, May 17, 1776, *LDC*, 4:24; ("Sickness absolutely . . .") Colonel Bedel's Defence, *NH Rolls*, 4:57.
15. ("want of Batteaus," private property) Colonel Bedel's Defence, *NH Rolls*, 4:59; ("many Difficulties . . .") "Extract of a Letter from Major Henry Sherburne, . . . June 18," *Providence Gazette*, June 29, 1776 [also *AA4*, 6:598].
16. ("unhappy situation," "500 Canadians . . . ," "This information . . .") "Extract of a Letter from Major Henry Sherburne, . . . dated New-York, June 18," *Providence Gazette*, June 29, 1776 [also *AA4*, 6:598]; May 19, 1776, Avery Journal. Historian Justin H. Smith offers additional details, apparently from an unlocated May 18 Sherburne to Paterson letter cited in *Our Struggle for the Fourteenth Colony*, 2:369n19, 372–73.
17. (violent wind, "compelled") "Extract of a Letter from Major Henry Sherburne, . . . dated June 18," *Providence Gazette*, June 29, 1776 [also *AA4*, 6:598]; (south wind) Elisha Porter, "Diary of Col. Elisha Porter of Hadley, Massachusetts," *Magazine of American History* 30 (1893): 194; (twelve men) May 20, 1776, Avery Journal; ("received the most humane . . .") May 20, 1776, Lewis Beebe, "Journal of a Physician on the Expedition against Canada, 1776," ed. Frederic R. Kirkland, *Pennsylvania Magazine of History and Biography* 59, no. 4 (Oct. 1935): 329.
18. ("would fall . . .") Pouchot, *Memoir*, 2:98; September 4, 1760, Jeffery Amherst, *The Journal of Jeffery Amherst: Recording the Military Career of General Amherst in America from 1758 to 1763*, ed. J. Clarence Webster (Toronto: Ryerson Press, 1931), 244.
19. ("the Six Nations . . .") Lorimier, *At War*, 50; Parke, *Authentic Narrative*, 22–23.
20. (ten o'clock) Cannon, *Historical Record of the Eighth*, 68; Lorimier, *At War*, 50.
21. ("great difficulties") "The following authentic account is communicated by an officer of the detachment it principally concerns," *New-York Journal*, June 20, 1776; ("in Montreal . . .") Sherburne Testimony, Papers of Thomas Jefferson, LOC (online) [also *PTJ*, 1:399–400].

Chapter 10

1. ("We marched as fast . . .") Lorimier, *At War*, 50; Parke, *Authentic Narrative*, 22–23.
2. ("they refused . . .") Lorimier, *At War*, 50–51.
3. ("would never . . . show them . . . ," "You and I . . .") Lorimier, *At War*, 51; Isabel T. Kelsay, "Tekawiroñte," *DCB*.
4. ("at a distance . . . ," "sang") Lorimier, *At War*, 51–52; (seven o'clock) Stevens, "Diary," 139. Stevens's diary noted only one soldier wounded in the shoulder.
5. Parke, *Authentic Narrative*, 23; Lorimier, *At War*, 51.
6. The author concurs with historian Paul L. Stevens's observation and conclusions: "One should note that the two major British [sic] narratives diverge here and elsewhere concerning the enthusiasm of various participants. Parke, et al. recall that in several instances the Indians showed no hurry to advance, while Lorimier remembers that Forster appeared overly cautious at times. Given the normally cautious nature of

most British officers and the consistent British practice from 1775 through 1783 of letting the Indians take the greatest risks, I am inclined to favor Lorimier's version." Stevens, "His Majesty's 'Savage' Allies," 620n5.

7. (four or five soldiers) Shepardson, "Reminscence," 5–6; Lorimier, *At War*, 52; ("obstinately...") Parke, *Authentic Narrative*, 23. Lorimier recounted one killed, four wounded; Shepardson remembered one killed and two wounded; while Parke reported the one captured soldier and one scalp delivered to Forster.

8. ("horrors of war") Shepardson, "Reminscence," 7; ("a mode of torture...") Long, *Voyages and Travels*, 31; ("principal object... to bring...") Pouchot, *Memoir*, 2:248; John Heckewelder, *The History, Manners, and Customs of the Indian Nations Who Once Inhabited Pennsylvania and the Neighbouring States* (Philadelphia: Historical Society of Pennsylvania, 1881), 215; ("proof of conquest...") Ian K. Steele, *Betrayals: Fort William Henry and the "Massacre"* (New York: Oxford University Press, 1990), 89. See also Nathaniel Knowles, "The Torture of Captives by the Indians of Eastern Northern America," *Proceedings of the American Philosophical Society* 82 (1940): 152; R. S. Stephenson, "Iroquois War and Warfare," in Sylvia Kasprycki, ed., *On the Trails of the Iroquois* (Bonn: Kunst- und Ausstellungshalle der Bundesrepublik Deutschland, 2013), 114; Fenton, *Great Law and the Longhouse*, 260; T. S. Abler, "Scalping, Torture, Cannibalism and Rape: An Ethnocultural Analysis of Conflicting Cultural Values in War," *Anthropologica* 34, no. 1 (1992): 4; Francis Assikinack, "Social and Warlike Customs of the Odahwah Indians," *Canadian Journal of Industry, Science, and Art* 3, no. 16 (July 1858): 303; Wayne E. Lee, *Barbarians and Brothers: Anglo-American Warfare, 1500–1805* (New York: Oxford University Press, 2011), 155; and McDonnell, *Masters of Empire*, 183.

9. Shepardson, "Reminiscence," 7; (detachment) Stevens, "Diary," 138; (twenty men) Lorimier, *At War*, 52.

10. (Charles Gillett) Stevens, "Diary," 139; *History of Litchfield County, Connecticut with Illustrations and Biographical Sketches of its Prominent Men and Pioneers* (Philadelphia: J. W. Lewis, 1881), 572, 578; ("defended themselves vigorously," "enraged and shouted...") Lorimier, *At War*, 52. Lorimier believed Bonheur (of unidentified nationality) was killed, but British accounts consistently mention a single Indian death at Fort Cedars, and circumstantial evidence places that battlefield death on the second day. It is still quite possible that Bonheur's wounds later proved fatal.

11. (Lewis presumed killed) Stevens, "Diary," 139; Lorimier, *At War*, 52; ("Lame and ulcerated leg") Jabez Lewis, S37169 p4, M804, and "List of certificates... of Invalid Prisoners...," *American State Papers: Documents, Legislative and Executive of the Congress of the United States, Class IX, Claims* (Washington, DC: Gales and Seaton, 1834), 115.

12. ("as near...") Charles Stedman, *History of the Origin, Progress, and Termination of the American War* (London, 1794), 1:171; ("we beheld...") Shepardson, "Reminiscence," 7.

13. ("secreted behind...") Shepardson, "Reminscence," 7; ("Forster would not budge") Lorimier, *At War*, 52; ("The success...") "Rules and Orders for the Discipline of the

Light Infantry Companies... in Ireland," May 15, 1772, in Raymond H. R. Smythies, *Historical Records of the 40th (2nd Somersetshire) Regiment*... (Devonport, UK, 1894), 550. In an anachronistic reference, Lorimier noted that Forster remained near "the new church," later built closer to the portage, the modern location of Les Cèdres village. Élie-J. Auclair, *Histoire de la paroisse de Saint-Joseph-de-Soulanges, ou Les Cèdres (1702–1927)* (Montreal: Sourds-Muets, 1927), 57; Brazeau, *Les Sépultures du coteau des Cèdres*, 20; Moise Mainville, *Histoire de la paroisse Saint-Joseph de Soulanges (des débuts à 1900)* (Quebec: Les Publications Généalogiques, 1995), 15, 19.

14. ("a few guns...") Hamtramck Testimony, 451; ("reduced," "the artillery men could not hit...," "concluded...") Shepardson, "Reminiscence," 7; (personnel) Muster Roll of a Part of a Company of Artillery... Commanded by Wm. Johnston, November 29, 1776, and Pay Roll of Capt John Lamb's Company of Artillery, September 1, 1775, r116 f19 p11, and r75 f122 p4, M246. It is unclear exactly what Shepardson meant by "reduced"—his description does not fit the field pieces captured at Fort St. Johns. Descriptions of available ammunition at Fort Cedars imply that the two pieces fired different weights of shot. Estabrook-Wilkins Testimony, 166. Inexperienced gunners would still be expected to hit a target at around four hundred yards' range, with most error in range rather than azimuth. Janice E. McKenney, *The Organizational History of the Field Artillery, 1775–2003* (Washington, DC: Center of Military History, United States Army, 2007), 12; Ian Hogg and John H. Batchellor, *Armies of the American Revolution* (Englewood Cliffs, NJ: Prentice-Hall, 1975), 114; William Stevens, *A System for the Discipline of the Artillery of the United States of America*... (New York: William A. Davis, 1797), 45; David McConnell, *British Smooth-bore Artillery: A Technological Study to Support Identification, Acquisition, Restoration, Reproduction, and Interpretation of Artillery at National Historic Parks in Canada* (Ottawa: Minister of Supply and Services Canada, 1988). Frank Cecala of John Lamb's Artillery Company (living history) provided technical expertise and additional background on this topic.

15. ("excellent men... first cannon...") Hunter, *Quebec to Carolina*, 73–74 (from a story related by one of William Butler's loyalist rangers); ("could rarely...") John K. Mahon, "Anglo-American Methods of Indian Warfare, 1676–1794," *Mississippi Valley Historical Review* 45 (1958): 257.

16. ("fine gentlemanly officer") Bailey, "Reminiscences," 40; Gilmore, *New Hampshire Men at Bunker Hill*, 77; Daniel F. Secomb, *History of the Town of Amherst, Hillsborough County New Hampshire*... (Concord, NH: Evans, Sleeper & Woodbury, 1883), 368; Pay Roll of Capt Josiah Crosbey's Company, Hammond, *NH Rolls*, 1:102; ("rushd out...") Shepardson, "Reminiscence," 7–8; ("superb" barn, "body of 180 Americans," "had sortied...") Lorimier, *At War*, 52.

17. ("summoned...," "should they not...") Parke, *Authentic Narrative*, 23; Lorimier, *At War*, 53.

18. ("shewed...") Sherburne Testimony, 1, Papers of Thomas Jefferson, LOC [also *PTJ*, 1:397]; ("but was Prevented...") Edward Payson Williams to Joseph Williams, August 27, 1776, MSS L1993.1.502, Society of the Cincinnati; Estabrook-Wilkins

Testimony, 166; (council, Wilkins and Stevens, "all the subalterns...," "cried...") Hamtramck Testimony, 451; (three hours) Parke, *Authentic Narrative*, 23.

19. (aware of reinforcements, "the Indians were...") Stedman, *History*, 1:171; ("menaced with destruction...," "boasted...") "From a number of persons lately arrived from Canada...," *New-York Journal*, June 27, 1776; Cannon, *Historical Record of the Eighth*, 68; Berthelot, "Mémoire," 236; ("with their arms") Parke, *Authentic Narrative*, 23; Hamtramck Testimony, 451; (honors of war) Timothy J. Shannon, "French and Indian Cruelty?: The Fate of the Oswego Prisoners of War, 1756–1758," *New York History* (Summer 2014): 387; (refusal of terms, "hostilities again commenced") Parke, *Authentic Narrative*, 23. This negotiation exchange comes mainly from secondary sources, but they seem plausible and consistent, conforming with the broad strokes in Parke's less detailed account. The only eyewitness source for the artillery threat is Shepardson, "Reminiscence," 10–11. See chap. 11 for further discussion.
20. ("a reinforcement...") Parke, *Authentic Narrative*, 23–24. Parke wrote that the Canadians told Sherburne that Fort Cedars had already fallen, while Sherburne recounted that he was warned about an attack by superior forces that night. "Extract of a Letter from Major Henry Sherburne,... dated New-York, June 18," *Providence Gazette*, June 29, 1776 [also *AA4*, 6:598].
21. ("but the Indians...," "worked like brave boys... without victuals...") Shepardson, "Reminiscence," 10, 8; ("loose" fire) Hamtramck Testimony, 451; Stevens, "Diary," 139; Shepardson, "Reminiscence," 8.
22. (redoubt) Stedman, *History*, 1:172; Berthelot, "Mémoire," 236; (fenceposts) Lorimier, *At War*, 52.

Chapter 11

1. (150 yards, "kept up a fire...") Parke, *Authentic Narrative*, 24; ("the Indians disapeard...") Shepardson, "Reminiscence," 9. Shepardson mentioned that the "chief" he saw killed was "buried under armes by the British," presumably the unnamed Abenaki Indian buried in Les Cèdres cemetery on May 20; burial record #564264, UMPRDH. The Abenaki was probably from Akwesasne, based on contextual clues in Lorimier's account and given that no primary sources mention participants from Odanak.
2. ("men from time to time...") Sherburne Testimony, 397; ("seeing himself...") Bailey, "Reminiscences," 34–35. Sherburne's and Bailey's accounts are secondhand but derived from direct contact with battle participants.
3. Shepardson, "Reminiscence," 9; Nathaniel Bacon, S45513 pp2, 6, M804.
4. (ten o'clock arrival, thirty Canadians) Parke, *Authentic Narrative*, 24; ("corps of loyal Canadians") Foretier, "Notes and Reminiscences," xxiv; ("there appeared...") Shepardson, "Reminiscence," 11. Montigny's brother is the only other volunteer known by name. François Béland, "Testard Louvigny de Montigny, Jean-Baptiste-Pierre, *DCB*; Transcript of Louvigny testimony, Francois J. Audet to J. B. Harkin, March 1, 1927, Historic Sites—Battle of Cidres [sic], 1775, fol. 342, Department of Canadian Heritage fonds, R5747-0-8-E, LAC.

5. ("If we stayed...") Lorimier, *At War*, 52.
6. Lorimier, *At War*, 52; (word from Quebec City) La Requête de Joseph La Mothe..., undated, RG1-L3L v118, fol. 57648, LAC; François-Auguste Magon de Terlaye, October 9, 1776, Parke, *Authentic Narrative*, 46.
7. Parke, *Authentic Narrative*, 24.
8. Shepardson, "Reminiscence," 10–11; (travelers' accounts) Hunter, *Quebec to Carolina*, 61; Hadfield, *Diary*, 53.
9. Two other historians were unable to verify or debunk this story: Butterfield, *Shadow of Cedars*, 124n56; Stevens, "His Majesty's 'Savage' Allies," 2078n6. See also Julia Shaw, *Memory Illusion: Remembering, Forgetting, and the Science of False Memory* (London: Random House, 2016), 198, 200; and Elizabeth F. Loftus, "Creating False Memories," *Scientific American* 277, no. 3 (Sept. 1997): 71, 75.
10. (desertion) George Pettibone deposition, (John Willard) S11848 p15, M804; Bailey, "Reminiscences," 35; Hamtramck Testimony, 452. Lieutenant Hamtramck identified Estabrook as one of the cowardly officers, but he may have confused him with Everett. Other sources identified Estabrook as a brave leader and "fine man" after the campaign, and Arnold relied on his testimony to indict Butterfield. Sherburne Testimony, 397; Bailey, "Reminiscences," 38; Estabrook-Wilkins Testimony, 166.
11. ("assembled the many chiefs") George Forster to Isaac Butterfield, May 19, 1776, *AA5*, 1:162; ("overcome the resolution...") [George Forster to] Major Butterfield, May 19, 1776, in Parke, *Authentic Narrative*, 25; (Indian casualties) "The following authentic Account of the Skirmish at the Cedars...," *Quebec Gazette*, August 29, 1776; Charles Douglas to Philip Stephens, May 24, 1776, William J. Morgan, ed., *Naval Documents of the American Revolution* (Washington, DC: U.S. Government Printing Office, 1970), 5:244–45. Only the *Quebec Gazette* account specifies that the death was an Indian; but the author believes all described casualties were Indians. The one Indian killed was probably the Abenaki chief reported by Shepardson on May 19; Lorimier's associate Bonheur was wounded on May 18. An Abenaki named Pierre (perhaps Bonheur) died on July 19, possibly from wounds, and was buried in the Les Cèdres parish cemetery eight days later. "Pierre: Abénaquis," individual record #564271, UMPRDH; Brazeau, *Les sépultures du coteau des Cèdres*, 38.
12. (surrender details) Lorimier, *At War*, 53; Shepardson, "Reminiscence," 9, 11; Stevens, "Diary," 139. Contrasting with the other accounts, Lieutenant Parke recorded that the Americans actually initiated this final parley. Parke, *Authentic Narrative*, 24.
13. ("as the disposition...") [George Forster to] Major Butterfield, May 19, 1776, in Parke, *Authentic Narrative*, 25; ("the artillery...") George Forster to Isaac Butterfield, May 19, 1776, *AA5*, 1:162; ("much terrified") Estabrook-Wilkins Testimony, 166; (council of war) Hamtramck Testimony, 451; ("very sick...") Bailey, "Reminiscences," 35; ("if their lives...") Parke, *Authentic Narrative*, 25; Westmoreland History Committee, *History of Westmoreland (Great Meadow), New Hampshire, 1741–1970, and Genealogical Data* (Westmoreland, NH: Westmoreland History Committee, 1976), 60. The two documented versions of the terms agree in substance but vary considerably in form and detail.

14. (Wilkins and Stevens opposition) Hamtramck Testimony, 451; Estabrook-Wilkins Testimony, 166; (Estabrook, "permission to sally . . . ," "might induce . . .") Sherburne Testimony, 397; (fire on Stevens) Electa Jones, *Stockbridge, Past and Present; or Records of an Old Mission Station* (Springfield, MA: Samuel Bowles, 1854), 173.
15. Shepardson, "Reminiscence," 11–12.
16. Parke, *Authentic Narrative*, 25; (Yankee Doodle) Shepardson, "Reminiscence," 12. "Yankee Doodle" lyrics were written by a British army doctor during the French and Indian War as a "satiric look" at New England provincial soldiers.
17. Shepardson, "Reminiscence," 12; ("the best muskets . . .") Committee of Safety to Artemas Ward, February 6, 1777, *DRNH*, 8:485; ("Now we are . . .") Stevens, "Diary," 139. Lieutenant Parke and Major Butterfield agree that 390 were taken prisoner, but only 340 are accounted for (see Fort Cedars Totals, appendix A)—the higher number might include camp followers, or it could reflect soldiers missing from exchange rolls and/or additional unidentified captives, Parke, *Authentic Narrative*, 28; Major Butterfield's testimony respecting a breach of the Convention at the Cedars, June 1776, *AA5*, 1:166 (hereafter cited as Butterfield Testimony).
18. Parke, *Authentic Narrative*, 25–26; ("all the plunder . . .") Estabrook-Wilkins Testimony, 166; Butterfield Testimony, 165.
19. (officers' baggage) Hamtramck Testimony, 451; Petition and Remonstrance of the Company Commanded by Capt Daniel Wilkins, March 10, 1779, *NH Rolls*, 1:476–77. Hamtramck said both Butterfield and Capt. John Stevens had specified that the terms protected officers' baggage.
20. (two chiefs, "to take the plunder . . .") Parke, *Authentic Narrative*, 25–26; Steele, *Betrayals*, 114; "Transactions at Fort William Henry during its Siege in August, 1757," in Ian K. Steele, "Suppressed Official Report of the Siege and 'Massacre' at Fort William Henry, 1757," *Huntington Library Quarterly* 55, no. 2 (Spring 1992): 347; MacLeod, *Canadian Iroquois in the Seven Years' War*, 94, 114.
21. (dissatisfied, "of some watches . . .") Parke, *Authentic Narrative*, 26.
22. ("Indians immediately") Hamtramck Testimony, 451; ("The savages did plunder . . .") Butterfield Testimony, 165.
23. ("365 of our men . . .") Shepardson, "Reminiscence," 13. Shepardson's description of 365 men possibly reflects 21 officer prisoners being kept in another building, or perhaps counts 25 camp followers in the 390-prisoner total provided by other sources (see above).
24. ("Nearly four hundred plucky fellows . . .") Smith, *Our Struggle for the Fourteenth Colony*, 2:371; Douglas R. Cubbison, *The American Northern Theater Army in 1776: The Ruin and Reconstruction of the Continental Force* (Jefferson, NC: McFarland, 2010), 95; Gustave Lanctot, *Canada and the American Revolution, 1774–1783*, trans. Margaret Cameron (Cambridge, MA: Harvard University Press, 1967), 141; (supplies) Estabrook-Wilkins Testimony, 166. One death came in the initial house fight on the first day, and Private Gillet was killed in the Cascades supply train ambush. At least one more was presumed dead but actually captured, Pvt. Jabez Lewis. One or two men were wounded by Lorimier and Tekawiroñte in the opening exchange,

and two more in the initial house fight. William Roby (Wilkins's company), and Joel Woodworth (Green's company) may have been among the wounded. Francis B. Heitman, *Historical Register of Officers of the Continental Army during the War of the Revolution, April, 1775, to December, 1783* (Washington, DC: Rare Book Shop, 1904), 471; Joel Woodworth pension claim, S45455 p7, M804. Howard H. Peckham, ed., *The Toll of Independence: Engagements & Battle Casualties of the American Revolution* (Chicago: University of Chicago Press, 1974), 17, records just two killed and one wounded.

25. (honorable defense) Ian K. Steele, "Surrendering Rites: Prisoners on Colonial North American Frontiers," in *Hanoverian Britain and Empire: Essays in Memory of Philip Lawson* (Woodbridge, UK: Boydell Press, 1998), 148; Shannon, "French and Indian Cruelty?," 387; ("The Iroquois cultivated . . .") Colin G. Calloway, "An Uncertain Destiny: Indian Captives on the Upper Connecticut River, *Journal of American Studies* 17 (1983): 199. Historian Charles Butterfield provides the most deliberate and balanced assessment of Isaac Butterfield's decision making; Butterfield, *Shadow of the Cedars*, 124, 126–27.

26. [Isaac Kimber] An Impartial Hand, *The History of England: From the Earliest Accounts to the Accession of His Present Majesty King George II* (London, 1762), 490; John Entick, *The General History of the Late War: Containing Its Rise, Progress, and Event* . . . (London, 1763), 2:401; Thomas Mante, *The History of the Late War in North-America and the Islands of the West-Indies* (London, 1772), 95–97; Robert G. Parkinson, *The Common Cause: Creating Race and Nation in the American Revolution* (Chapel Hill: University of North Carolina Press, 2016), 92–93; Charles Johnston to the New-Hampshire Congress, [undated, June 1775?], *DRNH*, 7:503; Thomas Jefferson to John Page, October 31, 1775, and Committee at Camp to George Washington, March 9, 1778, Smith, *LDC*, 2:279–80, 9:248–49; "Last evening arrived here John Brown . . . ," *Maryland Journal* (Baltimore), May 17, 1775.

27. (Cedars smallpox) Hamtramck Testimony, 1:451; (Butterfield smallpox) Bailey, "Reminiscences," 35; (potential concern for sick) Sherburne Testimony, 397; ("massacres") Steele, *Betrayals*, 79, 115; (Fort Oswego) [Anonymous], *The Military History of Great Britain for 1756, 1757, Containing a Letter from an English Officer at Canada Taken Prisoner at Oswego* (London: J. Millan, 1757), 41–42; (Fort William Henry) "Extract of a letter from Albany, dated August 15," *New-York Mercury*, August 22, 1757, and other contemporary reports.

28. ("The obstinate defence . . .") Stevenson, *Military Instructions*, 122–23.

Chapter 12

1. Sherburne reported having 100 men, Lorimier reported "about 120," while the author has accounted for only 80–89 (see appendix A). If the ranges of numbers killed in action at Quinchien (10–12) and promptly taken captive (0–8) are added to Lieutenant Parke's report of 97 prisoners of war, it appears Sherburne had somewhere from 107 to 117 men that day; "The following authentic account . . . , New-York, June 20,"

New-York Journal, June 20, 1776; Sherburne Testimony, 397; "Extract of a Letter from Major Henry Sherburne, ... dated New-York, June 18," *Providence Gazette*, June 29, 1776 [also *AA4*, 6:599]; Lorimier, *At War*, 55. Three New Hampshire Rangers are known Quinchien participants: Joseph Hadley, Solomon Cleveland, and James Derry. Bailey, "Reminiscences," 35; List of the Prisoners ... taken at Fort Cedars, Canada, *AA5*, 1:168; Report of the Secretary of War on the Petitions of James Derrey and Benjamin Hardison, June 23 and 25, 1790, in Kenneth Bowling, William C. DiGiacomantonio, and Charlene B. Bickford, eds., *Petition Histories: Revolutionary War Related Claims, Series: Documentary History of the First Federal Congress of the United States of America, March 4, 1789–March 3, 1791* (Baltimore: Johns Hopkins University Press, 1997), 7:417–18.
2. "Extract of a Letter from Major Henry Sherburne, ... dated New-York, June 18," *Providence Gazette*, June 29, 1776 [also *AA4*, 6:599]; Lorimier, *At War*, 55. The unidentified island may have been modern Île Todd, possibly known as Île Vaudreuil in the eighteenth century. Franquet, *Voyages et Memoirs*, 42.
3. "The following authentic account ... , New-York, June 20," *New-York Journal*, June 20, 1776; "Extract of a Letter from Major Henry Sherburne ... dated New-York, June 18," *Providence Gazette*, June 29, 1776 [also *AA4*, 6:598]. Sherburne reported a nine-mile march to the Cedars, but it is roughly eleven statute miles.
4. Jeanotte, *L'histoire de Vaudreuil*, 1 (author's translation); Pierre-Georges Roy, *Les Noms Géographiques de la Province de Québec* (Lévis, QC, 1906), 322; *Partez à la découverte de Vaudreuil-Dorion*, 6; Michel Bélisle, *De L'Isle-aux-Tourtes à Vaudreuil-Dorion* (Vaudreuil-Dorion, QC: Collectif pour l'histoire de Vaudreuil-Dorion, 2007), 2; William Kingsford, *The History of Canada* (Toronto: Rowsell & Hutchison, 1893), 6:48.
5. Parke, *Authentic Narrative*, 24; (Lefebvre) "Sous Trois Pavillons," *La Presqu'ile* [Montréal], date unknown, Fonds Robert-Lionel-Séguin, 5.13.41, Centre d'Archives Vaudreuil-Dorion; Lorimier, *At War*, 54; (Île Perrot participants) Michel Chartier de Lotbinière to Frederick Haldimand, March 5, 1779, Un Volontaire Canadien de 1775 [typescript, source unknown], Fonds de Beaujeu P03, H-368, Centre d'Archives Vaudreuil-Dorion.
6. (orders to Lorimier) Parke, *Authentic Narrative*, 26–27; Lorimier, *At War*, 53–54; ("ardent royalist," sergeant major) Gérard Malchelosse, "Les juifs dans l'histoire canadienne," *Cahiers des Dix* 4 (1939): 169–70; Jacob Maurer, individual record #2312238, UMPRDH; (Lorimier brother) Édouard-Zotique Massicotte, "La Famille de Lorimier: Notes généalogiques et historiques," *Bulletin des Recherches historiques* 21 (1915): 15; "Le Lorimier et Le Montigny," 37–38; Stevens, "His Majesty's 'Savage' Allies," 378; ("savages whooped ...") Stevens, "Diary," 139; Shepardson, "Reminiscence," 13. The Abenakis were almost certainly from Akwesasne, especially in consideration of minor details in Lorimier's memoirs.
7. (about twenty Canadians, muskets) Lorimier, *At War*, 54. Parke accounted for eighty Indians and eighteen Canadians with Lorimier. Parke, *Authentic Narrative*, 27. He apparently did not include those men that Lorimier recruited on the march.

8. Lorimier, *At War*, 54; (bridge) Bailey, "Reminiscences," 35; ("At the passage...") Stevenson, *Military Instructions*, 68. Bailey's account was informed by participant Joseph Hadley. Based on primary sources and period maps, the author believes the ambush occurred near the present-day northern intersection of Route de Lotbinière and Rue Meloche in Vaudreuil-Dorion, immediately north of Pointe-à-Valois. The author subsequently found a local history offering a similar conclusion, bounding the site "between the current Summerlea golf course and [rue] Bellerive" (author's translation). Bélisle, *Isle-aux-Tourtes à Vaudreuil-Dorion*, 103.
9. Lorimier, *At War*, 53–54; Parke, *Authentic Narrative*, 27; "On Their Discipline and Method of War," James Smith, *An Account of the Remarkable Occurrences in the Life and Travels of Col. James Smith, during his Captivity with the Indians...*, ed. William Darlington (Cincinnati: Robert Clarke, 1907), 152; ("usual flanking...") Leroy V. Eid, "'A Kind of Running Fight': Indian Battlefield Tactics in the Late Eighteenth Century," *Western Pennsylvania Historical Magazine* 71 (1988): 156; Stedman, *History*, 1:173–74; Greenwood, *Revolutionary Services*, 27; Bailey, "Reminiscences," 35.
10. ("As soon as...") Greenwood, *Revolutionary Services*, 27; David Grossman, *On Combat: The Psychology and Physiology of Deadly Conflict in War and Peace* (Belleville, IL: Warrior Science Publications, 2004), 67; George C. Neumann, *Battle Weapons of the American Revolution: The Historian's Complete Reference* (Texarkana, TX: Scurlock, 1998), 11. Greenwood was not actually present, but he presumably received this account through participants in his company.
11. ("At the first moment...") Pouchot, *Memoir*, 2:246; Lorimier, *At War*, 54; ("make the stoutest heart...") Scudder, *Journal*, 36; ("We stood...") "Extract of a Letter from Major Henry Sherburne,... dated New-York, June 18," *Providence Gazette*, June 29, 1776 [also *AA4*, 6:598]; Sherburne Testimony, 397; "The following authentic account..., New-York, June 20," *New-York Journal*, June 20, 1776; Bailey, "Reminiscences," 34–36.
12. ("first... their general maxim...") "Of the Temper and Genius of the Indians," William Smith, *Historical Account of Bouquet's Expedition against the Ohio Indians in 1764* (Cincinnati: Robert Clarke, 1868), 90; "On Their Discipline and Method of War," Smith, *Account of the Remarkable Occurrences*, 153.
13. ("maintained an obstinate...") "The following authentic account..., New-York, June 20," *New-York Journal*, June 20, 1776; Greenwood, *Revolutionary Services*, 27; ("done with the greatest Order") "Extract of a Letter from Major Henry Sherburne... dated New-York, June 18," *Providence Gazette*, June 29, 1776 [also *AA4*, 6:598–99]; Sherburne Testimony, 397. Sherburne believed his men fought for about an hour before retreating; but based on the flow of battle, casualties, and Indian tactics, he almost certainly experienced temporal distortion, remembering it lasting far longer than reality. Dawson, "Massacre at the Cedars," 14; Grossman, *On Combat*, 54–55, 96–97, 116.
14. ("proceeded methodically...") Eid, "Kind of Running Fight," 154.
15. ("fought like Lions!") May 24, 1776, Avery Journal; ("except when occasionally...") Sherburne Testimony, 397.

16. Lorimier, *At War*, 54; Bailey, "Reminiscences," 35. Hadley identified the Seneca as a chief because he was wearing a uniform coat and lace hat. Hadley's description of this encounter, recounted by Bailey, correlates well with Lorimier's, but the private's account before and after this firefight is an outright yarn, spun with heaping exaggerations and lies, presumably to make a better story.
17. ("One of my Indians . . . ," "had part of his nose . . . ," "I would not say . . .") Lorimier, *At War*, 54; (Kanughsgawiat) Minutes of Indian Affairs, January 28, 1780, MG19 RG10 ser. 2, v12, fol. 130 (microfilm C-1233), LAC; (buck-and-ball load) Berkeley R. Lewis, *Small Arms and Ammunition in the United States Service* (Washington, DC: Smithsonian Institution, 1956), 108. Aichinger's translation misidentifies "Tsonnotouan" and "Misisagué" as personal names—they are actually French for "Seneca" and "Mississauga" nationalities. Lorimier, *At War*, 54, *Mes Services*, 277–78.
18. ("I did not see . . .") "Extract of a Letter from Major Henry Sherburne . . . dated New-York, June 18," *Providence Gazette*, June 29, 1776 [also *AA4*, 6:599]; ("rushed forwards . . .") Sherburne Testimony, 397; ("active, energetic") Nathan Goold, *History of Col. James Scamman's Thirtieth Regiment of Foot* . . . (Portland, ME: Thurston Print, 1899), 45. The author estimates that the retreat was cut off at a stream bridge south of Pointe-aux-Chênes, about two miles from the ambush site. Primary accounts imply that Sullivan commanded the middle division. It is unclear which divisions McKinstry and Bliss led.
19. Lorimier, *At War*, 54; Parke, *Authentic Narrative*, 27; (Lefebvre) "Sous Trois Pavillons," *La Presqu'ile* [Montréal], date unknown, Fonds Robert-Lionel-Séguin, cote 5.13.41, Centre d'Archives Vaudreuil-Dorion; "Extract of a Letter from Major Henry Sherburne, . . . dated New-York, June 18," *Providence Gazette*, June 29, 1776 [also *AA4*, 6:598–99]; ("behaved . . . ," last to surrender) John Sullivan to John Hancock, undated, rg360 i160 r178 pp53–54, M247; (out of ammunition) Ebenezer Sullivan to Thomas Mifflin, January 1784, rg360 i42 r56 v7 p174, M247; (surrender) Stevens, "Diary," 139.
20. ("that Monsieur de Montigny . . . ," "made prisoners . . .") Parke, *Authentic Narrative*, 27; ("Just as I . . .") Lorimier, *At War*, 54; "The following authentic account . . . , New-York, June 20," *New-York Journal*, June 20, 1776.
21. Sherburne Testimony, 397; ("The story . . .") Kingsford, *History of Canada*, 61.
22. ("vile Conduct . . .") "Extract of a Letter from Major Henry Sherburne, . . . dated New-York, June 18," *Providence Gazette*, June 29, 1776 [also *AA4*, 6:599]; ("he had still . . .") Cubbison, *Northern Theater Army*, 97; Butterfield, *Shadow of Cedars*, 143. See also Charles H. Jones, *History of the Campaign for the Conquest of Canada in 1776* . . . (Philadelphia: Porter and Coates, 1882), 56.
23. (casualties) Sherburne Testimony, 398; "The following authentic account . . . , New-York, June 20," *New-York Journal*, June 20, 1776; "Extract of a Letter from Major Henry Sherburne, . . . dated New-York, June 18," *Providence Gazette*, June 29, 1776 [also *AA4*, 6:599]; ("10 only . . .") May 25, 1776, Avery Journal [Avery, "Northern Campaign," 18:239, fails to include "not one officer"]. From twenty pension applications submitted by soldiers at Quinchien, only Pvt. Jesse Hollister from McKinstry's

company reported being wounded. Jesse Hollister S39736 p5, M804. Only two officers are known to have been wounded: Capt. John McKinstry and Lt. Nathan Lord; Beebe. "Journal," 330; Heitman, *Historical Register*, 357. A casualty compilation for each Revolutionary War battle recorded five dead and no wounded, without citation. Peckham, ed., *Toll of Independence*, 17.

24. ("the Enemy lost . . .") "Extract of a Letter from Major Henry Sherburne, . . . dated New-York, June 18," *Providence Gazette*, June 29, 1776 [also *AA4*, 6:599]; Sherburne Testimony, 398; Lorimier, *At War*, 54; Hector Cramahé to George Germain, May 25, 1776, CO 42/35 (microfilm), fol. 48, LAC; Charles Douglas to Philip Stephens, May 25, 1776, Morgan, *Naval Documents of the American Revolution*, 5:244; Stedman, *History*, 1:173. British officers interpreted Forster's reports differently; the casualties were ambiguously from Fort Cedars, Quinchien, or both. Lieutenant Parke (not present at Quinchien) reported one killed and three wounded. Parke, *Authentic Narrative*, 28.

25. Parke, *Authentic Narrative*, 28; ("The collision . . .") Steele, *Warpaths*, 9. Parke reported that ninety-seven prisoners were consolidated with the others at Fort Cedars but did not quantify the "few" he reported being kept as Indian captives that day; Sherburne numbered them at seven or eight. "The following authentic account . . . , New-York, June 20," *New-York Journal*, June 20, 1776.

Chapter 13

1. ("their ability . . .") MacLeod, *Canadian Iroquois and the Seven Years' War*, 114.
2. ("There was no . . .") Preston, *Braddock's Defeat*, 299, ("the standard . . .") 301; McDonnell, *Masters of Empire*, 170, 173. For a 1776 example of Indians' Monongahela memory, in which an Indian chief and his son wear trophies of this victory to a British-hosted council, see William L. Stone, ed., *Memoirs and Letters and Journals of Major General Riedesel*, trans. Max von Eelking (Albany, NY: J. Munsell, 1868), 1:55.
3. ("The Barbarity . . .") "Extract of a Letter from Major Henry Sherburne, . . . dated New-York, June 18," *Providence Gazette*, June 29, 1776 [also *AA4*, 6:599–600]; ("savages who . . .") "An Oration; . . . ," *Boston Post Boy*, March 20, 1775; Alden T. Vaughan and Daniel K. Richter, "Crossing the Cultural Divide: Indians and New Englanders, 1605–1763," *Proceedings of the American Antiquarian Society* 90 (Oct. 1980): 81–82.
4. Stevens, "His Majesty's 'Savage' Allies," 623; Francis Jennings, *Empire of Fortune: Crowns, Colonies, and Tribes in the Seven Years War* (New York: Norton, 1988), 188, 202; ("Incidents of this kind . . .") Thomas Mante, *The History of the Late War in North-America and the Islands of the West-Indies* (London, 1772), 95–97; ("Scenes of violence . . .") Ari Kelman, *A Misplaced Massacre: Struggling over the Memory of Sand Creek* (Cambridge, MA: Harvard University Press, 2013), 8.
5. See Grossman, *On Combat*; Mark L. Howe and Laura M. Knott, "The Fallibility of Memory in Judicial Processes: Lessons from the Past and Their Modern

Consequences," *Memory* 23 (July 2015): 633–56; and Laura Engelhardt, "The Problem with Eyewitness Testimony, Commentary on a talk by George Fisher and Barbara Tversky," *Stanford Journal of Legal Studies* 1 (Dec. 1999): 25–29.
6. (captives) Pouchot, *Memoir*, 2:248; Knowles, "Torture of Captives," 211; (effects) Wendy Lucas Castro, "Stripped: Clothing and Identity in Colonial Captivity Narratives," *Early American Studies: An Interdisciplinary Journal* 6, no. 1 (2008): 127; ("touched") Lorimier, *At War*, 55.
7. ("You will have . . . ," What! . . . ," "Keep the bird . . .") Lorimier, *At War*, 55; (contested claims) Haefeli and Sweeney, *Captors and Captives*, 132; Viau, *Enfants du néant et mangeurs d'âmes*, 121–22.
8. Lorimier, *At War*, 55; (1757 service) Gardner, "Paterson's Regiment," 40.
9. (Lorimier-Portneuf exchange) Lorimier, *At War*, 55; Thomas-M. Charland, "Hertel de Saint-François, Joseph-Hippolyte," *DCB*. Based on Hertel's close ties with Akwesasne Abenakis, he may have had some form of kin relationship in the subcommunity.
10. ("a scene of Savage Barbarity . . .") "The following authentic account . . . , New-York, June 20," *New-York Journal*, June 20, 1776; ("fell to work . . . ," "The dead . . .") Greenwood, *Revolutionary Services*, 27; ("proof of valor") Knowles, "Torture of Captives," 210; Assikinack, "Social and Warlike Customs," 303; Pouchot, *Memoir*, 2:248. Greenwood was not present but his account was informed by participants.
11. ("before the Americans . . .") Lorimier, *At War*, 55–56. Lorimier's account seems plausible; American captive accounts ignore the incident altogether, perhaps tacitly silent in their complicity. Only a single Continental's secondhand account even mentions the island detachment's capture; Greenwood, *Revolutionary Services*, 27; ("After they had stripped us . . .") "Extract of a Letter from Major Henry Sherburne, . . . dated New-York, June 18," *Providence Gazette*, June 29, 1776 [also *AA4*, 6:599].
12. ("very unruly") Parke, *Authentic Narrative*, 27–28; Stevens, "Diary," 139; Shepardson, "Reminiscence," 13.
13. ("lost a principal . . . ," "savages . . .") Parke, *Authentic Narrative*, 28; Stedman, *History*, 1:173; Dawson, "Massacre at the Cedars," 11. See also Pouchot, *Memoir*, 2:252; Heckewelder, *History, Manners, and Customs*, 106; and Milton W. Hamilton, ed., "Guy Johnson's Opinions on the American Indian," *Pennsylvania Magazine of History and Biography* 77 (July 1953): 322.
14. ("most spirited . . .") Cannon, *Historical Record of the Eighth*, 58; (every effort) Parke, *Authentic Narrative*, 28; ("savages were determined . . .") Stevens, "Diary," 139; Greenwood, *Revolutionary Services*, 28; ("to stop their Outrage," "Eight Yoke . . .") "Narrative of John Peters," Colonel John Peters Papers, NYHS, 5; Stedman, *History*, 1:173–74. Peters was in Montreal but claimed to have communications with Captain Forster. Several details in Peters's narrative appear unreliable.
15. Sherburne Testimony, 398; Estabrook-Wilkins Testimony, 166; Hamtramck Testimony, 451; ("the whole evidence . . .") Dawson, "Massacre at the Cedars," 14. Even if they were mostly from the same regiment, many of Sherburne's men might not have

known each other by name, having been drawn from several companies into an ad hoc task force just a few days earlier. John Peters was not present, but he provided the sole dissenting loyalist view, suggesting that the Indians "killed several Captives." "Narrative of John Peters," Colonel John Peters Papers, NYHS, 5.

16. ("was first shot...") Sherburne Testimony, 398; ("a nation...") Heckewelder, *History, Manners, and Customs*, 218; Abler, "Scalping, Torture, Cannibalism and Rape," 10; Knowles, "Torture of Captives," 194–95; Smith, *Account of the Remarkable Occurrences*, 12; Butterfield, *Shadow of Cedars*, 145. For examples of expectations, see "Instances of Constancy..., when suffering the fiery Torture," *Essex Journal* (Newburyport, MA), October 6, 1775; and Scudder, *Journal*, 37.

17. ("uttered....") "Col. John McKinstry," *Dutchess Observer* (Poughkeepsie, NY), June 19, 1822; *Masonic Miscellany and Ladies' Literary Magazine* 2, no. 2 (Aug. 1822): 47–48; William L. Stone, *Life of Joseph Brant—Thayendanegea*, vol. 1 (New York: Alexander V. Blake, 1838), 153; David Harrison, "Joseph Brant: A Masonic Legend," *MQ Magazine* 23 (Oct. 2007), http://www.mqmagazine.co.uk/issue-23/p-33.php; Christopher Hodapp, *Freemasons for Dummies* (Hoboken, NJ: John Wiley & Sons, 2013).

18. "Brant's Visit to England, 1776," Draper Manuscripts, Series F, Joseph Brant, vol. 2, 78, Wisconsin Historical Society; Barbara Graymont, "Thayendanegea," *DCB*; (son's confirmation) Stone, *Life of Joseph Brant*, 155; Letter to Lyman Draper, Hudson, July 25, 1874, Draper Manuscripts, Series F, Joseph Brant, vol. 2, 112, Wisconsin Historical Society; ("imagination inflation") Loftus, "Creating False Memories," 74, 75; Isabel T. Kelsay, *Joseph Brant, 1743–1807: Man of Two Worlds* (Syracuse, NY: Syracuse University Press, 1984), 174; John L. Brooke, *Columbia Rising: Civil Life on the Upper Hudson from the Revolution to the Age of Jackson* (Chapel Hill: University of North Carolina Press, 2010), 536–37n40; "Captn. McKinstry & Brant, The Cedars, May 19th–20th 1776," Draper Manuscripts, Series F, Joseph Brant, vol. 2, 108, Wisconsin Historical Society. See also Shaw, *Memory Illusion*, xiv, 189, 200; Giuliana A. L. Mazzoni, Elizabeth F. Loftus, and Irving Kirsch, "Changing Beliefs about Implausible Autobiographical Events: A Little Plausibility Goes a Long Way," *Journal of Experimental Psychology: Applied* 7, no. 1 (2001): 51, 57; and Deryn Strange and Melanie K. T. Takarangi, "Memory Distortion for Traumatic Events: The Role of Mental Imagery," *Frontiers in Psychiatry* 6 (Feb. 2015): 1.

19. (Knox) Sylvia J. Sherman, ed., *Dubros Times: Selected Depositions of Maine Revolutionary War Veterans* (Augusta: Maine State Archives, 1975); C. C. Lord, *A History of the Descendants of Nathan Lord of Ancient Kittery, Me.* (Concord, N.H.: Rumford Press, 1912), 41.

20. ("designated for...," "misinformed...") William L. Stone, *Border Wars of the American Revolution* (New York: A. L. Fowle, 1900), 1:135; Steele, *Betrayals*, 115–16.

21. Steele, "Surrendering Rites," 138–39; (captive options) Knowles, "Torture of Captives," 211; Lee, *Barbarians and Brothers*, 155; Way, "Cutting Edge of Culture," 141; J. C. B., *Travels in New France by J. C. B.*, ed. Sylvester K. Stevens, Donald H. Kent, and Emma E. Woods (Harrisburg: Pennsylvania Historical Commission, 1941), 100;

Brett Rushforth, *Bonds of Alliance: Indigenous and Atlantic Slaveries in New France* (Chapel Hill: University of North Carolina Press, 2012), 19.

22. (ransom ascendance) James Axtell, *The Invasion Within: The Contest of Cultures in Colonial North America* (New York: Oxford University Press, 1985), 289; Viau, *Enfants du néant et mangeurs d'âmes*, 197; Vaughan, "Crossing the Cultural Divide," 84; Goodwin, *We Go as Captives*, 62–63; ("Individuals were bought...") Parke, *Authentic Narrative*, 28; ("Captain Forster...") Butterfield Testimony, 165.

23. ("All our endeavours...") Parke, *Authentic Narrative*, 28; (Senecas) Gregory Schaaf, *Wampum Belts & Peace Trees: George Morgan, Native Americans and Revolutionary Diplomacy* (Golden, CO: Fulcrum, 1990), 109–10; (Mississaugas) Philip Schuyler to George Washington, August 18, 1776, *PGWRWS*, 5:68; (seven or eight) "The following authentic account..., New-York, June 20," *New-York Journal*, June 20, 1776; ("several young...," "one young child," "all the blacks") Butterfield Testimony, 165–66; ("saleable plunder") Steele, "Surrendering Rites," 139. See also MacLeod, *Canadian Iroquois and the Seven Years' War*, 15; William R. Riddell, *The Slave in Canada* (Washington, DC: Association for the Study of Negro Life and History, 1920), 24n28; Kenneth W. Porter, *The Negro on the American Frontier* (New York: Amos Press, 1971), 25–26, 102; and Viau, *Enfants du néant et mangeurs d'âmes*, 196–97. Records document between eight and ten men from Sherburne's column carried into captivity, but the accounts are generally vague as to when they were specifically taken away; see chap. 18, appendix A, and appendix B.

24. ("trophies of their victory") Isaac Webster, *The Narrative of the Captivity of Isaac Webster* (New York: Garland Publishing, 1978), 11; Pouchot, *Memoir*, 2:248; (97 survivors, 487 total) Parke, *Authentic Narrative*, 28.

25. (church) Brazeau, *Les Sépultures du coteau des Cèdres*, 20; (forty-five pews) Auclair, *Histoire*, 47–48.

26. ("the savages insisting...") Parke, *Authentic Narrative*, 28–29; ("The indians...," "money silver...") Shepardson, "Reminiscence," 13; ("said it was not...") Butterfield Testimony, 165.

27. ("suf[f]ered s[a]vage Barbarity...") Petition of James Caldwell, Robert Campbell, John McNeill, and Josiah Warren, New Boston, December 1, 1795, *DRNH*, 9:661–62; "Individual accounts for losses in service," *NH Rolls*, 3:525–31; The Humble Petition and Remonstrance of the Company Commanded by Capt Daniel Wilkins," March 10, 1779, *NH Rolls*, 1:476–77; Thomas Gibbs's Losses at the "Cedars," *DRNH*, 11:329; ("naked") Aaron Smith, Nathl Bacon, Thomas Whitcomb, Eleazer Jordan, Thomas Gibbs to New Hampshire Council and House, October 16, 1779, Hammond, *NH Rolls*, 3:459; (britches) Petition of John Betton, January 17, 1778, *NH Rolls*, 4:211; Castro, "Stripped," 107, 114; ("stripped of every part...") Petition of the Officers of Colonel Bedel's Regiment to General Gates, July 17, 1776, *AA5*, 1:398.

28. Ian K. Steele, "When Worlds Collide: The Fate of Canadian and French Prisoners Taken at Fort Niagara, 1759," *Journal of Canadian Studies* 39, no. 3 (Fall 2005): 12, 15, ("effective broker") 28. Thanks to Jon Parmenter for mentioning this important parallel.

Chapter 14

1. ("Forster now found himself...") Stevens, "His Majesty's 'Savage' Allies," 622; Stevens, "Diary," 139.
2. Stevens, "Diary," 139; John Philip De Haas [to Commissioners?], May 31, 1776, Orderly Book of the 1st Pennsylvania Battalion of Foot, Society of the Cincinnati (hereafter cited as OB1P).
3. (all quotes) Shepardson, "Reminiscence," 14; Stevens, "Diary," 139; (Beaumont's) Lorimier, At War, 57.
4. (Canadians and Kanesatakes, "to take possession...") Parke, Authentic Narrative, 29; (Young) Bailey, "Reminiscences," 36. Kanesatakes were presumably traveling back and forth from their nearby village over these few days.
5. Sherburne Testimony, 398; "The following authentic account..., New-York, June 20," New-York Journal, June 20, 1776; Lorimier, At War, 57; De Terlaye, October 9, 1776, in Parke, Authentic Narrative, 29–30, 46; (officer numbers) Copy of the Cartel, Enclosed in by general Arnold, May 27, 1776, rg360 i162 v1 r179 pp78–81, M247; copy of the cartel, May 27, 1776, PRO 30/55/2/88 p4, National Archives (UK); Hamtramck Testimony, 452; Stevens, "Diary," 139; Parke, Authentic Narrative, 29; Shepardson, "Reminiscence," 14–15.
6. Parke, Authentic Narrative, 29; May 23, 1776, Stevens, "Diary," 139; Nos. 78, 79, 114, 116, and 117, "Court of Enquiry of Damages," MG23-GV7, LAC.
7. (word of attack) Robbins, Journal, 22; (Arnold at Sorel) Baldwin, Revolutionary Journal, 44; ("take them with...") May 19 and (Arnold return; Noble and 100 men; "Captain," "a few...") May 20, 1776, Avery Journal. The Kahnawake leader is clearly spelled as "Captain Eadcout" in Avery's original journal, but the name is not recognizable as any known chief—it could be a gross corruption of Atiatoharongwen. Louis Atiatoharongwen and Wendake (Lorette) Huron John Vincent were the two Indians most likely to be called "captain" at this time.
8. ("great vivacity...") Charles Carroll of Carrollton to Charles Carroll of Annapolis, April 30, 1776 [May 1 postscript], Hoffman, Dear Papa, Dear Charley, 2:902; Baldwin, Revolutionary Journal, 44; (one hundred regulars, thousand "Savages") Beebe, "Journal," 328–29; "Extract of a Letter... dated New-York, June 18," Providence Gazette, June 29, 1776 [also AA4, 6:598]; (one hundred men) Commissioners to Canada to John Hancock, May 27, 1776, Smith, LDC, 4:82; (two cannon) "New-York, June 8, Fresh News from Canada," Constitutional Gazette (New York), June 8, 1776; ("to stop...") James Wilkinson to Nathanael Greene, May 24, 1776, Greene, Papers, 1:217–18; ("cast up a small fort...") May 20, 1776, Avery Journal.
9. Léon Robichaud and Alan Stewart, Étude historique du site de la maison LeBer-LeMoyne (Lachine, QC: Remparts, 1999), 43; Perrault, Montréal en 1781, 206; Guy Pinard, Montréal, son histoire, son architecture (Montreal: Éditions du Méridien, 1991), 4:162, 164; (fortify warehouse) Lorimier, At War, 57–58, Mes Services, 282; James Wilkinson to Nathanael Greene, May 24, 1776, rg360 i78 v23 r104 pp285–86, M247 [also Greene, Papers, 1:217–18]; Bailey, "Reminscences," 36; Baldwin, Revolutionary Journal, 46–47; (ferry) Marthe Faribault-Beauregard, "Montréal, notre ile,

les passages de l'eau à la fin du XVIIIe siècle," in Société historique de Montréal, *Montréal, Activités, Habitants, Quartiers* (Montreal: Fides, 1984), 72.
10. ("goods & military stores...") May 23, 1776, Avery Journal; ("going up to supply...") Baldwin, *Revolutionary Journal*, 46–47.
11. (Noble) Joseph Badger, "Rev. Joseph Badger of Wood County, Ohio," *American Quarterly Register* 13 (1841): 318; (350 men) James Wilkinson to Nathanael Greene, May 24, 1776, rg360 i78 v23 r104 pp285–86, M247 [also Greene, *Papers*, 1:217–18]; ("under an arrest...") Bailey, "Reminiscences," 37; Wells, "Journal," 266; James Wilkinson, *Memoirs of My Own Times* (Philadelphia: Abraham Small, 1816), 1:39, 41. The self-serving Wilkinson's account must be carefully assessed, especially since it was written long after Arnold's turn. For Wilkinson's character issues, see Andro Linklater, *An Artist in Treason: The Extraordinary Double Life of General James Wilkinson* (New York: Walker Publishing, 2009).
12. (commissioners' order) Charles Carroll, *Journal of Charles Carroll of Carrollton, during His Visit to Canada in 1776*, ed. Brantz Mayer (Baltimore: John Murphy, 1876), 98–99; ("proceed to Fort St. Anns...") May 22, 1776, Jacob Shallus Journal, Nathanael Greene Papers, APS; (Pennsylvania troops) Commissioners to Canada to John Hancock, May 27, 1776, Smith, *LDC*, 4:83; Baldwin, *Revolutionary Journal*, 45; Roll of Captain John Nelson's Independent Company of Riflemen, Thomas L. Montgomery, ed., *Pennsylvania Archives*, 5th Series (Harrisburg, PA: Harrisburg Publishing Company, 1906), 2:75–78; (Williams, 160) May 22, 1776, Avery Journal; Joseph Vose, "Journal of Lieutenant-Colonel Joseph Vose," in *Publications of the Colonial Society of Massachusetts*, vol. 7, *Transactions, 1900–1902* (Boston: Colonial Society of Massachusetts, 1905), 255. The First Pennsylvania detachment included Josiah Harmar's and Marian Lamar's companies and Lt. John Butler's detachment. Montgomery, *Pennsylvania Archives*, 2:63.
13. Badger, "Rev. Joseph Badger," 318–19; (Arnold to Kahnawake) Wilkinson, *Memoirs*, 1:42; ("Militia Volunteers...") Moses Hazen to Committee of Congress, May 24, 1776, Perceval Maxwell Papers, MG23 B46, LAC; ("character of Beaver hunters") May 24, 1776, Avery Journal. At this point in the campaign, some secondary histories emphasize Brig. Gen. John Sullivan's report that the Kahnawakes were "demanding assistance, and threatening if they had not immediate relief, to join the enemy"; but the relevant primary source account is tied to a baseless report of the Kahnawakes losing sixty warriors while allegedly fighting Forster—there is no other primary account indicating that the Indians were really in such a panic. John Sullivan to Philip Schuyler, May 27, 1776, *AA4*, 6:609–10.
14. Lorimier, *At War*, 58; ("in quest of milk," "fell in the rear...") Wilkinson, *Memoirs*, 1:41–42; (thigh) James Wilkinson to Nathanael Greene, May 24, 1776, rg360 i78 v23 r104 pp285–86, M247 [also Greene, *Papers*, 1:217–18]; May 25, 1776, Avery Journal; James McElherron, S.28809 p5, and Joseph Welch S44029 pp7, 10, M804. Lorimier's memoirs are chronologically disjointed, but his geographic descriptions correlate with Wilkinson's account. Perreault, *Montréal en 1781*, 202–5. Lorimier recounted three soldiers involved; Wilkinson and Avery reported two.

15. Lorimier, *At War*, 58.
16. Parke, *Authentic Narrative*, 30; Lorimier, *At War*, 57–58; ("chamber and garret") Stevens, "Diary," 139.
17. (De Haas) "Narrative of John Peters," Colonel John Peters Papers, NYHS, 5; ("three hundred...") Sanguinet, "Témoin Oculaire," 132; ("incapable of misleading...") Lorimier, *At War*, 57, *Mes Services*, 282. Peters identifies one source as Mr. Ferguson, and Sanguinet identifies another as Dumilion, mistranscribed as "Carcassonne" and Dummonyon" in Lorimier's published memoirs.
18. ("that the rebels...") Parke, *Authentic Narrative*, 30; Long, *Voyages and Travels*, 26–27.
19. ("because they had...," "the fickle disposition...," "as their fancy...," eighty men) Parke, *Authentic Narrative*, 30–31.
20. ("with respect to the number...") François-Auguste Magon de Terlaye, October 9, 1776, in Parke, *Authentic Narrative*, 48. Arnold had about four hundred men, Hazen perhaps two hundred, and De Haas brought almost six hundred.
21. (Montigny transfers) Parke, *Authentic Narrative*, 30; May 24, 1776, Stevens, "Diary," 139; Angus, *Old Quebec*, 179; Benedict Arnold to Commissioners in Canada, May 25, 1776, *AA4*, 6:595; Lorimier, *At War*, 56–57; Kingsford, *History of Canada*, 52; ("desolate island...") "The following authentic account..., New-York, June 20," *New-York Journal*, June 20, 1776.
22. ("very scantily supplied...") "The following authentic account..., New-York, June 20," *New-York Journal*, June 20, 1776; Parke, *Authentic Narrative*, 31.
23. John Fifield W17500 p14, and Fifield deposition in Ephraim Chamberlain W25060 pp67–68, M804; (escapee intelligence) Benedict Arnold to Commissioners in Canada, May 25, 1776, *AA4*, 6:595; (other intelligence) May 25, 1776, Carroll, *Journal*, 99–100.
24. ("to cut off...") Moses Hazen to Committee of Congress, May 24, 1776, Perceval Maxwell Papers, MG23 B46, LAC; Benedict Arnold to Commissioners in Canada, May 25, 1776, *AA4*, 6:595; (delays for provisions) May 25, 1776, Carroll, *Journal*, 99; (scout) Greenwood, *Revolutionary Services*, 30–31.

Chapter 15

1. ("much incommoded...") Cannon, *Historical Record of the Eighth*, 70; Letter from a gentleman at Montreal..., August 4, 1776, *Scots Magazine* 38 (1776): 537; "The following authentic Account of the Skirmish at the Cedars...," *Quebec Gazette*, August 29, 1776.
2. (cartel text) Parke, *Authentic Narrative*, 31–35; Letter from a gentleman at Montreal..., August 4, 1776, *Scots Magazine* 38 (1776): 537; Sherburne Testimony, 2, Papers of Thomas Jefferson, LOC [also *PTJ*, 1:398]. Parke's published cartel text appears to be the earliest version, preceding the manuscript copy in the Papers of the Continental Congress; Prisoner Cartel, May 26, 1776, rg360 i29 r36 pp251–52, M247. For cartel text, see appendix C.

3. ("a surrender...," "in case of refusal...") Benedict Arnold to Commissioners in Canada, May 27, 1776, *AA4*, 6:595–96.
4. (six o'clock) Benedict Arnold to Commissioners in Canada, May 27, 1776, *AA4*, 6:595; (De Haas vanguard) Commissioners to Canada to John Hancock, May 27, 1776, Smith, *LDC*, 4:83; (strength) May 26, 1776, Avery Journal; (Kahnawakes, boats delayed) Greenwood, *Revolutionary Services*, 31; Charles Carroll of Carrollton to Charles Carroll of Annapolis, May 27, 1776, Hoffman, *Dear Papa, Dear Charley*, 2:912; Wilkinson, *Memoirs*, 1:44.
5. ("took some...," "attempted...") Stevens, "Diary," 139–40; May 26, 1776, Avery Journal; (dismissing claims) Parke, *Authentic Narrative*, 35. Multiple American accounts seem to independently describe these deaths. Survivors might not have been able to identify observed victims, since the hundreds of prisoners came from nineteen different companies drawn from five different colonies.
6. (Lynds, "that he had rather...") Shepardson, "Reminiscence," 18; ("a naked man...") Greenwood, *Revolutionary Services*, 31–32; Wentworth Lord S37192 p4, M804.
7. ("they would...," "torn by...") Benedict Arnold to Commissioners in Canada, May 27, 1776, *AA4*, 6:596; John Philip De Haas to Samuel Chase and Charles Carroll, June 12, 1776, OB1P.
8. ("ordered every man...") Badger, "Rev. Joseph Badger," 319; ("with zeal...") Wilkinson, *Memoirs*, 1:44–45; Parke, *Authentic Narrative*, 36; Stevens, "Diary," 140; "From a number of persons lately arrived from Canada...," *New-York Journal*, June 27, 1776; Shepardson, "Reminiscence," 15; (Kahnawakes) Greenwood, *Revolutionary Services*, 31.
9. Greenwood, *Revolutionary Services*, 31; ("ordered the boats...," "five unhappy...," "taken off...," "immediately ordered...") Benedict Arnold to Commissioners in Canada, May 27, 1776, *AA4*, 6:596; (cloudless) Wilkinson, *Memoirs*, 1:45.
10. ("could neither lye...") Shepardson, "Reminiscence," 15, 12; Wilkinson, *Memoirs*, 1:45; Lorimier, *At War*, 57; Stevens, "Diary," 140; Greenwood, *Revolutionary Services*, 31–32; ("well fortified") Benedict Arnold to Commissioners in Canada, May 27, 1776, *AA4*, 6:596. Primary sources imply a fluid, interspersed deployment, while early secondary accounts describe three distinct, segregated positions. Berthelot, "Mémoire," 237; Stedman, *History*, 1:174; Cannon, *Historical Record of the Eighth*, 69.
11. ("the detachment...") Wilkinson, *Memoirs*, 1:45; ("pushed on...") Greenwood, *Revolutionary Services*, 31–32; ("Some shot...") Badger, "Rev. Joseph Badger," 319. In this case, "musket-shot" probably meant a distance beyond effective range.
12. ("the Indians gave...," spent balls) Joseph Badger to John Frazer, September 5, 1839, "Plain Wood County, ...," Charles Cist, *Cincinnati Miscellany*... (Cincinnati: Caleb Clark, 1845), 1:143; Shepardson, "Reminiscence," 12; ("fire from one...," "We were eminently...") Wilkinson, *Memoirs*, 1:45; (eight shots) Stevens, "Diary," 140. Lieutenant Parke described the entire engagement in just one line: "In the evening they made a descent on our post, ... but were repulsed." Parke, *Authentic Narrative*, 36. Lorimier, late to the battle, only offered localized glimpses of Canadian and Indian action. Lorimier, *At War*, 57.

13. ("was so dark...") Benedict Arnold to Commissioners in Canada, May 27, 1776, *AA4*, 6:596; (rest on oars) Wilkinson, *Memoirs*, 1:45; Greenwood, *Revolutionary Services*, 31–32; Stevens, "Diary," 140. American accounts noted the absence of casualties, while Lorimier firmly believed Canadian artillery fire sank a bateau, and that the "enemy must have suffered heavy losses." Lorimier, *At War*, 57.
14. Benedict Arnold to Commissioners in Canada, May 27, 1776, *AA4*, 6:596; John Philip De Haas to Samuel Chase and Charles Carroll, June 12, 1776, OB1P; May 26, 1776, Avery Journal. Council secretary Capt. James Wilkinson's memoirs seem to offer a definitive insider's account. Details like personal tensions between Arnold, De Haas, and Hazen may be substantially true, but his conclusion, that Arnold reluctantly took the colonels' advice and decided *not* to attack the enemy, is overwhelmingly contradicted by contemporary records that agree Arnold issued orders to cross the lake and fight around dawn. Wilkinson, *Memoirs*, 1:45–46; Smith, *Our Struggle for the Fourteenth Colony*, 2:594. On Wilkinson's unreliability, see James K. Martin, *Benedict Arnold, Revolutionary Hero: An American Warrior Reconsidered* (New York: New York University Press, 2007), 213.
15. ("Natives' qualms...") Karim M. Tiro, *The People of the Standing Stone: The Oneida Nation from the Revolution through the Era of Removal* (Amherst: University of Massachusetts Press, 2011), 55–56; ("did not fight...") Karim M. Tiro, "A Civil War?: Rethinking Iroquois Participation in the American Revolution," *Explorations in Early American Culture* 4 (2000): 148, 149. See also Green, "New People in an Age of War," 300–301; and Parmenter and Robinson, "Perils and Possibilities of Wartime Neutrality," 187, 196. For other historical precedents, see February 23, 1745, Wraxall, *Abridgment of the Indian Affairs*, 244; Baron Dieskau to Count D'Argenson, September 14, 1755, *DRHNY*, 10:316–18; Goldsbrow Banyar to William Johnson, September 24, 1755, and Thomas Butler to William Johnson, May 3, 1756, *PSWJ*, 2:86, 9:446; and most recently and dramatically at Fort Niagara in 1759, Steele, *Warpaths*, 216–17.
16. ("continuum of cooperative acts") Karim M. Tiro, "Deconflicting Iroquoia," *Age of Revolutions* (October 18, 2017), https://ageofrevolutions.com/2017/10/18/deconflicting-iroquoia/; Green, "New People in an Age of War," 219–21; Parmenter and Robinson, "Perils and Possibilities of Wartime Neutrality," 188. Warriors might even have fired mud balls, instead of lead, as they did during the prisoner transfer.
17. ("even attempted...," "the door...") Shepardson, "Reminiscence," 15–16; Parke, *Authentic Narrative*, 36.
18. ("into a council...," "that it was...") Report of the Committee on the Cartel, July 10, 1776, *JCC*, 5:536; Benedict Arnold to Commissioners in Canada, May 27, 1776, *AA4*, 6:596; Commissioners to Canada to John Hancock, May 27, 1776 [May 28 postscript], Smith, *LDC*, 4:83; (McKinstry) Joseph Badger, *A Memoir of Rev. Joseph Badger: Containing an Autobiography, and Selections from His Private Journal and Correspondence* (Hudson, OH: Sawyer, Ingersoll, and Company, 1851), 9; Badger, "Rev. Joseph Badger," 319.
19. Benedict Arnold to Commissioners in Canada, May 27, 1776, *AA4*, 6:596; Wilkinson, *Memoirs*, 1:46; ("determined to kill...") Commissioners to Canada to John Hancock,

May 27, 1776 [May 28 postscript], Smith, *LDC*, 4:83–84; ("frustrate their...") Parke, *Authentic Narrative*, 36; ("extremely averse...," "was at length induced...") Report of the Committee on the Cartel, July 10, 1776, *JCC*, 5:537.

20. ("very insolent terms," "with disdain") "From a number of persons lately arrived from Canada...," *New-York Journal*, June 27, 1776; Benedict Arnold to Commissioners in Canada, May 27, 1776, *AA4*, 6:596; (terms) Parke, *Authentic Narrative*, 31–35. See appendix C for the initial and final agreement.
21. (hostages) Sherburne Testimony, 399.
22. ("as deserters...") Butterfield Testimony, 165; Hamtramck Testimony, 451–52; Petition of Jean Francois Hamtramck to Congress, July 11, 1776, rg360 i78 r96 v11 p72, M247; "Capt. Hamtramcks' recommendation," *Journal of the Provincial Congress, Provincial Conventions, Committee of Safety and Council of Safety of the State of New-York, 1775–1776–1777*, vol. 2 (Albany, NY: Thurlow Weed, 1842), 361; ("he had positive orders...") Benedict Arnold to Commissioners in Canada, May 27, 1776, *AA4*, 6:596–97.
23. Benedict Arnold to John Philip De Haas, May 27, 1776 [contemporary transcript], and John Philip De Haas to Samuel Chase and Charles Carroll, June 12, 1776, OB1P.
24. ("that it appeared...") Benedict Arnold to Commissioners in Canada, May 27, 1776, *AA4*, 6:596; Parke, *Authentic Narrative*, 36–37; ("hypocritical, insidious...," "British troops...," "If the commanders...," "no cause...") Commissioners to Canada to President of Congress, May 27, 1776 [May 28 postscript], *AA4*, 6:592.
25. ("the Cartel was...") Vose, "Journal," 255–56; ("Had my Opinion...") John Philip De Haas to Samuel Chase and Charles Carroll, June 12, 1776, OB1P; Baldwin, *Revolutionary Journal*, 52. See also William Thompson to George Washington, May 30, 1776, *AA4*, 6:628; Beebe, "Journal," 331; and Wilkinson, *Memoirs*, 1:47.

Chapter 16

1. Parke, *Authentic Narrative*, 37; (mud balls) Sherburne Testimony, 399.
2. ("looked as if...") Greenwood, *Revolutionary Services*, 32–33; Estabrook-Wilkins Testimony, 166; May 28, 1776, Avery Journal; ("It is Intirely...") George Forster to John Philip De Haas, May 29, 1776, and (four boats) John Philip De Haas to George Forster, May 28 [*sic*] [contemporary transcription], OB1P. Forster presumably used the opportunity to pack his own boats for retreat.
3. Shepardson, "Reminiscence," 16–18; Isaac Chamberlin S45836 pp5–6, M804; May 29, 1776, Avery Journal; Parke, *Authentic Narrative*, 37; Smith, *Our Struggle for the Fourteenth Colony*, 2:595nXCV. Parke audaciously suggested that "there was not the least insult offered to any prisoner, after the cartel was signed," while conceding that Indians, "amusing themselves by the water side, did fire several muskets... without the least intention to injure them, nor were any of them injured."
4. (retreat) Parke, *Authentic Narrative*, 28, 37; (twenty-three captives) Ebenezer Green to Israel Morey, August 14, 1776, i78 v10 r95 G pp25–26, M247; (Everett) John Philip De Haas [to Commissioners?], May 31, 1776, OB1P; May 31, 1776, Avery Journal; ("without

saying a word") Hamtramck Testimony, 451–52; Petition of Jean Francois Hamtramck to Congress, July 11, 1776, rg360 i78 r96 v11 p72, M247. One of the Canadians, young Claude Monty, appears to have been taken up-country as a captive before this; see appendix B.

5. Parke, *Authentic Narrative*, 37; Lorimier, *At War*, 58; ("under the necessity...") Guy Carleton to George Germain, June 2, 1776 [June 6 postscript], Davies, *Documents of the American Revolution*, 12:145.

6. ("an Officer...") Andrew Allen to Philip Schuyler, March 17, 1776, *LDC*, 3:393; ("been bred...") Henry Bouquet to James Hamilton, July 1, 1763, Sylvester K. Stevens, Donald H. Kent, and Autumn L. Leonard, eds., *The Papers of Henry Bouquet* (Harrisburg: Pennsylvania Historical and Museum Commission, 1972–94), 6:280; Robert P. Broadwater, *American Generals of the Revolutionary War: A Biographical Dictionary* (Jefferson, NC: McFarland, 2007), 29; David McNeely Stauffer, "Notes and Queries: General John Philip de Haas," *Pennsylvania Magazine of History and Biography* 2 (1878): 345–46; Abram Hess, *The Life and Services of General John Philip de Haas, 1735–1786* (Lebanon, PA: Lebanon County Historical Society, 1916), 76, 82–83; Henry M. M. Richards, *The Pennsylvania-German in the Revolutionary War, 1775–1783* (Lancaster: Pennsylvania-German Society, 1908), 403.

7. ("their Tribe...") John Philip De Haas to Samuel Chase and Charles Carroll, June 12, 1776 [contemporary transcript], OB1P; (allies) October 2 and October 29, 1764, Edward G. Williams, ed., *The Orderly Book of Colonel Henry Bouquet's Expedition against the Ohio Indians, 1764* (Pittsburgh: Mayer Press, 1960), 15, 39; (Bushy Run) Montgomery, *Pennsylvania Archives*, 2:61.

8. ("bring down all...") John Philip De Haas to Samuel Chase and Charles Carroll, June 12, 1776, and ("the War Hatchet") Memorandum of Colonel De Haas, [undated, June 1776], OB1P; (captives return) Badger, "Rev. Joseph Badger," 319; Solomon Calkin S23568 p3, M804. The chiefs also made an implausible promise to extradite "those of their own who had first commenced Hostilities."

9. ("to take ample vengeance") Benedict Arnold to Commissioners in Canada, May 27, 1776, *AA4*, 6:596; At a Council of War, Chambly, May 30, 1776, *AA4*, 6:628; ("Capt. Forster...") Samuel Chase to Philip Schuyler, May 31, 1776, Smith, *LDC*, 4:105; ("give not...") Benedict Arnold to John Philip De Haas, Montreal, May 29, 1776 [contemporary transcription], OB1P.

10. ("immediately take...," "surround...," "This I think...") Benedict Arnold to John Philip De Haas, May 31, 1776, and ("leave not one...") Benedict Arnold to John Philip De Haas, May 29, 1776 [contemporary transcription], OB1P; ("put *all* to the sword") June 1, 1776, Avery Journal.

11. (March 1776 uprising) Mark R. Anderson, *The Battle for the Fourteenth Colony: America's War of Liberation in Canada, 1774–1776* (Hanover, NH: University of New England Press, 2013), 281; ("It is my...") Jeffrey Amherst to Robert Rogers, September 13, 1759, Franklin B. Hough, ed., *Journals of Major Robert Rogers* (Albany, NY: Joel Munsell's Sons, 1883), 140; D. J. Beattie, "The Adaptation of the British Army to Wilderness Warfare, 1755–1763," in *Adapting to Conditions: War and Society in the*

Eighteenth Century, ed. M. Ultee (Tuscaloosa: University of Alabama Press, 1986), 80; ("the capture...") George Washington to John Sullivan, May 31, 1779, *PGWRWS*, 20:716; ("conciliate the Affections...") George Washington to Benedict Arnold, September 14, 1775, and George Washington, Instructions to Benedict Arnold, September 14, 1775, *PGWRWS*, 1:456, 458.

12. Lee, *Barbarians and Brothers*, 214; Wayne E. Lee, "From Gentility to Atrocity: The Continental Army's Ways of War," *Army History* 62 (Winter 2006): 11–12, 14, 15; Mark E. Lender and James K. Martin, "Liberty or Death! *Jus in Bello* and Existential Warfare in the American Revolution," Benjamin L. Carp, "'Disreputable among Civilized Nations': Destroying Homes during the Revolutionary War," and Daniel R. Brunstetter, "Neutrality, Race, and Wars of Extermination: Native Americans in the Aftermath of the American Revolution"—all in Glen A. Moots and Phillip Hamilton, eds., *Justifying Revolution: Law, Virtue, and Violence in the American War of Independence* (Norman: University of Oklahoma Press, 2018), 160, 176–77, 300–301; T. Cole Jones, *Captives of Liberty: Prisoners of War and the Politics of Vengeance in the American Revolution* (Philadelphia: University of Pennsylvania Press, 2020), 22; e-mail correspondence with James K. Martin, March 28, 2019. *Jus in bello* is "law in war," or law addressing the way war is conducted.

13. ("revenge the death," "slaughtered Brethren") June 1, 1776, Fort St. Ann, ("to take their opinion") June 2, 1776, Jacob Shallus Journal, Nathanael Greene Papers, APS; Memorandum of Colonel De Haas, [undated, June 1776], John Philip De Haas to Samuel Chase and Charles Carroll, June 12, 1776, and A Council of War held at Fort Ann, June 1, 1776, OB1P; Wilkinson, *Memoirs*, 47.

14. ("The Indians...," "humanity...") June 2, 1776, Jacob Shallus Journal, Nathanael Greene Papers, APS; ("General Arnold was unacquainted...") A Council of War held at Fort Ann, June 1, 1776, and Memorandum of Colonel De Haas, [undated, June 1776], OB1P; ("None but cowards...") Wilkinson, *Memoirs*, 47; ("very extraordinary") Benedict Arnold to Commissioners of Congress, June 2, 1776, *AA5*, 1:165.

15. ("wisely circumvented...") Stevens, "His Majesty's 'Savage' Allies," 630; see also George F. G. Stanley, *Canada Invaded, 1775–1776* (Toronto: A. M. Hakkert, 1977), 123. ("by destroying...") Moses Hazen to Committee of Congress, May 24, 1776, Perceval Maxwell Papers, MG23 B46, LAC. For a contrasting view, see Smith, *Our Struggle for the Fourteenth Colony*, 2:596nXCV.

16. Benedict Arnold to Commissioners of Congress, June 2, 1776, *AA5*, 1:165; (rain, "on account...") June 1, 1776, Avery Journal; Donald B. Webster, "Grenades at Fort Senneville," *Arms Collecting* 32, no. 3 (Aug. 1994): 94–95; "Court of Enquiry of Damages," September 15, 1777, MG23-GV7, LAC; ("in my opinion...") Jacob Shallus Journal, Nathanael Greene Papers, APS.

17. ("on a treaty of friendship...") June 2, 1776, Avery Journal; June 2, 1776, Memorandum of Colonel De Haas, [undated, June 1776], OB1P.

18. ("entered into...") Philip Schuyler to President of Congress, June 8, 1776, *AA4*, 6:763; Graymont, *Iroquois in the American Revolution*, 101; Stevens, "His Majesty's 'Savage' Allies," 587; ("You have requested...") Notes from a conference in Albany,

April 26 to May 7, 1776, PSP; At a meeting of some of the sachems and warriors of the Six Nations . . . on Thursday the 2d. day of May 1776, and Meeting in Albany, May 10, 1776, Penrose, *Indian Affairs Papers*, 53.
19. Oneida Chiefs to Philip Schuyler, May 22, 1776, SKC [also an intercepted copy in *DRHNY*, 8:689].
20. (thirteen Oneidas, sixty Kahnawakes killed, "Intreating Assistance") Philip Schuyler to Commissioners of Congress, May 28, 1776, PSP; Philip Schuyler to George Washington, May 31, 1776, *AA4*, 6:640; ("amongst the Canadian tribes . . .") "Extract of a letter from New York, dated June 7, 1776," *Pennsylvania Evening Post*, June 8, 1776.
21. ("after the usual . . . gave up . . .") Benedict Arnold to Philip Schuyler, June 10, 1776, *AA4*, 6:977; Stevens, "His Majesty's 'Savage' Allies," 637n16; ("The Caghnawaga Indians . . .") Sylvanus Ripley to Eleazar Wheelock, June 19, 1776, 776369, EWC. For Oneida accounts, see "At a meeting of thirteen Oneida Indians, upon their return from Canada," June 19, 1776, *AA4*, 6:977–78; and Henry B. Livingston to Philip Schuyler, June 16, 1776, Henry Livingston Collection, New York State Library.
22. ("Send up Some . . .") John Sullivan to George Washington, June 8, 1776 [June 12 postscript], *PGWRWS*, 4:467.
23. Timothy Bedel to John Sullivan, June 12, 1776, Hammond, *Papers of Major-General John Sullivan*, 1:233–34. Vincent is not identified by name, but the letter's description clearly matches him.
24. ("the Infamous Retreat . . .") John Sullivan to John Hancock, June 1, 1776, Hammond, *Papers of Major-General John Sullivan*, 1:213.
25. ("Americans had slaughtered . . .") Lorimier, *At War*, 58; Guillaume Lorimier to Frederick Haldimand, "praying to be promoted," 1779, 21878, HP.
26. ("took an affectionate leave . . .") Wilkinson, *Memoirs*, 54–55.

Chapter 17

1. ("immediately appoint . . .") John Sullivan to John Hancock, June 1, 1776, Hammond, *Papers of Major-General John Sullivan*, 1:213; Benedict Arnold to John Sullivan, June 5, 1776, *AA4*, 6:924; Colonel Bedel's Defence, Timothy Bedel Papers, Hammond, *NH Roll*, 4:57; Philip Schuyler to Israel Putnam, June 3, 1776, *AA4*, 6:692; Articles of War, June 30, 1775, *JCC*, 2:118; (evidence) Timothy Bedel to John Sullivan, June 12, 1776, Hammond, *Papers of Major-General John Sullivan*, 1:233–34; (references) Timothy Bedel Papers, fols. 55, 56, NHHS.
2. ("Conduct was as bad . . .") George Washington to Philip Schuyler, June 16, 1776, *PGWRWS*, 5:8; ("take proper . . . ," "If any Officer . . .") Philip Schuyler to John Sullivan, June 17, 1776, Hammond, *Papers of Major-General John Sullivan*, 1:249; Robert H. Berlin, "The Administration of Justice in the Continental Army during the American Revolution, 1775–1783" (PhD diss., University of California, Santa Barbara, 1976), 189–90, 202; Article XXV, Articles of War, June 30, 1775, *JCC*, 2:116.

3. ("If I did...") Petition of Samuel Young to Horatio Gates, [late July 1776], *AA5*, 1:698; General Orders at Ticonderoga, July 29, 1776, *AA5*, 1:658; Heitman, *Historical Register*, 611; The Commissioners of Indian Affairs to Col. Timothy Bedel, PSP.
4. July 18 and 19, 1776, General Orders, *AA5*, 1:654–55; (Scott) Ennis Duling, "Arnold, Hazen and the Mysterious Major Scott," *Journal of the American Revolution* (February 23, 2016), https://allthingsliberty.com/2016/02/arnold-hazen-and-the-mysterious-major-scott/.
5. Colonel Bedel's Defence, July 9, 1776, Hammond, *NH Rolls*, 4:57.
6. ("quitting his post...," "surrendering the Post...," "incapacitated for ever...") General Orders, August 1, 1776, *AA5*, 1:801; Berlin, "Administration of Military Justice," 187.
7. ("the disgraceful...") Horatio Gates to President of Congress, August 6, 1776, *AA5*, 1:795–96; ("the two Genius's...") "Extract of a Letter from an Officer at Ticonderoga,... dated August 1, 1776," *Maryland Journal* (Baltimore), August 28, 1776; ("broke with infamy") Thomas Jefferson to John Page, August 20, 1776, *PTJ*, 1:500; ("Our Commander...") Notes from a conference, August 1776, PSP.
8. Butterfield, *Shadow of Cedars*, 171–73, 194, 197, 199, 225; Westmoreland History Committee, *History*, 212; ("a numerous...") *The Farmer's Museum or Literary Gazette*, 10:427, Tuesday, June 9, 1801, cited in Butterfield, *Shadow of Cedars*, 236n34.
9. Calloway, "Sentinels of the Revolution," 294; Albert S. Batchellor, *The Ranger Service in the Upper Valley of the Connecticut and the Most Northerly Regiment of the New Hampshire Militia...* (Concord, NH: Rumford Press, 1900), 7–8, 28; William Whitcher, "Memorial to Col. Timothy Bedel," *The Granite Monthly: A New Hampshire Magazine* 47 (Nov.–Dec. 1915): 505; Introductory Biography, Timothy Bedel Papers, fol. 12, NHHS.
10. June 6, 10, 15, ("silence...") 17, 1776, *JCC*, 5:420, 428, 446, 455–58; Report of the Committee on the Cedars Cartel, [June 17, 1776], Boyd, *PTJ*, 1:401–4. Major Sherburne's known travel dates, and key narrative differences between the June 17 report and July 10 resolutions, make it clear that his committee testimony came after the first report. The Library of Congress gave this otherwise undated testimony an incorrect June 17 date, perpetuated in many subsequent histories. Henry Sherburne, Testimony to Continental Congress on Affair at the Cedars, June 17, 1776 [sic], Manuscript/Mixed Material, Library of Congress, https://www.loc.gov/item/mtjbib000151/.
11. (arrival) "Philadelphia, June 26," *Dunlap's Maryland Gazette* (Baltimore), July 2, 1776; ("to lay before...") "Extract of a Letter from Major Henry Sherburne... June 18," *Providence Gazette*, June 29, 1776 [also *AA4*, 6:600]; June 24, 1776, *JCC*, 5:476; Sherburne Testimony, 396.
12. Butterfield, *Shadow of Cedars*, 145–46.
13. June 11, 1776, *JCC*, 5:431; Pauline Maier, *American Scripture: Making the Declaration of Independence* (New York: Alfred A. Knopf, 1997), 79, 103; ("endeavoured to bring...") I. First Draft by Jefferson, [before June 13, 1776], Boyd, *PTJ*, 1:337–47; June 28, 1776,

JCC, 5:497; Parkinson, *Common Cause*, 236–38, 240–243; Jones, *Captives of Liberty*, 89; ("conspiratorial fears") Richter, *Facing East*, 217. Pauline Maier, Robert Parkinson, and T. Cole Jones are part of the minority that has connected the charge with the Cedars. An early Jefferson Declaration draft included cartel committee notes on the same page; see "Fragment of the Composition Draft of the Declaration of Independence," *PTJ*, 1:420–23, also available at https://jeffersonpapers.princeton.edu/selected-documents/fragment-composition-draft-declaration-independence. Jefferson was already familiar with, and thinking of, Indian atrocities before the Cedars—he owned a copy of an early Fort William Henry "massacre" account in John Entick's *General History of the Late War* (1763), and had referenced that infamous event in correspondence within the past year: Thomas Jefferson to John Page, October 31, 1775, Smith, *LDC*, 2:279–80; "1783 Catalog of Books," 47, Thomas Jefferson Papers, Massachusetts Historical Society, http://www.masshist.org/thomasjeffersonpapers/doc?id=catalog1783_47&mode=lgImg.

14. July 10, 1776, *JCC*, 5:533–36, 538–39; Jones, *Captives of Liberty*, 88.
15. July 10, 1776, *JCC*, 5:538–39.
16. ("hypocritical, insidious . . .") Commissioners to Canada to John Hancock, May 27, 1776 [May 28 postscript], Smith, *LDC*, 4:83; ("with safety . . .") William Thompson to George Washington, June 2, 1776, *PGWRWS*, 4:428–29; ("Commenced hostilities . . . ," "in my Opinion . . .") John Philip de Haas to Samuel Chase and Charles Carroll, June 12, 1776, OB1P.
17. ("null and void . . .") Steele, *Betrayals*, 145; ("Restitution . . .") Committee at Camp to George Washington, March 9, 1778, Smith, *LDC*, 9:248–49.
18. ("the indulgence of . . .") Stone, *Border Wars of the American Revolution*, 1:135–36.
19. Peter Silver, *Our Savage Neighbors: How Indian War Transformed Early America* (New York: Norton, 2008), 230, 232; Jones, *Captives of Liberty*, 88–89. The earliest newspaper printing was the *Pennsylvania Evening Post* (Philadelphia), July 25, 1776.
20. ("that the Facts . . .") William Howe to George Washington, July 16, 1776, *PGWRWS*, 5:341–42; ("notorious . . . ," "at a great price") Proclamation, August 4, 1776, *Quebec Gazette*, September 12, 1776.
21. *Quebec Gazette*, August 22 and 29, ("O! Shame . . .") September 19, 1776; "Dear Sir, Montreal, Aug. 4" and "Dear Sir, Montreal, Aug. 18," *Scots Magazine* 38 (Nov. 1776): 537–38.
22. ("no foundation . . .") Parke, *Authentic Narrative*, 21, 38; ("so strong . . . ," "serviceable . . .") Frederick Haldimand to Henry Clinton, September 28, 1779, in "Haldimand Papers," *Collections and Researches made by the Michigan Pioneer and Historical Society* (Lansing, MI: Robert Smith, 1892), 19:470; Holger Hoock, *Scars of Independence: America's Violent Birth* (New York: Crown, 2017), 398. Narrative extracts of Parke's pamphlet were reprinted in at least one American loyalist newspaper, concluding with *Newport Gazette*, December 11, 1777.
23. *Scots Magazine* 38 (Nov. 1776): 537–38, 590–91; J. Almon, *The Remembrancer; or Impartial Repository of Public Events*, pt. 2: *For the Year 1776* (London, 1776), 196, 303–4, 307–9; ("impolitic and anti-christian") "Account of the Proceedings of the

American Colonies," *Gentleman's Magazine* (1775) 45:446; Bickham, *Savages within the Empire*, 243–44, 246, 255, 258–59.
24. Bickham, *Savages within the Empire*, 264; Starkey, *European and Native American Warfare*, 111–12; Graymont, *Iroquois in the American Revolution*, 161; ("savages ...," "when a measure ...") Debate in the Commons, [November] 1777, and ("rewards of danger and warfare ...") Debate on Mr. Burke's Motion ..., February 6, 1778, *Parliamentary History of England, from the Earliest Period to the Year 1803* (London, 1814), 19:435, 695.
25. "The Closet," 1868,0808.4561, The British Museum; "Cartoon Prints, British," Library of Congress catalog description, http://www.loc.gov/pictures/item/2004673348/marc /; Silver, *Our Savage Neighbors*, 247.
26. ("forget not ...") "To the People ...," *Norwich (CT) Packet*, March 17, 1777; "Extract of a letter from Stillwater ...," *Philadelphia Evening Post*, August 12, 1777; "Extract of a letter from major gen. Gates ...," *Dunlap's Maryland Gazette* (Baltimore), September 23, 1777; "Extract of a Letter from Moses's Creek," *New-York Gazette and Weekly Mercury*, September 1, 1777; ("let loose ...") "Letter to the British Commissioners," *Independent Ledger* (Boston), October 5, 1778; Carp, "Destroying Homes during the Revolutionary War," 180; Hoock, *Scars of Independence*, 280. See general accusations in Thomas Paine, *The American Crisis* (London, 1819), (No. VII) 94, (No. XI) 146; and plans for Cedars-like themes in "Ideas for the Prints/List of British Cruelties," Barbara B. Oberg, ed., *The Papers of Benjamin Franklin* (New Haven, CT: Yale University Press, 1992), 29:591–92.

Chapter 18

1. (rejoin units) "From a number of persons ...," *New-York Journal*, June 27, 1776; Petition of the Officers of Col. Bedel's Regiment to Horatio Gates, July 17, 1776, *AA5*, 1:398–99; (clothes) James Hartshorn W14117 p5, John Wiley S41338 p24, and (sick comrades) John Fifield deposition in Ephraim Chamberlin W25060 p68—all in M804; Greenwood, *Revolutionary Services*, 32; (months) John Willard S11848 p8, Josiah Warren S43222 p3, Joseph Fellows W21112 p5 (Elias Abbott deposition), Nathaniel Chandler Abbot W15502 pp19–20, Jabez Spencer W22295 p6, and Joseph Beaman S38536 p4—all in M804; (informed) John Bellows to [Meschech Weare?], July 2, 1776, *DRNH*, 8:311–12 [also *AA5*, 1:479, dated July 30]; Hoadly, *Public Records of the Colony of Connecticut*, 527; (returns) Diary of Lieutenant Jonathan Burton, *NH Rolls*, 3:695.
2. Ken Miller, *Dangerous Guests: Enemy Captives and Revolutionary Communities during the War for Independence* (Ithaca, NY: Cornell University Press, 2014), 72, 79; ("so barbarously ...") Proceedings of the Lancaster Committee, August 5, 1776, *AA5*, 1:759–60.
3. William Howe to George Washington, September 21, 1776, *AA5*, 2:437; William Howe to George Washington, October 4, 1776, *PGWRWS*, 6:468 [also *AA5*, 2:893–94]; ("had taken ...") George Washington to William Howe, October 6, 1776, *AA5*, 2:919. See also "Extract of a Letter dated New-York," September 27, 1776, *AA5*, 2:562–63.

4. ("artifices and pretences...") "Extract of a Letter dated New-York," September 27, 1776, *AA5*, 2:562–63; Board of War to George Washington, November 19, 1776, *AA5*, 3:762; Miller, *Dangerous Guests*, 92; ("the 7th and 26th...") William Howe to George Germain, December 20, 1776, Davies, *Documents of the American Revolution*, 12:269; ("where a few cartouch boxes...") "Report of Col. Hyde and Capt. Andre," *Continental Journal* (Boston), June 3, 1779.
5. ("we will give...") Lorimier, *At War*, 55; George Washington to Joshua Loring, January 14 and March 13, 1777, *PGWRWS*, 8:67, 565; "Extrait des Subistances accordé...," Fonds de Beaujeu, P03, I057, Centre d'Archives Vaudreuil-Dorion; Guy Carleton to George Germain, May 27 and June 27, 1777, Davies, *Documents of the American Revolution*, 14:97, 123.
6. ("Hunger....") Ebenezer Sullivan to Thomas Mifflin, December 2, 1783, rg360 i42 r56 v7 pp174–76, M247.
7. (journey details, "frequently at the Door...") "Ebenezer Sullivan's Letter to be made publick when he shall be Redeemed," March 30, 1778, Papers of Charles Thomson, LOC.
8. ("be given up...") "Ebenezer Sullivan's Letter...," March 30, 1778, Papers of Charles Thomson, LOC. Sullivan misidentified Money as the commissary general; Edmund B. O'Callaghan, ed., *Orderly Book of Lieut. Gen. John Burgoyne* (Albany, NY: J. Munsell, 1860), 84n1.
9. (Burgoyne quotes) "Ebenezer Sullivan's Letter...," March 30, 1778, Papers of Charles Thomson, LOC. See chap. 19 for additional discussion about contemporary use of "massacre" for the Cedars affair.
10. ("setting forth...") Ebenezer Sullivan's Letter...," March 30, 1778, Papers of Charles Thomson, LOC. For American propaganda advantages, see Hoock, *Scars of Independence*, 100, 279, 398.
11. Ebenezer Sullivan to John Sullivan, August 14, 1776, Parke, *Authentic Narrative*, 39–42. Despite minor variations between different copies of this letter, Parke's version seems legitimate.
12. Ebenezer Green to Israel Morey, August 14, 1776, i78 v10 r95 G pp25–26, M247; Theodore Bliss to William Emerson, August 14, 1776, *AA5*, 1:1167–68.
13. *Scots Magazine* 38 (Nov. 1776): 538; Almon, *Remembrancer*, 307–8; *New-York Gazette*, December 23, 1776; Parke, *Authentic Narrative*, 39–42.
14. "Return of Rebell officers sent from Quebec... on their Paroles," undated, 21843, HP; (March 1777) George Washington to John Hancock, July 5, 1777, *PGWRWS*, 10:196; (end parole) Joseph Loring to Whom it May Concern (copy), February 11, 1782, rg360 v7 r56 p182, M247.
15. (Knox relationship) Lucy Knox to Henry Knox, August 28, 1777, in Phillip Hamilton, *The Revolutionary War Lives and Letters of Lucy and Henry Knox* (Baltimore: Johns Hopkins University Press, 2017), 121. Muster rolls inconsistently identify Bliss as a prisoner or hostage "on parole"; for examples, see Muster Roll of Capt. Thos. Theodore Bliss Compy, July 19, 1778, r118 f39 p5; and Return of the Officers in the Second or New York Regiment of Artillery, March 21, 1783, r120 f49 p63—both in M246. Francis B.

Heitman misinterpreted these annotations as evidence that Bliss was subsequently captured at Monmouth. Heitman, *Historical Register of Officers*, 89.
16. (pay) March 27, 1778, *JCC*, 10:288. For examples of the suffering and requests from the hostages, see John Sullivan to John Hancock, [August 1777], and John Sullivan to George Washington, March 2, 1778, Hammond, *Papers of Major-General John Sullivan*, 1:420, 2:27–28; March 19, 1779, *JCC*, 13:338; Petition of Capt. Ebenezer Green, January 12, 1781, *DRNH*, 9:505; Ebenezer Green Petition to New Hampshire House of Representatives, October [20], 1785, *NH Rolls*, 4:461–62; Report on the Petition of John Stevens, Office of Army Accounts, June 26, 1786, pp58–59, RG93, NARA; and Report of the Secretary of War on the Petition of John Stevens, March 22, 1790, in Bowling, DiGiacomantonio, and Bickford, *Petition Histories*, 7:410.
17. "Ebenezer Sullivan's Letter . . . ," March 30, 1778, Papers of Charles Thomson, LOC.
18. "Wethersfield, February 18, 1779," *Connecticut Courant* (Hartford), March 2, 1779; Muster Roll . . . 2d Regt. of Artilly, Novr and Decr 1779, r117, f37, p65, M246; Petition of Capt. Ebenezer Green, January 12, 1781, *DRNH*, 9:505.
19. (twenty-three Americans) Ebenezer Green to Israel Morey, August 14, 1776, i78 v10 r95 G pp25–26, M247; (Mississaugas) Philip Schuyler to George Washington, August 18, 1776, *PGWRWS*, 5:68; (Senecas) September 3, 1776, Samuel Kirkland, *The Journals of Samuel Kirkland: 18th-Century Missionary to the Iroquois, Government Agent, Father of Hamilton College*, ed. Walter Pilkington (Clinton, NY: Hamilton College, 1980), 111; (eleven purchased) Recapitulation . . . of the Rebel Prisoners taken . . . to 10th: August 1776, CO 42/35 (microfilm), fol. 147, LAC; Parke, *Authentic Narrative*, 28; ($16 each) Ebenezer Green to Israel Morey, August 14, 1776, i78 v10 r95 G pp25–26, M247; ("prisoners could still . . .") Lee, *Barbarians and Brothers*, 155–56; Rushforth, *Bonds of Alliance*, 4.
20. ("well used . . .") Hamtramck Testimony, 452; Scudder, *Journal*, 37, ("put to death by inches") 39; Neil Goodwin, "The Narrative of the Captive, George Avery, 1780–1782," *Vermont History* 80, no. 2 (Summer–Fall 2012): 120; Rushforth, *Bonds of Alliance*, 40–41; Axtell, *Invasion Within*, 309; ("no other prospect . . .") Steele, *Indian Captive*, 62, 56. Historian Len Travers provides a thorough analysis and great discussion of the up-country captive experience twenty years earlier during the French and Indian War in *Hodges' Scout*, 173–94. Cedars captives' experiences were presumably quite similar.
21. ("three Scalps . . .") John Butler to Western Indian Nations, June 5, 1776, and ("The Fiddle . . .") Paul Long to George Morgan, July 23, 1776, Morgan's Journal, 45–46, as cited in Schaaf, *Wampum Belts & Peace Trees*, 109–10; ("all the King's . . .") Frederick Haldimand to Daniel Claus, May 4, 1780, Daniel Claus Papers, MG19, LAC.
22. Miller, *Ogimaag*, 142–43; ("acted in such . . .") Nathaniel Segar, *A Brief Narrative of the Captivity and Sufferings of Lt. Nathan'l Segar . . .* (Paris, ME, 1825), 21. Nathaniel Segar was captured by Odanak Abenakis in the Maine District.
23. ("compelled to . . . ," "like a member . . . ," "doomed to serve . . .") Jones, *History of the Ojebway Indians*, 131; Lee, *Barbarians and Brothers*, 155; Viau, *Enfants du néant et mangeurs d'âmes*, 203–4; MacLeitch, *Imperial Entanglements*, 235–36; Rushforth, *Bonds of Alliance*, 4. A November 1776 muster roll of Capt. John Stevens's company

listed Uriah Bailey, Julius Davis, and Abner Spencer as "prisoner with the enemy, 19 May"; this is the same description given for retained captive Randal Hewit, discussed later in this chapter (r27 f198 pp2-4, M246), while Primus Chandler was allegedly "captured by the British at 'The Cedars' and was never afterwards heard from by his friends." Secomb, *History of the Town of Amherst*, 373.

24. ("to do the most menial...") J. C. B., *Travels*, 100; Rushforth, *Bonds of Alliance*, 60; ("scattered, semi-horticultural...") Schmalz, *Ojibwa of Southern Ontario*, 15; (liability, ransom) Steele, "Surrendering Rites," 139; Richard Smart S37406 p8, Jonathan Pasco S36209 p20, Ichabod Meacham S38204 pp3-4, Josiah Cleveland S37850 p5, John Glines W23356 pp13, 44, Rufus Payne (with Adonijah Pangman deposition) S36203 pp12-13, John James W11066 p4, Claud Monty S41017 p10, and John Wooster W26091 pp10-11—all in M804; (Meechum, Ichabod) Secretary of the Commonwealth, *Massachusetts Soldiers and Sailors of the Revolutionary War* (Boston: Wright and Potter, 1902), 10:599.

25. ("on condition...," "carried into the back country...," "the remote parts...") Report of the Secretary of War on the Petitions of James Derrey [sic] and Benjamin Hardison, June 23 and 25, 1790, and An Act for the relief of disabled Soldiers and Seamen..., August 11, 1790, in Bowling, DiGiacomantonio, and Bickford, *Petition Histories*, 7:417-18, 430, also 402; (British officer) Jane Hardison petition, Benjamin Hardison w22 p11, M804; ("revised his opinions...") Jesse E. Middleton, *The Municipality of Toronto: A History* (Toronto: Dominion Publishing, 1923), 1:75; Derry Certification, March 19, 1790, RG93, NARA.

26. (age) Randal Hewit S43664 p7, M804; (Mississaugas, John Grant) "The examination of Randal Hewit...," June 14, 1781, George Washington Papers, Series 4, General Correspondence, Manuscript/Mixed Material, https://www.loc.gov/item/mgw428504/.

27. ("proved himself...") Daniel Claus to Frederick Haldimand, July 5, 1781, Daniel Claus Papers, MG19, LAC; Return of Men's Names Employed as Rangers with the Mohawk Indians, April 8, 1782 [sic], HP; "Marriages and Deaths," *New England Historical & Genealogical Register* (Boston: Samuel Drake, 1850), 4:292; (Ballston Raid) Frank Mackey, *Done with Slavery: The Black Fact in Montreal, 1760-1840* (Montreal: McGill-Queens, 2010), 385.

28. (Oneida capture, Crown Point, "very much concernd...") Daniel Claus to Frederick Haldimand, July 5, 1781, Daniel Claus Papers, MG19, LAC; "The examination of William Empie..." and "The examination of Randal Hewit...," June 14, 1781, George Washington Papers, Series 4, General Correspondence, Manuscript/Mixed Material, https://www.loc.gov/item/mgw428504/; (Colonel Louis) Gavin K. Watt, *A Dirty, Trifling Piece of Business* (Toronto: Dundurn, 2009), 161; June 18 and July 8, 1781, Victor H. Paltstis, ed., *Minutes of the Commissioners for Detecting and Defeating Conspiracies in the State of New York: Albany County Sessions, 1778-1781* (Albany: State of New York, 1909), 2:737, 744; List of Persons for Exchange, [undated, 1781?], State of New York, *Public Papers of George Clinton, First Governor of New York: 1777-1795, 1801-1804* (Albany, NY: J. B. Lyon, 1902), 6:451; Randal Hewit S43664 pp7-8, M804.

29. Middleton's relatively uncommon name, race indicators, and common intermediary time as a Montreal servant link his American and British documentary trails. ("captured by...," "the sport...," "his bloody...") Petition of Reuben Middleton, 1786, Hammond, *DRNH*, 11:206–7; Mackey, *Done with Slavery*, 143; Robert Leake to R. Mathews, December 24, 1781, 21818, and R. Mathews to William Twiss[?], December 17, 1781, 21814—both in HP.
30. ("Pardon & release...," "came into the Province...") Petition of Rubin Middleton, November 26, 1781, in Mackey, *Done with Slavery*, 397; (Second Battalion) Robert Mathews to Edward William Gray, December 17, 1781, 21721, and ("usefull as an Artificer") Robert Leake to R. Mathews, December 24, 1781, 21818—both in HP; Ernest A. Cruikshank and Gavin K. Watt, *The History and Master Roll of the King's Royal Regiment of New York*, rev. ed. (Campbellville, ON: Global Heritage Press, 2006), 257. Cruikshank misidentifies Middleton's service start date.
31. Petition of Reuben Middleton, 1786, *DRNH*, 11:206–7; June 16, 1786, Albert S. Batchellor, ed., *Early State Papers of New Hampshire* (Manchester: John B. Clarke, 1891), 20:640; Cruikshank and Watt, *Master Roll of the King's Royal Regiment of New York*, 257. Cruikshank also misidentified Reuben Middleton as having received a postwar land grant. The actual grantee was *Robert* Middleton formerly of the Fifty-Third Regiment. Return of Disbanded Troops... Settled in Township No. 5, 4 October 1784, 21828, HP; Copy of the "Old U. E. List," *United Empire Loyalists, 1784-1884*... (Toronto: Rose Publishing, 1885), 211; WO 12/6316 Muster Roll of William Howe's Company, June 1777 (microfilm), David Library of the American Revolution.
32. ("was carried away a prisoner...," "adopted into...") Thomas Lamont, *A Brief Account of the Life at Charlotteville of Thomas William Lamont and His Family*... (New York: Duffield, 1915), 6–7; A List of the Prisoners... taken at the Cedars, June 2, 1776, rg360 i29 r36 p236, M247; McKinstry Pay Roll July 1776, f91 p3, M246; John Lamont S41746 pp7, 20, M804. The Irish-descended John Lamont was phonetically recorded on the prisoner list as John Leming, and on the pay roll as John Lemmon. A little more than a decade after the family account was published, a Lamont descendant critically analyzed the story and debunked many aspects. Charles H. Thompson, *John Lamont: My Grandmother's Grandfather* (unpublished, 1928), https://archive.org/details/johnlamontmanuscoothom, 11–16.

Chapter 19

1. Dawson further concluded that "as a political stratagem," Congress's account was "triumphantly successful." Dawson, "Massacre at the Cedars," ("the event...") 2, ("mythical," "... political stratagem...") 15; George L. Parker, "Dawson, Samuel Edward," *DCB*.
2. George Bancroft, *History of the United States from the Discovery of the American Continent* (Boston: Little, Brown, 1860), 8:427–28. In 1852, Canadian historian François-Xavier Garneau made a fleeting description of "the massacre of many prisoners by

the Indians" (author's translation) in the only identified historical Cedars "massacre" reference preceding Bancroft's; and in the same year that Bancroft published his history, fellow American historian Benson J. Lossing also referred to the Cedars as a "massacre." F.-X. Garneau, *Histoire du Canada depuis sa découverte jusqu'à nos jours* (Quebec: John Lovell, 1852), 3:27; Benson J. Lossing, *The Pictorial Field Book of the Revolution* (New York: Harper & Brothers, 1860), 1:207-8. The mid-eighteenth-century American reemergence of "massacre" to describe the Cedars might have more to do with contemporary developments and perceptions in Indian relations.

3. July 10, 1776, *JCC*, 5:539.
4. "Dear Sir, Montreal, Aug. 4. . . . ," *Scots Magazine* 38 (1776): 537; Ebenezer Sullivan to John Sullivan, August 14, 1776, *AA5*, 1:1167; Ebenezer Green to Israel Morey, August 14, 1776, i78 v10 r95 G pp25-26, M247; "Ebenezer Sullivan's Letter to be made publick when he shall be Redeemed," March 30, 1778, Papers of Charles Thomson, LOC; Parke, *Authentic Narrative*, 39-42.
5. *A Dictionary of the English Language*, Digital Edition of the 1755 Classic by Samuel Johnson, https://johnsonsdictionaryonline.com/search-johnsons-dictionary/?SearchValue=massacre; Noah Webster, *A Compendious Dictionary of the English Language* (New Haven, CT, 1806), 186; *Le Dictionnaire de l'Académie française, Quatrième Édition*, vol. 2 (1762), https://artflsrv03.uchicago.edu/philologic4/publicdicos/query?report=bibliography&head=massacre (author's translation). Johnson's dictionary did not have a "massacre" entry.
6. See detailed discussion of these events in chaps. 12 and 13.
7. ("war of wounds . . .") Hoock, *Scars of Independence*, 176.
8. ("sachems") "The following authentic Account of the Skirmish at the Cedars . . . ," *Quebec Gazette*, August 29, 1776.
9. Kahnawake headmen conveniently blamed elderly sachem Jean-Baptiste Ogagragighte for the village's "bad conduct"—a pretense that was ritualistically accepted by colonial officials and other Native leaders; see Stone, *Journals of Major General Riedesel*, 47-48; and Stevens, "His Majesty's 'Savage Allies,'" 464-50.
10. Graymont, "Atiatoharongwen," *DCB*. Louis's Oriskany participation is commonly accepted, but documentation appears to be indirect, coming secondhand in Jeptha R. Simms, *Frontiersmen of New York* . . . (Albany, NY: George C. Riggs, 1883), 2:108-9; notably, Graymont did not include it in her biographical article.
11. ("the whole frontier . . .") Bowler and Wilson, "Butler, John (d. 1796)," *DCB*; "Narrative of Lt. Col. Butler's Services in America," May 1785, 21875, HP.
12. Leighton, "Lorimier, Claude-Nicolas-Guillaume de," *DCB*; Lorimier, *At War*, 63-73; (Fort Schuyler expedition) Alexander Fraser to Frederick Haldimand, July 12, 1779, and "The Particulars of a Conference held by a Deputation from Mr. Lorrimier's [sic] scout, with a party of Oneidas . . . ," August 7, 1779, 21780—both in HP; William Scudder, *The Journal of William Scudder, an Officer in the Late New-York Forces Who Was Taken Captive by the Indians at Fort Stanwix* . . . (New York, 1794), 37-40.
13. Potter, "Redcoats on the Frontier"; Stevens, "His Majesty's 'Savage Allies,'" 1114-16; Memorandum Book of Henry Bird, July 28, 1777, in Peter Gansevoort Jr., *Hero of*

Fort Schuyler: Selected Revolutionary War Correspondence of Brigadier General Peter Gansevoort, Jr., ed. David A. Ranzan and Matthew J. Hollis (Jefferson, NC: McFarland, 2014), 64-65.
14. (Bedel and Atiatoharongwen) Horatio Gates to Timothy Bedel, October 4, 1777 (transcript), Timothy Bedel Papers, NHHS; (Arnold) Martin, *Benedict Arnold*, 365-66; (Schuyler) Don R. Gerlach, *Proud Patriot: Philip Schuyler and the War of Independence, 1775-1783* (Syracuse, NY: Syracuse University Press, 1987), passim; Graymont, *Iroquois in the American Revolution*, 163, 219, 242-43, 264.
15. ("the event itself...," "felt it a duty...") Kingsford, *History of Canada*, 6:64; M. Brook Taylor, "Kingsford, William," *DCB*.

Appendix D

1. July 10, 1776, *JCC*, 5:534-37.
2. The enemy force was still at Akwesasne on May 15 and did not close to within nine miles until late on May 17.
3. The attack began on May 18.
4. The combined Indian contingent was closer to 250 men at maximum strength.
5. Actual casualties were two dead and three or four wounded. See chap. 11.
6. The combined Indian and Canadian force was fewer than two hundred men even when joined by the Canadian militia at battle's end. See chap. 12.
7. See chaps. 13 and 19 for assessment of postbattle killings.
8. Forster did not make direct threats against the prisoners himself; he only relayed Indian threats. See chap. 16.
9. The cartel committee's June 17 report included a convoluted and legally unfounded contention that the prisoners from Fort Cedars did not warrant an exchange because they had not fought; Cartel committee report, June 17, 1776, *JCC*, 5:455-58.

BIBLIOGRAPHY

Archival Sources

American Philosophical Society, Philadelphia
    Nathanael Greene Papers, 1777–1780
    Cooke, Charles. Iroquois personal names, 1900–1951
Bibliothèque et Archives nationales de Québec, Montreal
    Fonds Ministère des Terres et Forêts, E21
    Fonds Ministère de la Culture et des Communications, E6
    Collection Élisée Choquet, P60
Boston Public Library, Boston
    Richard H. Brown Revolutionary War Era Maps Collection of the Norman B. Leventhal Map Center
British Library, London
    Great Britain. Colonial Office 42
    Haldimand, Sir Frederick (1718–1799). Unpublished Papers and Correspondence, 1758–1784
    Public Records Office, War Office WO4
Centre d'Archives de Vaudreuil-Soulanges, Vaudreuil-Dorion, Quebec
    Fonds Robert-Lionel-Séguin, cote 5.13.41
    M04 Fonds Seigneurie de Vaudreuil
    M18 Fonds Paroisse St-Michel de Vaudreuil
    P03 Fonds Beaujeu
Connecticut Historical Society, Hartford
    American Revolution Collection, 1776–1786, call # AMREV
    David Avery Papers, 1771–1817
    Explanation of his prints of Battle of Bunker Hill and Attack of Quebec, n.d., John Trumbull (artist) Papers
    Robbins Family Papers, 1724–ca. 1803
Dartmouth College, Hanover, NH
    Eleazar Wheelock Collection (MS-1310)
    Microfilm Edition of the Papers of Eleazar Wheelock
David Library of the American Revolution, Washington Crossing, PA. Since February 2020, incorporated into the American Philosophical Society as the David Center for the American Revolution.
    Sol Feinstone Collection (microfilm)

Gilder Lehrman Institute of American History, New York City
Hamilton College Library, Clinton, NY
    Samuel Kirkland Collecton, http://elib.hamilton.edu/kirkland
Historical Society of Pennsylvania, Philadelphia
    Anthony Wayne Orderly Books
Houghton Library, Harvard University, Cambridge, MA
    Jared Sparks collection of American manuscripts
        "Henry Hamilton Drawings of North American Scenes and American Indians, 1769–1778," https://hollisarchives.lib.harvard.edu/repositories/24/resources/1371
Huntington Library, San Marino, CA
    Orderly book of Philip John Schuyler, 1775, June 28–1776, April 18, New York, Fort Ticonderoga, Albany, Fort St. George, http://catalog.huntington.org/record=b1625602
Library and Archives Canada, Ottawa
    MG17A, Archives of the Seminary of St-Sulpice, Série II
    MG18 H7, Famille Testard de Montigny
    MG23 B46, Perceval Maxwell Papers
    MG23 GV7, "Second Book of Minutes of the Court of Enquiry of Damages, Occasioned by the Invasion of the Rebels," March 10, 1777, Fonds Hospice-Anthelme Jean-Baptiste Verreau
    MG23 K10, Durell Saumarez papers, 1777–1779
    R5236-0-7-E (116-020019-X) Daniel Claus and Family Fonds
    R5443-0-1-E, General Twiss Journal commencing May 1st 1779 and ending July 31st 1781 while surveying Canada, 6303–05/1 Transcript CR/JS 11–89
    R5747-0-8-E, Department of Canadian Heritage fonds, Historic Sites—Battle of Cidres [Cedars], 1775 [sic] (microfilm T14030)
    R5747-7-0-E, Department of Canadian Heritage fonds, Historic Sites—Quebec—Fort Senneville (microfilm T14025).
    RG1-L3L, Lower Canada Land Papers, v118 fol. 57648–57649 (Joseph La Mothe) (microfilm C-2538)
Library of Congress, Washington, DC
    Papers of Charles Thomson, 1765–1845, MSS42861 (microfilm), Box 1/Reel 1
    Testimony on Canadian Campaign, Continental Congress, July 1776, The Thomas Jefferson Papers at the Library of Congress: Series 1: General Correspondence. 1651 to 1827, www.loc.gov
    Peter Force Papers
Massachusetts Historical Society, Boston
    John Thomas Papers, 1724–1776
National Archives, London
    Great Britain. Colonial Office. America and West Indies. Original Correspondence: North America CO 5, Colonial Office, America and West Indies, original correspondence, etc., 1606–1807, CO 5/253–54.

Great Britain. Colonial Office. Canada. Original Correspondence, Quebec. CO 42/35.
   War Office, WO 12
National Archives and Records Administration, Washington, DC
   M246, Revolutionary War Rolls
   M247, The correspondence, journals, committee reports, and records of the Continental Congress (1774–1789)
   M804, Revolutionary War Pension and Bounty-Land Warrant Application Files
   Papers of the War Department (1784–1800), https://wardepartmentpapers.org/s/home/page/home
New Hampshire Historical Society, Concord
   Timothy Bedel Papers, 1880.001
New-York Historical Society, New York City
   Colonel John Peters Papers
   Joseph Reed Papers, 1757–1784, https://cdm16694.contentdm.oclc.org/digital/collection/p16124coll1/id/48136/rec/3
New York Public Library, New York City
   Philip Schuyler Papers
   Samuel Adams Papers
   Digital Collections—Thomas Addis Emmet collection, 1483–1876, bulk 1700–1800 [microform], https://digitalcollections.nypl.org/collections/thomas-addis-emmet-collection
New York State Archives, Albany
   Papers of Franklin B. Hough
New York State Library, Albany
   Henry Livingston Collection, 1751–1833
   Miscellaneous Manuscripts
Society of the Cincinnati, Washington, DC
   Orderly book kept by First Lieutenant Samuel Smith, dated from June 11 to September 22, 1776
   Commission of Henry Sherburne as major of a regiment to be raised in the counties of Newport and Bristol, R.I. Newport, 12 May 1775
University of Manchester, John Rylands Library, Manchester, UK
   Bagshawe Family Muniments
Université de Montréal Archives, Montreal
   Collection Louis-François-George Baby (P0058)
   Le Programme de recherche en démographie historique, https://www.prdh-igd.com/en/Acces
University of California, San Diego
   William Bond Papers, 1768–1777, MSS.80, http://libraries.ucsd.edu/speccoll/findingaids/mss0080.html
Vermont Historical Society, Montpelier
   MS B Sh47 Zephaniah Shepardson Papers—Reminiscence of Shepardson's military service in 1776 in Vermont and Canada, and his observations on the evils of drink

Wisconsin Historical Society, Madison
   Draper Manuscripts, Series F, Joseph Brant
Yale University, Beinecke Rare Book and Manuscript Library, New Haven, CT
   Guy Johnson Papers

Published Sources

Abbot, W. W., ed. *The Papers of George Washington, Colonial Series*. Vol. 1. Charlottesville: University Press of Virginia, 1983.

———, ed. *The Papers of George Washington, Revolutionary War Series*. Charlottesville: University Press of Virginia, 1985– .

Abler, Thomas S., ed. *Chainbreaker: The Revolutionary War Memoirs of Governor Blacksnake as Told to Benjamin Williams*. Lincoln: University of Nebraska Press, 1989.

———. "Scalping, Torture, Cannibalism and Rape: An Ethnocultural Analysis of Conflicting Cultural Values in War." *Anthropologica* 34, no. 1 (1992): 3–20.

Abler, Thomas S., and Elisabeth Tooker. "Seneca." In Trigger, *Handbook of North American Indians*, vol. 15: *Northeast*.

[Adair, James]. "An Account of the North-American Indians Barbarity to their Captives, and their Manner of devoting them to Death, Extracted from 'The History of the North-American Indians, their customs, &c.,' just published." *London Magazine* 44 (April 1775): 184–86.

Akweks, Aren. *History of the St. Regis Akwesasne Mohawks*. Malone, NY: Lanctot, 1948.

Aldrich, Edgar. "The Affair of the Cedars and the Service of Colonel Timothy Bedel in the War of the Revolution." *Proceedings of the New Hampshire Historical Society* 3, pt. 2 (June 1897–June 1899): 194–231.

———. "Memorial to Col. Timothy Bedel." *Granite Monthly: A New Hampshire Magazine* 47 (November–December 1915): 496–503.

Alfred, Gerald R. *Heeding the Voices of Our Ancestors: Kahnawake Mohawk Politics and the Rise of Native Nationalism*. Toronto: Oxford University Press, 1995.

———. "The Meaning of Self-Government in Kahnawake." Research Program of the Royal Commission on Aboriginal Peoples. July 1994.

Alfred, [Gerald R.] Taiaiake. "A Different View: A Descendant Recounts the 1704 Attack, 1995." In Evan Haefeli and Kevin Sweeney, *Captive Histories: English, French, and Native Narratives of the 1704 Deerfield Raid*, 244–52. Amherst: University of Massachusetts Press, 2006.

Algonquins of Ontario. "History of the Algonquins." http://www.tanakiwin.com/wp-system/uploads/2013/10/a-History-of-the-Algonquins.pdf.

Allaire, J-B A. *Dictionnaire biographique du clergé canadien-français*. Vol. 1. Montreal: Imprimerie de l'École catholique des sourds-muets, 1910.

Allen, Robert S. "The British Indian Department and the Frontier in North America, 1755–1830." In *Canadian Historic Sites: Occasional Papers in Archaeology and History No. 14*, 5–125. Ottawa: Parks Canada, 1975.

Almon, J. *The Remembrancer; or Impartial Repository of Public Events*. Pt. 2, *For the Year 1776*. London, 1776.

American State Papers: Documents, Legislative and Executive, of the Congress of the United States. Class IX: Claims. Washington, DC: Gales and Seaton, 1834.

Amherst, Jeffery. *The Journal of Jeffery Amherst: Recording the Military Career of General Amherst in America from 1758 to 1763*. Edited by J. Clarence Webster. Toronto: Ryerson Press, 1931.

Anburey, Thomas. *Travels through the Interior Parts of America in a Series of Letters by an Officer*. Vol. 1. London, 1789.

Anderson, Mark R. *The Battle for the Fourteenth Colony: America's War of Liberation in Canada, 1774–1776*. Hanover, NH: University of New England Press, 2013.

———, ed. *The Invasion of Canada by the Americans, 1775–1776: As Told through Jean-Baptiste Badeaux's Three Rivers Journal and New York Captain William Goforth's Letters*. Translated by Teresa L. Meadows. Albany: State University of New York Press, 2016.

Andrews, Robert J., ed. *The Journals of Jeffery Amherst, 1757–1763*. Vol. 1, *The Daily and Personal Journals*. East Lansing: Michigan State University Press, 2015.

Angus, Alexander D. *Old Quebec in the Days before Our Day*. Montreal: Louis Carrier, 1949.

Annual Register . . . for the Year 1776. London: J. Dodsley, 1777.

Annual Register . . . for the Year 1777. London: J. Dodsley, 1778.

[Anonymous]. *The Military History of Great Britain for 1756, 1757, Containing a Letter from an English Officer at Canada Taken Prisoner at Oswego*. London: J. Millan, 1757.

Aquila, Richard. *The Iroquois Restoration: Iroquois Diplomacy on the Colonial Frontier, 1701–1754*. Detroit: Wayne State University Press, 1983.

Assikinack, Francis. "Social and Warlike Customs of the Odahwah Indians." *Canadian Journal of Industry, Science, and Art* 3, no. 16 (July 1858): 297–309.

Auclair, Élie-J. *Histoire de la paroisse de Saint-Joseph-de-Soulanges, ou Les Cèdres (1702–1927)*. Montreal: Sourds-Muets, 1927.

Avery, David. "The Northern Campaign. From the Diary of the Rev. David Avery, Chaplain in Col. John Paterson's Regiment." *American Monthly Magazine* 18–19 (1901): 235–40, 20–22.

Axtell, James. "Forked Tongues: Moral Judgments in Indian History." *Perspectives: American Historical Association Newsletter* 25, no. 2 (February 1987): 11–13.

———. *The Invasion Within: The Contest of Cultures in Colonial North America*. New York: Oxford University Press, 1985.

———. "The White Indians of Colonial America." *The William and Mary Quarterly* 32, no. 1 (January 1975): 55–88.

Badger, Joseph. *A Memoir of Rev. Joseph Badger: Containing an Autobiography, and Selections from His Private Journal and Correspondence*. Hudson, OH: Sawyer, Ingersoll, and Company, 1851.

———. "Rev. Joseph Badger of Wood County, Ohio." *American Quarterly Register* 13 (1841): 317–28.

Bailey, De Witt. "British Military Small Arms in North America, 1755–1783." *Bulletin of the American Society of Arms Collectors* 17 (1994): 3–13.
Bailey, Frye. "Colonel Frye Bailey's Reminiscences." In *Proceedings of the Vermont Historical Society for the Years 1923, 1924 and 1925*, 22–45. Bellows Falls, VT: P. H. Gobie Press, 1926.
Baldwin, Jeduthan. *The Revolutionary Journal of Col. Jeduthan Baldwin, 1775–1778*. Edited by Thomas William Baldwin. Bangor, ME: The De Burians, 1906.
Bancroft, George. *History of the United States from the Discovery of the American Continent*. Vol. 8. Boston: Little, Brown, 1860.
Bartlett, Josiah. *The Papers of Josiah Bartlett*. Edited by Frank C. Mevers. Hanover, NH: University Press of New England, 1979.
Batchellor, Albert S., ed. *Miscellaneous Revolutionary Documents of New Hampshire*. Manchester, NH: John B. Clarke, 1910.
———. *The Ranger Service in the Upper Valley of the Connecticut and the Most Northerly Regiment of the New Hampshire Militia* . . . Concord, NH: Rumford Press, 1900.
Baxter, James P. *Documentary History of the State of Maine*. Vol. 14. Portland, ME: Lefavor-Tower Company, 1910.
Beattie, D. J. "The Adaptation of the British Army to Wilderness Warfare, 1755–1763." In *Adapting to Conditions: War and Society in the Eighteenth Century*, edited by M. Ultee, 56–83. Tuscaloosa: University of Alabama Press, 1986.
Beaulieu, Alain, and Jean-Pierre Sawaya. "L'importance stratégique des Sept-Nations du Canada (1650–1860)." *Bulletin d'histoire politique* 8 (2000): 87–107.
Beaulieu, Alain, Stephanie Bereau, and Jean Tanguay. *Les Wendats du Québec: Territoire, Économie et Identité, 1650–1930*. Quebec City: Les Editions GID, 2013.
Beauregard, Ludger. "Géographie historique des côtes de l'île de Montréal." *Cahiers de géographie du Québec* 28, nos. 73–74 (1984): 47–62.
Béchard, Henri. *The Original Caughnawaga Indians*. Montreal: International Publishers, 1976.
Becker, Ann M. "Smallpox in Washington's Army: Strategic Implications of the Disease during the American Revolutionary War." *Journal of Military History* 68, no. 2 (April 2004): 381–430.
Becker, Mary Druke. "Linking Arms: The Structure of Iroquois Intertribal Diplomacy." In *Beyond the Covenant Chain: The Iroquois and Their Neighbors in Indian North America, 1600–1800*, edited by Daniel K. Richter and James H. Merrill, 29–39. University Park: Pennsylvania State University Press, 2003.
———. "'We Are an Independent Nation': A History of Iroquois Sovereignty." *Buffalo Law Review* 46, no 3 (October 1998): 981–99.
Beebe, Lewis. "Journal of a Physician on the Expedition against Canada, 1776." Edited by Frederic R. Kirkland. *Pennsylvania Magazine of History and Biography* 59, no. 4 (October 1935): 321–61.
Bélisle, Michel. *De L'Isle-aux-Tourtes à Vaudreuil-Dorion*. Vaudreuil-Dorion, QC: Collectif pour l'histoire de Vaudreuil-Dorion, 2007.

———. *Saint-Michel de Vaudreuil: Une Église Seigneuriale*. Vaudreuil, QC: Le Centre d'Histoire La Presqu'île, 1993.

Berlin, Robert H. "The Administration of Justice in the Continental Army during the American Revolution, 1775–1783." PhD diss., University of California, Santa Barbara, 1976.

Berthelot, Michel-Amable. "Extraits d'un Mémoire de M. A. Berthelot sur l'Invasion du Canada en 1775." In *Invasion du Canada: Collection des Mémoires Recueillis et Annotes*, edited by Hospice-Anthelme Jean-Baptiste Verreau, 225–40. Montreal: Eusèbe Senécal, 1873.

Bickham, Troy. *Savages within the Empire: Representations of American Indians in Eighteenth-Century Britain*. New York: Oxford University Press, 2005.

Bilharz, Joy. *Oriskany: A Place of Great Sadness, a Mohawk Valley Battlefield Ethnography*. Boston: Northeast Region Ethnography Program, National Park Service, 2009.

Blair, Emma Helen, ed. *The Indian Tribes of the Upper Mississippi Valley and Region of the Great Lakes, as described by Nicolas Perrot . . .* 2 vols. Cleveland: Arthur H. Clark, 1911–12.

Blanchard, David. *Kahnawake: A Historical Sketch*. Kahnawake, QC: Kanien'kehaka Raoititiohkwa Press, 1980.

———. *Seven Generations: A History of the Kanienkehaka*. Kahnawake, QC: Kahnawake Survival School, 1980.

Blau, Harold, Jack Campisi, and Elisabeth Tooker. "Onondaga." In Trigger, *Handbook of North American Indians*, vol. 15: *Northeast*.

Bonaparte, Darren. "Colonel Louis at Oriskany and Valley Forge." http://www.wampumchronicles.com/oriskanyandvalleyforge.html.

———. "The First Families of Akwesasne." http://www.wampumchronicles.com/firstfamilies.html.

———. "The History of Akwesasne from Pre-Contact to Modern Times." http://www.wampumchronicles.com/history.html.

———. "The History of the St. Regis Catholic Church and the Early Pastors." http://www.wampumchronicles.com/catholicchurch.html.

———. "Louis Cook: A French and Indian Warrior." http://www.wampumchronicles.com/frenchandindianwarrior.html.

———. "Louis Cook: A 'Colonel' of Truth?" http://www.wampumchronicles.com/coloneloftruth.html.

———. "The Missions of Atiatonharongwen." http://www.wampumchronicles.com/missionsofatiatonharongwen.html.

———. "St. Regis Mission Established 250 Years Ago This Year." http://www.wampumchronicles.com/missionestablished.html.

———. "The Seven Nations of Canada: The Other Iroquois Confederacy." http://www.wampumchronicles.com/sevennations.html.

Bouchette, Joseph. *A Topographical Dictionary of the Province of Lower Canada*. London: Longman, Rees, Orme, Brown, Green, and Longman, 1832.

Bougainville, Louis Antoine. *Adventure in the Wilderness: The American Journals of Louis Antoine de Bougainville, 1756–1760*. Edited and translated by Edward P. Hamilton. Norman: University of Oklahoma Press, 1964.

Bouton, Nathaniel, ed. *Provincial and State Papers. Miscellaneous Documents and Records Relating to New Hampshire at Different Periods*. Vol. 10. Concord, NH: Edward A. Jenks, 1877.

———, ed. *Provincial Papers. Documents and Records Relating to the Province of New-Hampshire from 1764 to 1776*. Vol. 7. Nashua, NH: Orren C. Moore, 1873.

———, ed. *State Papers. Documents and Records Relating to the State of New-Hampshire from 1776 to 1783*. Vol. 8. Concord, NH: Edward A. Jenks, 1874.

Bowling, Kenneth, William C. DiGiacomantonio, and Charlene B. Bickford, eds. *Petition Histories: Revolutionary War Related Claims, Series: Documentary History of the First Federal Congress of the United States of America, March 4, 1789–March 3, 1791*. Vol. 7. Baltimore: Johns Hopkins University Press, 1997.

Boyd, Julian P., ed. *The Papers of Thomas Jefferson*. Vol. 1, *1760–1776*. Princeton, NJ: Princeton University Press, 1950.

Brazeau, Jean-Luc, and Isabelle Aubuchon. *Les sépultures du coteau des Cèdres, 1750–1780*. Vaudreuil-Dorion, QC: Centre d'histoire La Presqu'île, 2014.

Brown, Thomas. "A Plain Narrativ [*sic*] of the Uncommon Sufferings, and Remarkable Deliverance of Thomas Brown, of Charlestown, in New England." *Magazine of History with Notes and Queries*, extra no. 4 (1908): 207–21.

Brumwell, Stephen. "The British Army and Warfare with the North American Indians." *War in History* 5 (1998): 147–75.

Brunstetter, Daniel R. "Neutrality, Race, and Wars of Extermination: Native Americans in the Aftermath of the American Revolution." In Moots and Hamilton, *Justifying Revolution*.

Burgoyne, John. *A State of the Expedition from Canada . . .* London, 1780.

Burnett, Kristin, and Geoff Read, eds. *Aboriginal History: A Reader*. 2nd ed. Toronto: Oxford University Press, 2016.

Butler, John. "Declaration of Colonel John Butler Received by Notary Beek, Montreal, 27 October 1787." *Rapport de l'Archiviste de la Province de Quebec pour 1924–1925* (Quebec: Ls-A. Prouls, 1925): 393–96.

Butterfield, Charles. *In the Shadow of Cedars*. Keene, NH: Historical Society of Cheshire County, 2013.

Calloway, Colin G. *The American Revolution in Indian Country*. Cambridge: Cambridge University Press, 1995.

———. *The Indian History of an American Institution: Native Americans and Dartmouth*. Hanover, NH: Dartmouth College Press, 2010.

———. *The Indian World of George Washington: The First President, the First Americans, and the Birth of the Nation*. New York: Oxford University Press, 2018.

———. "Sentinels of the Revolution: Bedel's New Hampshire Rangers and the Abenaki Indians on the Upper Connecticut." *Historical New Hampshire* 45, no. 4 (Winter 1990): 271–95.

———. *The Western Abenakis of Vermont, 1600–1800: War, Migration, and the Survival of an Indian People*. Norman: University of Oklahoma Press, 1990.

Campbell, Patrick. *Travels in the Interior Inhabited Parts of North America, in the Years 1791 and 1792*. Edinburgh, 1793.

Campbell, William W. *Annals of Tryon County; or, The Border Warfare of New-York during the Revolution*. New York: J. & J. Harper, 1831.

Campisi, Jack. "The Iroquois and the Euro-American Concept of Tribe." *New York History* 63 (April 1982): 165–82.

Cannon, Richard. *Historical Record of the Eighth, or the King's Regiment of Foot*. London, 1837.

Cardy, Michael, ed. "The Iroquois in the Eighteenth Century: A Neglected Source." *Man in the Northeast* 39 (Fall 1989): 1–20.

Carp, Benjamin L. "'Disreputable among Civilized Nations': Destroying Homes during the Revolutionary War." In Moots and Hamilton, *Justifying Revolution*.

Carroll, Charles. *Journal of Charles Carroll of Carrollton, during His Visit to Canada in 1776*. Edited by Brantz Mayer. Baltimore: John Murphy, 1876.

Carter, Clarence Edwin, ed. *The Correspondence of General Thomas Gage . . . 1763–1775*. 2 vols. New Haven, CT: Yale University Press, 1931.

Carver, Jonathan. *Travels through the Interior Parts of North America, in the Years 1766, 1767, and 1768*. London, 1781.

Cascades 300: 1684–1984 Vers L'Avenir. Pointe des Cascades, QC: 1984.

Castro, Wendy Lucas. "Stripped: Clothing and Identity in Colonial Captivity Narratives." *Early American Studies: An Interdisciplinary Journal* 6, no. 1 (2008): 104–36.

Chamberlain, A. F. "Notes on the History, Customs, and Beliefs of the Mississaugas." *Journal of American Folk-Lore* 1 (July 1888): 150–60.

Chartrand, René. *The Forts of New France in Northeast America 1600–1763*. New York: Osprey, 2008.

———. *French Fortresses in North America, 1535–1763: Québec, Montréal, Louisbourg and New Orleans*. New York: Osprey, 2005.

Chase, Frederick. *A History of Dartmouth College and the Town of Hanover, New Hampshire*. Vol. 1. Cambridge, MA: University Press, 1891.

Chet, Guy. *Conquering the American Wilderness: The Triumph of European Warfare in the Colonial Northeast*. Boston: University of Massachusetts Press, 2003.

Claus, Daniel. *Daniel Claus' Narrative of His Relations with Sir William Johnson and Experiences in the Lake George Fight*. New York[?]: Society of Colonial Wars in the State of New York, 1904.

Colden, Cadwallader. *The History of the Five Indian Nations of Canada, which Are Dependent on the Province of New-York in America*. 3rd ed. London, 1755.

Coleman, Emma L. *New England Captives Carried to Canada between 1677 and 1760 during the French and Indian Wars*. 2 vols. Portland, ME: Southworth Press, 1925.

Corbett, Theodore G. *A Clash of Cultures on the Warpath of Nations: The Colonial Wars in the Hudson-Champlain Valley*. Fleischmanns, NY: Purple Mountain Press, 2002.

Couture, Claude, Denis Gravel, and Jean-Marc Grenier. *Histoire de Ville de LaSalle*. Montreal: Éditions du Méridien, 1988.
Crouch, Christian A. "Surveying the Present, Projecting the Future: Reevaluating Colonial French *Plans* of Kanesatake." *William and Mary Quarterly* 75, no. 2 (April 2018): 323–42.
Cruikshank, Ernest. *The Story of Butler's Rangers and the Settlement of Niagara*. Welland, ON: Tribune Printing House, 1893.
Cubbison, Douglas R. *The American Northern Theater Army in 1776: The Ruin and Reconstruction of the Continental Force*. Jefferson, NC: McFarland, 2010.
Davies, Kenneth. *Documents of the American Revolution, 1770–1783*. Colonial Office Series. Vols. 11, 12, and 14 (Transcripts 1775 July–December, Transcripts 1776, and Transcripts 1777). Dublin: Irish University Press, 1976.
Dawson, Samuel E. "The Massacre at the Cedars." *Canadian Monthly* 5 (April 1874): 305–23.
Day, Gordon M. *The Mots Loups of Father Mathevet*. Publications in Ethnology no. 8. Ottawa: National Museums of Canada, National Museum of Man, 1975.
———. "Nipissing." In Trigger, *Handbook of North American Indians*, vol. 15: *Northeast*.
———. "Rogers' Raid in Indian Tradition." *Historical New Hampshire* 17 (1962): 3–17.
Day, Gordon M., and Bruce G. Trigger. "Algonquin." In Trigger, *Handbook of North American Indians*, vol. 15: *Northeast*.
Delage, Denys, and J-P Sawaya. "Les origines de la Fédération des Sept-Feux." *Recherches amérindiennes au Québec* 31, no. 2 (2001): 43–54.
De Peyster, Arent Schuyler. *Miscellanies by an Officer*. Dumfries, UK: C. Munro, 1813.
Devine, E. J. *Historic Caughnawaga*. Montreal: Messenger Press, 1922.
Dickinson, John A., and Jan Grabowski. "Les Populations Amérindiennes de la Vallée Laurentienne, 1608–1765." *Annales de Démographie Historique* (1993): 51–65.
Dictionary of Canadian Biography (online). http://www.biographi.ca/en/.
Digby, William. "Campaign of 1776, by an Officer in the Northern Army under the Command of His Excellency General Guy Carleton." In *The British Invasion from the North: The Campaigns of Generals Carleton and Burgoyne from Canada, 1776–1777*, edited by James Phinney Baxter, 77–361. Albany, NY: Joel Munsell's Sons, 1887.
Doughty, Arthur G., ed. "Appendix B—Papers Relating to the Surrender of Fort St. John's and Fort Chambly." In *Report of the Work of the Public Archives for the Years 1914 and 1915*. Ottawa: J. de L Taché, 1916.
Dowd, Gregory E. *Groundless: Rumors, Legends, and Hoaxes on the Early American Frontier*. Baltimore: Johns Hopkins University Press, 2015.
Dunn, Walter S. *Opening New Markets: The British Army and the Old Northwest*. Westport, CT: Praeger, 2002.
Du Ponceau, Peter S. "The Autobiography of Peter Stephen Du Ponceau." Edited by James L. Whitehead. *Pennsylvania Magazine of History and Biography* 63, no. 2 (April 1939): 189–227.
Eastburn, Robert. *The Dangers and Sufferings of Robert Eastburn, and His Deliverance from Indian Captivity*. Reprint of the original edition of 1758. Edited by John R. Spears. Cleveland: Burrows Brothers, 1904.

Eccles, W. J. *The Canadian Frontier, 1534–1760*. Rev. ed. Albuquerque: University of New Mexico Press, 1983.
Egleston, Thomas. *The Life of John Paterson, Major-General in the Revolutionary Army*. New York: G. P. Putnam's Sons, 1894.
Eid, Leroy V. "The Cardinal Principle of Northeast Woodland Indian War." In *Papers of the Thirteenth Algonquian Conference*, edited by William Cowan, 243–50. Ottawa: Carleton University, 1982.
———. "'A Kind of Running Fight': Indian Battlefield Tactics in the Late Eighteenth Century." *Western Pennsylvania Historical Magazine* 71 (1988): 147–71.
———. "National War among the Indians of Northeastern America." *Canadian Review of American Studies* 16 (1985): 125–54.
Entick, John. *The General History of the Late War: Containing Its Rise, Progress, and Event* . . . Vol. 2. London, 1763.
Everest, Allen S. *Moses Hazen and the Canadian Refugees in the American Revolution*. Syracuse, NY: Syracuse University Press, 1976.
Ewing, William S., and J[ames] F[urnis]. 1961. "An Eyewitness Account by James Furnis of the Surrender of Fort William Henry, August 1757." *New York History* 42, no. 3 (July 1961): 307–16.
Faribault-Beauregard, Marthe. "Montréal, notre ile, les passages de l'eau à la fin du XVIIIe siècle." In *Montréal, Activités, Habitants, Quartiers*, 64–80. Société historique de Montréal. Montreal: Fides, 1984.
Fenn, Elizabeth A. "Biological Warfare in Eighteenth-Century North America: Beyond Jeffery Amherst." *Journal of American History* 86, no. 4 (2000): 1552–80.
———. *Pox Americana: The Great Smallpox Epidemic of 1775–82*. New York: Hill and Wang, 2001.
Fenton, William N. "Factionalism in American Indian Society." In *Actes du IVe Congrès International des Sciences Anthropologiques et Ethnologiques, Vienne, 1–8 Septembre 1952*. Vol. 2, 230–40. Vienna: Adolf Holzhausen, 1965.
———. *The Great Law and the Longhouse: A Political History of the Iroquois Confederacy*. Norman: University of Oklahoma Press, 1998.
———. "Leadership in the Northeastern Woodlands of North America." *American Indian Quarterly* 10, no. 1 (Winter 1986): 21–45.
Fenton, William N., and Elisabeth Tooker. "Mohawk." In Trigger, *Handbook of North American Indians*, vol. 15: *Northeast*.
Filion, Mario. *Histoire du Haut-Saint-Laurent*. Sainte-Foy, QC: Les Éditions de l'Institut québécois de recherche sur la culture, 2000.
Fisher, Samuel. "Fit Instruments in a Howling Wilderness: Colonists, Indians, and the Origins of the American Revolution." *William and Mary Quarterly* 73, no. 4 (October 2016): 647–80.
Fitz, Caitlin A. "'Suspected on Both Sides': Little Abraham, Iroquois Neutrality, and the American Revolution." *Journal of the Early Republic* 28, no. 3 (Fall 2008): 299–335.
Forbes, J-G. "St-François-Xavier de Caughnawaga." *Bulletin des Recherches Historiques* 5 (1899): 131–35.

Force, Peter, ed. *American Archives*. 4th and 5th Series. Washington, DC: M. St. Clair Clarke and Peter Force, 1837–53.

Ford, Worthington C. *British Officers Serving in the American Revolution, 1774–1783*. Brooklyn, NY: Historical Printing Club, 1897.

———, ed. *Journals of the Continental Congress, 1774–1789*. Washington, DC, 1904–37.

Foretier, Pierre. "Notes and Reminiscences of an Inhabitant of Montreal during the Occupation of That City by the Bostonians from 1775 to 1776." *Annual Report of the Department of Public Archives for the Year 1945* (1946): xxiii–xxvi.

"Fort de la Présentation—History of the Fort." https://www.fort1749.org/fort-history/.

Foucher, Antoine. "Journal Tenu pendant le Siege du Fort Saint-Jean, en 1775, par Feu M. Foucher, Ancien Notaire de Montreal." *Le Bulletin des Recherches Historiques* 40 (March–April 1934): 135–59, 197–222.

Fournier, Marcel. *De la Nouvelle-Angleterre à la Nouvelle-France: L'histoire des captifs anglo-américaines au Canada entre 1675 et 1760*. Montreal: Société généalogique canadienne-française, 1992.

Fraser, John. *Historic Canadian Ground: The Lasalle Homestead of 1666 and Other Old Landmarks of French Canada on the Lower Lachine Road*. Montreal: Witness, 1892.

Frazier, Patrick. *The Mohicans of Stockbridge*. Lincoln: University of Nebraska Press, 1992.

Frey, Sylvia. *The British Soldier in America: A Social History of Military Life in the Revolutionary Period*. Austin: University of Texas Press, 1981.

Frisch, Jack A. "The Abenakis among the St. Regis Mohawks." *Indian Historian* 4 (Spring 1971): 27–29.

———. "Tribalism among the St. Regis Mohawks: A Search for Self-Identity," *Anthropologica*, n.s., 12, no. 2 (1970): 207–19.

Frye, Joseph. "Journal of the Attack of Fort William Henry, on the 3d of August, and the Surrender of It on the 9th of the Same Month, 1757." *Port Folio* 7, no. 5 (May 1819): 359–68.

Gabriel-Doxtater, Brenda Katlatont, and Arlette Kawanatatie Van den Hende. *At the Woods' Edge: An Anthology of the History of the People of Kanehsatà:ke*. Kanesatake, QC: Kanesatake Education Center, 1995.

Gardner, Frank A. "Colonel John Paterson's Regiment." *Massachusetts Magazine* 8, no. 1 (January 1915): 27–41; no. 2 (April 1915): 75–83.

Garneau, François-Xavier. *Histoire du Canada depuis sa découverte jusqu'à nos jours*. Vol. 3. Quebec: John Lovell, 1852.

The Gentleman's Magazine and Historical Chronicle 47 (1776).

Gerlach, Don R. *Proud Patriot: Philip Schuyler and the War of Independence, 1775–1783*. Syracuse, NY: Syracuse University Press, 1987.

Gibb, Harley L. "Colonel Guy Johnson, Superintendent General of Indian Affairs, 1774–82." *Papers of the Michigan Academy of Science, Arts and Letters* 27 (1941): 596–600.

Gibson, Marian M. *In the Footsteps of the Mississaugas*. Mississauga, ON: Mississauga Heritage Foundation, 2006.

Gilbert, Benjamin. *A Narrative of the Captivity and Sufferings of Benjamin Gilbert and His Family Who Were Taken by the Indians in the Spring of 1780*. Philadelphia, 1848.

Gilmore, George C. *State Senators, 1784–1900: New Hampshire Men at Bunker Hill.* Manchester, NH: John B. Clarke, 1899.

Girouard, Désiré. *Lake St. Louis, Old and New.* Montreal: Poirier, Bessette, 1893.

———. *Supplement to "Lake St. Louis," &c. &c. from Many Unpublished Documents.* Montreal: Poirier, Bessette, 1903.

Glasson, William H. *Federal Military Pensions in the United States.* New York: Oxford University Press, 1918.

Glatthaar, Joseph T., and James Kirby Martin. *Forgotten Allies: The Oneida Indians and the American Revolution.* New York: Hill and Wang, 2006.

Goodwin, Neil. "The Narrative of the Captive, George Avery, 1780–1782." *Vermont History* 80, no. 2 (Summer–Fall 2012): 112–40.

———. *We Go as Captives: The Royalton Raid and the Shadow War on the Revolutionary Frontier.* Barre: Vermont Historical Society, 2010.

Grant, Francis. "Journal from New York to Canada, 1767." *New York History* 30 (1932): 181–96, 305–22.

Graymont, Barbara. *The Iroquois in the American Revolution.* Syracuse, NY: Syracuse University Press, 1988.

———. "The Six Nations in the Revolutionary War." In *The Iroquois in the American Revolution, 1976 Conference Proceedings*, 25–36. Rochester, NY: Rochester Museum and Science Center, 1981.

Green, Gretchen Lynn. "A New People in an Age of War: The Kahnawake Iroquois, 1667–1760." PhD diss., College of William and Mary, 1991.

Greene, Nathanael. *The Papers of Nathanael Greene.* Vol. 1. Edited by Richard K. Showman. Chapel Hill: University of North Carolina Press, 1976.

Greenwood, John. *The Revolutionary Services of John Greenwood, of Boston and New York, 1775–1783.* Edited by Isaac J. Greenwood. New York: Devine Press, 1922.

Grenier, John. *The First Way of War: American War Making on the Frontier.* New York: Cambridge University Press, 2005.

Griffin, Martin I. J. "Catholic Indians and the American Revolution." In *Catholics and the American Revolution.* Vol. 2, 97–134. Philadelphia: Self-published, 1909.

Grossman, David. *On Combat: The Psychology and Physiology of Deadly Conflict in War and Peace.* Belleville, IL: Warrior Science Publications, 2004.

Grundset, Eric G., ed. *Forgotten Patriots: African American and American Indian Patriots in the Revolutionary War.* Washington, DC: National Society Daughters of the American Revolution, 2008.

———, ed. *Forgotten Patriots: African American and American Indian Patriots in the Revolutionary War—Supplement 2008–2011.* Washington, DC: National Society Daughters of the American Revolution, 2011.

Guzzardo, John C. "The Superintendent and the Ministers: The Battle for Oneida Allegiances, 1761–75." *New York History* 57 (July 1976): 255–83.

Hadden, James M. *Hadden's Journal and Orderly Books: A Journal Kept in Canada and upon Burgoyne's Campaign in 1776 and 1777, by Lieut. James M. Hadden, Roy. Art.* Edited by Horatio Rogers. Albany, NY: Joel Munsell's Sons, 1884.

Hadfield, Joseph. *An Englishman in America, 1785: Being the Diary of Joseph Hadfield.* Edited and annotated by Douglas S. Robertson. Toronto: Hunter-Rose, 1933.

Haefeli, Evan, and Kevin Sweeney. *Captive Histories: English, French, and Native Narratives of the 1704 Deerfield Raid.* Amherst: University of Massachusetts Press, 2006.

———. *Captors and Captives: The 1704 French and Indian Raid on Deerfield.* Amherst: University of Massachusetts Press, 2003.

Hagan, William T. *Longhouse Diplomacy and Frontier Warfare: The Iroquois Confederation in the American Revolution.* Albany, NY: New York State Bicentennial Commission, 1976.

Hagedorn, Nancy L. "'A Friend to Go between Them': The Interpreter as Cultural Broker during Anglo-Iroquois Councils, 1740–70." *Ethnohistory* 35, no. 1 (1988): 60–80.

Hagist, Don N. "Untangling British Army Ranks." *Journal of the American Revolution* (19 May 2016). https://allthingsliberty.com/2016/05/untangling-british-army-ranks/.

"Haldimand Papers." *Collections and Researches Made by the Michigan Pioneer and Historical Society.* Vols. 19 and 20. Lansing, MI: Robert Smith, 1892.

Hämäläinen, Pekka, and Samuel Truett. "On Borderlands." *Journal of American History* 98 (September 2011): 338–61.

Hamilton, Edward P. "Unrest at Caughnawaga, or The Lady Fur Traders of Sault St.-Louis." *Bulletin of Fort Ticonderoga Museum* 11 (1963): 155–60.

Hamilton, Milton W., ed. "Guy Johnson's Opinions on the American Indian." *Pennsylvania Magazine of History and Biography* 77 (July 1953): 311–27.

Hamilton, Phillip. *The Revolutionary War Lives and Letters of Lucy and Henry Knox.* Baltimore: Johns Hopkins University Press, 2017.

Hammond, Isaac W., ed. "Correspondence between Rev. Eleazar Wheelock and Others, of Dartmouth College, and John Phillips, LL.D., 1765 to 1787." *Collections of the New Hampshire Historical Society* 9 (1889): 68–122.

———, ed. *State of New Hampshire: Rolls and Documents Relating to Soldiers in the Revolutionary War.* Vols. 3 and 4 of War Rolls. Manchester, NH: John B. Clarke, 1887–89.

———, ed. *State of New Hampshire: Rolls of the Soldiers in the Revolutionary War, 1775, to May, 1777 . . .* Vol. 1 of War Rolls. Vol. 14 of Series. Concord, NH: Parsons B. Cogswell, 1885.

———, ed. *Town Papers: Documents Relating to Towns in New Hampshire.* Vols. 11–13. Concord, NH: Parsons B. Cogswell, 1882–84.

Hammond, Otis G., ed. *Letters and Papers of Major-General John Sullivan, Continental Army.* Vols. 1 and 2. Concord: New Hampshire Historical Society, 1930–31.

Hanson, J. Howard, and Samuel Ludlow Frey, eds. *The Minute Book of the Committee of Safety of Tryon County.* New York: Dodd Mead, 1905.

Hays, I. Minis. "A Journal Kept during the Siege of Fort William Henry, August 1757." *Proceedings of the American Philosophical Society* 37 (1898): 143–50.

Heagerty, John J. *Four Centuries of Medical History in Canada, and a Sketch of the Medical History of Newfoundland.* Vol. 1. Toronto: Macmillan, 1928.

Heckewelder, John. *The History, Manners, and Customs of the Indian Nations Who Once Inhabited Pennsylvania and the Neighbouring States.* Philadelphia: Historical Society of Pennsylvania, 1881.

Heitman, Francis B. *Historical Register of Officers of the Continental Army during the War of the Revolution, April, 1775, to December, 1783.* New, Revised, and Enlarged Edition. Washington, DC: Rare Book Shop, 1904.

Henry, Alexander. *Alexander Henry's Travels and Adventures in the Years 1760–1776.* Edited by Milo Milton Quaife. Chicago: Lakeside Press, 1921.

Heriot, George. *Travels through the Canadas, Containing a Description of the Picturesque Scenery on Some of the Rivers and Lakes* . . . Philadelphia: M. Carey, 1813.

Herrmann, Rachel B. "'No Useless Mouth': Iroquoian Food Diplomacy in the American Revolution." *Diplomatic History* 41, no. 1 (2017): 20–49.

Hess, Abram. *The Life and Services of General John Philip de Haas, 1735–1786.* Lebanon, PA: Lebanon County Historical Society, 1916.

Hinman, Royal R. *Historical Collection from Official Records, Files, &c. of the Part Sustained by Connecticut during the War of the Revolution.* Hartford, CT: E. Gleason, 1842.

Historical Section of the General Staff. *A History of the Organization, Development and Service of the Military and Naval Forces of Canada from the Peace of Paris in 1763 to the Present Time.* Vol. 2. Quebec: King's Printer, 1919.

History of Berkshire County, Massachusetts, with Biographical Sketches of Its Prominent Men. Vol. 2. J. B. Beers, 1885.

History of Litchfield County, Connecticut with Illustrations and Biographical Sketches of Its Prominent Men and Pioneers. Philadelphia: J. W. Lewis, 1881.

Hoadly, Charles J. *The Public Records of the Colony of Connecticut, from May, 1775 to June, 1776, inclusive* . . . Hartford, CT: Case, Lockwood, and Brainard, 1890.

Hoffman, Ronald. *Dear Papa, Dear Charley: The Peregrinations of a Revolutionary Aristocrat as Told by Charles Carroll of Carrollton and His Father, Charles Carroll of Annapolis* . . . Vol. 2. Chapel Hill: University of North Carolina Press, 2001.

Holliday, Francis. *An Easy Introduction to Fortification and Practical Gunnery.* London: G. Robinson, 1774.

Hollister, Josiah. *The Journal of Josiah Hollister: A Soldier of the American Revolution and a Prisoner of War in Canada.* Edited by Romanzo Norton Bunn. [Chicago]: Romanzo Norton Bunn, 1928.

Hoock, Holger. *Scars of Independence: America's Violent Birth.* New York: Crown, 2017.

Hoskins, Nathan. *A History of the State of Vermont, from Its Discovery and Settlement to the Close of the Year MDCCCXXX.* Vergennes, VT: J. Shedd, 1831.

Hough, Franklin B. *A History of St. Lawrence and Franklin Counties, New York* . . . Albany, NY: Little, 1853.

Houlding, J. A. *Fit for Service: The Training of the British Army, 1715–1795.* Oxford: Clarendon Press, 1981.

Huden, John Charles. "The White Chief of the St. Francis Abnakis: Some Aspects of Border Warfare, 1690–1790." *Vermont History* 24 (July–October 1956): 199–210, 337–55.

Hughes, Ben. *The Siege of Fort William Henry: A Year on the Northern Frontier.* Yardley, PA: Westholme, 2011.

Hunter, Robert, Jr. *Quebec to Carolina in 1785–1786: Being the Travel Diary and Observations of Robert Hunter, Jr., a Young Merchant of London.* Edited by Louis B. Wright and Marion Tinling. San Marino, CA: Huntington Library, 1943.

Igartua, José E. "The Merchants and *Négociants* of Montreal, 1750–1775: A Study in Socio-Economic History." PhD diss., Michigan State University, 1974.

Ingram, James. *Indians and British Outposts in Eighteenth-Century America.* Gainesville: University Press of Florida, 2012.

Innis, Harold A. *The Fur Trade in Canada.* Toronto: University of Toronto Press, 1956.

Jacobs, Wilbur R. *Diplomacy and Indian Gifts: Anglo-French Rivalry along the Ohio and Northwest Frontiers, 1748–1763.* Stanford, CA: Stanford University Press, 1950.

———. *Wilderness Politics and Indian Gifts: The Northern Colonial Frontier, 1748–1763.* Lincoln: University of Nebraska Press, 1966.

J. C. B. *Travels in New France by J. C. B.* Edited by Sylvester K. Stevens, Donald H. Kent, and Emma E. Woods. Harrisburg: Pennsylvania Historical Commission, 1941.

Jeannotte, Adhémar. *L'histoire de Vaudreuil.* Société de Généalogie Vaudreuil-Cavagnal, 2015.

Jennings, Francis. *Empire of Fortune: Crowns, Colonies, and Tribes in the Seven Years War.* New York: Norton, 1988.

———. "The Imperial Revolution: The American Revolution as a Tripartite Struggle for Sovereignty." In *The American Indian and the American Revolution*, edited by Francis P. Jennings, 42–59. The Newberry Center for the History of the American Indian Occasional Papers no. 6. 1983.

———, ed. *Iroquois Indians: A Documentary History.* Reels 30, 31, 32, 33. Woodbridge, CT: Research Publications, 1984.

Jezierski, John V., ed. and trans. "A 1751 Journal of Abbé François Picquet." *New-York Historical Society Quarterly* 54 (1970): 361–81.

Johnston, Basil. *Ojibway Heritage.* Lincoln: University of Nebraska Press, 1990.

Johnston, Henry P. *The Record of Connecticut Men in the Military and Naval Service during the War of the Revolution, 1775–1783.* Hartford, CT, 1889.

Jones, Electa Fidelia. *Stockbridge, Past and Present, or, Records of an Old Mission Station.* Springfield, MA: Samuel Bowles, 1854.

Jones, Peter. *History of the Ojebway Indians; with Especial Reference to Their Conversion to Christianity.* London: A. W. Bennett, 1861.

Jones, T. Cole. *Captives of Liberty: Prisoners of War and the Politics of Vengeance in the American Revolution.* Philadelphia: University of Pennsylvania Press, 2020.

Journal of the Provincial Congress, Provincial Conventions, Committee of Safety and Council of Safety of the State of New-York, 1775–1776–1777. Vol. 2. Albany, NY: Thurlow Weed, 1842.

Kahkewaquonaby [Jones, Peter]. "The Indian Nations: A Short Account of the Customs and Manners of the North American Indians, Particularly the Chippeway Nation." *Monthly Review Devoted to the Civil Government of Canada* 1, no. 5 (May 1841): 318–26.

Kahnawake Longhouse. "History and Culture." http://www.kahnawakelonghouse.com/index.php?mid=2&p=1.

Kaplan, Sidney, and Emma Nogrady Kaplan. *The Black Presence in the Era of the American Revolution*. Amherst: University of Massachusetts Press, 1989.

Ke-che-ah-gah-me-qua. *The Life of Captain Joseph Brant, (Thayendanegea)*. Brantford, ON: B. H. Rothwell, 1850.

Kelly, Eric P. "The Dartmouth Indians." *Dartmouth Alumni Magazine* 22 (December 1929): 122–25.

[Kimber, Isaac] An Impartial Hand. *The History of England: From the Earliest Accounts to the Accession of His Present Majesty King George II*. London, 1762.

King, Titus. *Narrative of Titus King of Northampton, Mass.: A Prisoner of the Indians in Canada, 1755–1758*. Hartford: Connecticut Historical Society, 1938.

Kingsford, William. *The History of Canada*. Vol. 6. Toronto: Rowsell & Hutchison, 1893.

Kirkland, Samuel. *The Journals of Samuel Kirkland: 18th-century Missionary to the Iroquois, Government Agent, Father of Hamilton College*. Edited by Walter Pilkington. Clinton, NY: Hamilton College, 1980.

Knoblock, Glenn A. *"Strong and Brave Fellows": New Hampshire's Black Soldiers and Sailors of the American Revolution, 1775–1784*. Jefferson, NC: McFarland, 2003.

Knowles, Nathaniel. "The Torture of Captives by the Indians of Eastern Northern America." *Proceedings of the American Philosophical Society* 82 (1940): 151–225.

Knox, John. *An Historical Journal of the Campaigns in North America for the Years 1757, 1758, 1759, and 1760*. Vol. 2. London, 1769.

Lafitau, Joseph François. *Customs of the American Indians Compared with the Customs of Primitive Times*. Edited by William N. Fenton and Elizabeth L. Moore. 2 vols. Toronto: Champlain Society, 1974.

Lainey, Jonathan, and Thomas Peace. "Louis Vincent Sawatanen: A Life Forged by Warfare and Migration." In *Aboriginal History: A Reader*, edited by Kristin Burnett and Geoff Read, 106–16. 2nd ed. Toronto: Oxford University Press, 2016.

Lanning, Michael Lee. *Defenders of Liberty: African Americans in the Revolutionary War*. New York: Kensington, 2000.

Lapause de Margon, Jean-Guillaume Plantavit de. "Relation de Mr. Poulariès Envoyée à Mr. le Marquis de Montcalm." *Rapport de l'archiviste de la province de Québec* (1932–33): 47–65.

Lee, Arthur. "Extracts of Some Letters, from Sir William Johnson, Bart. to Arthur Lee, M.D. F.R.S. on the Customs, Manners, and Language of the Northern Indians of America." *Philosophical Transactions of the Royal Society of London* 63, no. 1: 142–48.

Lee, Wayne E. *Barbarians and Brothers: Anglo-American Warfare, 1500–1805*. New York: Oxford University Press, 2011.

———. "From Gentility to Atrocity: The Continental Army's Ways of War." *Army History* 62 (Winter 2006): 5–19.

Lee, William Henry. "An Address on the Life and Character of Major-General John Patterson . . ." *The New York Genealogical and Biographical Record* 21, no. 3 (July 1890): 99–112.

Lefferts, Charles M. *Uniforms of the American, British, French, and German Armies in the War of the American Revolution, 1775–1783.* Edited by Alexander J. Wall. Old Greenwich, CT: WE, 1972.

Lender, Mark E., and James K. Martin. "Liberty or Death! *Jus in Bello* and Existential Warfare in the American Revolution." In Moots and Hamilton, *Justifying Revolution.*

Lepage, Jean-Denis G. G. *French Fortifications, 1715–1815: An Illustrated History.* Jefferson, NC: McFarland, 2010.

Léry McDonald, Archibald Chaussegros de. *Les Seigneuries de Vaudreuil et Rigaud.* Quebec: Les Publications Généalogiques, 1995.

Levinson, David. "An Explanation for the Oneida-Colonist Alliance in the American Revolution." *Ethnohistory* 23, no. 3 (1976): 265–89.

A List of the Officers of the Army . . . London: War Office, 1757–84.

Livingston, Henry. "Journal of Major Henry Livingston, of the Third New York Continental Line, August to December, 1775." *Pennsylvania Magazine of History and Biography* 22 (1898): 9–33.

Loescher, Burt G. *Genesis: Rogers' Rangers: The First Green Berets.* San Mateo, CA: 1969.

———. *The History of Rogers' Rangers.* Vol. 3, *Officers and Non-Commissioned Officers.* Burlingame, CA: Self-published, 1957.

Loftus, Elizabeth F. "Creating False Memories." *Scientific American* 277, no. 3 (September 1997): 70–75.

Long, John. *John Long's Voyages and Travels, in the Years 1768–1788.* Edited by Milo Milton Quaife. Chicago: Lakeside Press, 1922.

Lorimier, Claude-Nicholas-Guillaume de. *At War with the Americans: The Journal of Claude-Nicolas-Guillaume de Lorimier.* Translated and edited by Peter Aichinger. Victoria, BC: Press Porcepic, 1987.

———. *Mes Services pendant la Guerre Americaine de 1775: Memoire de M. de Lorimier.* Edited by Hospice-Anthelme Jean-Baptiste Verreau. Montreal: Eusèbe Senecal, 1871.

"Le Lorimier et Le Montigny des Cèdres." *Le Bulletin des Recherches historiques* 47, no. 4 (February 1941): 33–47.

Loskiel, George Henry. *The History of the Mission of the United Brethren among the Indians in North America, in Three Parts.* Translated by Christian Ignatius La Trobe. London: Brethren's Society for the Furtherance of the Gospel, 1794.

Lozier, Jean-François. "History, Historiography, and the Courts: The St Lawrence Mission Villages and the Fall of New France." In *Remembering 1759: The Conquest of Canada in Historical Memory,* edited by Phillip Buckner and John G. Reid, 110–35. Toronto: University of Toronto Press, 2012.

———. "In Each Other's Arms: France and the St. Lawrence Mission Villages in War and Peace, 1630–1730." PhD diss., University of Toronto, 2012.

———. "Mission Villages on the St. Lawrence." In *On the Trails of the Iroquois,* edited by Sylvia Kasprycki, 128–31. Bonn: Kunst- und Ausstellungshalle der Bundesrepublik Deutschland, 2013.

Lunn, Jean. "The Illegal Fur Trade Out of New France, 1713–1760." *Canadian Historical Association Report* (1939): 61–76.

Lynch, James. "The Iroquois Confederation and the Adoption and Administration of Non-Iroquoian Individuals and Groups Prior to 1756." *Man in the Northeast* 30 (Fall 1985): 83–99.

Mackenzie, Alexander. *Voyages from Montreal through the Continent of North America to the Frozen and Pacific Oceans in 1789 and 1793 with an Account of the Rise and State of the Fur Trade.* 2 vols. New York: A. S. Barnes, 1903.

Mackey, Frank. *Done with Slavery: The Black Fact in Montreal, 1760–1840.* Montreal: McGill-Queens, 2010.

MacLeitch, Gail D. *Imperial Entanglements: Iroquois Change and Persistence on the Frontiers of Empire.* Philadelphia: University of Pennsylvania Press, 2011.

MacLeod, D. Peter. "The Anishinabeg Point of View: The History of the Great Lakes Region to 1800 in Nineteenth-Century Mississauga, Odawa, and Ojibwa Historiography." *Canadian Historical Review* 73, no. 2 (June 1992): 194–210.

———. *The Canadian Iroquois and the Seven Years' War.* Toronto: Dundurn, 1996.

———. "Microbes and Muskets: Smallpox and the Participation of the Amerindian Allies of New France in the Seven Years' War." *Ethnohistory* 39, no. 1 (Winter 1992): 42–64.

Mahon, John K. "Anglo-American Methods of Indian Warfare, 1676–1794." *Mississippi Valley Historical Review* 45 (1958): 254–75.

Mainville, Moise. *Histoire de la paroisse Saint-Joseph de Soulanges (des débuts à 1900).* Quebec: Les Publications Généalogiques, 1995.

Malchelosse, Gérard. "Les juifs dans l'histoire canadienne." *Cahiers des Dix* 4 (1939): 167–95.

Mante, Thomas. *The History of the Late War in North-America and the Islands of the West-Indies.* London, 1772.

Manual Exercise, as Ordered by His Majesty, in the Year 1764. Philadelphia: J. Humphreys, 1776.

"Marriages and Deaths." *New England Historical and Genealogical Register* 4, no. 3 (July 1850): 292.

Marshall, Peter. "The Government of the Quebec Fur Trade: An Imperial Dilemma, 1761–1775." In *Le Castor Fait Tout: Selected Papers of the Fifth North American Fur Trade Conference, 1985.* Montreal: Lake St. Louis Historical Society, 1987.

Martin, James K. *Benedict Arnold, Revolutionary Hero: An American Warrior Reconsidered.* New York: New York University Press, 2007.

———. "A Contagion of Violence: The Ideal of *Jus in Bello* versus the Realities of Fighting on the New York Frontier during the Revolutionary War." *Journal of Military Ethics* 14, no. 1 (May 2015): 57–73.

Massachusetts Muster, Payrolls & Various Papers, 1763–1808 of the Revolutionary War. 44 microfilm rolls. Boston: Massachusetts Archives, 1993.

Massicotte, Édouard-Zotique. "Le bourgeois Pierre Fortier." *Bulletin des Recherches historiques* 47 (1941): 176–79.

———. "La Famille de Lorimier: Notes généalogiques et historiques." *Bulletin des Recherches historiques* 21 (1915): 10–16, 33–45.

Maurault, Olivier. "Oka: Les vicissitudes d'une mission sauvage." *Revue Trimestrielle Canadienne* 16 (June 1930): 121–49.

———. "Quand Saint-Sulpice allait en guerre . . ." *Cahiers des Dix* 5 (1940): 11–30.

Mayer, Holly A. *Belonging to the Army: Camp Followers and Community during the American Revolution.* Columbia: University of South Carolina Press, 1996.

———. "Wives, Concubines, and Community: Following the Army." In *War and Society in the American Revolution: Mobilization and Home Fronts,* edited by John Resch and Walter Sargent, 235–62. DeKalb: Northern Illinois University Press, 2007.

McCallum, James Dow, ed. *The Letters of Eleazar Wheelock's Indians.* Hanover, NH: Dartmouth College Publications, 1932.

McConnell, Michael N. *Army and Empire: British Soldiers on the American Frontier, 1758–1775.* Lincoln: University of Nebraska Press, 2004.

McDonnell, Michael A. *Masters of Empire: Great Lakes Indians and the Making of America.* New York: Hill and Wang, 2015.

McHenry, Chris, comp. *Rebel Prisoners at Quebec, 1778–1783.* Lawrenceburg, IN: Self-published, 1981.

Merrell, James H. "Second Thoughts on Colonial Historians and American Indians." *William and Mary Quarterly* 69, no. 3 (July 2012): 451–512.

Merrill, Georgia Drew. *History of Coos County, New Hampshire.* Syracuse, NY: W. A. Fergusson, 1888.

Metcalf, Seth. *Diary and Journal (1755–1807) of Seth Metcalf.* Boston: Historical Records Survey, 1939.

Metzger, Charles H. *The Prisoner in the American Revolution.* Chicago: Loyola University Press, 1971.

Mileham, Patrick. *"Difficulties Be Damned," The King's Regiment, 8th, 63rd, 96th: A History of the City Regiment of Manchester and Liverpool.* Knutsford, UK: Fleur de Lys, 2000.

Miller, Cary. *Ogimaag: Anishinaabeg Leadership, 1760–1845.* Lincoln: University of Nebraska Press, 2010.

Ministère de la Culture et des Communications [Québec]. *Les Carnets du Patrimoine: Site Historique et Archéologique du Fort-Senneville.*

Mintz, Max M. *Seeds of Empire: The American Revolutionary Conquest of the Iroquois.* New York: New York University Press, 1999.

Mohawk Council of Kahnawake. *Seigneury of Sault St. Louis.* Kahnawake, QC, 2004.

Mohr, Walter H. *Federal Indian Relations, 1774–1788.* Philadelphia: University of Pennsylvania Press, 1933.

Montgomery, Thomas L. *Pennsylvania Archives,* 5th Series. Vols. 1 and 2. Harrisburg, PA: Harrisburg Publishing Company, 1906.

Moore, Steven C. "'Our Brothers in This Country': Captivity and Kinship in the Colonial Northeast." Master's thesis, University of Massachusetts Boston, 2013.

Moots, Glen A., and Phillip Hamilton, eds. *Justifying Revolution: Law, Virtue, and Violence in the American War of Independence.* Norman: University of Oklahoma Press, 2018.

Morgan, Lewis H. *League of the Ho-dé-no-sau-nee, or Iroquois.* New York: Dodd, Mead, 1922.

Morgan, William J., ed. *Naval Documents of the American Revolution*. Vol. 5. Washington, DC: U.S. Government Printing Office, 1970.
Neimeyer, Charles P. *America Goes to War: A Social History of the Continental Army*. New York: New York University Press, 1996.
———. "No Meat, No Soldier: Race, Class and Ethnicity in the Continental Army." PhD diss., Georgetown University, 1993.
Newman, Andrew. *Allegories of Encounter: Colonial Literacy and Indian Captivities*. Chapel Hill: University of North Carolina Press, 2019.
Newman, Debra L., comp. *List of Black Servicemen Compiled from the War Department Collection of Revolutionary War Records*. National Archives Special List no. 36. Washington, DC: National Archives and Records Service, 1974.
Norton, David J. *Rebellious Younger Brother, Oneida Leadership and Diplomacy, 1750–1800*. DeKalb: Northern Illinois University Press, 2009.
Norton, Thomas E. *The Fur Trade in Colonial New York, 1686–1776*. Madison: University of Wisconsin Press, 1974.
O'Callaghan, Edmund B., ed. *The Documentary History of the State of New York*. Vol. 1. Albany, NY: Weed, Parsons, 1849.
———, ed. *Documents Relative to the Colonial History of the State of New-York*. Vols. 6–10. Albany, NY: Weed, Parsons, 1855–58.
———, ed. *Orderly Book of Lieut. Gen. John Burgoyne, from His Entry into the State of New York until His Surrender at Saratoga, 16th Oct., 1777*. Albany, NY: J. Munsell, 1860.
O'Donnell, James H. "The World Turned Upside Down: The American Revolution as a Catastrophe for Native Americans." In *The American Indian and the American Revolution*, edited by Francis P. Jennings, 80–93. The Newberry Center for the History of the American Indian Occasional Papers no. 6. 1983.
Osborne, Brian, and Michael Ripmeester. "Kingston, Bedford, Grape Island, Alnwick: The Odyssey of the Kingston Mississauga." *Historic Kingston* (1995): 84–112.
———. "The Mississaugas between Two Worlds: Strategic Adjustments to Changing Landscapes of Power." *The Canadian Journal of Native Studies* 17, no. 2 (1997): 259–91.
Ostola, Lawrence. "The Seven Nations of Canada and the American Revolution, 1774–1783." Master's thesis, Université de Montréal, 1989.
Otten, William L., Jr. *Colonel J. F. Hamtramck: His Life and Times*. Vol. 1, *1756–1783*. Port Aransas, TX: William L. Otten, 1997.
Paltstis, Victor H., ed. *Minutes of the Commissioners for Detecting and Defeating Conspiracies in the State of New York: Albany County Sessions, 1778–1781*. Vol. 2. Albany: State of New York, 1909.
Parke, Andrew. *An Authentic Narrative of Facts Relating to the Exchange of Prisoners Taken at the Cedars*. London, 1777.
Parker, John, ed. *The Journals of Jonathan Carver and Related Documents, 1766–1770*. St. Paul: Minnesota Historical Society Press, 1976.
Parkinson, Robert G. *The Common Cause: Creating Race and Nation in the American Revolution*. Chapel Hill: University of North Carolina Press, 2016.

Parliamentary History of England, from the Earliest Period to the Year 1803. Vols. 18 and 19. London, 1814.

Parmenter, Jon W. "After the Mourning Wars: The Iroquois as Allies in Colonial North American Campaigns, 1676–1760." *William and Mary Quarterly* 64, no. 1 (2007): 39–82.

———. "At the Wood's Edge: Iroquois Foreign Relations, 1727–1768." PhD diss., University of Michigan, 1999.

Parmenter, Jon W., and Mark P. Robinson. "The Perils and Possibilities of Wartime Neutrality on the Edges of Empire: Iroquois and Acadians between the French and British in North America, 1744–1760." *Diplomatic History* 31, no. 2 (April 2007): 167–206.

Partez à la découverte de Vaudreuil-Dorion. Vaudreuil-Dorion, QC: Ville de Vaudreuil-Dorion, 2008.

Pastore, Ralph T. "The Board of Commissioners for Indian Affairs in the Northern Department and the Iroquois Indians, 1775–1778." PhD diss., University of Notre Dame, 1972.

———. "Congress and the Six Nations, 1775–1778." *Niagara Frontier* 20 (1973): 80–95.

Paudash, Robert. "The Coming of the Mississagas." Prepared by J. Hampden Burnham. *Ontario Historical Society, Papers and Records* 6 (1905): 7–11.

Peace, Thomas G. M. "Maintaining Connections: Lorette during the Eighteenth Century." In *From Huronia to Wendakes: Adversity, Migration, and Resilience, 1650–1900*, edited by Thomas Peace and Kathryn M. Labelle, 74–110. Norman: University of Oklahoma Press, 2016.

———. "Two Conquests: Aboriginal Experiences of the Fall of New France and Acadia." PhD diss., York University, 2011.

Peckham, Howard H., ed. *The Toll of Independence: Engagements & Battle Casualties of the American Revolution.* Chicago: University of Chicago Press, 1974.

Penrose, Maryly B., ed. *Indian Affairs Papers: American Revolution.* Franklin Park, NJ: Liberty Bell Associates, 1981.

Perrault, Claude. *Montréal en 1781: Déclaration du fief et seigneurie de L'ile de Montréal . . .* Montreal: Payette Radio, 1969.

Perrot, Nicolas. *Mémoire sur les mœurs coutumes et religion des sauvages de l'Amérique Septentrionale.* Leipzig: Libraire A. Franck, 1864.

Pickering, Timothy. *An Easy Plan of Discipline for a Militia.* Salem, MA, 1775.

Pinard, Guy. *Montréal, son histoire, son architecture.* Vol. 4. Montreal: Éditions du Méridien, 1991.

Pioneer and Historical Society of the State of Michigan. *Collections and Researches Made by the Pioneer and Historical Society of the State of Michigan.* Vols. 9, 10, and 25. Lansing, 1886–88, 1896.

Plotnik, Arthur. *Man behind the Quill: Jacob Shallus, Calligrapher of the United States Constitution.* Washington, DC: National Archives and Records Administration, 1987.

Porter, Elisha. "Diary of Col. Elisha Porter of Hadley, Massachusetts." *Magazine of American History* 30 (1893): 187–205.

Porter, Kenneth W. *The Negro on the American Frontier.* New York: Amos Press, 1971.

Potter, William L. "Redcoats on the Frontier: The King's Regiment in the Revolutionary War." *Selected Papers from the 1983 and 1984 George Rogers Clark Trans-Appalachian Frontier History Conferences.* Edited by Robert J. Holden. Vincennes, IN: Eastern National Park and Memorial Association, 1985. http://npshistory.com/series/symposia/george_rogers_clark/1983-1984/sec3.htm.

Pouchot, Pierre. *Memoir from the Late War in North America between the French and English.* Vols. 1 and 2. Translated by Franklin B. Hough. Roxbury, MA: W. Elliot Woodward, 1866.

Preston, David L. *Braddock's Defeat: The Battle of the Monongahela and the Road to Revolution.* New York: Oxford University Press, 2015.

———. *The Texture of Contact: European and Indian Settler Communities on the Frontiers of Iroquoia, 1667–1783.* Lincoln: University of Nebraska Press, 2009.

Priest, Josiah. *The Fort Stanwix Captive, or New England Volunteer, Being the Extraordinary Life and Adventures of Isaac Hubbell among the Indians of Canada and the West, in the War of the Revolution . . .* Albany, NY: J. Munsell, 1841.

Reagen, James E. *Warriors of La Presentation.* Ogdensburg, NY: Oswegatchie Press, 1999.

Rees, John U. "Black in Blue: African Americans in the Continental Army." *Patriots of the American Revolution* 4, no. 4 (July–August 2011): 40–45.

———. "'. . . the Multitude of Women': An Examination of the Numbers of Female Camp Followers with the Continental Army." *Brigade Dispatch*, pt. 1, 23 (Autumn 1992): 5–17; pt. 2, 24 (Winter 1993): 6–16; pt. 3, 24 (Spring 1993): 2–6.

Reid, Gerald F. *Kahnawà:ke: Factionalism, Traditionalism, and Nationalism in a Mohawk Community.* Lincoln: University of Nebraska Press, 2004.

Reid, Marjorie G. "The Quebec Fur-Traders and Western Policy, 1763–1774." *Canadian Historical Review* 6 (March 1925): 15–32.

Reid, W. Max. *The Story of Old Fort Johnson.* New York: G. P. Putnam's Sons, 1906.

Resch, John. "The Revolution as a People's War: Mobilization in New Hampshire." In *War and Society in the American Revolution: Mobilization and Home Fronts*, edited by John Resch and Walter Sargent, 70–102. DeKalb: Northern Illinois University Press, 2007.

Richter, Daniel K. *Facing East from Indian Country: A Native History of Early America.* Cambridge, MA: Harvard University Press, 2003.

———. *Ordeal of the Longhouse: The Peoples of the Iroquois League in the Era of European Colonization.* Chapel Hill: University of North Carolina Press, 1992.

———. "War and Culture: The Iroquois Experience." *William and Mary Quarterly*, 3rd ser., 40, no. 4 (October 1983): 528–59.

Richter, Daniel K., and James H. Merrill, eds. *Beyond the Covenant Chain: The Iroquois and Their Neighbors in Indian North America, 1600–1800.* University Park: Pennsylvania State University Press, 2003.

Riddell, William R. *The Slave in Canada.* Washington, DC: Association for the Study of Negro Life and History, 1920.

Ritzema, Rudolphus. "Journal of Col. Rudolphus Ritzema." *Magazine of American History* 1 (1877): 98–107.

Robbins, Ammi R. *Journal of the Rev. Ammi R. Robbins, a Chaplain in the American Army in the Northern Campaign of 1776.* New Haven, CT: Yale College, 1850.

Robichaud, Léon, and Alan Stewart. *Étude historique du site de la maison LeBer-LeMoyne.* Lachine, QC: Remparts, 1999.

Robinson, Percy J. *Toronto during the French Regime.* Toronto: University of Toronto Press, 1965.

Robinson, Willard B. *American Forts: Architectural Form and Function.* Chicago: University of Illinois Press, 1977.

Robson, Eric. "British Light Infantry in Mid-Eighteenth Century: The Effect of American Conditions." *Army Quarterly* 62 (1952): 209–22.

Rogers, E. S. "Southeastern Ojibwa." In Trigger, *Handbook of North American Indians*, vol. 15: *Northeast*.

Rogers, Gerald A. "Mohawks of Quebec." *Loyalist Gazette* 29, no. 2 (Fall 1991): 40–44.

Rogers, Greg. "*Petite Politique*: The British, French, Iroquois, and Everyday Power in the Lake Ontario Borderlands, 1724–1760" (2016). *Electronic Theses and Dissertations* 2506. http://digitalcommons.library.umaine.edu/etd/2506.

Rolls and Lists of Connecticut Men in the Revolution, 1775–1783: Collections of the Connecticut Historical Society. Vol. 8. Hartford: Connecticut Historical Society, 1901.

Rushforth, Brett. *Bonds of Alliance: Indigenous and Atlantic Slaveries in New France.* Chapel Hill: University of North Carolina Press, 2012.

Saffell, W. T. R., ed. *Records of the Revolutionary War: Containing the Military and Financial Correspondence of Distinguished Officers.* Philadelphia: G. G. Evans, 1860.

Sanguinet, Simon. "Témoin Oculaire de l'Invasion du Canada par les Bastonnois: Journal de M. Sanguinet." In *Invasion du Canada: Collection des Mémoires Recueillis et Annotes*, edited by Hospice-Anthelme Verreau, 1–156. Montreal: Eusèbe Senécal, 1873.

Sawaya, Jean-Pierre. *Alliance et dépendance: Comment la Couronne britannique a obtenu la collaboration des Indiens de la vallée du Saint-Laurent entre 1760 et 1774.* Sillery, QC: Septentrion, 2002.

———. "Les Amérindiens domiciliés et le protestantisme au XVIIIe siècle: Eleazar Wheelock et le Dartmouth College." *Historical Studies in Education/Revue d'histoire de l'éducation* 22, no. 2 (Fall 2010): 18–38.

———. *La Fédération des Sept Feux de la Vallée du Saint-Laurent: XVIIe au XIXe Xiècle.* Sillery, QC: Septentrion, 1998.

Schaaf, Gregory. *Wampum Belts & Peace Trees: George Morgan, Native Americans and Revolutionary Diplomacy.* Golden, CO: Fulcrum, 1990.

Schieffelin, Hannah Lawrence. "Hannah Lawrence Schieffelin's Letter." *New York Genealogical and Biographical Record* 72, no. 2 (April 1941): 120–23.

Schmalz, Peter. *The Ojibwa of Southern Ontario.* Toronto: University of Toronto Press, 1991.

Schmidt, Ethan A. *Native Americans in the American Revolution: How the War Divided, Devastated, and Transformed the Early American Indian World.* Santa Barbara, CA: Praeger, 2014.

Schoolcraft, Henry R. *Notes on the Iroquois; or Contributions to American History, Antiquities, and General Ethnology.* Albany, NY: Erastus H. Pease, 1847.

Scots Magazine 38 (1776).

Scott, James. "The Raid on Ballston, 1780, Memoranda of Reminiscences, 1846." *Bulletin of the Fort Ticonderoga Museum* 7, no. 4 (July 1946): 12–24.

Scudder, William. *The Journal of William Scudder, an Officer in the Late New-York Forces Who Was Taken Captive by the Indians at Fort Stanwix, on the 23d of July 1779 . . .* New York, 1794.

Seaver, James E. *Life of Mary Jemison: Deh-he-wa-mis; The White Woman of the Genesee.* New York: Miller, Orton & Mulligan, 1856.

Secomb, Daniel F. *History of the Town of Amherst, Hillsborough County New Hampshire . . .* Concord, NH: Evans, Sleeper & Woodbury, 1883.

Secretary of the Commonwealth. *Massachusetts Soldiers and Sailors of the Revolutionary War.* 17 vols. Boston: Wright and Potter, 1896–1908.

Segar, Nathaniel. *A Brief Narrative of the Captivity and Sufferings of Lt. Nathan'l Segar, Who Was Taken Prisoner by the Indians and Carried to Canada during the Revolutionary War.* Paris, ME: 1825.

Séguin, Robert-Lionel. "Les miliciens de Vaudreuil et Soulanges." In *Rapport de l'archiviste de la province de Québec pour 1955–1956 et 1956–1957,* 225–52. Quebec: Rédempti Paradis, 1957.

Severance, Frank H. *An Old Frontier of France: The Niagara Region and Adjacent Lakes under French Control.* 2 vols. New York: Dodd, Mead, 1917.

Shannon, Timothy J. "French and Indian Cruelty?: The Fate of the Oswego Prisoners of War, 1756–1758." *New York History* (Summer 2014): 381–407.

Shaw, Julia. *Memory Illusion: Remembering, Forgetting, and the Science of False Memory.* London: Random House, 2016.

Shea, John G. *History of the Catholic Missions among the Indian Tribes of the United States, 1529–1854.* New York: P. J. Kennedy, 1854.

Shepperd, Alan. *The King's Regiment.* Oxford: Osprey, 1973.

Siebert, W. H. *The Loyalists and Six Nations Indians in the Niagara Peninsula.* Ottawa: Royal Society of Canada, 1915.

Silver, Peter. *Our Savage Neighbors: How Indian War Transformed Early America.* New York: Norton, 2008.

Silverman, David J. *Red Brethren: The Brothertown and Stockbridge Indians and the Problem of Race in Early America.* Ithaca, NY: Cornell University Press, 2010.

Simmons, David A. "Military Architecture on the American Frontier." In *Selected Papers from the 1983 and 1984 George Rogers Clark Trans-Appalachian Frontier History Conferences,* edited by Robert J. Holden. Vincennes, IN: Eastern National Park and Memorial Association, 1985. http://npshistory.com/series/symposia/george_rogers _clark/1983-1984/sec5.htm.

Smith, Donald B. "The Dispossession of the Mississauga Indians: A Missing Chapter in the Early History of Upper Canada." *Ontario History* 78, no. 2 (June 1981): 67–89.

———. *Sacred Feathers: The Reverend Peter Jones (Kahkewaquonaby) and the Mississauga Indians*. Toronto, ON: University of Toronto Press, 1987.

———. "Tales of the Mississauga, Part I: How They Viewed the 'Golden Horseshoe.'" *Ontario Indian* 4, no. 2 (February 1981): 12–13.

———. "Who Are the Mississauga?" *Ontario History* 67, no. 4 (December 1975): 211–12.

Smith, James. *An Account of the Remarkable Occurrences in the Life and Travels of Col. James Smith, during His Captivity with the Indians . . .* Edited by William Darlington. Cincinnati: Robert Clarke, 1907.

Smith, James G. E. "Leadership among the Indians of the Northern Woodlands." In *Currents in Anthropology: Essays in Honor of Sol Tax*, edited by Robert Hinshaw, 305–24. The Hague: Mouton, 1979.

Smith, Justin H. *Our Struggle for the Fourteenth Colony: Canada and the American Revolution*. 2 vols. New York: Knickerbocker Press, 1907.

Smith, Paul H., ed. *Letters of Delegates to Congress, 1774–1789*. 25 vols. Washington, DC: Library of Congress, 1976–2000.

Smy, William A. *The Butler Papers: Documents and Papers Relating to Colonel John Butler and His Corps of Rangers, 1711–1977*. Vol. 1. Victoria, BC: W. Smy, 1994. https://dr.library.brocku.ca/handle/10464/9243.

Sosin, Jack M. "The Use of Indians in the War of the American Revolution: A Reassessment of Responsibility." *Canadian Historical Review* 46 (1965): 101–21.

Sossoyan, Matthieu. "Les Indiens, les Mohawks et les Blancs: Mise en contexte historique et sociale de la question des Blancs à Kahnawake." *Recherches amérindiennes au Québec* 39, nos. 1–2 (2009): 159–71.

Spring, Matthew H. *With Zeal and with Bayonets Only: The British Army on Campaign in North America, 1775–1783*. Norman: University of Oklahoma, 2008.

Stanley, George F. G. "The Six Nations and the American Revolution." *Ontario History* 56, no. 4 (December 1964): 217–32.

Starkey, Armstrong. *European and Native American Warfare, 1675–1815*. Norman: University of Oklahoma Press, 1998.

Stauffer, David McNeely. "Notes and Queries: General John Philip de Haas." *Pennsylvania Magazine of History and Biography* 2 (1878): 345–47.

Stearns, Ezra S. *Genealogical and Family History of the State of New Hampshire: A Record of the Achievements of Her People in the Making of a Commonwealth and the Founding of a Nation*. Vol. 3. New York: Lewis Publishing, 1908.

Stedman, Charles. *History of the Origin, Progress, and Termination of the American War*. Vol. 1. London, 1794.

Steele, Ian K. *Betrayals: Fort William Henry and the "Massacre."* New York: Oxford University Press, 1990.

———. "Suppressed Official Report of the Siege and 'Massacre' at Fort William Henry, 1757." *Huntington Library Quarterly* 55, no. 2 (Spring 1992): 339–52.

———. "Surrendering Rites: Prisoners on Colonial North American Frontiers." In *Hanoverian Britain and Empire: Essays in Memory of Philip Lawson*, 126–51. Woodbridge, UK: Boydell Press, 1998.

———. *Warpaths: Invasions of North America*. New York: Oxford University Press, 1994.

———. "When Worlds Collide: The Fate of Canadian and French Prisoners Taken at Fort Niagara, 1759." *Journal of Canadian Studies* 39, no. 3 (Fall 2005): 9–39.

Steele, Zadock. *The Indian Captive; or a Narrative of the Captivity and Suffering of Zadock Steele* . . . Montpelier, VT: E. P. Walton, 1818.

Stephenson, R. S. "Iroquois War and Warfare." In *On the Trails of the Iroquois*, edited by Sylvia Kasprycki, 112–15. Bonn: Kunst- und Ausstellungshalle der Bundesrepublik Deutschland, 2013.

Stevens, Benjamin. "Diary of Benjamin Stevens, of Canaan, Conn." *Daughters of the American Revolution Magazine* 45, nos. 2–3 (August–September 1914): 137–40.

Stevens, Paul L. "His Majesty's "Savage" Allies: British Policy and the Northern Indians during the Revolutionary War, the Carleton Years, 1774–1778." PhD diss., State University of New York at Buffalo, 1984.

———. *A King's Colonel at Niagara, 1774–1776*. Youngstown, NY: Old Fort Niagara Association, 1987.

Stevens, William. *A System for the Discipline of the Artillery of the United States of America* . . . New York: William A. Davis, 1797.

Stevenson, Roger. *Military Instructions for Officers Detached in the Field: Containing a Scheme for Forming a Corp of a Partisan, Illustrated with Plans of the Manoeuvres Necessary in Carrying on the Petite Guerre*. Philadelphia, 1775.

Stobo, Robert. *Memoirs of Major Robert Stobo of the Virginia Regiment*. Pittsburgh, 1854.

Stone, William L. *Border Wars of the American Revolution*. Vol. 1. New York: A. L. Fowle, 1900.

———. *Letters of Brunswick and Hessian Officers during the American Revolution*. Albany, NY: Joel Munsell's Sons, 1891.

———. *Life of Joseph Brant—Thayendanegea* . . . Vol. 1. New York: Alexander V. Blake, 1838.

———, ed. *Memoirs and Letters and Journals of Major General Riedesel*. Vol. 1. Translated by Max von Eelking. Albany, NY: J. Munsell, 1868.

St-Onge, Nicole. "'He Was Neither a Soldier Nor a Slave: He Was under the Control of No Man': Kahnawake Mohawks in the Northwest Fur Trade, 1790–1850." *Canadian Journal of History* 51, no. 1 (Spring–Summer 2016): 1–32.

Strachan, Hew. *British Military Uniforms, 1768–96: The Dress of the British Army from Official Sources*. London: Arms and Armour Press, 1975.

Sullivan, James, ed. *Minutes of the Albany Committee of Correspondence, 1775–1778*. Vol. 1. Albany: University of the State of New York, 1923.

———, ed. *The Papers of Sir William Johnson*. 14 Vols. Albany: University of the State of New York, 1921–65.

Surtees, Robert J. "The Iroquois in Canada." In *The History and Culture of Iroquois Diplomacy: An Interdisciplinary Guide to the Treaties of the Six Nations and Their League*, edited by Francis Jennings and William Fenton, 67–84. Syracuse, NY: Syracuse University Press, 1985.

Taylor, Alan. *The Divided Ground: Indians, Settlers, and the Northern Borderland of the American Revolution*. New York: Alfred A. Knopf, 2006.

Taylor, Gordon Garfield. "The Mississauga Indians of Eastern Ontario, 1634–1881." Master's thesis, Queen's University, 1981.

Taylor, Robert J., ed. *Papers of John Adams*. Vols. 3 and 4. Cambridge, MA: Belknap Press, 1979.

Têtu, Henri. *Notices biographiques; les évêques de Québec*. Quebec, 1889.

Thomas, Cyrus. *History of the Counties of Argenteuil, Que. and Prescott, Ont*. Montreal: John Lovell & Son, 1896.

Tiro, Karim Michel. "Ambivalent Allies: Strategy and the Native Americans." In *Strategy in the American War of Independence: A Global Approach*, edited by Donald Stoker, Kenneth J. Hagan, and Michael T. McMaster, 120–40. New York: Routledge, 2010.

———. "A Civil War?: Rethinking Iroquois Participation in the American Revolution." *Explorations in Early American Culture* 4 (2000): 148–65.

———. "Deconflicting Iroquoia." *Age of Revolutions* (October 18, 2017). https://ageofrevolutions.com/2017/10/18/deconflicting-iroquoia/.

———. "The Dilemmas of Alliance: The Oneida Indian Nation in the American Revolution." In *War and Society in the American Revolution: Mobilization and Home Fronts*, edited by John Resch and Walter Sargent, 215–34. DeKalb: Northern Illinois University Press, 2007.

———. "James Dean in Iroquoia." *New York History* 80 (October 1999): 397–422.

———. *The People of the Standing Stone: The Oneida Nation from the Revolution through the Era of Removal*. Amherst: University of Massachusetts Press, 2011.

Tooker, Elisabeth. "Eighteenth Century Political Affairs and the Iroquois League." In *The Iroquois in the American Revolution, 1976 Conference Proceedings*, 1–12. Rochester, NY: Rochester Museum and Science Center, 1981.

———. "The League of the Iroquois: Its History, Politics, and Ritual." In Trigger, *Handbook of North American Indians*, vol. 15: *Northeast*.

Travers, Len. *Hodges' Scout: A Lost Patrol of the French and Indian War*. Baltimore: Johns Hopkins University Press, 2015.

Trigger, Bruce G. "The Historians' Indian: Native Americans in Canadian Historical Writing from Charlevoix to the Present." *Canadian Historical Review* 67, no. 3 (September 1986): 315–42.

———, ed. *Handbook of North American Indians*, vol. 15: *Northeast*. Washington, DC: Smithsonian Institution, 1978.

Trudel, Marcel. *Canada's Forgotten Slaves: Two Hundred Years of Bondage*. Translated by George Tombs. Montreal: Véhicule Press, 2013.

———. *Dictionnaire des Esclaves et de Leurs Propriétaires au Canada Français*. Ville LaSalle, QC: Éditions Hurtubise, 1990.

Trumbull, Benjamin. "A Concise Journal or Minutes of the Principal Movement towards St. John's of the Siege & Surrender of the Forts There in 1775." *Collections of the Connecticut Historical Society* 7 (1899): 137–73.

Trussell, John B. B., Jr. *The Pennsylvania Line: Regimental Organization and Operation, 1776–1783*. Harrisburg: Pennsylvania Historical and Museum Commission, 1977.

Turgeon, Charles. "Monseigneur, Pardonnez-moi parce que j'ai peché: La regulation de la dissidence au sein du clergé canadien, au moment de l'invasion americaine de 1775–1776." Master's thesis, Université de Montréal, 2010.

United States House of Representatives. *Reports of Committees of the House of Representatives Made during the First Session of the Thirty-Sixth Congress, 1859–'60*. Washington, DC: Thomas H. Ford, 1860.

Van Buskirk, Judith L. *Standing in Their Own Light: African American Patriots in the American Revolution*. Norman: University of Oklahoma Press, 2017.

Vaughan, Alden T. *Narratives of North American Captivity: A Selective Bibliography*. New York: Garland Publishing, 1983.

Vaughan, Alden T., and Daniel K. Richter. "Crossing the Cultural Divide: Indians and New Englanders, 1605–1763." *Proceedings of the American Antiquarian Society* 90 (October 1980): 23–99.

Venables, Robert W. "'Faithful Allies of the King': The Crown's Haudenosaunee Allies in the Revolutionary Struggle for New York." In *The Other Loyalists: Ordinary People, Royalism, and the Revolution in the Middle Colonies, 1763–1787*, edited by Joseph S. Tiedemann, Eugene R. Fingerhut, and Robert W. Venables, 131–57. Albany: State University of New York Press, 2009.

Verreau, Hospice-Anthelme Jean-Baptiste, ed. *Invasion du Canada, Collection de Mémoires Recueillis et Annotes*. Montreal: Eusèbe Senecal, 1873.

Viau, Roland. *Enfants du néant et mangeurs d'âmes: Guerre, culture et société en Iroquoisie ancienne*. Cap-Saint-Ignace, QC: Boréal, 1997.

Vivian, James F., and Jean H. Vivian. "Congressional Indian Policy during the War for Independence: The Northern Department." *Maryland Historical Magazine* 63 (1968): 241–74.

Vose, Joseph. "Journal of Lieutenant-Colonel Joseph Vose." In *Publications of the Colonial Society of Massachusetts*, vol. 7: *Transactions, 1900–1902*, 248–62. Boston: Colonial Society of Massachusetts, 1905.

Wallace, Anthony F. C. *The Death and Rebirth of the Seneca*. New York: Vintage Books, 1972.

Watt, Gavin K. "Action at Sabbath Day Point, March 20, 1777." *Journal of the American Revolution* (June 5, 2017). https://allthingsliberty.com/2017/06/action-sabbath-day-point-march-20-1777/.

———. *The Burning of the Valleys: Daring Raids from Canada against the New York Frontier in the Fall of 1780*. Toronto: Dundurn, 1997.

———. *Poisoned by Lies and Hypocrisy: America's First Attempt to Bring Liberty to Canada, 1775–1776*. Toronto: Dundurn, 2014.

———. *Rebellion in the Mohawk Valley: The St. Leger Expedition of 1777*. Toronto: Dundurn, 2002.

Way, Peter. "The Cutting Edge of Culture: British Soldiers Encounter Native Americans in the French and Indian War." In *Empire and Others: British Encounters with Indigenous Peoples, 1600–1850*, edited by Martin Daunton and Rick Halpern, 123–48. Philadelphia: University of Pennsylvania Press, 1999.

Webster, Donald B. "Grenades at Fort Senneville." *Arms Collecting* 32, no. 3 (August 1994): 94–95.

Webster, Isaac. *The Narrative of the Captivity of Isaac Webster.* New York: Garland Publishing, 1978.

Weld, Isaac. *Weld's Travels through the States of North America, and the Provinces of Upper and Lower Canada during the Years 1795, 1796, and 1797.* 2 vols. London, 1807.

Wells, Bayze. "Journal of Bayze Wells of Farmington, May, 1776–February, 1777, at the Northward and in Canada." *Collections of the Connecticut Historical Society* 7 (1899): 240–67.

Wells, Frederic P. *History of Newbury, Vermont, from the Discovery of the Coos Country to Present Time.* St. Johnsbury, VT: Caledonian Company, 1902.

Westmoreland History Committee. *History of Westmoreland (Great Meadow), New Hampshire, 1741–1970, and Genealogical Data.* Westmoreland, NH: Westmoreland History Committee, 1976.

Wheelock, Eleazar. *A Continuation of the Narrative of the Indian Charity School, Begun in Lebanon in Connecticut; Now Incorporated with Dartmouth-College, in Hanover, in the Province of New-Hampshire.* Hartford, CT, 1773.

———. *A Continuation of the Narrative of the Indian Charity School, Begun in Lebanon in Connecticut; Now Incorporated with Dartmouth-College, in Hanover, in the Province of New-Hampshire.* Hartford, CT, 1775.

Whitcher, William. *History of the Town of Haverhill, New Hampshire.* Concord, NH: Rumford Press, 1919.

———. "Memorial to Col. Timothy Bedel." *Granite Monthly: A New Hampshire Magazine* 47 (November–December 1915): 503–5.

White, Bruce M. "Montreal Canoes and Their Cargoes." In *Le Castor Fait Tout: Selected Papers of the Fifth North American Fur Trade Conference, 1985,* 164–92. Montreal: Lake St. Louis Historical Society, 1987.

White, David O. *Connecticut's Black Soldiers, 1775–1783.* Chester, CT: Pequot Press, 1973.

White, Richard. *The Middle Ground: Indians, Empires and Republics in the Great Lakes Region, 1650–1815.* New York: Cambridge University Press, 1991.

Wilkinson, James. *Memoirs of My Own Times.* Vol. 1. Philadelphia: Abraham Small, 1816.

Williamson, Peter. *French and Indian Cruelty: Exemplified in the Life and Various Vicissitudes of Fortune of Peter Williamson, a Disbanded Soldier.* London, 1757.

Winthrop, William. *Military Law and Precedents.* Washington, DC: W. H. Morrison, 1886.

Witgen, Michael. *An Infinity of Nations: How the Native New World Shaped Early North America.* Philadelphia: University of Pennsylvania Press, 2012.

Worthen, Samuel C. "Bedel's Rangers at the Siege of St. Johns." *Granite Monthly: New Hampshire State Magazine* 52, no. 11 (November 1920): 448–51.

Wraxall, Peter. *An Abridgment of the Indian Affairs.* Cambridge, MA: Harvard University Press, 1915.

Zaboly, Gary. *American Colonial Ranger: The Northern Colonies, 1724–64.* New York: Osprey, 2004.

INDEX

Page numbers in *italics* indicate illustrations or maps.

Abenakis, 6, 31, 157, 190n14; warriors from, 84, 92, 102. *See also* Akwesasne; Odanak
Aboyderroy, 61
active neutrality, 6, 25, 33, 155
adoption, captive, 7–8, 147
Akwesasne, 4, 46, 54, 127, 155; Abenakis in, 66, 84, 92, 102, 218n21; cautious chiefs from, 65, 66; intelligence from, 60, 69; origins of, 66; pro-American faction in, 66, 156, 218n19; spelling of, 209n7; war party stops in, 65–66, 75, 126; warriors from, 66, 84, 92, 102, 156. *See also* Indian war party (Cedars)
Albany: council fire at, 17; Kahnawake historical ties with, 6–7; Six Nations councils in, 17–19, 25, 42
Algonguians, 6, 190n14. *See also* Arundaks; Mississaugas; Nipissings
Allen, Ethan, 1, 33; Indian diplomacy of, 25, 193n31
Amherst, Jeffery, 74, 127
Anishinaabeg. *See* Algonquians
Arnold, Benedict, 3, 37, 42, 133, 135, 157; and cartel, 122–23, 138; field command of, 110–11, 115–16, 117–18, 123; Indian diplomacy of, 111, 117, 118, 130, 193n31; in Montreal, 54, 55, 70, 109–10, 131; Quinchien advance by, 119, 121; vengeance plans of, 117, 118, 127–28; western threat assessment of, 72
Arnold's corps (Island of Montreal), 109–11, 115–21

Articles of War, 132
artillery, 126; Continental, 55, 79, 81; inaccuracy of, 79, 81, 121; militia use of, 119, 121; ruse involving, 82, 86
Arundaks, 14, 20, 130, 195n9
Atiatoharongwen, Louis, 2, 17, 25, 29; Albany-Cambridge trip (second) by, 38, 39, 40–41; army liaison work by, 18, 28, 31; background of, 1, 3–4, 7; Cambridge trip (first) by, 1–4, 6, 14, 16, 31; as captain, 55, 60, 69, 109–10, 131, 236n7; post-Cedars career of, 148, 156, 157
atrocities, 100, 124, 151, 152. *See also* captives; plundering; ritual killing; scalping
Ayonwahta, John Stacey, 8

Baker, Remember, 18, 20, 26
bateaux, 109, 118, 125, 126; shortages of, 71, 73, 74, 115
Beaumont, Louis, 64, 73, 85, 108
Bedel, Timothy, 30; arrest and court martial of, 131, 132–33; field command of (1775 campaign), 30–31, 37; and Fort Cedars, 54–55, 59, 70, 71, 72; as Indian agent (1775 campaign), 31–32, 37, 39–40; as Indian agent (1776 campaign), 54–55, 69–70, 131, 133; post-Cedars career of, 134, 157; regimental command challenges of, 40–42, 55; and smallpox, 55–56, 59, 70, 72, 220n5

285

Bird, Henry, 52–53, 86–87, 117, 157
Bliss, Theodore, 73, 91, 231n18; as hostage, 123, 142–44, 145
Boucherville, Pierre de, 119
Brant, Joseph Thayendanegea, 24, 27, 34, 104
British Army, 9, 17, 33, 126; reluctance to engage by, 22, 24, 75, 79, 222–23n6. *See also* Eighth Regiment of Foot; Forster's company; Seventh Regiment of Foot; Twenty-Sixth Regiment of Foot
Brown, John, 28, 109
Burgoyne, John, 139, 140, 143–44
Burrall's Regiment (Connecticut), 55, 119, 147; Fort Cedars detachment from, 55–56, 78–79, 82. *See also* Fort Cedars
Butler, John, 34, 146; Indian diplomacy of, 17, 34, 43–44, 45, 50, 129; post-Cedars career of, 156
Butterfield, Isaac, 56–57; captivity of, 109, 117; court martial of, 132, 133–34; at Fort Cedars, 57–58, 69–70, 82, 86–87, 88; judgment of, 89–90, 134, 135, post-Cedars life of, 134; terrorized, 81–82, 84, 86, 87, 90

Caldwell, John, 36, 48, 49, 50, 62; Indian diplomacy of, 43, 146
Cambridge, Massachusetts, 1, 37, 39–40, 72
Campbell, John, 26–27, 101
Canadians. *See* loyalists, Canadian; militia, Canadian; Second Canadian Continental Regiment; volunteers, Canadian
captives, 7–8, 99, 157; claiming of, 98, 101; escapes by, 113, 115, 118, 119, 147; experiences of, 88–89, 103–7, 115, 118, 146–49; historical memory regarding, 100–101, 146, 147; Indian customs toward, 7, 102, 105–6, 118; as measure of victory, 62, 78, 153; officers treatment as, 109, 117; reintegration of, 141; repatriation of, 125, 127, 137; threats to kill, 103, 118, 122, 123, 124
Carillon, 54, 55, 60
Carleton, Guy, 21, 144; Indian ally recruiting by, 4, 14; Indian diplomacy of, 13, 24, 33; Indian restraint policy of 15–16; military leadership by, 34–35, 68, 126; Montreal evacuation by, 35–36, response to Cedars resolutions of, 137–38
cartel, Cedars: cease fire, 123, 124, 125, 137; criticism of, 123, 124; Indian calls for, 117, 153; negation of, 136, 137, 143; negotiation of, 117, 122–23
Cascades landing. *See* Les Cascades
Caughnawaga. *See* Kahnawake
Cayuga nation, 10; chiefs of, 43; warriors from, 34, 50, 62, 154, 216n6
The Cedars (parish), 53, 54, 57, 76, 106; loyalist support in, 52, 53. *See also* Fort Cedars
chiefs, Indian, 6, 9, 39, 50, 94, 190n15; prestige of, 24, 61; restraining influence of, 66, 86, 104, 117, 122; tactical leadership of, 22, 93, 96, 108
clan matrons, 13, 50
Claus, Daniel, 13, 17, 27, 148
commissioners to Canada (Continental Congress), 71–72, 74, 111, 124, 136–37
confederacy, Indian. *See* Seven Nations; Six Nations
Continental Army, 111. *See also* Arnold's corps (Island of Montreal); artillery; Burrall's Regiment (Connecticut); Fifteenth Continental Regiment (Massachusetts); First Pennsylvania Regiment (Continental); Nelson's Pennsylvania Rifle Company; New Hampshire Ranger companies (Continental); New Hampshire

Ranger Regiment (Continental); scouts, Kahnawake; Second Canadian Continental Regiment; Second Continental Regiment (New Hampshire); Sherburne's detachment

Continental Congress, 45; approves Canadian invasion, 4, 14; cartel committee of, 134–36; Cedars resolutions of, 136, 137–38, 143, 151, 153; commissioners to Canada, 71–72; 74; 111, 124, 136–37; hostage accommodations by, 145; Indian policy of, 4, 38

Cook, Louis. *See* Atiatoharongwen, Louis

Coteau-des-Cèdres, 57, 75

Coteau-du-Lac, 126; rapids, 53, 66, 68, 73–74, 75

courts-martial, 131, 132–34

Crown Point, 37, 42, 131, 133, 141; capture of, 1, 3

Dartmouth College, 8, 40–41, 70, 130

Dean, James, 17, 42, 70

death song, 32, 65, 66, 74, 75; meaning of, 62

Declaration of Independence, 135–36, 137

De Haas, John Philip, 64, 124, 133, 137; background of, 126; conducts council of war, 128; at Fort Ste Anne, 118–19, 125, 126–29, 240n14; Indian relations of, 126–27, 130; Sorel detachment command of, 111, 113, 116

Denaut, Pierre, 52, 53, 57

Denis, Thomas, 52, 76

Derry, James, 148

Downs, David, 86

drunkenness, Indian, 32, 33, 211n22

Eighth Regiment of Foot (British), 36, 63, 157; garrison life of, 49, 63; light infantry of, 47, 79. *See also* Forster's company

Estabrook, Joseph, 70, 87; spelling of, 220n3

Everett, Edward, 86, 126

Fifteenth Continental Regiment (Massachusetts), 71, 109, 110, 111, 119. *See also* Sherburne's detachment

First Pennsylvania Regiment (Continental), 64, 111, 113, 116

Foretier, Pierre, 64

Forster, George, 47–48; 51, 52, 141, 157; advances on Island of Montreal, 108–9, 113–14; arranges cartel, 117, 122–24, 138; extradition demands for, 136, 138, 143, 144; at Fort Cedars battle, 76, 79, 81–83, 85, 92; and Fort Cedars surrender, 86–87, 88–89, 100; Indian coordination by, 62–63, 66, 86, 92, 122; Indian threats conveyed by, 81, 84, 86, 122–23, 125; leads campaign, 63, 74; manages prisoners, 88, 103–4, 105–6, 108–9, 117–19; at Pointe-de-Quinchien battle, 119, 121; ransoms captives, 105, 138, 146; retreats, 125–26

Forster's company, 47; descends St. Lawrence, 63, 65; at Fort Cedars battle, 76, 79, 82–83; guards prisoners, 106, 118, 122; on Island of Montreal, 109, 114; at Pointe-de-Quinchien, 119; retreat of, 125–26

Fort Cedars, 54, 55, 80; battle of, 79–81, 82–83, 84–85; casualties at, 89, 226n11; construction of, 58–60, morale in, 86, 87; preparation for battle at, 69–70, 74, 78, 89; prisoners kept at, 108, 125–26; reports of attack on, 70–71, 72, 109; skirmishes around, 76, 77–79; surrender negotiations at, 81–82, 86–88

Fort Niagara, 146; battle of (1759), 107; councils at, 43–44, 45, 50; Indian trade stores at, 11, 34; as military base, 36, 48, 49, 154, 156; war party assembles at, 50–51, 129

Fort Ontario, 11, 13
Fort Oswegatchie, 13, 36, 47, 143, 146; Indian war party gathers at, 61–63; loyalist coordination at, 46–48, 52, 54; retreat to, 126
Fort Oswego, 89, 107
Fort Schuyler (Stanwix), 148, 156, 157
Fort Senneville. See Fort Ste. Anne
Fort Ste. Anne, 56, 116; Arnold's operations from, 118–19, 121, 123–24; British operations from, 109, 113, 115; captives returned to, 125; Continentals abandon, 109, 129; Continental garrison at, 56, 60, 64, 73, 91; De Haas's command at, 126, 128; destruction of, 129; Kanesatake visits to, 126–27
Fort St. Johns, 9, 20, 22, 131; Indian scouts at, 14, 16, 18, 49; prisoners from, 117, 142; raids on, 3, 4, 21; siege of, 32, 36; skirmishes outside, 22, 24, 28–30
Fort Ticonderoga, 4, 48, 131, 133, 141; capture of 1, 3, 8
Fort William Henry, 101, 102, 105, 107, 137; historical memory of, 88, 89, 246n13
French and Indian War, 100, 154; historical memory of, 89, 124. See also Fort William Henry; Monongahela, Battle of the
fur trade ban, 45, 50, 71

Gananoque, 49, 61
Gates, Horatio, 133, 134
Goddard, James Stanley, 46–48, 49, 50–51
Green, Ebenezer, 57, 86; as hostage, 123, 142–43, 144–45, 151

Haldimand, Frederick, 138, 147, 149
Hamtramck, Jean-François, 89, 123, 126, 146
Hardison, Benjamin, 148
Haudenosaunee. See Six Nations Confederacy

Hazen, Moses, 54, 111, 113, 115; disagrees with Arnold, 128, 240n14
Hertel de Saint François, Joseph-Hippolyte, 101–2
Hewit, Randall, 148, 250n23
hostages, 123, 125, 142–46; letters by, 144–45, 151
Howe, William, 137, 141–42
Hurons. See Wendake

Ile aux Noix, 19, 22, 25, 26, 27
Ile aux Tourtes, 115, 118, 153
Ile Perrot, 92, 115
Indian Department officers. See Northern Indian Department
Indian policy: British, 15–16, 34, 136, 137, 138–39; Continental, 4, 17–18, 38
Indians: casualty aversion of, 24, 68; diplomatic customs of, 9, 19, 24, 42; neutrality preference of, 4, 6, 18, 43; restraining forces among, 13, 34, 50; restraint by, 104, 107, 117, 122, 153–54; tactics of, 79, 81, 84, 96, 119, 121; terror used by, 89, 102, 108, 125; trade concerns of, 11, 43, 45, 50, 154; war customs of, 117, 118, 146, 147; warrior prestige among, 49, 50, 61–62, 153. See also by nation or confederacy; Indian war party (Cedars); presents, Indian diplomatic
Indian war party (Cedars), 100, 126, 146; assembles, 61–63; composition of, 217n11; descends St. Lawrence, 65–68, 73–74; at Fort Cedars, 75–78, 84–89, 92, 103–6; on Island of Montreal, 108, 109, 113, 114; at Pointe-de-Quinchien, 117, 118, 119, 121, 125; at Quinchien ambush, 92–93, 95–98, 101–3
inoculation, 55–56; 111
Iroquois. See Six Nations Confederacy

Jefferson, Thomas, 134, 135
Jesuits, 6, 8

Johnson, Guy, 12, 17, 31, 50, 62; background of, 10–11, frustrated by Carleton, 26–27, 33–34; manages warrior allies, 16, 17, 24–25; recruits Indian allies, 11, 13, 24, 42
Johnson, William. *See* Tekawiroñte
Johnson, William, Sir, 10, 20, 107, 196n16; father of Tekawiroñte, 24, 76; mentor to Butler, 34, 156

Kachnectago, Thomas Wildman, 25, 32
Kahnawake, 1–3, *16*, 65, 66; American-allied warriors from, 109–10, 111, 118–19, 130; British-allied warriors from; 14, 20, 22, 24, 25, 28–29, 156; British calls to arms at, 4, 13–14, 25, 189–90n13; councils at, 17, 25, 69–71, 126, 128, 130, 133; diplomatic outreach from, 1–4, 37–40, 130, 237n13; intelligence to Continentals from, 54, 111, 117, 118, 122; interactions with Continental army, 18, 27, 28, 31–33, 111, 129; neutrality of, 27, 31–32, 38–39, 70, 130; offers to provide warriors to Americans, 38, 39, 41, 55; Oneida cooperation with, 42, 43, 129, 154; post-Cedars experiences of, 131, 155; pro-American faction in, 4, 6–9, 25, 32, 35, 130, 134, 155–56; scout company from, 55, 60, 67, 68, 69, 70, 74; Seven Nations council fire at, 1, 17, 25, 126, 128, 130; spelling of, 188n3; and Stockbridge incident, 9; strategic interests of, 1–3; trade connections of, 7, 31
Kanesatake, 14–15, *15*, 63; captives in, 109, 117, 126–27, 142; destruction threat to, 127–28; interests of, 14–15, 24–25; neutrality of, 126–27, 130; prisoners from, 35, 48; pro-British commitment of, 14–15, 24–25, 48, 130, 155; spelling of, 195n9; villagers peaceful interactions with Continentals, 60, 126–27; warriors from, 20, 24, 35, 48, 85, 109, 155, 156. *See also* Arundaks; Indian war party (Cedars); Nipissings
Kanughsgawiat, 61, 93, 97
Kaquatanawajey, 61
Kirkland, Samuel, 17, 42, 196n15
Kontítie, Joseph, 28–29, 32

Lachine, 56, 72, 129, 130; defenses at, 110–11, 113–14, 117–18; Lorimier home in, 20, 46, 131
Lake Champlain, 1, 19, 37, 42; scouting missions on, 11, 18, 20, 195n11
Lake of Two Mountains, 14, 57, 60, 64, 109, 118; as military obstacle, 73, 74, 99, 115. *See also* Kanesatake
Lake St. Francis, 66, 74
Lake St. Louis, 57, 113
Lamont, John, 149–50
Laprairie, 31, 32, 33, 109
Laurentian Indians. *See* Seven Nations Confederacy
Lefebvre, Jean-Baptiste, 92, 98, 101, 119
Les Cascades, 57, 76, 78, 93
Longue Pointe, 33
Longueuil, 31, 35
Lorette. *See* Wendake
Lorimier, Claude, 20, *21*, 22, 113, 131; at Battle of Longueuil, 35; Carleton coordination with, 36, 46; in Cedars advance, 63, 65, 66–67, 74, 75–76; coordinates supplies, 52–54; escapes Montreal, 46–47; at Fort Cedars battle, 79, 81, 85; as Indian officer, 14, 21, 22, 25, 28–29; Indian ally coordination by, 48–49, 54, 61, 66; Kahnawake ties of, 21–22, 32; post-Cedars career of, 156–57; at Quinchien ambush, 92–93, 97–98, 101–3, 142; scouting by, 20, 32, 113, 195n11
Lorimier, François-Thomas de Verneuil, 35, 92

loyalists, Canadian, 45, 73; gather supplies, 52–53, 60, 63, 64–65, 85; pass intelligence, 74, 82, 92, 93, 113–15. *See also* militia, Canadian; volunteers, Canadian

massacre, 42, 140, 152; Cedars as a, 143, 144, 151–53; memories of, 89, 101. *See also* Fort Oswego; Fort William Henry
Mathevet, Jean-Claude, 25, 85, 109
Maurer, Jacob, 92, 93
McKinstry, John, 91, 102, 122, 231n18; and Brant legend, 104–5, 149, 150
memory errors, 86, 101, 104
Middleton, Reuben, 149
militia, Canadian, 35, 64, 98, 109, 113; at Fort Cedars, 85, 92; at Pointe-de-Quinchien, 98, 119, 121
Mississaugas, 13, 48–49, 62; as captors, 105, 146, 147, 148; warriors from, 34, 49, 52, 61, 63, 92, 97, 114, 157; western bands of, 50–51, 61, 63. *See also* Indian war party (Cedars)
Mohawk (nation in Six Nations), 10, 11, 43, 50; warriors from, 22, 24, 28, 50, 62, 148, 154. *See also* Indian war party (Cedars)
Mohawks (ethno-linguistic group in Seven Nations), 6, 14, 66. *See also* Akwesasne; Kahnawake; Kanesatake
Mongongahela, Battle of the, 3, 100, 107
Montgomery, Richard, 19, 22, 35, 37; death of, 29, 39, 54; Indian diplomacy of, 25, 27, 28, 31, 33, 37
Montigny, Jean-Baptiste Testard de, 56, 64, 129; manages captives, 113, 115; organizes loyalists, 63–64, 85, 92, 109; at Quinchien ambush, 98, 101
Montreal: Continental occupation of, 37, 38, 45, 72, 110, 131; fur trade importance in, 45; Indian conference at, 10, 13; loyalists in, 45, 64; as objective for Cedars expedition, 48, 49, 63, 108–9, 113

Nelson's Pennsylvania Rifle Company, 111, 119
New Hampshire Ranger companies (Continental), 30, 37, 41
New Hampshire Ranger Regiment (Continental), 54, 55, 56, 219n23; captives from, 148–49; formation of, 40–42; Young's detachment from, 60, 64, 91, 109, 110–11. *See also* Fort Cedars
Nipissings, 14, 15, 190n14, 199n7
Noble, David, 109, 110
Northern Army. *See* Continental Army
Northern Indian Department (British), 10; officers of, 22, 24, 33, 51, 61
Northern Indian Department (Continental), 17, 19, 25–26, 38, 43, 129. *See also* Schuyler, Philip

Odanak, 3, 8, 66, 130; pro-American faction in, 6, 134, 155, 157, 191n19, 211n20; Raid on (1759), 66, 127
Ogagragighte, Jean-Baptiste, 7, 38, 40, 252n9
Ohquandageghte, 28, 35, 219n21
Oka, 195n9. *See also* Kanesatake
Oneida nation, 10; ambassadors to Seven Nations from, 19, 25–27, 129–30; American-allied warriors from, 148, 154, 156, 157; British-allied warriors from, 50, 62; Kahnawake ties with, 42, 129, 154; as neutrality advocate, 17–18, 27, 42–43, 154
Onondaga nation, 10; council fire in, 18, 26, 42–43, 129; war commitment of, 13; warriors from, 50, 61, 62. *See also* Indian war party (Cedars)
Oriskany, 154, 156, 157
Oswegatchies, 46–47, 66

Oswego. *See* Fort Ontario; Fort Oswego
Ottawa River, 14, 54, 60

parallel warfare, 61–62, 153–54, 155; tensions in, 85, 99, 100, 107
Parke, Andrew, 74–76, 103, 105, 114, 210n12; cartel negotiations by, 122, 123; pamphlet by, 138, 144, 152–53
Paterson, John, 71, 72, 109, 110, 133. *See also* Fifteenth Continental Regiment (Massachusetts)
plundering, 3, 101, 108, 136, 142–43, 153; at Fort Cedars, 88–89, 106–7; promised to Cedars war party, 62, 88, 103
Pointe-au-Diable, 69, 74, 75, 76
Pointe-au-Foin, 53, 66, 67
Pointe Claire, 113, *114*
Pointe-de-Quinchien, 57, 76, 92, 115; Arnold's reconnaissance of, 119, *120*, 121; captives at, 108, 119, 125, 137; Sherburne's detachment landings at, 73, 91–93, 103
Pointe du Lac, 190n14
presents, Indian diplomatic: American, 19, 27, 31, 40; British, 11, 13, 34, 43, 62
Presqu'ile, 57, 64, 73, 91, 103
prisoners of war, 35; British soldiers as, 117, 141–42; Canadian loyalists as, 57, 142; Indian, 35, 48. *See also* captives
propaganda, 137–40, 144–45, 151

Quebec City: Continental retreat from, 68, 69, 71, 85, 155; siege of, 37, 39, 42, 54, 55
Quinchien, 91. *See also* Quinchien, Battle of
Quinchien, Battle of, *95*, 96–98, 135; aftermath of; casualties at, 97, 99; site of, 93, 230n8, 231n18; war party approach to, 92–93

ransom, 105, 138, 146, 147, 148, 153
ritual killing, 7, 105, 147, 154; by fire, 104–5, 135, 136, *139*, 140, 153; after Quinchien, 103–5, 149, 152

"roasting." *See* ritual killing
Roundocks. *See* Arundaks

sachems, 13, 50, 66, 153, 190n15
Sagoouike, Louise, 21, 46
Sanórese, Philip, 7, 8, 219n23
Saratoga: campaign (1777), 139, 142, 154, 156, 157; raid (1745), 7, 198n5
Sawatanen, Louis Vincent, 54
scalping, 78, 102, 139, 156–57; in memory, 100–101; as war trophy, 78, 146, 153–54
Schuyler, Philip: comments on Cedars surrender, 132; 134; as Indian commissioner, 17–19, 26, 38, 129–30, 157, 209n3; Kahnawake warrior offer handling by, 39, 40, 41, 156; as Northern Army commander, 4, 22
scouts, Kahnawake, 55, 60, 67, 68, 69, 70, 74
Second Canadian Continental Regiment, 54, 55, 123, 125–26
Second Continental Regiment (New Hampshire), 111
Seneca nation, 10, 43, 62; as captors, 105, 146; war commitments of, 13, 50, 154; warriors from, 34, 61, 62, 92, 93, 103, 104, 157. *See also* Indian war party (Cedars)
Seven Nations Confederacy, 3, 5, 31, 37; member nations of, 4, 6, 190n14; neutrality of, 6, 14, 26, 31–32, 128, 130; politics of, 4, 6, 24, 50, 155; Six Nations ties to, 10, 19, 26, 31–32, 44, 67, 121–22, 200n16; warriors of, 14, 18, 20, 22, 35, 114. *See also* Akwesasne; Kahnawake; Kanesatake; Odanak; Pointe du Lac; Wendake; Wôlinak
Seventh Regiment of Foot (British), 22, 117, 141–42
Sherburne, Henry, 72; captivity experiences of, 101–3, 104, 109, 117, 122–23; detachment command of, 72–73, 74, 91, 93–99, 135; reports and testimony, 98–99, 104, 105, 135

Sherburne's detachment, 72–73, 74, 91; ambush of, 93–99; battlefield captivity experiences of, 101–6
Six Nations Confederacy, 3, 10, *11*; councils of, 18, 26, 42–44, 129; councils with, 11, 13, 17–18, 19, 50, 134; factions/tensions in, 42, 43–44, 129, 154; neutrality of, 17–18, 19, 26, 42–43, 157; Seven Nations ties to, 10, 19, 26, 31–32, 44, 67, 121–22, 200n16; strategic interests of, 6, 11, 18, 60; warriors from, 20, 28–29, 50–51, 61–63, 74, 75, 77, 114, 154. *See also* Cayuga nation; Indian war party (Cedars); Mohawk nation (in Six Nations); Oneida nation; Onondaga nation; Seneca nation; Tuscarora nation
smallpox, 55, 59, 70, 90, 111, 220n5
Sorel, 71, 109, 111, 124, 132
Stacey, John. *See* Ayonwahta, John Stacey
Ste. Anne (parish), 56
Stevens, John, 56, 60, 82, 84, 87; as hostage, 123, 142–43, 144, 145–46
St. Francis. *See* Odanak
Stockbridges, 9, 27, 41
St. Regis. *See* Akwesasne
stripped captives, 101–3, 106–7, 108, 115, 136, 143
Sullivan, Ebenezer, 73, 91, 98, 123, 142–46; hostage letter, 144–45, 151
Sullivan, John, 130, 132, 237n13; as brother of Ebenezer Sullivan, 73, 143, 144, 145
Sulpicians, 6, 15, 25

tacit neutrality, 44, 67, 121–22, 155, 156, 219n1
Tekawiroñte, William Johnson, 24, 50, 76

Terlaye, François-Auguste Magon de, 25, 85, 109, 114
Thayendanegea. *See* Brant, Joseph Thayendanegea
Tuscarora nation, 10, 18, 43, 154, 157
Twenty-Sixth Regiment of Foot (British), 22, 117, 141–42

Vaudreuil, 82, 85, 92, 108, 109; presbytery-chapel, 64, 73, 85, 119, 122
Vincent, Jean, 25, 28, 30, 31, 131, 236n7
Vincent, Louis (Sawatanen), 54
volunteers, Canadian, 63, 76, 85, 92, 98, 109, 114; as prisoners of war, 57, 142; in 1775 campaign, 22, 33

Walker, Richard, 46–47, 48
wampum, 193n31; British-Indian diplomacy, 33; Indian-American diplomacy, 27, 31, 38, 129; Indian-Indian diplomacy, 9, 26, 130. *See also* war belt
war belt, 13, 14, 42, 127, 130
war song. *See* death song
war whoop, 93, 96, 121
Washington, George, 41–42, 127, 132, 137, 142; Indian diplomacy of, 3–4, 39–40, 156
Wendake (Lorette), 4, 8, 131, 190n14; British cooperation from, 24, 126, 155, 219n26. *See also* Vincent, Jean; Vincent, Louis (Sawatanen)
Wheelock, Eleazar, 8, 40
Wilkins, Daniel, 58, 81, 82, 87
Wilkinson, James, 111, 121, 131, 240n14
Wôlinak, 190n14
Wooster, David, 38, 45, 50, 54, 218n19

Young, Samuel, 60, 64, 109, 110–11; court martial of, 132, 133

www.ingramcontent.com/pod-product-compliance
Lightning Source LLC
Chambersburg PA
CBHW031430160426
43195CB00010BB/673